of children as well as of adults. Helene Deutsch has spoken recently of the warm interest all analysts felt in the early child work in Vienna; this annual has played an important role in closing the gap built up in the intervening years between child analysis and adult analysis."

American Journal of Psychiatry—"The appearance of a new volume of *The Psychoanalytic Study of the Child* is always a welcome addition to the library of many who work with disturbed children. The range of topics covered in these volumes has been wide and the authors include many of the most prominent in the field."

Childhood Education—"This annual of exceptional merit will interest and gratify all child educators who believe in the unconscious, who step beyond observing behavior to take cognizance of symbols and meanings, who value education as an evocative process, or who simply respect the child's inner life. . . . Many teachers will find this a book of unparalleled richness and helpfulness in their work."

Archives of Internal Medicine—"Each year there are just a few volumes that achieve eminence and represent a unique contribution. This volume is in such a category. Not only does this text stimulate and enlighten the reader, but it is a serendipitous experience in personality development.

"The papers are written lucidly, and only rarely is one trapped by technical jargon. Such diverse topics as functioning of the mind, archaic thinking in schizophrenia, and learning disabilities are woven into a glittering psychoanalytic fabric. It is a text that will appeal to those who are intrigued with the metaphysics of personality development, yet the practical minded physician will enjoy the clinical gems that are concerned with pathological development and clinical application.

"This is a reference book that will be constantly used and will satisfy the most exacting reader."

Robert Coles, Harvard University Health Services—"Twenty years is a generation's time, reason enough for reflection on the history of any annual. . . . The twentieth volume in what has come to be one of the most scholarly and fertile of the psychoanalytic publications [contains] unprejudiced observations, papers on psychoanalytic theory [that] are unusually stimulating . . . excellent clinical reports. In sum, this year's issue offers richness and diversity (yes, even a touch of humility), a promising way indeed for an annual to celebrate a significant anniversary."

The Psychoanalytic Study of the Child

VOLUME XXII

The Psychoanalytic Study of the Child

VOLUME XXII

INTERNATIONAL UNIVERSITIES PRESS, INC.
New York New York

Library of Congress Catalog Card Number: 45:11304

Manufactured in the United States of America

CONTENTS

Problems of Psychopathology and Therapy

Contributions to Psychoanalytic Theory

Contributions to Normal and Pathological Development

Clinical Contributions

PROBLEMS OF PSYCHOPATHOLOGY AND THERAPY

ABOUT LOSING AND BEING LOST

ANNA FREUD, LL.D., D.Sc. (London)

Interpretations of Losing: Dynamic and Libido-Economic

Losing and mislaying objects came under analytic scrutiny at an early date. In 1901, in *The Psychopathology of Everyday Life,* we find it mentioned for the first time, and, further, more explicitly in the chapters on "Parapraxes" of the *Introductory Lectures* (1916-1917). In both publications, Freud explained losing, as he did the other common errors such as forgetting, slips of the tongue, etc., on the basis of a conscious intention being interfered with by a wish which arises from the unconscious. In the case of losing this means that we have the unconscious desire to discard something which consciously we wish to retain. The unconscious tendency makes use of some favorable moment (when our attention is turned elsewhere, when we are tired, preoccupied, etc.) to have its own way. We then lose the object in question; i.e., we throw it away, or put it away, without realizing that we are doing so.

A number of examples of such happenings were collected in *The Psychopathology of Everyday Life,* aiming, above all, "at paving the way for the necessary assumption of *unconscious yet operative* mental processes" (p. 272, n.).

For our metapsychological thinking, on the other hand, it is significant that Freud's interest in the phenomenon of losing went, as early as 1916, beyond the explanation of two forces interfering with each other as well as beyond the need to prove the existence of an operative unconscious. In the *Introductory Lectures* he wrote: *"Losing and mislaying* are of particular interest to us owing to the many

Based on a paper that was read at the 18th Congress of the International Psycho-Analytical Association, London, 1953. This version was written in 1966 and is simultaneously published in German as "Über Verlieren und Verlorengehen." In: *Hoofdstukken uit de hedendaagse psychoanalyse.* Arnhem: Van Loghum Slaterus, 1967.

meanings they may have—owing, that is, to the multiplicity of purposes which can be served by these parapraxes. All cases have in common the fact that there was a wish to lose something; they differ in the basis and aim of that wish. We lose a thing when it is worn out, when we intend to replace it by a better one, when we no longer like it, when it originates from someone with whom we are no longer on good terms or when we acquired it in circumstances we no longer want to recall. . . . The preserving of *things* may be subject to the same influences as that of children" (p. 77).

Insight into "the basis and aim" of losing led here from the dynamics of mental life to the libido-economic aspects of it, with which we are equally familiar. As Freud did then, we now take it for granted that our material possessions are cathected with libido (and aggression) and that retaining, mislaying, losing, and rediscovering them are caused by either quantitative or qualitative alterations in this cathexis.

Our material possessions may represent for us parts of our own body, in which case we cathect them narcissistically; or they may represent human love objects, in which case they are cathected with object libido. We increase or decrease cathexis, or change it from positive to negative, from libido to aggression, according to the vicissitudes of our attitude to our own body on the one hand and to the objects in the external world on the other hand.

So far as the symbolic links between body parts and material possessions are concerned, these have been studied most closely with regard to the anal product. Here psychoanalysis has established a direct line leading from the high value attributed to excrements in infantile life to the value attributed to money in adulthood. Many attitudes of the adult which would otherwise remain puzzling are open to explanation on this basis, such as the urge to collect, miserliness, avariciousness, or their opposites.

A new chapter in the understanding of losing and retaining was opened when analysts began to concentrate their attention on the events of the first year of life and the earliest interactions between infants and their mothers. There is general agreement that the infant directs value cathexis to any object from which satisfaction can be obtained, irrespective of the object being animate or inanimate, part of the internal or of the external world: as observation confirms, the mother's breast, the bottle, the child's own fingers, etc., are periodically searched for, found, lost, recaptured, etc.

On the other hand, it depends on the individual author's theoretical orientation whether the dawning differentiation between the self and the object world is conceived of as happening very early or comparatively late in infancy; and whether inanimate objects (such as the bottle) and body parts (such as fingers) are seen as objects in their own right or merely as derivatives of and substitutes for the mother. It seems to me that any decision in this respect (or the continuing indecision) needs to be based on the fact that we deal here with undifferentiated and unstructured human beings; that this is a period of life when there are no whole objects, only part objects; when there are only anaclitic, i.e., need-satisfying, object relationships; and when even external objects are included in the child's internal, narcissistic milieu.[1]

We are greatly helped in our dilemma by the concept of the "transitional object" as it was introduced by D. W. Winnicott (1953). Winnicott traced the line which connects the mother's breast as a source of pleasure with the thumb which is sucked and the blanket, pillow, or soft, cuddly toy which is played with. He showed convincingly that all these early objects are cathected doubly, narcissistically and with object love, and that this enables the child to transfer his attachments gradually from the cathected figure of the mother to the external world in general.

Thus, human beings are flexible where their attachments are concerned. Narcissistically colored ties alternate with object ties proper; libidinal with aggressive cathexis; animate with inanimate objects. This creates multiple possibilities for discharge, which remain important far beyond childhood. Children who are frustrated, dissatisfied, jealous, etc., but unable for internal or external reasons to react aggressively to their parents, may turn this same aggression toward material things and become destructive of their toys, their clothing, the furniture, etc. In a temper or rage individuals of all ages may choose as their point of attack either their own bodies, or other people, or any objects within their reach. Children in separation distress may cling to any of their possessions which they invest, for the time being, with cathexis displaced from their human objects.

[1] According to a term introduced by W. Hoffer (1952).

When we analyze adolescents who pass through a phase of withdrawal from the object world, or who suffer from the aftereffects of an unhappy love affair, we often find that they are obsessed with holding on to what is left, in the form of compiling lists either of their remaining friends, or of their valuables. People with obsessional characters are well known to displace the reaction formations against their hostile impulses and death wishes from human beings to material things, thereby becoming unable to discard anything, down to the most valueless, useless, and superfluous matters.

There is no doubt in our mind that the libido-economic aspects of the interpretation of losing add considerably to its dynamic explanation and that, on this basis, we advance from the mere understanding of phenomena such as losing, mislaying, discarding, destroying, recapturing, etc., to some theory concerning the attitude of human beings to their possessions. We begin to understand, further, why losing things is the exception rather than the rule, in spite of the multitude of items which we own. Obviously, it is the distribution of our libido between the animate and the inanimate world and the resulting positive cathexis of material objects which assures that our possessions remain tied to us, or, rather, we to them.

We understand, further, why some people become chronic losers. If their libidinal processes are seriously altered, they cease to have a hold on their possessions, without the latter having changed for the worse in any respect. We see this happen, for example, in individuals whose whole interest is concentrated on one particular subject (such as a scientific inquiry) and who become "abstracted" as a result; or in states of high emotional involvement such as mourning, or being in love, when cathexis is similarly sent out in one particular direction only and withdrawn from other uses.

Certain other phenomena may be mentioned in the same connection. We are familiar with the *fear of impoverishment* which appears as a symptom in a number of prepsychotic states, and we understand it, on the basis of the foregoing, as the result of the individual's libidinal withdrawal from his material possessions and the ensuing fear of losing hold of them; obviously, this is not unlike the graver psychotic delusion of the destruction of the world, which we interpret as a reflection in consciousness of the withdrawal of libido from the object world in general. We know severe states of *negativ-*

ism in which the individual withdraws cathexis not only from material possessions but also from his body, which as a consequence is utterly neglected (dirty, unkempt, starved, etc.). We are familiar, further, with the concept of *voluntary poverty,* an attitude which is practiced by many religious, political, and social bodies where it is meant to assure that their members will cathect only ideals and not waste cathexis on material matters. Also, we expect poets, writers, members of the medical profession, and others to be *"high-minded,"* i.e., at least to be partially uninterested in material reward.

Some Reactions to Losing: Identification with the Lost Object

We take it for granted that we feel unhappy and miserable after losing one of our possessions, even if these moods are hardly justified by the circumstances themselves.

We feel *deprived,* in the first instance, not necessarily because of the objective value of the lost item but more frequently because of its subjective value, as representative of an important body part (penis symbol) or an important love object (the giver of it). On this basis we go through a period of detaching ourselves from it, almost as we do when *mourning* a dead person. Also, we feel *guilty,* as if we had not lost the thing unintentionally but discarded it in full consciousness.

Nevertheless, this accumulation of castration distress, mourning, and guilt still does not suffice to explain all of the loser's distress. There are further elements involved which originate in deeper layers of the mind and become visible only where losing occurs either during an analysis, or at least in full view of an analyst. When this happens, we notice, first, that the loser seems to ascribe some independent action to the lost object. He can be heard to say not only, "I have lost something, mislaid it, forgotten where I put it," etc., but equally often: "It got lost," or "It is gone," or "It has come back." Obviously this signifies a displacement: the libidinal withdrawal responsible for the loss is shifted from the inner world of the loser to the item which has been lost, personifying the latter in the process. We notice, secondly, that the loser's emotions do not confine themselves to his own regrets about the loss, but extend to feelings which allegedly belong to the lost object. Here, projection has led to personification, which in its turn is followed by identification.[2]

I remember in this connection an early observation of my own which left me with a lasting impression of the processes concerned. The central figure of the incident was a young girl, an ardent mountaineer, whose walking trip had taken her high into the Alps. Resting near a waterfall, she had forgotten her cap in the camping area. The loss was insignificant in itself and did not seem to concern her much in the beginning. But this changed during the night which followed the excursion. Lying sleepless in her bed, she was suddenly compelled to imagine the lost cap, exposed and deserted in the dark solitude of the mountain scenery. The misery created by this picture became extreme and intolerable until she sobbed herself to sleep.

Identification of the loser with the lost object, as demonstrated by the above example, can be confirmed by us on the basis of numerous other observations. In child analysis we are struck by the fact that certain children—especially those with increased ambivalence and strong defenses against aggression—cling to their possessions, not only to collect and amass them, but because they fear to hurt the imagined feelings of the toys if they consent to their being given away or thrown away. There are many dolls and teddy bears which are preserved in this manner until adolescence or even adulthood, not because their owners have remained "childish" in this respect, but because they have remained too identified with these former transitional objects to withdraw feeling from them altogether.

Such displacements of affect from the loser to the lost become still more obvious when the lost object is a human one. In our work with separated children during wartime, we had many occasions to observe those who experienced not their own, very real separation distress but the imagined distress, loneliness, and longing of the mother whom they had left behind. "I have to telephone my Mummy, she will feel so lonely," was a frequent wish, expressed especially in the evening. Children who went home on short holidays from the residential institution used to try and diminish the imagined distress of their nurses by promising to "send them parcels," as their mothers did to comfort them when they left home. Nursery school children often ask their teacher after a weekend or holiday what she has done

2 "Projective identification," a concept introduced by Melanie Klein (1932).

"all alone," whether she has "missed" them. Patients in analysis confirm this attitude in the transference when they experience the imagined distress of the analyst in place of their own during a break in treatment.

It is not difficult in analysis to understand and interpret such displacements of feeling. When traced back to their source, they reveal themselves as based on early childhood events when the loser was himself "lost," that is, felt deserted, rejected, alone, and experienced in full force as his own all the painful emotions which he later ascribes to the objects lost by him.

The Child as Lost Object and as Loser of Objects

We remember the hint given by Freud in the *Introductory Lectures* with regard to children, and we understand that their protection from danger, or exposure to danger, proceeds on lines similar to the preservation or losing of material things. The parents, as owners of the children, cathect them with libido or aggression. We assume that the younger the child, the greater is the part played by narcissistic libido in this respect; as the child grows older, he becomes increasingly part of his parents' object world, cathected with object libido proper. There is a gap in our theoretical understanding when we try to imagine the ways and means by which this cathexis, of whichever kind, reaches its object. We fall back here on the practical experience that children feel secure, happy, and content while they are loved by their parents, and that they become insecure, unhappy, and hurt in their narcissism if this love is withdrawn, or diminished, or changed into aggression.

As in the case of material objects, for a child to get lost is the exception rather than the rule, which is surprising in view of the lack of reality orientation in our toddlers and under-fives, and of the boisterousness and adventurous spirit of those who are slightly older. Here the children's urge to cling seems to unite with the parents' high valuation of their offspring and, combined, to set limits to the area in which the latter roam freely.

It is only when parental feelings are ineffective or too ambivalent, or when their aggression is more effective than their love, or when the mother's emotions are temporarily engaged elsewhere, that children not only feel lost but, in fact, get lost. This usually happens under conditions which make rationalization easy, but which, on the other hand, are much too common to explain the specific event: such as crowds, a full department store, etc. It is interesting that children usually do not blame themselves for getting lost but instead blame the mother who lost them. An example of this was a little boy, lost in a store, who, after being reunited with his mother, accused her tearfully: "You losted me!" (not "I lost you!").

Matters are different when the looseness and breaking of the emotional tie originate with the child, not with the parents. We know children of all ages whose capacity for object love is underdeveloped for either internal or external, innate or acquired reasons. This defect may become manifest in the symptoms of early wandering, frequently getting lost, truanting, etc. In these instances, the children do not accuse other people, nor do they feel guilty themselves.

It is a fact, well known especially to schoolteachers, that children become chronic losers if they feel unloved at home or are unloved in fact. They do not turn to possessions to compensate themselves for what they miss in their lives. On the contrary, they are singularly unable to establish or to retain ownership. They come to school without the necessary implements, and they forget in the classroom the items which should be taken home. They forget and mislay their money, their caps and articles of clothing wherever they are. We feel tempted to say that not only are their possessions strewn around, but they actually run away from the children. What we discover in their analyses first is an inability to cathect the inanimate, owing to the general damage done to their capacity for involvement with objects; next, that they direct to their possessions the whole hostility aroused by the frustrations and disappointments imposed on them by their parents. It is only behind these fairly obvious causes that a further, even more far-reaching motive comes into view: by being chronic losers, they live out a double identification, passively with the lost objects which symbolize themselves, actively with the parents whom they experience to be as neglectful, indifferent, and unconcerned toward them as they themselves are toward their possessions.

The Lost Object in Dreams and Folklore

The significance of losing some item which may be of small value in itself differs greatly from that of losing through death a person who plays an important role in our lives such as a parent, a marital partner, a child. Such differences in the magnitude of an event may altogether change the quality of the accompanying emotions, and therefore should not be taken lightly. Nevertheless, certain similarities or even identities between the two types of happenings are open to view in the specific case of losing.

We assume that the process of mourning for a loved person will last while the emotions of the mourner are concentrated on the loss, as well as on the necessity of withdrawing feeling from the inner image of the dead. So far as this means withdrawing from the external world, the task of mourning interferes with life itself. So far as it signifies a reunion with the dead by means of reviving and reliving the memories concerning him, mourning is known to be as absorbing and fulfilling as it is painful.

In analysis, we have occasion to notice that in some persons the later stages of mourning are characterized by a series of typical dreams, the latent content of which is fairly easy to interpret. In these dreams the dead person appears, either manifestly or slightly disguised, and makes every effort to bring himself to the notice of the survivor. He searches for him, or pleads with him, or beseeches him to come and stay; he expresses longing, or complains about being alone and deserted. The dreamer feels in the grip of conflicting emotions and alternates between pure joy about the reunion and remorse and guilt for having stayed away from the dead, neglected him, etc. He wakes up, usually, with anxiety and finds it difficult to realize that the whole experience has "only been a dream."

It seems to me that the latent content of these dreams has much in common with the mental processes ascribed above to the person who loses a material possession. Here too a part is played by the interference of two opposite tendencies with each other, the simultaneous wishes to retain and to discard being replaced in this instance by the simultaneous urges to remain loyal to the dead and to turn toward new ties with the living. Here, as in the former examples, the survivor's desolation, longing, loneliness are not acknowledged as his own feelings, but displaced onto the dream image of the dead, where they are experienced in identification with the dead. As above, it can be shown here, when the dream is submitted to interpretation, that identification with the "lost object," the deserted person, is derived from specific infantile experiences when the dreamer, as a child, felt unloved, rejected, and neglected.

There is no doubt about the dream wish here, of course, since its fulfillment is brought about openly by the reappearance of the dead and accompanied by the positive emotions which characterized the lost relationship. The painful accusations, regrets, etc., in the manifest content correspond to the dreamer's realization that he is on the point of becoming disloyal to the dead and his guilt about this. The anxiety which interrupts the dream corresponds to the defense against the opposite wish: to yield to the dream image's invitation, turn away from life altogether, and follow the lost object into death.

Loyalty conflicts with regard to the dead are frequent motifs, not only in dream life but equally in fairy tales, myths, and folklore in general.

Many popular beliefs, for example, are concerned with the figure of a dead person who reappears, usually at nighttime, and beckons to the living. Such figures are invested with dread, obviously to the degree to which the survivor has to ward off the wish to accept the invitation.

Further, we are familiar with innumerable ghost stories, which have a different origin. In these tales, the spirit of the dead person appears in the role of avenger, threatening punishment. Analytic interpretation suggests that tales of this kind are based on the survivor's ambivalence and that such large measures of anxiety are aroused by them because this corresponds to the intensity of the warded-off death wishes which had been directed toward the former love object in life.

The connection is still closer between our subject of losing and another common myth, that of the "lost," "poor," or "wandering" soul. Such lost souls are depicted as being unable to rest in their burial places and condemned instead to wander aimlessly, especially at nighttime, when they moan, sigh, and complain, and beseech the living to help them find release. Some act—often left indefinite—needs to be performed to bring this about.

"Lost souls" are pitiable rather than threatening and uncanny rather than outrightly frightening. They are "poor," since they symbolize the emotional impoverishment felt by the survivor. They are "lost" as symbols of object loss. That they are compelled to "wander" reflects the wandering and searching of the survivor's libidinal strivings which have been rendered aimless, i.e., deprived of their former goal. And, finally, we understand that their "eternal rest" can be achieved only after the survivors have performed the difficult task of dealing with their bereavement and of detaching their hopes, demands, and expectations from the image of the dead.

BIBLIOGRAPHY

Freud, S. (1901), The Psychopathology of Everyday Life. *Standard Edition,* 6. London: Hogarth Press, 1960.

—— (1916-1917 [1915-1917]), Introductory Lectures on Psycho-Analysis. *Standard Edition,* 15 & 16. London: Hogarth Press, 1963.

Hoffer, W. (1952), The Mutual Influences in the Development of Ego and Id: Earliest Stages. *This Annual,* 7:31-41.

Klein, M. (1932), *The Psycho-Analysis of Children.* London: Hogarth Press.

Winnicott, D. W. (1953), Transitional Objects and Transitional Phenomena: A Study of the First Not-Me Possession. *Int. J. Psa.,* 34:89-97.

ON OBSTACLES STANDING IN THE WAY OF PSYCHOANALYTIC CURE

JEANNE LAMPL-DE GROOT, M.D. (Amsterdam)

Among the many unsolved problems in psychoanalysis I have chosen one that is of practical as well as theoretical importance. It was raised by Freud in 1937 in "Analysis Terminable and Interminable." He suggested that instead of investigating in which way psychoanalytic treatment accomplishes a cure (which is sufficiently known), we should ask ourselves: which are the obstacles standing in the way of achieving a cure? This question is still as interesting as it was thirty years ago. In the meantime, however, our experience and our theoretical knowledge have grown. These can be applied to work out some of Freud's points and to add new ones.

I shall not discuss untimely interruptions of analysis due to external circumstances, or the impatience or inexperience of the analyst, or unforeseen deteriorations in the patient's mental condition, e.g., the outbreak of severe psychosis, which demands discontinuation of analytic treatment and hospitalization. I shall limit myself to those situations in which the patient is sufficiently intelligent and able to cooperate, in which there is a good working alliance that has helped to uncover a considerable part of the unconscious conflicts, and in which the therapeutic effect has nevertheless failed to come about after patient working through in prolonged treatment.

Freud mentioned some of the factors responsible. Among them are the following:

1. A strong need for punishment that leads to the negative therapeutic reaction.

2. An incapacity to "tame" the instinctual drives and a particularly unfortunate relationship between sexual (libidinal) and aggressive drives.

3. An ego alteration or impairment which makes the patient in-

capable of coping with the instinctual demands in a favorable way; or, put in another way, an irregular development of ego functions.

4. A clash between passive and active tendencies, a repudiation of femininity in the sexual sphere.

I shall try to examine these different factors, especially in their interaction with each other.

Need for Punishment

Freud discovered quite early that neurotic patients are not born as degenerates but are suffering from acquired illnesses that originate in childhood and are due to a failure to resolve the oedipus complex in a normal way. In this, traumatic experiences, e.g., the sexual use or seduction of small children by adults, play an important role. The uncovering of such repressed experiences was originally expected to result in mental health. The fate of the oedipal situation was seen as the core of neurosis.

The bringing into consciousness of the repressed oedipal conflicts did indeed sometimes lead to the expected recovery. In many cases, however, both analyst and patient were disappointed. The neurotic symptoms did not disappear or were replaced by others. The increased experience gained in analysis of adults and children, and especially by direct observation of infants, began to reveal the importance of the preoedipal phase of development, i.e., not only of the maturational processes of the instinctual drives, but also of the development of object relationships and of the gradual unfolding of ego functions. In the area of drive development, the recognition of the aggressive drives was of special significance. In the area of the ego functions, the gradual organization of the primary autonomous functions, the defense mechanisms, the structures leading to secondary autonomy, and the emergence of the superego as a subsystem of the ego organization greatly furthered the understanding of harmonious as well as disturbed mental development. Early object relations, the infant's first tie to his mother, proved to exert great influence on the course of further development in nearly every area. The mother-child dyad determines to a large extent the state of the infant's physical and mental well-being. Yet I do not believe that this increase in our knowledge has decisively added to the number of successes of analytic treatment during the last decades.

On the other hand, there has been a positive change in the type and range of psychic disturbances that we try to influence by psychoanalysis. We no longer limit therapeutic efforts to the "ordinary" (transference) neuroses. We analyze character neuroses, borderline cases, and even psychotics and delinquents, although these conditions may sometimes require the introduction of "parameters" in our technique (Eissler, 1953). This extension of the application of psychoanalysis has become possible through the increase in our knowledge. At the same time it has altered the goals and the expectations of the psychoanalytic procedure. We no longer are content with removing neurotic symptoms; we now look for character distortions and, if possible, try to alter disharmonies in the mental structure. This is especially necessary in training analyses.

Character traits are essentially shaped in the first years of life, in the preoedipal and the oedipal phases of development. It is true that they unfold on the basis of genetically determined factors inherent in drive equipment as well as in the potentialities out of which ego qualities, functions, and capacities gradually develop. It is the growing interaction of these given factors that can proceed harmoniously only if the mother-infant relationship provides the necessary favorable climate. For this reason we need to look into that archaic preoedipal phase, the period immediately following birth. We must examine the "prehistory" of patients who, suffering from a strong need for punishment, show the negative therapeutic reaction. This symptom is due to a very strict superego, which does not permit the enjoyment of a state of well-being. The superego, which becomes established as an internal system after the passing of the oedipus complex, has taken over the norms and the prohibitions of the parents. The severity of the superego partly mirrors the strictness of the parental demands, but these are not the only source of its cruelty. As is well known, this is to a large extent due to the turning inward of aggression that cannot be discharged in the outer world. This process, however, has its precursors in the preoedipal phase and it seems worthwhile to examine its fate during this period.

All of us have treated patients suffering from unconscious guilt and a strong need for punishment; we succeed in improving their condition by uncovering their adherence to the severe parental demands, thus enabling the mature person to choose his own norms and restrictions in a healthier way. However, this success, which sometimes already occurs in the initial phase of an analysis, is often followed by a regressive tendency and a renewed clinging to the feeling of inferiority and guilt-laden worthlessness. If we then try to unravel the superego *precursors* in the preoedipal phase, where single parental prohibitions were accepted and even internalized, we may be confronted with the child's overwhelming anxiety concerning his own *aggressive* impulses. After the superego demands have been attenuated, the sexual wishes are no longer experienced as quite so dangerous unless they are completely fused with aggression and have become transformed into sadistic fantasies and actions. But the *aggressive* impulses are, in any event, experienced as too dangerous. In the first place, the infant has at some time or other learned that an attack on or the destruction of some object or other, e.g., a pet or a toy, while originally providing intense joy and satisfaction, usually leads to loss or at least to damage of the object. This experience is especially threatening when the impulse is directed toward a living person, initially the mother. As a consequence of the child's magic thinking, he experiences his impulses as though they were real actions. The conflict between love and hate means to him: to keep or to destroy his mother, an unsolvable problem.

This brings me to a second source of anxiety. The little child's magic world includes the narcissistic fantasy of his omnipotence as well as that of his parents. His inability to solve the love-hate conflict is a severe threat to his inner equilibrium. In order to ameliorate the narcissistic injury he again clings to reinforced fantasies of grandeur, and a vicious circle emerges.

Some patients apparently find it less painful to keep their neurotic suffering in self-punishment than to face the primitive fear of their own aggressive drives and the destruction of their omnipotence fantasies. In other cases a real improvement in the patient's condition may occur, provided he is able to accept a certain *powerlessness,* as it exists in every human's life, and to find other ways of handling his aggressive impulses. Such a favorable outcome is by no means a regular occurrence. If we fail, we must ask ourselves: what other obstacles stand in the way of a patient's recovery?

Incapacity to Tame the Instinctual Drives

My previous reference to a successful analysis of the preoedipal love-hate conflicts already implied that the infantile nature of the child's ego organization—i.e., his magical and wishful thinking—greatly influences his ability to deal with the drive impulses. We all know that it does not make sense to speak of the "strength" of the drives. What matters is the *relation* between the power of the drives and the forces available to the gradually developing ego functions, which will ultimately be organized in what we call the system ego. Quantitative considerations (which are often neglected) are of utmost importance, provided we realize that we are dealing with *relative* quantities or intensities.

What do we mean by the "taming" of the drives? It is not suppression, repression, or warding off of the instinctual impulses. Human beings cannot live and grow without a certain amount of direct satisfaction. However, living in a community with fellowmen demands considerable limitations of drive discharge. For this reason certain transformations of the *modes* of gratification are imperative. These must occur both in the original narcissistic state of the libido and its later investment in object relations and in the aggressive drive. We have conceptualized such transformations as processes of desexualization and deaggressivization or neutralization of the mental energy of the instinctual drives (Hartmann, 1964).

I am aware of the fact that the term "mental energy" may give rise to criticism on the part of psychologists, psychiatrists, and psychoanalysts. One of the arguments of those who oppose the concept of mental energy reads: the term "energy" is not applicable in mental life; it is borrowed from physics and therefore too mechanistic. I would counter this argument by maintaining that, as I see it, it may rather be the other way round. Since human languages have existed, words such as "force," "power," and "energy" have been used to designate certain activities and qualities of human beings. When the science of physics began to develop, from where did the physicists take their terminology? Is it not conceivable that they chose their terms for describing physical phenomena on the basis of an (unconscious) anthropomorphism? It is true that as analysts we cannot specify the sources of "mental energy," that we do not know whether its nature is chemical, hormonal, electrical, etc.; nor can we measure it. However, in psychology—as in physics and other sciences —there are many unknown areas and limitations of knowledge. As long as we do not have a better term to account for our observations, therefore, I see no advantage in discarding a concept that has proved to be of heuristic usefulness.

The "tamability" of drives seems to be dependent upon a certain degree of flexibility, which permits neutralization of a portion of their energy as far as the drives themselves are concerned. It is difficult to decide whether *aggression* is more inflexible and harder to neutralize than *libido* or whether the danger inherent in its destructive component is responsible for the strength of the countermeasures adopted against aggressive manifestations. Surveying man's history, one is strongly impressed by the numerous breakthroughs of violent, unneutralized, aggressive and destructive acts among fellowmen. The final outcome of the mental process that leads to a restriction of direct discharge is, however, equally dependent upon the qualities of the mediating and organizing ego organization. In early childhood the immature ego functions are not yet organized in a coherent system. The ego is therefore "weak" in relation to the imperative demands of the powerful drive impulses. In coping with them, the ego of the infant and the little child is strongly dependent on the mother's support.

Irregular Ego Development

The study of ego development is meaningful only if it is viewed in its interaction with drive development, because both ego and id develop out of an initially undifferentiated matrix. While the drives as well as the core of the gradually emerging ego functions are inborn, both developments are decisively influenced by the first experiences in the mother-child dyad and especially by the infant's reactions to external and internal stimuli. For theorizing in this field we cannot resort to information gained in psychoanalytic treatment but must turn to the careful observational studies on newborns and infants, such as those carried out by Spitz, Anna Freud, Bowlby, Margaret Mahler, Ernst and Marianne Kris, Winnicott, and many others.

I shall start with the observations made by Spitz, which he described in many papers but most comprehensively in his book *The First Year of Life* (1965). On the basis of many careful investigations Spitz depicts the newborn as having a high stimulus barrier which shields him against stimuli from the external world. His sensory organs begin to function only some time after birth. The newborn "receives" stimuli from inside, e.g., hunger, thirst, etc., and reacts to them with reflex movements, but he does not yet experience sensory *perceptions*. The *reception* of stimuli is accompanied by sensations of unpleasure; the removal of tensions provides pleasure. This original reception system is termed the *coenesthetic organization*. Later on the *diacritic organization* comes into being. The infant gradually develops his faculty of perception by way of making a "distance contact" with his mother. He now "recognizes" her face (or at least part of her face, a so-called Gestalt), and the diacritic organization begins to unfold. The mode of functioning of the coenesthetic organization is the primary process, whereas the diacritic organization gradually switches over to secondary-process functioning.

From the very beginning the reactions of individual infants differ remarkably. Some infants remain more or less passive, others seem to crave passionately for the satisfaction of their bodily needs, the gaining of pleasure and the removal of unpleasure. These observations highlight the constitutional differences in drive equipment. However, the infant's active behavior, manifested in his body movements, his crying, his grasping, etc., not only reveals something about his drives, it also indicates how and at what rate his ego functions of perception, memory, primitive awareness of an outer world, motility, etc., begin to develop. The individual differences in the timing and the speed of development point to inborn potentialities or qualities of the gradually emerging ego as well.

It is well known that the infant's complete dependence on the mother's care for survival is complicated by the fact that he is also dependent on the mother's *love* for his physical and mental growth. If he is deprived of loving mothering, the infant is hampered or even totally disturbed in the development of the various functions. This is valid not only for the sensory functions and the active responses to stimuli (diacritic organization) but also for the passive receptive state of the earlier coenesthetic organization. In the course of development the diacritic mode of functioning more or less replaces and sometimes represses the earlier mode of functioning. Normally, however, both organizations continue to exist throughout life.

In one instance the coenesthetic organization is clearly revived, namely, in the healthy mother who is nursing her newborn child. The mother's coenesthetic way of functioning enables her to "understand" the newborn's signals which indicate his needs, to "respond" to them, to communicate with her baby in an adequate way. The question then arises: what is an *adequate way?* Since the newborn can function only in the passive receptive mode, that is what the mother must react to. However, the mother's understanding and furthering of the gradually developing diacritic organization are equally important. Her capacity to stimulate this unfolding is necessary as well. I believe we have to evaluate the "adequacy" of the mother's behavior in terms of a well-balanced interplay between the revived coenesthetic and the diacritic modes of reacting. We have always known that too much frustration as well as too much indulgence can lead to disturbed development. One explanation may be sought in an unharmonious relation of the two ways of functioning in the mother's personality. Apart from the fact that an infant's inborn passivity-activity pattern may be an unfortunate one, it seems to be highly dependent upon the nature of the "dialogue" between mother and child, upon the mother's competence to use both modes of functioning in accordance with the special needs of her baby. Spitz remarks that in many adults the coenesthetic organization is so deeply repressed or even abolished that it cannot be revived. If this is the case in a mother, her newborn will be frustrated from birth, with deleterious effects on his growth.

Spitz believes that the coenesthetic mode of functioning is retained not only in a healthy mother in her relation to the newborn but also in specially talented people, artists, musicians, composers, dancers, acrobats, etc. However, I believe that every person who in some way or other is performing original work must retain or reacquire the capacity to "regress" to the receptive mode of functioning, to the coenesthetic organization. This regression is a "regression in the service of the ego," to use Kris's concept (1952), a regression in the service of all nonautomatic functioning. Of course, the diacritic organization, the secondary-process functioning, must be developed as well, to arrange, regulate, and shape the person's final performance. In the last decades many authors have written about creativity and the related phenomena of intuition and empathy. I mention, among others, Bornstein (1948), Burlingham (1935), Greenacre (1957), Greenson (1960, 1966), Kohut (1966), Kris (1952), Olden (1958), Schafer (1959), and Spitz (1965). Greenacre draws attention to the "collective alternates," the talented child's "love affair with the world" in addition to the love for his mother. Kohut describes "transformations of narcissism," which he believes are responsible for creativity and empathy in connection with the development of a child's grandeur fantasies into adult ideals. Others stress the importance of the early mother-child relationship. Spitz especially points to the importance of both modes of functioning, the passive, receptive, and the active, ordering modality, which originate in the coenesthetic and in the diacritic organizations. In addition, Spitz draws attention to the observation that many highly creative persons exhibit disturbances in certain areas of their personalities, often in their emotional, sexual, and social life. Owing to the complex nature of mental development, it seems to be very difficult to achieve and to retain a harmonious balance between the two modes of functioning. On the one side derangements in the interaction between the processes of id and ego growth, and on the other side a lack of intensive support from the mother in this complicated interplay may lead to manifold disturbances in the child's development and the later adult disorders.

My special interest in this interplay concerns the case in which the mother fails to respond to the newborn's original coenesthetic mode of functioning, with the consequence that it is rigidly repressed and buried. For I believe that the capacity to revive the original receptive passive modality is of great significance in a variety of circumstances—*the psychoanalytic situation being one of them.* In psychoanalytic treatment a working alliance between analyst and patient is indispensable. It is a "dyadic" relationship in which both participants play their role.

It is well known that verbal communication between patient and analyst is not the only way in which they collaborate. Speech may suffice to uncover a patient's unconscious neurotic conflicts as they reveal themselves in the actual situation and can be traced back to their origin in the oedipal situation. The analyst's psychological knowledge, his technical skill, his adherence to the basic rule, his listening with free-floating (suspended) attention, and his self-knowledge enable him to avoid contamination of the analytic situation by his personal problems and peculiarities. These basic prerequisites may be sufficient to achieve the goal of working through the patient's *oedipal* conflicts. However, in the many cases in which development in the preoedipal phase was decisively distorted or hampered, non-verbal modes of communication become unavoidable. In these cases, I believe, the analyst's intuitive empathic understanding remains incomplete if he cannot revive his own coenesthetic organization. He must be able passively to receive signals sent out by the patient's behavior, his posture, his movements, his nonverbally expressed emotions and affects, his mimicry, his stammering, etc. This applies especially to those cases where the very first relation between newborn and mother was severely disturbed. Of course, the analyst must also be capable of alternatingly using the diacritic mode of functioning in order to verbalize what is going on in the patient's inner world. It is understandable that this verbalization may be difficult. Words can express inner experiences only approximately and often insufficiently. Attempts in this direction frequently proceed by trial and error. Sometimes the analyst's communication succeeds in reviving a patient's archaic personality residues and thus has a beneficial effect; sometimes it may fail to do so. But without the capacity to use the primitive receptive mode of functioning, the analyst cannot succeed. This mode is, I believe, one of the deepest layers of empathy.

There is a parallel need for the *patient* to retain or revive his coenesthetic, receptive way of functioning. Although this capacity is based on innate factors, it may have been either furthered or impaired by the mother's intervention. If it has been suffocated at the very beginning, it may remain buried forever. In this case, the patient is unable to re-experience and to work through the very first conflicts, with the result that further conflicts affecting, in some cases, every area of the personality cannot be recovered. It is sometimes difficult to determine whether a failure in psychoanalytic treatment is due to the analyst's rigidity or to the patient's incapacity to overcome his resistance against the unearthing of his most primitive conflicts, because of the great amount of *anxiety* that has to be mastered. Initially the lack of the mother's response causes the infant unpleasure, but after a certain distance contact and a first narcissistic object relation have been established, anxiety comes into the picture. The development of the instinctual life, of the object relationships, and particularly of the primitive ego functions is hampered. The situation has become a traumatic one.

External events, provided they are not too life threatening, need not per se constitute an infantile trauma. They become traumatic when the infant's inner world has remained chaotic. In later phases, after ego functioning has been acquired, it becomes possible to determine whether an external event which was considered to be traumatic by the observer actually traumatized the child or not (Anna Freud and others). On the other hand, certain constellations usually have detrimental effects, especially a succession of states of unpleasure and lack of satisfaction which may arouse so much anxiety that a passive, receptive attitude is experienced as a danger. This may constitute the basis of the subsequent fear of passivity. In the phallic-oedipal situation, a passive attitude may acquire the meaning of passive *sexual* surrender. This implies, for the little boy, giving up masculinity and his male organ, in order to acquire his mother's position. The passive sexual wishes then engender great castration anxiety. If this meaning persists, every passive attitude may be experienced as a danger and may be repressed completely. Later in life, when passive receptivity is still indispensable in many situations, e.g., in learning processes, the maturing personality may become blunted to such an extent that the original capacities are more or less suffocated. As mentioned previously, this process is enhanced and reinforced by *aggressive* impulses, which are mobilized by experiences of unpleasure, lack of satisfaction, and disappointment. These are experienced as dangers during the phase of development in which the child is struggling with the conflict between love and hate, between the need to keep the love object and the wish to destroy it. If the latter predominates, every activity may be experienced as *destructive* aggression, with the result that the child is utterly dependent upon the mother's empathic understanding and her support in overcoming these anxiety-ridden inner conflicts. Whenever this support is lacking, *autoaggression* is unavoidable.

This may be one of the factors underlying the resistances of some neurotics in whom "the instinct of self-preservation has actually been reversed. They [these patients] seem to aim at nothing other than self-injury and self-destruction. It is possible too that the people who in fact do in the end commit suicide belong to this group" (Freud, 1940, p. 180).

I shall now summarize what we have so far learned about the different obstacles standing in the way of a psychoanalytic cure. It has become clear that a strong need for punishment, leading to negative therapeutic results, has a prehistory in the very first days and years of life. In the analysis of patients suffering from this disturbance, we must look for this prehistory and attempt to revive their most primitive modes of experiencing and functioning, and help them find more favorable ways of acting and reacting. In doing so we also come up against the archaic drives, in their unmitigated intensity, especially the *aggressive, destructive* impulses and the concomitant clinging to the earliest omnipotent fantasies. As I mentioned before, I am far from optimistic about the therapeutic results that can be achieved in such cases. There are, e.g., patients whose mother-infant dyadic relationship was so disturbed and engendered so much anxiety that one does not dare to go too deep into the primitive, chaotic inner life and therefore cannot revive the oldest reaction patterns. We must then limit our therapeutic efforts to the improvements that can be attained by virtue of working through the actual and oedipal conflicts. All we can do in such cases is to continue to wonder about the chief causes of the failure: whether it was due to an inherent incapacity to tame the instinctual drives, to a lack of ego potentialities, unevenness of ego development, disturbed reality testing; or whether it was the mother's incapacity to "understand" the infant's needs and to respond to them in a well-balanced way. This also involves the question whether the analyst was capable of the necessary empathy to gain insight into the archaic mother-infant interaction. A psychoanalyst who has a rigid personality and who in his training analysis has not acquired the capacity to revive his own coenesthetic organization, his personal receptive mode of functioning, will be unable to carry out this special part of the treatment.

A further complicating factor lies in the fact that not only severe *frustrations* in the original dyad may lead to the burial of the archaic receptive mode of functioning and thus to a distorted development.

As I mentioned before, too much giving in, "spoiling," may bring about a developmental disturbance as well. Too much and too instantaneous satisfaction of the infant in the receptive state may hamper the development of his active strivings and thus impair the coming into being of the diacritic, active functioning and result in similar disturbances of development. This outcome is less well described and understood than the pathogenic result of frustrations and lack of loving mothering. At first, it seems strange that love can have a deleterious effect. However, on second thought, we realize that a spoiling mother is an overanxious person who wards off her own unconscious hostile feelings in an active quasi-loving but domineering attitude. The infant then has no outlet for his own aggressive impulses, and his need to acquire some kind of independence is frustrated. Most of his active attempts are experienced as hostile attacks by both mother and child. In order not to lose the mother's love, the little child has to give up his strivings for independent activities and to cling to the passive modes of gaining satisfaction. The resentment caused by the mother's suppression of his genuine need to become a person in his own right is firmly repressed. His diacritic mode of functioning may not develop adequately. According to Spitz, the outcome of a crippled diacritic development is much less frequent in our Western culture than the suffocation of the coenesthetic organization.

In connection with the psychoanalytic profession, Spitz therefore recommends that an investigation into a candidate's capacity to revive his coenesthetic organization should be a prerequisite for the decision whether to admit him to psychoanalytic training or not. Theoretically, I am in complete agreement with Spitz, but I do not know how to carry out this requirement. In the selection of candidates we try to evaluate a number of personality traits, among them a certain constancy, but also a certain flexibility of character. However, on the basis of a few interviews, it is extremely difficult to form a well-founded opinion of a candidate's suitability in this respect. Sometimes a person who has what appears to be a very rigid character profits a great deal from analysis and is then able to revive the necessary receptive empathy. In other cases, an intuitive person, who is apparently full of understanding and empathy, persists in clinging so tenaciously to a primitive, passive attitude that he becomes involved in acting out his own conflicts in the patient's analysis. In these cases it is only the personal analysis that can decide whether the necessary balance between the two modes of functioning will finally be achieved. I hope that at some time we shall be able to find more appropriate ways of evaluating the giftedness of the future analysts.

Reviewing the points I have raised so far, we can conclude that some of the obstacles to analytic cure mentioned by Freud can in part be traced back to the earliest developmental phases. The need for punishment and the unevenness of ego development are better understood if we view them in terms of the interaction of drive and ego growth and the mother's reaction to her infant in the dyadic relationship. The precursors of a cruel superego are to be found in the relative intensity and the fate of the *aggressive impulses*. If they cannot find appropriate outlets, initially in direct discharge and gradually in a more or less neutralized form, they will finally shape the superego into a sadistic, self-punishing agency. Although the innate properties of the drive equipment may be responsible for the fact that the drives cannot be tamed, other factors may also be of decisive significance: a deficiency in the possibilities for neutralization which depend on the interaction of certain drive properties with specific ego potentials, the presence or absence of a faculty for sublimated activities in the ego organization, and the influence of the mother on this process of interdependent development. The balance or imbalance that the mother has achieved between the two modes of functioning may further or hamper this threefold interaction. The same is true for the "clash" between passivity and activity. As we have already seen, passive and active tendencies are normal constituents of personality; they have their place in the mental life of healthy adults.

Repudiation of Femininity

I now turn to the last point mentioned by Freud: the struggle between femininity and masculinity on the basis of innate bisexuality, the so-called anatomical "bedrock." Masculinity and femininity were originally more or less equated with activity and passivity. This view has been abandoned, although this has not always been made explicitly clear. I think we should make a very plain distinction. Passive and active modes of functioning manifest themselves in every human being from birth throughout life; both are indispensable for normal, harmonious development. Masculinity and femininity refer to *sexual* life and its derivatives in love life. Although the relation between the sexes is a model for many other performances in life, it coincides with active and passive behavior only when these behavior patterns are sexualized or, more accurately, invested with nonneutralized drive energy. Repudiation of femininity does not automatically imply repudiation of passivity. Freud's original idea that the psychic manifestations of bisexuality, the girl's wish for a penis and the boy's castration fear, were anatomically based (on the assumption that the clitoris is a rudimentary penis) has been disputed by more recent embryological discoveries. The female clitoris apparently is *not* a phylogenetically atrophied penis, since all mammalian embryos are morphologically female in the first days or weeks of their existence. The male-female struggle is genetically determined and unfolds hormonologically. The biological foundation of the woman's strong penis envy and the man's overwhelming castration fear—manifestations which we regularly observe in children and adult patients—must therefore be looked for in the genetic endowment and not in anatomy. However, the child's observation of the anatomical difference between the sexes is the trigger for the individual's sexual difficulties. In the treatment of male patients with intense castration fear, and in that of female patients who appear to be unable to conquer their penis envy and wish for a penis, we have to make the attempt to reach the forerunners of these phenomena in the preoedipal phase. In some instances we may be able to uncover the little child's intense fear not only of losing the mother's love but also, and sometimes predominantly, of losing his "own personality," his still unstable ego organization. The passive wish to "merge with the mother" may have become a severe danger to the gradually emerging need for independence. His growing, but still feeble self-esteem may have been threatened by the mother's domineering influence. It then may happen that in the phallic phase *every* passive wish is sexualized and acquires the meaning of sexual surrender, implying the acceptance of *castration,* as a consequence of which the faculties responsible for the neutralization of energy may become arrested.

These faculties have to be freed and restored in the course of psychoanalytic treatment. If the analyst succeeds in supporting these processes, the patient may be able to conquer his current castration fear as a result of having worked through these primitive anxieties.

I want to stress once again that the increase in our knowledge of early mental development does not always bring us an increase in the desired therapeutic successes, but it enables us to make a more knowledgeable attempt. In training analyses, where we aim at liberating the future analyst's capacity for empathy, our effort cannot be confined to a mere attempt—its success is a prerequisite of our profession.

BIBLIOGRAPHY

Bornstein, B. (1948), Emotional Barriers in the Understanding and Treatment of Young Children. *Amer. J. Orthopsychiat.*, 18:691-697.

Burlingham, D. (1935), Die Einfühlung des Kleinkindes in die Mutter. *Imago*, 21:429-444.

Eissler, K. R. (1953), The Effect of the Structure of the Ego on Psychoanalytic Technique. *J. Amer. Psa. Assn.*, 1:104-143.

Freud, A. (1952), The Mutual Influences in the Development of Ego and Id: Introduction to the Discussion. *This Annual*, 7:42-50.

—— (1965), *Normality and Pathology in Childhood: Assessments of Development*. New York: International Universities Press.

Freud, S. (1937), Analysis Terminable and Interminable. *Standard Edition*, 23:209-253. London: Hogarth Press, 1964.

—— (1940), An Outline of Psycho-Analysis. *Standard Edition*, 23:141-207. London: Hogarth Press, 1964.

Greenacre, P. (1957), The Childhood of the Artist: Libidinal Phase Development and Giftedness. *This Annual*, 12:47-72.

Greenson, R. R. (1960), Empathy and Its Vicissitudes. *Int. J. Psa.*, 41:418-424.

—— (1966), That "Impossible" Profession. *J. Amer. Psa. Assn.*, 14:9-27.

Hartmann, H. (1964), *Essays on Ego Psychology: Selected Problems in Psychoanalytic Theory*. New York: International Press; see esp. Chapts. 9 and 12.

Kohut, H. (1966), Forms and Transformations of Narcissism. *J. Amer. Psa. Assn.*, 14:243-272.

Kris, E. (1952), *Psychoanalytic Explorations in Art*. New York: International Universities Press; see esp. Chapts. 6 and 14.

Lampl-de Groot, J. (1965), *The Development of the Mind: Psychoanalytic Papers on Clinical and Theoretical Problems*. New York: International Universities Press.

Olden, C. (1958), Notes on the Development of Empathy. *This Annual*, 13:505-518.

Schafer, R. (1959), Generative Empathy in the Treatment Situation. *Psa. Quart.*, 28:342-373.

Spitz, R. A. (1957), *No and Yes: On the Beginnings of Human Communication*. New York: International Universities Press.

—— (1965), *The First Year of Life: A Psychoanalytic Study of Normal and Deviant Development of Object Relations*. New York: International Universities Press.

ON AFFECT CONTROL

ANDREW PETO, M.D. (New York)

Anxiety has been in the center of attention since Freud's earliest writings, and the clinical and theoretical insights attained have vindicated this interest. The other affects have never been subject to a comparable systematic investigation, although their paramount role has been stressed in various publications (Jones, 1929; Glover, 1939; Hartmann, 1939; Hartmann and Loewenstein, 1962; Fenichel, 1941; Rapaport, 1953, 1960; Schur, 1958; Jacobson, 1957; Novey, 1961; Arlow and Brenner, 1964; and other authors). Schafer's paper (1964) shows that a clinical-theoretical approach that takes into consideration all the actually operating factors creates a task which can hardly be mastered, even in a long series of systematic observations.

This paper is an inquiry into the first noticeable phases of affect mobilization, affect change, and affect control as observed in the analytic session. The patients had already settled down in their transference neurosis and had acquired the necessary introspection for reporting their inner experiences. As a matter of course the analytic setup contributed to a slowdown and to a better registration of what was going on. The spontaneity and immediacy of the communications enhanced the directness of the patients' reports. In the first part of this paper I shall investigate some clinical-theoretical aspects of control and mobilization of the affect of "sadness."

I

As a point of departure I use a phenomenon that we often encounter in our daily practice. We hear from our patients that they have a definite control over affect mobilization during the analytic

An abridged version of this paper was presented at the 25th International Psycho-Analytical Congress in Copenhagen, July, 1967.

Clinical Professor, Department of Psychiatry, Albert Einstein College of Medicine, New York.

session. They refer on such occasions to their capacity to choose between two possibilities, namely, to slip deeper into an already present affect state or to "snap out" of it. This control is applicable only in the earliest phases of affect mobilization in the session. My observations prove that our patients are mostly correct in judging this capacity of their egos. I found that this ability may be present in all neurotic as well as in certain schizophrenic patients. The most important precondition of snapping out seems to be that the affect should be attached at its most superficial functional level to a well-circumscribed, isolated mental representation (image, thought, attitude, etc.). The moment this stage is passed, snapping out becomes increasingly difficult, and eventually the ego loses this capacity for active control.

In the process of the mobilization of a certain affect, a variety of "being sad" is experienced and reported by the patient. These affect signals are always attached to a corresponding variety of images and thoughts. While these "sadnesses" may eventually form an affect compound in which individual elements are no longer discernible, at the beginning, while not too many elements are operating, the snapping out, the complete affect change, may succeed.

The central observing ego agency is able to watch these affective signal mobilizations. There are multiple "splits" between the functioning and oscillating ego units that carry these signals. These splits enable the ego to observe and experience specific shades of "sadness" separately from one another. However, when too many shades of affect attached to a multiplicity of ego carriers are operating simultaneously, integrated self-observation and self-awareness are abandoned. The control, the feeling of "being able to snap out," is lost and a compound affect complex takes over the operational field. The control of the central, optimally adapted ego ceases to operate and even a well-integrated ego becomes transiently the passive victim of an uncontrollable mood or affect storm.

The problem of mood mobilization and demobilization is conceived in the present frame of reference in the following way: To snap out of a sad mood is feasible only if a mood of very brief duration is attached to a clear-cut thought, image or action. Beyond a certain narrow limit, however, the patient becomes a victim of his own mood.

We often observe the reverse process when after a successful interpretation series the ego is able to focus on a specific genetic, dynamic, or other aspect of the mood and this may pave the way for a particular affect signal. Thereafter the hitherto complex mood that always contains superego and id sources may be replaced by a single affect, which represents a relatively clear ego signal.

This process represents the main thesis of this paper, i.e., that the decisive factor in affect control after beginning mobilization is whether the affect operates as an ego signal proper or as an affect complex that is more in the nature of a drive derivative or discharge. The latter represents an intersystemic process, the former a relatively less complex intrasystemic ego signaling. However, we are unable to differentiate clinically between intrasystemic archaic ego signaling and intersystemic affect complexes of drive origin or having discharge qualities.

A mood is analytically approachable and subsequently demobilizable only on the condition that the interpretations succeed in focusing on some specific affect signal in the texture of the mood. This promotes the transition from an intersystemic affect state toward a gradual intrasystemic affect state, which in turn is more approachable for systematic resistance analysis. It also opens up an additional avenue for the understanding of content material and its gradual interpretation.

II

To illustrate my thesis I present first certain aspects of affect mobilization and affect control in three cases.

Case 1

A young male patient with a not too severe character neurosis came into the session and said that he was sad because the day was the anniversary of his father's death. He shed a few tears and then the thought of the analyst's impending vacation came to his mind. He recognized the transference implications of this thought, which put him into a mood of less sadness; "it was a bargain," compared with his previous sadness.

Both types of sadness were present simultaneously, and soon two additional shades of sadness signal joined them and were kept separated from the previous signal affects. Thus the patient experienced the following sadnesses simultaneously or oscillating in quick succession:

1. sadness about father's death;
2. sadness about analyst's vacation;
3. sadness about wife's instability;
4. sadness about his son's exaggerated dependency on his wife.

In addition more affect shades of sadness joined in the loose complex:

5. sadness about his mother's present plight;
6. sadness about his mother's ailing cousin.

There was the conspicuous presence of a central reality-adapted ego agency which constantly weighed the changing types of sadness and made a running selection among them. Thus the patient had a rather well-established feeling both of being in control over these oscillations of sadnesses and of being able to snap out of any of them if he really wanted to.

This type of mobilization and demobilization went on for a while, accompanied by a feeling of control over snapping out and slipping in. However, with the progress of free association and the concomitant spreading of cathexes and increasing emergence of new representations carrying additional signals of sadness, the central ego's control gradually decreased. Although the patient, on this occasion, tried to snap out of his developing mood, he failed; and eventually the mood of sadness was overshadowed by a pervasive feeling of loneliness and finally by a feeling of being depressed. It is of interest to note that the same ego units that previously carried the isolated "sad" signals emerged again, but their original affect load was overshadowed by a variety of affect shades that added up to the feeling of being depressed.

We may state that at this stage of affect mobilization the sphere of conflicts transgressed the boundaries of the ego, and this was indicated *and* promoted by the emergence of substantial archaic superego functions (i.e., depressive mood). The ego's adaptability in the transference became reduced (a depressive mood appeared) and the whole character of the resistance changed. It became lessened by the above-described transgression of the ego boundaries (and concomitant regression) on the one hand, but on the other hand the emergence of superego-induced affects stiffened it. Feelings of bitterness and loneliness brought to the fore aggressive drives accompanied by additional affects. The previous signal affects of the ego gave way to affects that were closer to aggressive drive derivatives as manifested by oppressive superego presence in the depressive mood.

Case 2

A married male patient suffered from obsessional ruminations about being a potential homosexual. He had compulsive thoughts about the anus of men whom he met socially. In phases of severe preoccupation with his obsessional thinking he was often caught in confusional ego states. He found relief when he passed from this condition of his "big obsession" into what he called his "little obsession," when he was able to consider his ruminations and his compulsive thoughts as alien bodies in his mind.

At times he was able to exert some control on slipping into the "big obsession." He asked me to refrain from any interpretation on such occasions and leave him alone so that he could attempt to snap out of the developing depression which would follow his acutely experienced sadness about his condition.

These changes were closely interrelated with oscillations in his affective manifestations of sadness. He was frequently in transient sad moods, which often turned into bitterness and subsequent depression.

When he came to his sessions in such a transient state of sadness, the current transference phase determined whether he let himself slip into an eventual depressive mood or whether he attempted and sometimes succeeded, in snapping out of his sadness. He was able to snap out if the upsurging thoughts or images were close to reality and carried sad signals that were attached to realistically sad events of his past or present. As long as this type of sadness prevailed, he was able to keep himself within the limits of his "little obsession." The nature of his sadness changed, however, when superego-induced affects (shame, guilt, humiliation) or id derivatives (strong heterosexual and homosexual desires) came to the fore. He became their victim, whereas previously there had been a distinct feeling of control. The difference was created by the prevalence of sadness which on the one hand was mainly ego contained and on the other hand was attached to nonego representations as well. It goes without saying that this presentation offers only a specific facet of the dynamics with the purpose of showing the detailed process of control and mobilization of a certain affect, sadness, by the ego.

Case 3

In a twenty-eight-year-old woman obsessional rumination and constant doubt represented the defensive superstructure against confusion, paranoid fears, thought disorder, and unclear auditory and visual hallucinations. I propose to discuss only certain aspects of her affect states.

a. The most controlled condition was that of outspoken mistrust of the analyst, whose remarks might upset the patient's precarious balance. Whenever she allowed herself to discuss her serious problems, she became sad. This sadness kept her apart from her analyst and also represented an affect signal which kept her general mood in a low key. Her sadness had another ego-syntonic aspect: she thought it was the only thing she could control to some extent. She was often able to snap out of it with a smile, and it enabled her to look with some detachment at her ruminations.

b. If outside pressure was increased through the most cautious interpretations, the sadness gave way to a pervading mood of dejection and severe depression which took the place of the preceding sadness and was uncontrollable. The prevailing archaic images carried corresponding archaic affect loads of diffuse dejection and depression which indicated the presence of threatening superego operations of extremely aggressive character. The intrasystemic affect control gave way to intersystemic flooding with archaic affects which could scarcely be differentiated from the accompanying drive representations.

c. Increasing confusion led to disjointed imagery and transient thought disorders of changing magnitude. At this juncture there was no way to differentiate the specific elements of the accompanying affect conglomerate that took over the originally well-controlled ego signal system. Apart from increasing aggressive and libidinal drive representations and their affect facets, sudden drive discharge phenomena of rage and somatic-libidinal manifestations came to the fore. Archaic superego representation of oral and anal origin and rather untamed id representations flooded the psyche with corresponding infantile affects.

III

As my material illustrates, the ego controls and mobilizes affect (sadness in my examples) in such a way that first it tries to keep the affect mobilization within controlled intrasystemic boundaries of the ego. It attempts to keep the signaling and mobilization within the boundaries of shade changes. If this intrasystemic control breaks down, whether suddenly or gradually, the affect formations become intersystemic phenomena with the participation of superego-induced affects and drive-discharge affects. Their nature is very different from the original ego signals, since they represent drive and discharge phenomena to a much higher degree and extent than the original ego signals. Therefore it is doubtful whether they should be classified as signals carried by the most archaic ego units or as drive derivatives and discharge phenomena.

The material discussed so far suggests the following theoretical considerations:

1. The first stages of affect mobilization appear as intrasystemic events if relatively nontraumatic circumstances prevail.

2. As a next step in affect change a different shade of the same affect appears which is attached to a new group of images, thoughts, or self and object representations. This new affect shade may be of a regressive or of a more adaptive nature. Soon additional shades of the same affect (in my cases, the affect of sadness) appear. One can then observe an oscillation between the simultaneously operating affect carrying ego units that have a definite anticipatory signal character. There develops a contest on the one hand between the central regulating ego agency, its affect signaling and these upsurging units, and on the other hand between the emerging units themselves.

3. These affect carriers represent mainly intrasystemic mobilization and demobilization events as indicated by their relative maturity, adaptive capacity, and controllability from the point of view of anticipatory affect signaling. Gradually the affective coloring is changed by additional affects that definitely bear the signs of superego-induced signaling or are the affective accompaniment of rela-

tively direct drive representations of libidinal and aggressive nature.

4. At this juncture the well-adapted reality ego becomes increasingly helpless, i.e., its original "sad" signals disappear completely; instead either sad affects of a more archaic coloring manifest themselves or the originally well-defined affect changes into a mood. This is a sign that the central agency has lost its control over affect mobilization and demobilization and that newly emerging superego functions and id derivatives have taken over the field of affective action.

At this stage the previously almost completely intrasystemic mobilization processes become increasingly intersystemic ones. Blurring of the structural boundaries and a general tendency to regression take place. Strong superego-induced affects, guilt and a variety of other feelings appear; at the same time drive representations carry affect components which overcome the well-adapted signal regulations of the ego, and in their turn secondarily provoke defensive affects on the part of the still operating well-adapted ego components.

5. A further important characteristic of this transition from intrasystemic to intersystemic affect mobilization is the disappearance of the "splits" between the operating representations which carry the affect signals. These splits enable the observing agencies of the ego to experience and to keep affects apart. As a consequence of these splits, the individual affect carriers and their signaling do not become overwhelming and there is an obstacle to the formation of a pervading mood. The affects are clearly separated from one another and the patient has a distinct feeling of a certain control ability, i.e., of being able to snap out or to let himself go. At this stage of affect control these splits operate on a relatively superficial level and seem to represent adaptive and integrative aspects of isolation. Freud (1925) referred to the importance of isolation in thinking; Eissler (1959) hypothesized on the biological models of isolation. The moment the process becomes predominantly intersystemic these splits disappear and the feeling and actual capacity of control cease to operate.

Jacobson (1957) seems to assume that this "inner dichotomy" (as she calls what may correspond to these splits) is characteristic of states of sadness and grief. If I interpret her text correctly, she attributes them to intersystemic events.

IV

To add further support to my hypothesis I shall describe certain forms of affect mobilization in the syndromes of depressive mood and depersonalization. I wish to emphasize that this presentation does not deal with the metapsychological aspects of these entities. Furthermore, it disregards the differences or degrees of pathology between neurotic and psychotic depression on the one hand and depersonalization and related ego states (derealization, *déjà vu,* etc.) on the other hand. My basic purpose is to discuss certain aspects of affect mobilization and demobilization.

Mobilization of Anger in the Course of the Formation of a Depressive Mood

In the course of slipping into and emerging from a transient or lasting depressive mood our patients traverse a complicated gamut of feelings which often cannot be unraveled. Only sophisticated and especially intuitive patients are capable of following the entwined pathways of their affects. Although it is probable that several pathways of affect mobilization and demobilization exist, the following brief sketch from an analytic session presents only one specific aspect of one particular affect mobilization.

The patient was aware of her capacity to snap out or let herself slip into a certain affect complex, a capacity she often experienced on her way into or out of a depressive mood.

At the beginning of a session she reported that she had gone through a bad state of depression during the preceding weekend, and she did not want to come to her session because she was worried about precipitating a repetition of her depressive mood. However, because of the broad overlapping of transference and external events, she could not resist talking about the weekend; and, indeed, inevitably she again went through the mood changes of the past few days. The sequence in the mobilization of anger was the following:

1. Irritation and subsequently growing anger against the analyst.

2. Change of color of the anger when it became attached, as a signal, to humiliating transference experiences at the hands of the analyst and of past images. It showed a distinct signal character point-

ing to well-circumscribed objects; furthermore, there existed clear "splits" between the affect-carrying images.

3. Anger of a changed quality attached to variations of decreasing self-esteem, which was reality *and* transference determined.

4. Emergence of a strong effort to snap out of these well-contained affect signals and to "fight it" instead of "wallowing in it."

5. A transient feeling of victory ("it does not have me in its grip"), among oscillating anger signals coming from a variety of ego levels.

6. The appearance of hate and rage against the analyst and her husband.

7. A sudden turning of these affects against herself; and, as a result of this change in the affect mobilization, a transformation of the whole picture.

8. She experienced increasing hatred directed against several self representations and a feeling of being overcome by self-defeat created by the atmosphere of guilt and of a complicated intersystemic affect discharge process. While this was at the beginning fairly well structured, it nevertheless gradually turned into an affect storm. The latter was intensified by the appearance of aggressive and libidinal drive derivatives, archaic forms of hate and longing toward analyst and husband.

9. In the transference this phase was followed by a feeling of emptiness and exhaustion and the usual, frequently experienced complex feeling of "being depressed."

This brief sketch amply supports the complexity of Jacobson's metapsychological formulation (1953, 1954, 1964). It also indicated that certain forms of depressive mood formation are accompanied by intrasystemic and subsequent intersystemic affect mobilizations, the former representing ego signals of a well-circumscribed character, the latter being superego-induced affects or manifestations of discharge and drive phenomena.

It is of particular interest in this context that according to Bibring (1953), depression represents an intrasystemic conflict, i.e., the loss of self-esteem. Jacobson (1957) is also of the opinion that the earliest phases of the depressive process influence self representations that are contained within the system ego.

Mobilization of Anger in Depersonalization

The next example is drawn from a transient depersonalization syndrome that developed in the course of the transference in a neurotic patient. I shall again limit the discussion to the mobilization of a particular affect series that preceded the syndrome. Although Freud (1936) stressed the split in the ego, he also referred to splits in the superego, as did Oberndorf (1939). However, recent publications (Peto, 1955; Jacobson, 1959; Arlow, 1963) stress a complex splitting process in the ego.

The patient had become increasingly tense and edgy in the weeks preceding the reported session. The interaction of external events and the developing transference paved the way for an increasing series of projective phenomena in the transference. A remark of the analyst indicated that the patient was unable to handle her son's aggression properly because of her own conflicting identifications. This interpretation provoked irritation, which became attached to a masculine self image. Subsequent intensive hate signals indicated that clearly defined self images from her tomboy past were the carriers of the affect signals (hate against the analyst). Eventually infantile death wishes against the father and contemporary ones against the analyst emerged. This broad spectrum of the well-defined hate signals which was attached to a variety of self images originated in many developmental phases. Finally, the intersystemic barriers were disrupted and superego-induced affects appeared. Guilt, self-punishing hate and self-abasing feelings appeared. Subsequently two discernible trends emerged in the session.

1. In addition to affects provoked by the superego, a variety of hate affects appeared that represented a definite and direct participation of instinctual drives. Oral aggressive fantasies about hunger and rage came into consciousness as well as corresponding memories about eating until she became sick.

2. A transient frightening syndrome of depersonalization occurred. It consisted of giddiness, strange body sensations, disorientation, a feeling of eeriness and detachment from the self. Similar experiences in the patient's past had led to drive-discharge phenomena (attacks of rage and pseudoconvulsions). The depersonalization represented both faulty adaptation and a failing defense against

dangerous affective discharge phenomena. The splitting in the frame of the depersonalization aimed at sloughing off the threatening intersystemic affect load of object- and self-directed hate originating in superego and id dynamics.

The main point of these two examples is to demonstrate the mobilization of affect from intrasystemic signaling into intersystemic flooding with superego-induced affects, discharge phenomena, and drive representations. I attempt to show that this process is discernible in the course of the formation of such complex events as depression or depersonalization.

V

These observations encouraged me to turn my attention to the affect that is, of course, of the greatest importance to the analyst: to anxiety. In certain instances, anxiety mobilization must, I believe, proceed under conditions similar to those reported above. I also believe that different forms of anxiety have a changing pattern of mobilization and demobilization. Further observations are needed to establish the differences from and the similarities with the formation of other affects. Maturation and developmental determinants play a role and individual variations in certain autonomous ego functions are of importance. I have particularly in mind adaptation, integrations, and neutralizing ability (Hartmann, 1939; Hartmann and Loewenstein, 1962).

As an illustration I shall discuss the formation of anxiety during dreaming as it was reflected in a patient's manifest dream. While he reported the dream in the session the affect process that formed itself during dreaming was repeated in the state of consciousness. The analysis of the dream caused a repetition of the anxiety mobilization.

In the dream the patient was involved in some sort of antigovernment plot and had a secret meeting with a young man who was one of the conspirators. The patient looked around furtively and anxiously and noticed with great relief that the streets were completely empty. Finally, the young man left him and the dreamer walked in another direction and found himself approaching Central Park. When he reached the edge of the Park, he saw a mounted policeman on horseback slowly walking his horse closer and closer to him. The dreamer stood petrified. The policeman reached him and dismounted from his horse. The patient knew that he would be arrested because of his part in the conspiracy. The policeman pointed to a teen-age boy standing nearby and told the patient that this boy had complained that the dreamer had made a homosexual "pass" at him. Great relief came over the dreamer. He knew that the very absurdity of the accusation would make it easy for him to clear himself. He woke up and, in a twilight state of anguish and vindictiveness, began to plan how he would force the boy's parents to go with him to the principal of the boy's school and make their son admit he had lied. Then he woke up completely and immediately understood the main latent elements of the dream and the affects that were operating.

I wish to emphasize the transition from intrasystemically contained signal anxiety to intersystemic flooding of the dreaming ego with anxieties of different origins. At the beginning of the dream there are anxiety signals, but they are well contained, intrasystemic, and their success is mirrored in the ego's achievement in keeping secondary revision under control with the help of anxiety signaling. Therefore, in the first part of the dream, anxiety transiently disappears and, after the conspirator in the manifest dream left, a feeling of relief is apparent. The "snapping out" from the anxiety situation and from the increasing spread of anxiety is symbolized in the manifest dream by "walking away" from the danger situation that originally had provoked anxiety signals.

In this period of dreaming the self and object images that carried the affect signals were well-defined and reality-adapted images (i.e., the way the dreamer looked around furtively and eventually left the scene). Under such conditions the anxiety signaling was kept intrasystemic and, as the quiet walking away in the manifest dream proved, this intrasystemic signaling achieved a reduction of tension and a transient demobilization of affect.

This brief anxiety-free period was ended by the appearance of the mounted policeman. It indicated the presence of emerging superego elements and it brought about rising feelings of guilt about a crime committed against higher authority. The broadening affect mobilization burst the ego containment, flooded the whole functioning ego, and eventually led to a paralyzing anxiety attack. This intersystemic flooding by superego-induced anxiety petrified the dreamer's self representation in the manifest dream. The manifest charge of homosexuality and the sudden presence of the young boy indicated that instinctual drives were also present in the uncontrollable affect-discharge eruption. Their character vastly differed from the ego-contained signaling in the first part of the dream.

The ego's adaptive capacity failed and affect signals of anxiety were replaced by affect flooding of drive and discharge nature (Rapaport, 1953), i.e., anxiety affects that were very close to homosexual drives.

The observations indicate that one can also differentiate between intrasystemic signaling and intersystemic flooding in the instance of anxiety mobilization. In the former, the ego actively operates the signals; in the latter, it more or less passively experiences the onslaught that originates mainly from nonego sources.

Freud (1933) took cognizance of what I have attempted to describe as the two modes of affect mobilization with particular respect to anxiety: "The first and original repressions arise directly from traumatic moments, when the ego meets with an excessively great libidinal demand; they construct their anxiety afresh, although it is true, on the model of birth. The same may apply to the generation of anxiety in anxiety neurosis owing to somatic damage to the sexual function. We shall no longer maintain that it is the libido itself that is turned into anxiety in such cases. But I can see no objection to there being a twofold origin of anxiety—one as a direct consequence of the traumatic moment and the other as a signal threatening a repetition of such a moment" (p. 94f.).

A further ambiguous line from the *Outline* (1940) may have some relevance to the topic :"It [the ego] makes use of the sensations of anxiety as a signal to give a warning of dangers that threaten its integrity" (p. 199). The wording "makes use of the sensation" leaves open for speculation whether the affect is generated by the ego or whether the latter is passively exposed to this experience and then secondarily uses it.

VI

These considerations indicate that Rapaport's metapsychological formulations (1953, 1960) on affect hierarchy have a certain clinical validity. The observed phenomena are "new editions" of developmental and maturational processes. The regression in the transference as well as the transient traumatic effect of well-timed transference interpretations bring about changes that disrupt the hitherto established structures. This process precipitates affect mobilizations which go beyond ego signaling and are the replica of early stages when the relatively undifferentiated ego-id system reacted with affective drive derivatives and affect discharge.

The original maturational trend can be observed when the patient recovers from a confused affect state and a specific affect signal takes over the field of action. This very same process is also indicative of improving adaptation in analysis. I think that, apart from infantile traumatic experiences of an extreme nature, the inborn individual potential for adaptiveness plays the most significant role in affect control and mobilization. These functions are autonomous (Hartmann) and play an important role in the establishment of appropriate object relationships. While the neurotic may benefit a great deal from analysis in this respect, borderlines and schizophrenics often show no sign of improvement in affect control, although substantial insights might have been achieved.

VII

The observations and assumptions I have made have technical implications which can be briefly summarized as follows:

The efficiency of the ego in affect control, as long as the mobilization processes are intrasystemic, vindicates the systematic, layer-by-layer analysis of resistances, since the latter represent the successful control of the ego. Our interpretative technique aims at breaking through this intrasystemic control in order to broaden transiently the conflicts and to reach the less integrated superego structures and id derivatives. We work against the intrasystemic control and attempt to broaden the affect signaling into an intersystemic mobilization which almost inevitably, as I attempted to show, precipitates changes in affect formations in two ways: (1) the emerging ego units have a more archaic affect character; (2) they are intimately connected to drive representations and possible drive discharge.

Thus a technique which alternates, with good timing, between a systematic resistance analysis and a properly adapted drive-derivative empathy is a replica of a particular sphere of mental functioning

(Freud, 1940). The latter consists, from the point of view presented here, of oscillations of affective signal mobilization within the boundaries of the well-adapted ego on the one hand, and on the other hand of the constant upsurge of affects which show an increasing closeness to drive representations and discharge if excitation increases.

BIBLIOGRAPHY

Arlow, J. A. (1963), In: Panel on Depersonalization, rep. W. A. Stewart. *J. Amer. Psa. Assn.,* 12:171-186.

—— & Brenner, C. (1964), *Psychoanalytic Concepts and the Structural Theory.* New York: International Universities Press.

Bibring, E. (1953), The Mechanism of Depression. In: *Affective Disorders,* ed. P. Greenacre. New York: International Universities Press, pp. 13-48.

Brenner, C. (1953), An Addendum to Freud's Theory of Anxiety. *Int. J. Psa.,* 34:18-24.

Eissler, K. R. (1959), On Isolation. In: Panel on Isolation, rep. H. F. Marasse. *J. Amer. Psa. Assn.,* 7:163-172.

Fenichel, O. (1941), The Ego and the Affects. *The Collected Papers of Otto Fenichel,* 2:215-227. New York: Norton, 1954.

Freud, S. (1925), Negation. *Standard Edition,* 19:235-239. London: Hogarth Press, 1961.

—— (1933 [1932]), New Introductory Lectures on Psycho-Analysis. *Standard Edition,* 22:81-111. London: Hogarth Press, 1964.

—— (1936), A Disturbance of Memory on the Acropolis. *Standard Edition,* 22:239-248. London: Hogarth Press, 1964.

—— (1940 [1938]), An Outline of Psycho-Analysis. *Standard Edition,* 23:141-207. London: Hogarth Press, 1964.

Glover, E. (1939), The Psycho-Analysis of Affects. *On the Early Development of Mind.* New York: International Universities Press, 1956, pp. 297-306.

Hartmann, H. (1939), *Ego Psychology and the Problem of Adaptation.* New York: International Universities Press, 1958.

—— & Loewenstein, R. M. (1962), Notes on the Superego. *This Annual,* 17:42-81.

Jacobson, E. (1953), Contribution to the Metapsychology of Cyclothymic Depression. In: *Affective Disorders,* ed. P. Greenacre. New York: International Universities Press, pp. 49-83.

—— (1954), Contribution to the Metapsychology of Psychotic Identifications. *J. Amer. Psa. Assn.,* 2:239-262.

—— (1957), On Normal and Pathological Moods: Their Nature and Functions. *This Annual,* 12:73-113.

—— (1959), Depersonalization. *J. Amer. Psa. Assn.,* 7:581-610.

—— (1964), *The Self and the Object World.* New York: International Universities Press.

Jones, E. (1929), Fear, Guilt, and Hate. *Int. J. Psa.,* 10:383-397.

Novey, S. (1961), Further Considerations on Affect Theory in Psycho-Analysis. *Int. J. Psa.,* 42:21-31.

Oberndorf, C. P. (1939), On Retaining the Sense of Reality in States of Depersonalization. *Int. J. Psa.,* 20:137-147.

Peto, A. (1955), On So-called "Depersonalization." *Int. J. Psa.,* 36:379-386.

Rapaport, D. (1953), On the Psycho-Analytic Theory of Affects. *Int. J. Psa.,* 34:177-198.

—— (1960), *The Structure of Psychoanalytic Theory: A Systematizing Attempt* [*Psychological Issues,* Monogr. 6]. New York: International Universities Press.

Schafer, R. (1964), The Clinical Analysis of Affects. *J. Amer. Psa. Assn.,* 12:275-299.

Schur, M. (1958), The Ego and the Id in Anxiety. *This Journal,* 13:190-220.

CONTRIBUTIONS TO PSYCHOANALYTIC THEORY

THE DEVELOPMENT OF FREUD'S CONCEPT OF PRIMAL REPRESSION

ALVIN FRANK, M.D. (St. Louis) and
HYMAN MUSLIN, M.D. (Chicago)

The concept of "primal repression" currently occupies an uncertain niche in psychoanalytic psychology. Originally a cornerstone of the theory of the neuroses, its significance has become blurred, its limits and definition ambiguous, its importance subject to debate. For example, a meeting of the Regional Committee on the Psychoanalysis of Children and Adolescents in Philadelphia in April, 1953, led to this decision: "that the use of the word primal caused the disagreement between the various definitions, and that primal repression should not be understood in the sense of time. Freud was considering the mind of the adult when he wrote on repression" (Pearson, 1953, p. 42). Similarly, in the chapter entitled "The Mechanisms of Defense" in *The Psychoanalytic Theory of Neurosis* Fenichel does not mention primal repression as such, but states that repression proper is a derivative of childhood "denial": "the tendency to deny painful sensations and facts" (1945, p. 148). In contrast, Nunberg assigns primal repression a central role in repression theory: "*Each new repression does not represent a new act without a psychic prototype, but a repetition of the primal repression*" (1932, p. 234). And, in agreement, Glover says of "primary repression": "It is a necessary complement to the theory of actual repression" (1939, p. 71).

While some of these examples may involve differences in terminology, it is clear that even in the basic area of definition serious disagreement and confusion exist. Some of the historical causes of this

---

Portions of this paper were presented at the Annual Meeting of the American Psychoanalytic Association, Detroit, May, 1967.

The comments and helpful suggestions of Dr. Heinz Kohut are gratefully acknowledged.

ambiguity are easily discerned; for example, Freud's more than occasional interchangeable use of the terms "defense" and "repression." But most important, a characteristic pattern in Freud's creative work was to develop a given theory or proposition, lay it aside, and at some later time revise it in the light of new discoveries or theoretical developments. In such cases it is sometimes difficult to determine what of the theory originating in the early stages was retained, what was refuted, and what was discarded as no longer relevant. Primal repression constitutes such a case.

It is our wish in reviewing Freud's writings on primal repression to re-evaluate the concept's development and evolution in the perspective of other concurrent theoretical developments. In this way we shall arrive at a formulation which is, in our opinion, consistent with Freud's later writings and thinking.[1]

Specifically, we are interested in the role of primal repression from the perspective of the early development of mind. How are we to understand primal repression as distinguished from repression proper? If we assume that primal denotes early repression, how early? When, how, and why does it begin? When, how, and why is it superseded by (later) repression proper? And in what ways do the earlier (presumably more primitive) and later (presumably more mature) forms of repression differ?

Primal Repression: The Beginnings

A prototype of the concept of primal repression is found as early as 1895 in the *Studies on Hysteria.* This earliest theory involved an explanation of some cases of hysteria. In an attempt to understand the sequence of events in the case of Miss Lucy R. Freud proposed a time lag between the original "traumatic" experience, which had led to structural changes in the psychic apparatus, and the "auxiliary" experience(s) which precipitated the symptom. In this case both "traumatic" and "auxiliary" experiences occurred in adulthood and

[1] Unfortunately it is impractical to review comprehensively previous similar studies in an article of this length. The two similar surveys are those of Brenner (1957) and Madison (1961). Brenner's evaluation, while limited in depth because of his examination of the broader areas of repression theory development, led to general conclusions very much in agreement with ours. On the other hand, Madison's interpretations were very dissimilar to those of this study.

the interval involved was only months (p. 123f.). Within a short time Freud was considering the deferred action of still earlier trauma in a more comprehensive way (1950, pp. 410-416). He proposed in a series of papers that the specific etiologies of both hysteria and obsessional neurosis involved incidents of actual sexual stimulation during childhood (1896a, 1896b, 1896c, 1898), the memories of which were revived by sexual excitement following puberty: "*The traumas of childhood operate in a deferred fashion as though they were fresh experiences; but they do so unconsciously*" (1896b, p. 167, n.).

The Evolution of the Concept (1900-1915)

Soon, however, as revealed by Freud's letters to Fliess (1950), the "childhood seduction theory" of the etiology of the neuroses was abandoned (Letter 69, September 21, 1897). The discovery of normal infantile sexuality (Letter 75, November 14, 1897) and the oedipus complex (Letter 71, October 15, 1897) gave new and universal relevance to infantile sexual memories. With the development of topographical concepts and the elaboration of the phenomena of energy transference and primary and secondary processes Freud could propose an integrated and comprehensive theory of repression in *The Interpretation of Dreams.* Although he did not use the term "primal repression" for another fifteen years, the following statement might well be considered Freud's first definitive formulation of the theory:

> When I described one of the physical processes occurring in the mental apparatus as the 'primary' one, what I had in mind was not merely considerations of relative importance and efficiency; I intended also to choose a name which would give an indication of its chronological priority. It is true that, so far as we know, no psychical apparatus exists which possesses a primary process only and that such an apparatus is to that extent a theoretical fiction. But this much is a fact: the primary processes are present in the mental apparatus from the first, while it is only during the course of life that the secondary processes unfold, and come to inhibit and overlay the primary ones; it may even be that their complete domination is not attained until the prime of life. In consequence of the belated appearance of the secondary processes, the core of our being, consisting of unconscious wishful impulses, remains inaccessible to the understanding and inhibition of the precon-

scious; the part played by the latter is restricted once and for all to directing along the most expedient paths the wishful impulses that arise from the unconscious. These unconscious wishes exercise a compelling force upon all later mental trends, a force which those trends are obliged to fall in with or which they may perhaps endeavour to divert and direct to higher aims. A further result of the belated appearance of the secondary process is that a wide sphere of mnemic material is inaccessible to preconscious cathexis.

Among these wishful impulses derived from infancy, which can neither be destroyed nor inhibited, there are some whose fulfilment would be a contradiction of the purposive ideas of secondary thinking. The fulfilment of these wishes would no longer generate an affect of pleasure but of unpleasure; and *it is precisely this transformation of affect which constitutes the essence of what we term 'repression'*. The problem of repression lies in the question of how it is and owing to what motive forces that this transformation occurs; but it is a problem that we need only touch upon here. It is enough for us to be clear that a transformation of this kind does occur in the course of development—we have only to recall the way in which disgust emerges in childhood after having been absent to begin with—and that it is related to the activity of the secondary system. The memories on the basis of which the unconscious wish brings about the release of affect were never accessible to the *Pcs.*, and consequently the release of the affect attaching to those memories cannot be inhibited either. It is for the very reason of this generation of affect that these ideas are now inaccessible even by way of the preconscious thoughts on to which they have transferred their wishful force. On the contrary, the unpleasure principle takes control and causes the *Pcs.* to turn away from the transference thoughts. They are left to themselves—'repressed'—and thus it is that the presence of a store of infantile memories, which has from the first been held back from the *Pcs.*, becomes a *sine qua non* of repression [1900, p. 603f.].

In this first exposition of primal repression Freud proposes a number of both general principles and specific characteristics of the process. The general are:

1. That a quantity of "infantile memories" and "wishful impulses" inaccessible to later conscious recall and direction exists in the mental apparatus.

2. That this phenomenon is the result of an ubiquitous developmental process; namely, "the belated appearance of the secondary

process" (rather than a response to a stimulus evoking a defensive reaction).

3. That the memories and impulses thus estranged from the later personality are forgotten only in a literal sense; actually they exert a powerful influence on all later mental events through their "wishful force."

4. That these memories and impulses, thus estranged from later conscious recall and direction, are necessary for later repression to occur.

Inasmuch as the subject matter of this formulation includes much more than chance isolated traumata it differs markedly from those of the 1890s (Freud, 1895, 1896a, 1896b, 1896c, 1898). The latter deal with specific unique phenomena rather than a ubiquitous process in mental development leading to a universal process, repression. For this reason the propositions of the '90s can be considered prototypical only of this formulation.

Without a concept such as this Freud would have been at a loss to explain what was now obvious to him: that primitive infantile processes exert an undue influence on rational behavior; that the existence of these processes is largely unknown to the subject; that they account for a variety of phenomena including dreams, what he termed "the psychopathology of everyday life," the dynamics of jokes, and neurotic symptomatology; finally, that some connection exists between later mental events and processes and those primitive processes which cannot be discerned by ordinary introspection or observation.

In regard to the specific characteristics of the process:

1. These infantile memories and wishes never had, and continue to lack, preconscious ideational representation.

2. Preconscious thought processes, the vehicles of the secondary process, are defined elsewhere in *The Interpretation of Dreams* as being themselves "without quality" and of acquiring "quality" with acquisition of verbal memories (1900, p. 617). Freud here associated the establishment of the secondary process, the beginnings of the adult preconscious, and the onset of primal repression with the acquisition of language.

3. In consequence of the introduction of "secondary process" (the psychical processes of the preconscious), fulfillment of some in-

fantile wishes later leads to "a transformation of affect." Consequently, the gratification of these wishes results in unpleasure. The example given is of disgust. It should be noted that actually two factors are alluded to and condensed herein—secondary process and internalized prohibition (i.e., in later terminology corresponding to the ego and the ego-ideal aspect of the superego).

This formulation, while representing a great advance, has its shortcomings. Assuming that this process begins with the acquisition of language, when is it completed? On the one hand Freud maintains that the secondary process may not attain "complete domination . . . until the prime of life." Is he implying that the process of early repression (leading to amnesia) described in consequence of the delayed appearance of the secondary process continues until sometime in adulthood? Or does it stop at some point along the way? His contemporary writings provide an inferential indication of his clinical views at this time. In the "Screen Memory" paper, he states that while some persons can remember to the end of the first year, the earliest recollections of others are of the eighth (1899, p. 304). In *The Psychopathology of Everyday Life,* he quotes several studies to the effect that the range is from the sixth month to the end of the sixth or even the eighth year (1901, p. 46). Finally, in *Three Essays on Sexuality,* he asserts that for most people the period of infantile amnesia extends to the sixth or eighth year (1905, p. 174). But this clarification leads to more questions. Why does the process stop at six or eight? Is there some factor involved other than that cited: "the belated appearance of the secondary processes"? And is this comparatively lengthy period of time consistent with the characterization of the process as the passive sequela of development rather than an active defensive process. Obviously, Freud lacked the conceptual tools to approach these questions at this time.

In the Schreber paper Freud expanded his 1900 formulation from a clinical perspective with great consistency. He divided repression into three phases:

> (1) The first phase consists in *fixation,* which is the precursor and necessary condition of every 'repression'. Fixation can be described in this way. One instinct or instinctual component fails to accompany the rest along the anticipated normal path of development, and, in consequence of this inhibition in its development,

> it is left behind at a more infantile stage. The libidinal current in question then behaves in relation to later psychological structures like one belonging to the system of the unconscious, like one that is repressed. . . .
>
> (2) The second phase of repression is that of repression proper —the phase to which most attention has hitherto been given. It emanates from the more highly developed systems of the ego—systems which are capable of being conscious—and may in fact be described as a process of 'after-pressure'. It gives an impression of being an essentially active process, while fixation appears in fact to be a passive lagging behind. . . .
>
> (3) The third phase, and the most important as regards pathological phenomena, is that of failure of repression, of *irruption*, of *return of the repressed*. This irruption takes its start from the point of fixation, and it implies a regression of the libidinal development to that point [1911, p. 67f.].

Freud considered two possibilities in regard to repression proper. First, the derivatives of the original instinct may be reinforced and thus introduce conflict with the "ego" or "ego-syntonic instincts" leading to repression. He did not mention here the question of preconscious representation. Second, a later psychical trend "capable of arousing strong aversion" from the conscious system may be connected with the "primarily repressed."[2] Then the "attraction" of the unconscious and the "repulsion" from the system *Cs.* ("after-pressure") would combine to produce repression. Without this connection, however, no repression would occur. Freud concludes by stating that these two possibilities may be one and the same, the only difference being the proportion of either factor in any given case (1911, p. 67f.).

This exposition is also very consistent with the formulations in the *Three Essays on Sexuality* (1905). The "primarily repressed" instinct or derivative is fixated as the result of some "inhibition in its development" and "left behind at a more infantile state," presumably lacking access to the preconscious system. Again the process is described as a passive, i.e., developmental, phenomenon.

The term itself, "primal repression," first appears in the 1915

[2] Freud's use of this phrase in the Schreber paper is probably Brenner's reason for dating the titling of the concept to 1911 (Brenner, 1957). We cannot really strongly disagree, although in our judgment it was first used in this, rather than a purely temporal, sense in 1915 (see below).

metapsychology papers. In the papers entitled "Repression" and "The Unconscious," Freud gives his most detailed and integrated presentation of primal repression. He begins in the first by delineating repression. Repression is seen as originating from internal instinctual impulses and differs from "condemnation" which represents "rejection based on judgement." Rather, it is "a preliminary stage of condemnation, something between flight and condemnation." He repeats his earlier proposition that in order to undergo a process such as repression an instinct's attainment of its aims must potentially lead to unpleasure rather than pleasure. Using pain as an example of an internalized external stimulus, he concludes that the tension produced from such a stimulus does not evoke repression. Similarly, when "an instinctual stimulus such as hunger remains unsatisfied" and can be relieved only by a specific action it leads to "nothing in the nature of a repression":

> Let us rather confine ourselves to clinical experience, as we meet with it in psycho-analytic practice. We then learn that the satisfaction of an instinct which is under repression would be quite possible, and further, that in every instance such a satisfaction would be pleasurable in itself; but it would be irreconcilable with other claims and intentions. It would, therefore, cause pleasure in one place and unpleasure in another. It has consequently become a condition for repression that the motive force of unpleasure shall have acquired more strength than the pleasure obtained from satisfaction. Psycho-analytic observation of the transference neuroses, moreover, leads us to conclude that repression is not a defensive mechanism which is present from the very beginning, and that it cannot arise until a sharp cleavage has occurred between conscious and unconscious mental activity—that *the essence of repression lies simply in turning something away, and keeping it at a distance, from the conscious.* This view of repression would be made more complete by assuming that, before the mental organization reaches this state, the task of fending off instinctual impulses is dealt with by the other vicissitudes which instincts may undergo—e.g., reversal into the opposite or turning round upon the subject's own self [1915a, p. 147].[3]

[3] Freud periodically differentiated in this way between "repression," "defense," and other specific defenses. The most comprehensive formal clarification appears in *Inhibitions, Symptoms and Anxiety* (1926, p. 163f.). Despite these clarifications Freud continued to use the term "repression" in the generic as well as the specific sense, a source of some of the confusion and disagreement alluded to in the introduction to this paper. For example, as late as 1937, he wrote: "It is familiar ground that the work

In this context he then uses the term "primal repression" for the first time: "We have reason to assume that there is a *primal repression,* a first phase of repression, which consists in the psychical (ideational) representative of the instinct being denied entrance into the conscious.[4] With this a *fixation* is established; the representative in question persists unaltered from then onwards and the instinct remains attached to it" (1915a, p. 148).

Freud continues here by describing repression proper in the same way as in the Schreber paper. He notes that if instinctual derivatives are sufficiently distant (either sufficiently distorted or by virtue of enough intermediate associative links) from the primally repressed, they may gain access to the conscious.

The metapsychology of repression is considered in detail in another of the 1915 theoretical papers, "The Unconscious." Freud begins by asserting that repression occurs to "ideas on the border between the systems *Ucs.* and *Pcs.* (*Cs.*)" (p. 180). Inasmuch as the repressed idea in the system *Ucs.* is capable of exerting continuing influence on the psychic apparatus it must have retained its libidinal cathexis. In repression proper the ideas in the system *Pcs.* have been decathected; i.e., the *Pcs.* cathexis has been withdrawn. In order to explain why the repressed idea does not persist in its attempts to penetrate into the system *Pcs.* Freud turns to the mechanisms involved in primal repression:

> . . . when it comes to describing *primal* repression, the mechanism just discussed of withdrawal of preconscious cathexis would fail to meet the case; for here we are dealing with an unconscious idea which has as yet received *no* cathexis from the *Pcs.* and therefore cannot have that cathexis withdrawn from it.
>
> What we require, therefore, is another process which maintains the repression in the first case [i.e. the case of after-pressure] and, in the second [i.e. that of primal repression], ensures its being established as well as continued. This other process can only be found in the assumption of an *anticathexis,* by means of which

of analysis aims at inducing the patient to give up the repressions (*using the word in the widest sense*) belonging to his early development" (1937b, p. 257; our italics). Unfortunately, he was rarely that conscientious in defining his use of the term, and in this work we have inferred his meaning from the context of the immediate reference.

4 This sentence contains a hint that Freud now thinks of primal repression as originating as an active process, in contrast to the 1900 formulation. However, he is obviously still committed to the earlier approach at this time.

> the system *Pcs.* protects itself from the pressure upon it of the unconscious idea. We shall see from clinical examples how such an anticathexis, operating in the system *Pcs.*, manifests itself. It is this which represents the permanent expenditure [of energy] of a primal repression, and which also guarantees the permanence of that repression. Anticathexis is the sole mechanism of primal repression; in the case of repression proper ('after-pressure') there is in addition withdrawal of the *Pcs.* cathexis. It is very possible that it is precisely the cathexis which is withdrawn from the idea that is used for anticathexis [1915b, p. 180f.].

At this phase in the evolution of the theory, the findings can be summarized in the following manner:

1. Maturational and Developmental: As a result of the belated appearance of secondary-process thinking (characteristic of the system preconscious), associated with the development of verbal symbols, a large store of infantile wishful impulses and memories lack preconscious representation and cathexis. Furthermore, the fulfillment of these wishes would at a later time result in unpleasure as well as pleasure due to the discrepancies between primary and secondary processes and certain acquired standards and prohibitions. These impulses and memories are said to be "primally repressed" and "fixated." They are a *sine qua non* for later repression, "repression proper."

2. Topographic: What is repressed is unconscious both in the sense of being inaccessible to consciousness (a quality) and in the sense of belonging to the "system *Ucs.*" The process of repression takes place "on the border between the system *Ucs.* and *Pcs.* (*Cs.*)."

3. Dynamic and Economic: Any repressed idea retains its cathexis in the unconscious. Primal repression is maintained only by a permanent expenditure of energy operating in the system *Pcs.*, an anticathexis. This force opposes that of the unconscious pressures associated with the primally repressed (unavailable to preconsciousness) idea. In the case of repression proper, in addition to preconscious anticathexis, the repression is also maintained by withdrawal of preconscious cathexis from the preconscious ideational representative. This may be the source of some anticathectic energy. Because of its associative links with what has been primally repressed, what is repressed later (repression proper) is subjected to the same repressing

forces as the older material (the "push-pull" concept) (Jones, 1955, p. 184).

The four general principles inherent in the 1900 exposition of primal repression still stand, although there are hints of their inadequacy. If primal repression does indeed provide the explanation of an infantile amnesia extending quite regularly to the sixth year, some correction or addition is needed. The relationship between *the onset* of primal repression and the unfolding of the preconscious secondary processes is consistent with the theory as a whole, but there is still no rationale for the duration of the process if the explanation is limited to the vicissitudes of preconscious development. Similarly, at least a portion of these primally repressed instinctual derivatives must have word representation at the age of six. In that case an exception to the specific characteristic of the primally repressed, lack of preconscious word representation, exists. Furthermore, it is difficult to conceive of this process as involving only a passive developmental nondefensive "lagging behind" at the more advanced age.[5] Is the process more complex than that described? Or are these apparent discrepancies the result of an overlapping between primal repression and repression proper; i.e., is there no sharp dividing line in time between the cessation of the first and the initiation of the second?

The New Theory of Anxiety (1926) and Primal Repression in Freud's Later Writings

The major theoretical works immediately following the 1915 papers on metapsychology contribute no explicit answers to these questions. Freud did not return to the subject of primal repression until 1926. Whereas previously a basic assumption of the primal repression theory had been that repressed libido is transformed into anxiety, this assumption was now reversed. It is anxiety which initiates repression or other defensive mechanisms. Furthermore, the concept of "the system *Pcs.*" is no longer in evidence. It was supplemented by structural hypotheses involving relatively stable groups of functions —id, ego, and superego. With the advantage of the theoretical advances Freud could now propose equally revolutionary changes in repression theory:

[5] See Footnote 4.

> As I have shown elsewhere, most of the repressions with which we have to deal in our therapeutic work are cases of *after*-pressure. They presuppose the operation of earlier, *primal repressions* which exert an attraction on the more recent situation. Far too little is known as yet about the background and preliminary stages of repression. There is a danger of over-estimating the part played in repression by the super-ego. We cannot at present say whether it is perhaps the emergence of the super-ego which provides the line of demarcation between primal repression and after-pressure. At any rate, the earliest outbreaks of anxiety, which are of a very intense kind, occur before the super-ego has become differentiated. It is highly probable that the immediate precipitating causes of primal repressions are quantitative factors such as an excessive degree of excitation and the breaking through of the protective shield against stimuli [1926, p. 94].

A few chapters later, in discussing the ego as the site of anxiety, he amplifies one of these points:

> The id cannot have anxiety as the ego can; for it is not an organization and cannot make a judgement about situations of danger. On the other hand it very often happens that processes take place or begin to take place in the id which cause the ego to produce anxiety. Indeed, it is probable that the earliest repressions as well as most of the later ones are motivated by an ego-anxiety of this sort in regard to particular processes in the id. Here again we are rightly distinguishing between two cases: the case in which something occurs in the id which activates one of the danger-situations for the ego and induces the latter to give the anxiety-signal for inhibition to take place, and the case in which a situation analogous to the trauma of birth is established in the id and an automatic reaction of anxiety ensues. The two cases may be brought closer together if it is pointed out that the second case corresponds to the earliest and original danger-situation, while the first case corresponds to any one of the later determinants of anxiety that have been derived from it [p. 140f.].

Consider these paragraphs in the order of Freud's certainty regarding his statements.

First, primal repressions are still considered a necessary condition for later repression.

Second, "the immediate precipitating causes of primal repressions are probably quantitative factors." Something happens in the id evoking "an ego-anxiety," "an automatic reaction of anxiety" (rather than an "anxiety signal"). This excessive excitation in turn may lead to primal repression. Freud introduces here a formulation which was impossible prior to this time. Primal repression is presented from the time of its onset as an active, defensive, responsive process. But what of the older theory? Has he discarded the idea that in passive consequence of the belated development of the secondary processes a store of early memories and impulses is withheld from consciousness while actively continuing to influence later mental life? Is primal repression now considered to be a defense of the first days, weeks, or months, i.e., prior to the establishment of the preconscious? How can this later theory of primal repression be reconciled with the earlier one, if indeed Freud still considers the earlier pertinent? What of the relationship between the process he just described, the preconscious state, and verbal symbols?

Third, Freud is least definite concerning the role of the superego vis-à-vis primal repression and whether superego formation should be considered the dividing line between primal repression and repression proper.

Unfortunately, this is Freud's last explicit statement regarding primal repression.[6] From this point two sources of information are available regarding his possible views—remarks probably involving primal repression (although the process is not so labeled) and inferences from his work in other areas. Using the statements and questions raised previously as a guide we shall attempt a synthesis of this material. In so doing, we intend to approximate his final views on primal repression in the context of the psychoanalytic psychology of his later writings.

Freud's 1926 formulation, that the earliest repressions constitute an active process stimulated by an economic factor (i.e., the overwhelming of the ego by excitation) remains unchanged in his later writings (e.g., 1933, p. 94f.; 1937a, p. 227). In addition, in a later series of isolated expositions he continues to reconcile in longitudinal perspectives the consequences of the unfolding of the "preconscious state" of the ego. A passage from *Moses and Monotheism* is instructive in demonstrating the transition to functional ego concepts:

[6] In "Analysis Terminable and Interminable" Freud refers to "a 'primal repression' " in summarizing Ranks "birth trauma" theory (1937a, p. 216). However, there is no discussion of the concept or his use of it in this context.

> The *repressed* is to be counted as belonging to the id and is subjected to the same mechanisms; it is distinguished from it only in respect to its genesis. The differentiation is accomplished in the earliest period of life, while the ego is developing out of the id. At that time a portion of the contents of the id is taken into the ego and raised to the preconscious state; another portion is not affected by this translation and remains behind in the id as the unconscious proper. In the further course of the formation of the ego, however, certain psychical impressions and processes in the ego are excluded [i.e., expelled] from it by a defensive process; the characteristic of being preconscious is withdrawn from them, so that they are once more reduced to being component portions of the id. Here then is the 'repressed' in the id. . . . The fact that later on a special region—that of the 'super-ego'—is separated off in the ego lies outside our present interest [1939, p. 96f.].

This exposition is repeated in *An Outline of Psycho-Analysis:*

> In the course of this slow development certain of the contents of the id were transformed into the preconscious state and so taken into the ego; others of its contents remained in the id unchanged, as its scarcely accessible nucleus. During this development, however, the young and feeble ego put back into the unconscious state some of the material it had already taken in, dropped it, and behaved in the same way to some fresh impressions which it *might* have taken in, so that these, having been rejected, could leave a trace only in the id. In consideration of its origin we speak of this latter portion of the id as *the repressed.* It is of little importance that we are not always able to draw a sharp line between these two categories of contents in the id. They coincide approximately with the distinction between what was innately present originally and what was acquired in the course of the ego's development [1940, p. 163].

There can be no question that what Freud refers to in both statements as "the repressed" is the repression of infantile and childhood impressions. In the first case, its relationship to adult repression is clearly indicated three paragraphs earlier (1939, p. 95).

Now we are in a position to view the relationship between Freud's earlier and later formulations of primal repression. That which was described as primally repressed prior to 1926 (i.e., repressed passively in consequence of secondary-process elaboration) is now referred to in structural rather than dynamic terms. It is that portion of the id to which nothing has happened in this connection, the "unconscious proper" in the id. On the other hand, Freud now uses the terms "repression" and "repressed" (as applied to infancy and childhood) only in an active sense. He thus connotes the early defensive efforts of the mental apparatus (in line with the new theory of anxiety propounded in 1926). For example:

> All repressions take place in early childhood; they are primitive defensive measures taken by the immature, feeble ego. In later years no fresh repressions are carried out; but the old ones persist, and their services continue to be made use of by the ego for mastering the instincts. New conflicts are disposed of by what we call 'after-repression' [1937a, p. 227].

This passage obviously refers to primal as opposed to adult repression. The previous impression that Freud no longer uses the term to include certain early impressions and forces left lagging behind secondary-process development is confirmed. But he has not negated the significance of the impressions and impulses which are thus excluded from the preconscious state. As a matter of fact, he minimizes the need for a sharp operational distinction between the categories of id contents.[7]

Other questions, previously posed, can now be approached. What of the relationship between the onset of primal repression and the development of the preconscious state? First, did Freud conceive of the active defensive process described in *Inhibitions, Symptoms and*

[7] It is not our intention to minimize the significance of the earlier formulation, which by virtue of its differentiation from active defensive primal repression can now be approached in a less confused way. Whether or not we consider that variety of id contents which is without preconscious representation as the result of the delayed development of the secondary processes as "repressed" seems to us largely a semantic issue. Using Freud's later diagrammatic models of the mental apparatus (1923, p. 24; 1933, p. 78) as a frame of reference, it is probable that we are referring here to the area where ego and id are not sharply separated but gradually merge, designated by Kohut (1961) as the "area of progressive neutralization" (see also Kohut and Seitz, 1963). In contrast, that which is now termed (actively) primally repressed would be quite sharply separated from the preconscious ego by the repression barrier. It would seem likely that these two processes continue side by side in the developing mental apparatus. As discussed below, it is probable that new (active) primal repressions cease in normal development in association with superego formation. The end point for the other phenomenon, corresponding to Freud's earlier concept, would in turn be associated with the vicissitudes of secondary-process development. The fact that two distinct processes are involved in childhood amnesia must account in part for its variability.

Anxiety as dependent on preconscious development in the same way as was the primal repression of his earlier formulation (i.e., 1900-1915)? Or was the 1926 primal repression independent of preconscious development, i.e., a defensive process of the first days or weeks of life? In *Inhibitions, Symptoms and Anxiety* Freud clearly includes some degree of ego development (1926, p. 140f.). The quotations above from *Moses and Monotheism* (1939, p. 96f.) and *An Outline of Psycho-Analysis* (1940, p. 163) are more explicit. Inasmuch as the (primally) "repressed" is differentiated from the "unconscious proper" on the basis of this different specific relationship to the preconscious state, it is only reasonable to assume that primal repression—i.e., the active defensive process first defined in 1926—cannot begin until the preconscious state exists.[8] Prior to the time of this development, other mechanisms are used as defenses against instinctual impulses (see above).

Second, the original exclusive association between the preconscious state (originally system *Pcs.*) and mnemic speech residues is eventually contradicted. In the *Outline* Freud states: "It would not be correct, however, to think that connection with the mnemic residues of speech is a necessary precondition of the preconscious state. On the contrary that state is independent of a connection with them, though the presence of that connection makes it safe to infer the preconscious nature of a process" (1940, p. 162).[9] The true nature of the preconscious, Freud later concludes, is to be found in those laws which in their totality comprise the "secondary process" (1940, p. 164).

Third, what is now referred to as "childhood" (presumably an equivalent term for "primal") repression may involve impressions which once had preconscious representation. In *The Interpretation of Dreams* Freud states explicitly that these memories were never accessible to the preconscious system. Until 1926 his expositions implicitly confirm the 1900 formulation; in no other way could one explain the memories' preconscious inaccessibility in the context of

[8] For this reason we are in disagreement with the interpretation of, for example, K. Eissler (1953, pp. 220-224) and M. Klein (1932, p. 183f.). They describe phenomena which antedate preconscious ego state development.

[9] This is not the first statement to this effect, merely the most comprehensive. For example, see Freud (1923, p. 20f.).

a theory emphasizing that primal repression occurred passively as the result of a developmental lag. Now, however, Freud views primal repression as an active defensive process and this further change is consistent with the theory as a whole. The groundwork for this development may well be in "The Dissolution of the Oedipus Complex," where Freud speaks of "a destruction and an abolition of the complex"; "more than a repression" (1924, p. 177). In any event, in the passages quoted above from *Moses and Monotheism* and the *Outline* he is most explicit in this regard.[10]

A final consideration—what can we consider the dividing line in time between primal repression and repression proper? Here we find little to guide us in Freud's later works and must be content to debate the advantages and disadvantages of the possibility suggestively presented in 1926. In *Inhibitions, Symptoms and Anxiety* Freud very tentatively proposed superego formation as the end point of new primal repressions (p. 94). In this context the following scheme is implied: primal repression is a possible response to internal overstimulation (quantitatively defined); repression proper (secondary repression) is one of the mechanisms available in response to anxiety signaled by the ego upon recognizing an incipient overstimulation related to a corresponding danger situation. There is an overlapping developmental series of danger situations related to particular instinctual overstimulation—the dangers of loss of object, loss of love, castration, and of the superego (1926, pp. 134-142; 1933, p. 87f.).

Hence, there are two implied dividing lines between primal repression and repression proper. First, whenever the ego develops the capacity to recognize and successfully respond to a given state of instinctual overstimulation related to a danger situation by a signal of anxiety, primal repression is pre-empted by repression proper or other defenses for that given situation. Second, the instinctual drives appropriate to the oedipus complex are the last of the series detailed above and lead to superego formation and the last in the series of danger situations (danger of the superego). Consequently superego formation represents the end of the possibility of new primal repressions in normal development. It would therefore be implied that repression proper could be used in response to signal anxiety corre-

[10] For further confirmation see Freud (1939, p. 97f.).

sponding to an incipient danger situation prior to superego formation.[11]

The clinical advantages of considering primal repression to end, normally, with superego formation are compelling. If we were to consider it to end prior to this time, we could not satisfactorily account for the oedipus complex as neurosogenic. Neurosis is the consequence of the return of the repressed as the result of the combination of what is primally repressed and what is later secondarily repressed (repression proper). If new primal repressions arose after superego formation, we would expect to find novel neurotic configurations clinically.[12] Furthermore, allowing for some retrospective distortion and error in dating by adult subjects, superego formation as a dividing line coincides with the usual length of infantile amnesias. The variability in the degree and duration of such childhood amnesias could also be partially explained by considering two overlapping dividing lines as above.[13] But at this point we have reached the reasonable limits of the task of reviewing and interpreting the concept of primal repression as developed by Freud.[14]

Summary and Discussion

In reviewing the development of the concept of primal repression in Freud's writings we observed three distinct phases.

The first, from about 1895 to 1898, could be regarded as *prototypical.* Trauma could affect later mental life through deferred, unconscious activity. The trauma was overt (e.g., sexual seduction), and the results were specific (e.g., hysteria). This schema was limited to specific neuroses.

[11] Inasmuch as signal anxiety corresponding to the danger of loss of object appears somewhere between the sixth and ninth month (Spitz, 1965, pp. 150-162; Benjamin, 1963), it is safe to assume that primal repression must begin before this time. Again, the association between primal repression and language acquisition is weakened. However, we cannot assume that it would be the only defense available or even the predominant defense in such a situation.

[12] The obvious rare exception, that of certain traumatic neuroses, is satisfactorily accounted for without weakening this argument (see Freud, 1920, pp. 12-14, 31-35). It is also inherent in the 1926 statement that primal repression can be precipitated by "the breaking through of the protective shield against stimuli" (1926, p. 94).

[13] See also footnote 7.

[14] Work in progress represents an attempt further to elaborate on Freud's concept of primal repression in the light of more recent advances in psychoanalysis (specifically ego psychology) and child development.

The second phase, from 1900 to 1915, could be aptly titled a theory of *passive primal repression.* As the result of a ubiquitous process in psychic development, the deferred development of the secondary processes, certain early impressions and forces are left lagging behind. While these forces continue to exert an indirect effect on mental life, the ideational representatives, because of their lack of preconscious representations, are inaccessible to consciousness. In addition, the fulfillment of these wishful impulses would at a later date result in unpleasure (as well as the pleasure of discharge) because of the discrepancies between secondary and primary processes and certain standards and prohibitions acquired in the interim. Later associatively connected impulses would be subjected to the same repressive forces; hence primal repression is a necessary precondition for later adult repression (repression proper, secondary repression).

The primal repression in this formulation is maintained by system *Pcs.* anticathexes. It is clear in the context of concurrent psychoanalytic psychology that the development of the system preconscious and of the secondary process is considered intimately associated with verbal mnemic symbols. Hence, the onset of the processes which leave the primally repressed in their wake is initiated by the acquisition of the mnemic residues of speech.

Repression is here explicitly defined as an exclusion of ideational content from consciousness. In contrast to the (first) prototypical phase in the development of the theory, Freud now describes a universal defense and its role in "normal" development. This formulation has a high degree of internal consistency, with the shortcomings mentioned previously. It is also highly consistent with the psychoanalytic clinical practice of its period; i.e., a technique primarily directed toward the overcoming of resistances in order to recover infantile repressed memories.

The third phase in the development of the concept of primal repression, from 1926 on, involves a total change in perspective as the result of other theoretical advances. At first glance it would seem that Freud has discarded his earlier theory of the primally repressed as occurring passively. Only a close examination of his later writings demonstrates that he now presupposes the existence of this phenomenon and that the newer theory represents an addition. In line with the new anxiety theory he focuses on what he now terms primal repression as, from the first, an active defensive process. Previously he had proposed no motive for primal repression; only after the establishment of the secondary processes and the primally repressed could once pleasurable fulfillment lead to unpleasure. Now a motive, a specific stimulus for the production of unpleasure responsible for the primal repression, is explicitly defined. *Active defensive primal repression* occurs as the result of unpleasure associated with overstimulation of the immature mental apparatus analogous to the birth trauma. Thus, the first active primal repressions are from the beginning no less the consequences of unpleasure than later secondary repressions. But the unpleasure of these earliest defensive repressions is the result of an economic factor.

While Freud repeatedly associates the earliest outbreaks of anxiety (i.e., associated with overstimulation of the mental apparatus rather than signal anxiety) with the earliest repressions, we cannot infer that active defensive primal repression is a defense present in the first days or weeks of life. He also repeatedly associates this defense with a certain degree of ego organization, specifically with the preconscious state. Our interpretation of Freud's later formulation is accordingly that active primal repression cannot begin until the preconscious state exists. As noted, the connection between the preconscious state and verbal mnemic symbols is no longer considered as crucial in this regard. Furthermore, in contrast to the 1900-1915 concept, the ideational representatives which are primally repressed may once have possessed and subsequently lost, for all practical purposes, preconscious representation.

In the absence of further comment by Freud we believe we are justified in considering two dividing lines between primal repression and repression proper in normal development. The first is associated with the stable establishment of the danger-situation signal-anxiety sequence for any given situation of instinctual overstimulation. The second involves the end of the usual developmental series of such situations which is in turn associated with the formation of the superego.

BIBLIOGRAPHY

Benjamin, J. D. (1963), Further Comments on Some Developmental Aspects of Anxiety. In: *Counterpoint: Libidinal Object and Subject,* ed. H. S. Gaskill. New York: International Universities Press, pp. 121-153.

Brenner, C. (1957), The Nature and Development of the Concept of Repression in Freud's Writings. *This Annual,* 12:19-46.

Breuer, J. & Freud, S. (1893-1895), Studies on Hysteria. *Standard Edition,* 2. London: Hogarth Press, 1955.

Eissler, K. R. (1953), Notes upon the Emotionality of a Schizophrenic Patient and Its Relation to Problems of Technique. *This Annual,* 8:199-251.

Fenichel, O. (1945), *The Psychoanalytic Theory of Neurosis.* New York: Norton.

Freud, S. (1896a), Heredity and the Aetiology of the Neuroses. *Standard Edition,* 3:141-156. London: Hogarth Press, 1962.

—— (1896b), Further Remarks on the Neuro-Psychoses of Defence. *Standard Edition,* 3:159-185. London: Hogarth Press, 1962.

—— (1896c), The Aetiology of Hysteria. *Standard Edition,* 3:189-221. London: Hogarth Press, 1962.

—— (1898), Sexuality in the Aetiology of the Neuroses. *Standard Edition,* 3:261-285. London: Hogarth Press, 1962.

—— (1899), Screen Memories. *Standard Edition,* 3:301-322. London: Hogarth Press, 1962.

—— (1900), The Interpretation of Dreams. *Standard Edition,* 4 & 5. London: Hogarth Press, 1958.

—— (1901), The Psychopathology of Everyday Life. *Standard Edition,* 6. London: Hogarth Press, 1960.

—— (1905), Three Essays on the Theory of Sexuality. *Standard Edition,* 7:125-243. London: Hogarth Press, 1953.

—— (1911), Psycho-Analytic Notes on an Autobiographical Account of a Case of Paranoia (Dementia Paranoides). *Standard Edition,* 12:3-82. London: Hogarth Press, 1958.

—— (1915a), Repression. *Standard Edition,* 14:141-158. London: Hogarth Press, 1957.

—— (1915b), The Unconscious. *Standard Edition,* 14:159-215. London: Hogarth Press, 1957.

—— (1920), Beyond the Pleasure Principle. *Standard Edition,* 18:3-64. London: Hogarth Press, 1955.

—— (1923), The Ego and the Id. *Standard Edition,* 19:3-66. London: Hogarth Press, 1961.

—— (1924), The Dissolution of the Oedipus Complex. *Standard Edition,* 19:173-179. London: Hogarth Press, 1961.

—— (1926 [1925]), Inhibitions, Symptoms and Anxiety. *Standard Edition,* 20:77-175. London: Hogarth Press, 1959.

—— (1933 [1932]), New Introductory Lectures on Psycho-Analysis. *Standard Edition,* 22:3-182. London: Hogarth Press, 1964.

—— (1937a), Analysis Terminable and Interminable. *Standard Edition,* 23:209-253. London: Hogarth Press, 1964.

—— (1937b), Constructions in Analysis. *Standard Edition,* 23:255-269. London: Hogarth Press, 1964.

—— (1939 [1934-1938]), Moses and Monotheism: Three Essays. *Standard Edition,* 23:3-137. London: Hogarth Press, 1964.

—— (1940 [1938]), An Outline of Psycho-Analysis. *Standard Edition,* 23:141-207. London: Hogarth Press, 1964.

—— (1950), *The Origins of Psycho-Analysis: Letters to Wilhelm Fliess, Drafts and Notes: 1887-1902,* ed. M. Bonaparte, A. Freud, & E. Kris. New York: Basic Books, 1954.

Glover, E. (1939), *Psycho-Analysis: A Handbook for Medical Practitioners and Students of Comparative Psychology.* London & New York: Staples Press.

Jones, E. (1955), *The Life and Work of Sigmund Freud.* Vol. 2: *1901-1919, Years of Maturity.* New York: Basic Books.

Klein, M. (1932), *The Psycho-Analysis of Children.* London: Hogarth Press.

Kohut, H. (1961), Discussion of D. Beres' Paper, "The Unconscious Fantasy," Abstr. in: *Bull. Phila. Assn. Psa.*, 11:194.

—— & Seitz, P. (1963), Concepts and Theories of Psychoanalysis. In: *Concepts of Personality*, ed. J. Wepman & R. Heine. Chicago: Aldine Publishing Co., pp. 113-141.

Madison, P. (1961), *Freud's Concept of Repression and Defense: Its Theoretical and Observational Language*. Minneapolis: University of Minnesota Press.

Nunberg, H. (1932), *Principles of Psychoanalysis*. New York: International Universities Press, 1955.

Pearson, G. H. J., rep. (1953), A Note on Primal Repression. *Bull. Phila. Assn. Psa.*, 3:42.

Spitz, R. A. (1965), *The First Year of Life: A Psychoanalytic Study of Normal and Deviant Development of Object Relations*. New York: International Universities Press.

THE CONCEPTS OF STRUCTURE AND STRUCTURALIZATION

Psychoanalytic Usage and Implications for a Theory of Learning and Creativity

HUMBERTO NAGERA, M.D. (London)

The need for the conceptual clarification undertaken in this paper arose from the application of the developmental Profile (diagnostic Profile) to a large number of children with a wide range of psychopathology studied and treated at the Hampstead Clinic. The ambiguity of some terms and assumptions of the structural theory as formulated for the adult personality hindered to some extent our progress in the understanding of the normal and psychopathological processes in the development of children. I believe that clarification of our conceptual tools and present theories in respect of so important an area of the personality as that represented by the ego structure cannot fail to help in furthering our understanding of the normal and the psychopathological processes of children at any given age. The significant role played by the ego in normal adaptation, in the solution of conflicts, in symptom formation, etc. justifies this attempt.

Psychoanalytic Usage

The term structure derives from the Latin *structura* meaning to build. Structure is defined in Webster's Third New International Dictionary as:

> the action of building; something constructed or built; something made up of more or less interdependent parts or elements; the

---

The present paper is part of a larger series entitled "The Structural Theory: Some Clarifications and Reformulations." It forms part of the ongoing research on "Assessment of Pathology in Childhood" conducted at the Hampstead Child-Therapy Clinic in London. The investigation is supported in part by Public Health Service Research Grant, M-5683-0405 from the National Institute of Mental Health, Washington.

> manner of construction; the arrangement of particles or parts in a substance or body; the arrangement and mode of particles or parts in a substance or body; the arrangement and mode of union of the atoms in a molecule; the interrelation of parts as dominated by the general character of the whole; the elements or parts of an entity or the position of such elements or parts in their external relationships to each others.
>
> *Structural* [is defined as]: of or relating to structure or a structure; affecting structure.
>
> *Structuralization* [is defined as]: the process of structuralizing.
>
> *Structuralizing* [is defined as]: embodying in structural or material form.

All these different connotations seem to be implicit in psychoanalytic terminology.

Structure is defined by Lewis (1965) in the following terms: "By *structure* we mean an ordered arrangement of elements, which may be perceptions, events, thoughts, reactions, etcetera of sufficient stability to give some predictability. It is important to note that structure may refer to sequential, as well as to simultaneous, relations among elements" (p. 151).

Beres, discussing "Structure and Function in Psycho-Analysis" (1965, p. 55) states, quite rightly I think, that a "distinction must be made between the 'structural theory' of psycho-analysis and the use of the term 'structure' by some authors in the attempt to set up a psycho-analytic psychology." He further pointed to three areas requiring clarification in this respect: first, the tendency to reify id, ego, and superego; secondly, the confusion that arises when the concept of structure is used in a sense that differs from Freud's limited structural formulations without defining such differences; and thirdly, the need to emphasize constantly the *functional basis of structure* in psychoanalysis.

We also talk of organic or physical structures and of psychological, philosophical, and social structures, etc. The main implication seems to be that a certain manner or order, a certain organization of the elements involved, is in existence. According to this definition, a mental mechanism can be considered a structure, mental processes of the most diverse kind can be considered structures too, an ego function is a structure (this will be qualified later), an idea is a structure, a memory trace is a structure, etc. At least on one occasion

Freud (1915, p. 178) even referred to affective structures. Beres states that on the basis of these definitions, concepts, theories, and scientific laws are structures; at the same time he warns that these psychological structures are not physical entities and are not to be treated as such (p. 54). The last point is also stressed in Colby's definition of structure. He says: "By 'structure' we do not mean any material substance, but again a hypothetical ordering of psychic elements which must await further description" (1955, p. 16).

Schur (1966, p. 13) points out too that the "structural point of view has been the center of our interest to such an extent that we often encounter the term 'structural theory' as a substitute for 'the structural point of view of metapsychology,'" a situation that no doubt further contributes to the ambiguity of the terms and concepts used.

Viewing the difference between structures from one angle, I believe it can be said to consist in how many elements are involved in any given structure and in the complexity with which the different elements are organized. Some structures are simple because they contain few elements or because the elements they contain are organized in very simple ways. Others can be considered complex structures because they contain numerous elements and/or because the relationship between these elements is multidimensional and of great complexity.

As is well known, the topographical theory aimed at describing or classifying mental processes as belonging in one of three systems according to their relationship to the phenomena of consciousness. These systems were named the unconscious, the preconscious, and the conscious. When this guideline proved unsatisfactory, Freud put forward a theory (later called the structural theory) that defines three mental agencies (now called id, ego, and superego) on the basis *of their different functions.* The characteristics of these functions or of the mental processes underlying them vary greatly according to the degree and quality of structuralization that is typical of each one of the agencies. It is for these reasons that Beres (1965, p. 12) has proposed to call the structural theory the "functional theory of psychoanalysis" since the different structures are to be understood in reference to their different functions.

The ambiguity of the term structure when utilized in psychoanalysis is partly due to the fact that in reality all things that can be said to exist have a structure of their own, no matter how primitive it may be. This applies to inorganic and organic matter on the one hand as well as to processes of whatever nature on the other hand. Thus, in psychoanalysis, what we really mean when we speak of structuralization is the steps taken from relatively little or primitive structuralization to more complex forms of it, more complex functional organizations than those existing to start with. On the basis of these steps further structuralization can take place. Thus we are making a relative statement and not an absolute one. Strictly speaking, we do not start from nothing (no structuralization whatsoever) to structuralization. Perhaps the best example of this is the contrast between the id and the ego. That the id is structured seems to me beyond question since the processes that take place in its realm follow primary-process laws, which are themselves a form of organization, of regulation of mental processes. Nevertheless, we generally speak of the id as a chaotic agency (ignoring that this is chaos with an order of its own) in contrast to the ego, which we consider as a highly organized agency. When Freud referred to these two agencies in those terms, he proceeds as if he had decided to call the degree of more primitive organization of the id the absolute zero (in terms of order, structure, and organization), with which he then compared the degree of organization and structuralization of the other agencies[1] (see Schur, 1966).

As useful as the concepts of structure and structuralization are, they inevitably carry with them some degree of ambiguity.

As we have seen, the different agencies of the mind are structures, although we speak most often of the ego structures.[2] The ego apparatuses are themselves structures; the ego functions are structures as

[1] Colby (1955) too has some objections in this respect. He said: "One theoretical drawback to the tripartite model concerns the concept of id. Freud conceived of this entity with its impersonal pronoun as being completely chaotic and unorganized. This does not seem theoretically possible if metapsychology is to remain logically consistent. A structure by definition is an organization, and each part of it must, therefore, also be organized. Organization within the parts of a structure may differ from system to system, but all the systems must possess some kind of order" (p. 76).

[2] Occasionally the term substructure is applied to this agency; for example, Hartmann (1950, p. 114) stated that the ego "is a substructure of personality and is defined by its functions."

well; even primary processes are structures, and so are secondary processes, according to a number of analysts whose views will be discussed later.

Survey of the Literature

A cursory review of psychoanalytic writings shows that Rapaport was among those who made a more liberal use of the terms structure, structuralization, control structures etc.; moreover, there is much evidence of his influence on the writings of many of the so-called ego psychologists. For these reasons I shall discuss his monograph on *The Structure of Psychoanalytic Theory* (1960c) in greater detail.

According to Rapaport, it was the realization of the contrast between "the drive processes, whose rate of change is fast and whose course is paroxysmal, [and these forces] which conflict with them and . . . appeared to be invariant, or at least of a slower rate of change," that laid the foundation on which the concept of structure was built, the latter relatively abiding elements being the prototype of it (p. 53). Rapaport considered that the study of the forces that opposed or delayed drive discharge (the defenses) with their permanent deployment of countercathexis marked the beginning of the structural conception. He added that "An explicit formulation of the structural conception became necessary when it was realized that not only the drives but also most of these invariant factors which interfere with drives are unconscious" (p. 53f.).

The recognition of the structure building and structural role played by the process of identification (Freud, 1923) was soon followed by the recognition of the ego's defensive *substructures*. In addition, psychoanalytic ego psychology came to recognize other *substructures* such as orienting (perceptual), processing (conceptual), and executive (motor) substructures that are ready-made tools available to ego processes (Hartmann, 1939; Rapaport, 1951b). Rapaport refers to Hartmann's concept of inborn ego apparatuses (such as memory, perception, motility) as *structural givens* clarifying that by *structural givens* he means neither the muscular apparatuses of motility, nor the end organs used for perception, "but rather their psychological regulations: for instance, those psychological structures through which the control and triggering of the motor apparatus is effected" (p. 53, n. 13).[3]

As I have already noted, Rapaport refers to the defenses as "structures": "they are the most extensively studied structures," and for this reason many analysts may have gained the incorrect impression "that all structures are conflict-born and all controls are defenses" (p. 56).[4] He further states that, to begin with, psychoanalysis assumed that all psychologically relevant structures arise in ontogeny and are conflict-born; today, however, we accept that some of these structures are inborn givens, for example, Hartmann's ego apparatuses of primary autonomy. Rapaport contrasts these with the group of functions or structures that were born out of conflict or subserved drive gratification but later underwent what Hartmann called a "change of function," thus becoming means of adaptation in the service of the ego. Quoting Hartmann (1939) Rapaport refers to this group as *structures of secondary autonomy*. Hartmann, however, uses the term *functions* and not *structures* of secondary autonomy.

Rapaport summarizes this section of his discussion by stating that "inborn structures and acquired structures are apparatuses of primary and secondary autonomy. Structure-building transforms motivations and thus gives rise to new (more neutralized) motivations" (p. 56).

Rapaport concluded that "The concepts of structure and relative autonomy (Hartmann) are indispensable to the theory, and at present it is not possible to foresee changes in the theory which could eliminate them. But the concepts of id, ego, superego, and the differentiation of the ego into defense-, control-, and means-structures are neither as indispensable to nor as independent from the theory. However, a variety of subordinate structural concepts (e.g., specific primary-process and defense mechanisms, like displacement, condensation, substitution, symbolization, repression, isolation, reaction

[3] Rapaport's formulations could be misleading or misunderstood. The existence of the inborn ego apparatuses is perhaps self-evident, but this must not be taken to imply that the psychological structures that control them (and it is to these that Rapaport is referring) are inborn as well and present in their final form from the beginning. All evidence demonstrates that they are only primitive to start with and have to be built up, acquired later on, and that this happens only very gradually.

[4] A fuller account of defenses as stable structures playing a number of different roles in the mental economy is to be found in his paper, "On the Psychoanalytic Theory of Motivation" (1960a). See also Gill (1963).

formation, projection) which are more directly related to observations and of a lesser generality, are likely to survive" (p. 128).

Some further understanding of Rapaport's ideas about structure can be gained by his considerations concerning *cognitive structures.* He defines them as "those quasipermanent means which cognitive processes use and do not have to create *de novo* each time and those quasipermanent organizations of such means that are the framework for the individual cognitive processes" (1957, p. 157).

He thinks of memory organizations as possibly the most common cognitive structures, which are organized in terms of spatial and temporal contiguity, in terms of the drives, interest, and affects, as well as conceptually. He describes other forms of cognitive organizations such as cognitive styles, styles of perceiving, conversing, dreaming, etc., which show striking interindividual differences. According to him, all these cognitive organizations or structures do not constitute a random assembly but are closely interrelated in a multiple complex hierarchy.

He believes that "A distinction between cognitive processes on the one hand and the structured (patterned and persisting) tools of cognition and their organizations on the other can probably be made by the criterion of rates of change; the processes may be defined as showing a high rate of change, the tools and their organization as showing a low one. In other words, the processes are temporary and unique, the tools and their organizations permanent and typical" (1957, p. 161).

As Rapaport himself remarks, he focused on the relatively enduring forms in contrast to passing processes, because "we need concepts of organization- or structure-character to account for all these quasistable enduring forms" existing in the personality. His stress upon this relatively enduring organization parallels, as he says, a change of emphasis in psychoanalysis, that is, the development of psychoanalytic ego psychology, a development that added to the earlier emphasis on motivation and gratification processes an equal stress upon the study of defensive organizations, controls, and structures. "It seems that with this stress on relatively enduring controlling- and means-organizations, psychoanalytic psychology finds itself again in a pioneering role" (p. 194).

Rapaport concludes this 1957 paper with a clear statement of his views of the concept of structures and the conceptual difficulties involved: "The specific cognitive organizations or structures that I discussed were meant only as illustrations. My study of these is still in the initial stage and I hold no brief for them, except insofar as they illustrate my general point. Nor for that matter do I hold a brief for any specific psychoanalytic concept that refers to relatively enduring structures. Further study may well replace these concepts. But it cannot abolish the phenomena to which the present structure-concepts refer. So far psychoanalysis is the only theory that has attempted to take account of these phenomena" (p. 194).

In his paper "On the Psychoanalytic Theory of Motivation" (1960a), Rapaport makes a number of interesting points in relation to structures and their maintenance. He thinks that sufficiently consolidated structures are self-sustaining, but he acknowledges that evidence to show actual instances where this is the case is difficult to come by. In an earlier publication (1958) he had suggested, and he repeats the suggestion here (1960a), that structures do not stand in isolation but are in fact integrated with other structures and are nourished and maintained through their relations to one another. He further suggested that activation by external stimuli makes a contribution to the maintenance of the structures (including the defensive structures and other types). It is the environment that provides "stimulus nutriment" for structures, a term that according to Holt (1965, p. 158) Rapaport has taken and adapted from Piaget's concept aliment.[5] Rapaport categorically stated that there is "independent evidence available indicating that it is the development and maintenance of structures rather than a special kind of motivation which prompts the organism to reach out for stimulation" (1960a, p. 223f.). Thus Rapaport's concept of "stimulus-nutriment" includes nutriment both from without and from within. According to Miller (1962, p. 8), Rapaport's "stimulus-nutriment from the environment includes all that is perceived in the external world, while nutriment from within is provided by ego- and superego-structures and ultimately by drives."

Although I cannot include an extensive discussion of Rapaport's concept of ego autonomy (see 1951b, 1958), it is necessary to refer

[5] Cf. Rapaport (1960a, p. 221ff.) where he makes this link.

to it briefly because it is closely related to his ideas about ego structures and their maintenance. He conceived of an autonomy of the ego from the id (as seen in the ego's capacity to postpone drive discharge, modify it, etc.), and of a relative autonomy of the ego from external reality (as seen in the ego's capacity to adapt in different ways or to postpone its reactions to external stimuli). Since on the one hand this autonomy of the ego is dependent on the ego structures and their stability and on the other hand the latter depends on the reception of appropriate quantities of stimulus nutriment, the interference with stimulus nutriment or the lack of stimulus nutriment disrupts—by affecting the structure's stability—the autonomy of the ego, especially that from the id.

As Holt (1965, p. 155) points out, Rapaport cited sensory deprivation and hypnosis as examples of instances in which the stability of structures can be seen to suffer. Further, Rapaport conceived of a complementary relationship between these two types of autonomy; that is, the ego relations to reality guarantee autonomy from the id; consequently, excessive autonomy from reality impairs the autonomy from the id; and, similarly, an excessive autonomy from the id (since the drives are the ultimate guarantee of autonomy from the environment) may impair the autonomy from the environment (1958, p. 24).

According to Holt (1965, p. 154), Rapaport does not distinguish clearly between the role of stimuli in *structure building* in contrast to their role in *structure maintenance*. Holt does not agree with Rapaport that all structures are in need of stimulus nutriment "lest they wither away," giving as examples memory-trace structures, disused for many years, which are found intact and recovered by means of hypnotic suggestion, brain stimulation, and psychoanalytic treatment. He also refers to psychic structures involved in seasonal activities (i.e., ice skating) which after months of lack of nutriment show no sign of decompensation. He nevertheless concedes that Rapaport's point of view applies to a limited number of structures, describing as an example the disruption of perceptual structures in experiments of isolation. Holt adds an interesting qualification: if there is a change in the type of stimulus input, the perceptual structure not only is disrupted after some time but starts to rebuild itself on the basis of the new conditions. This type of structure if deprived of input lies quietly in storage and remains relatively unchanged; however, if it is fed the wrong or an insufficient diet of stimuli it begins to rebuild itself on a new plan.

Holt says: "the psychic apparatus is capable of re-writing its programmes continuously and automatically to take account of changes in the information fed to it. Introduce any kind of systematic distortion, and, soon, or later, a new programme is written that makes the old sense out of the new information. . . . The fact that we have such structures requiring nutriment is one reason that organisms become so profoundly incapacitated when they are brought up during the critical early stages of development in impoverished environments; the psychic apparatus that develops may get a built-in rigidity and inability to cope with stimuli as chaotic as the average expectable environment if it is fed highly simplified information for a long enough time" (p. 162).

Holt concludes that the "principal role of structures is to widen the tolerable range of inputs (whether of urge, press, inner and outer information, or tonic support)," while pointing at the same time to the existence of what he calls *maladaptive structures,* such as those involved in a phobia, which "may narrow the range of inputs, as do inhibitory structures generally" (p. 164).

It should be noted that Rapaport stated that Piaget's structure concept, "just like the psychoanalytic, assumes a hierarchic layering of progressively differentiating structures" (1960a, p. 222).

He also described some of the economic factors involved in the building of structures, using memory traces as an example. He thus explained how an excitation capable of attracting a sufficient amount of attention for a sufficient length of time gives rise to a structure such as a memory trace. Structures so built retain only a small quantity of the attention cathexis that was necessary in their formation process (the energy becoming bound in the structure), while the rest becomes available again to deal with other excitations (1960a, p. 229).

I also want to note that in this paper (1960a, p. 231) Rapaport refers to learning as a process of structure formation, a point to which I shall come back later.

A comparison between Rapaport's and Hartmann's uses of the terms structure and apparatus (ego structures or ego apparatuses) seems to me to show clearly that Rapaport greatly favors the term structure. He uses it, generally speaking, as synonymous with ego apparatuses. In fact, in quoting Hartmann, Rapaport occasionally substitutes structure for apparatus. Hartmann, on the other hand, favors the term apparatuses, most certainly so in his book *Ego Psychology and the Problem of Adaptation* (1939), in which the term structure appears only rarely.[6]

Nevertheless, it is in most cases feasible (in the writings of both Hartmann and Rapaport) to use these terms interchangeably without greatly altering the meaning of the statements. Indeed, on page 26 (of the above-mentioned book) Hartmann uses the terms interchangeably. He writes: "An attitude which arose originally in the service of defense against an instinctual drive may, in the course of time, become an *independent structure,* in which case the instinctual drive merely triggers this *automatized apparatus. . . . Such an apparatus* may, as a relatively *independent structure,* come to serve . . ." (my italics).

Further, Hartmann (1964, p. xii) stated that the "differential study of the ego suggests also a broadening of the concept of structure, and it has become meaningful to speak of 'structures in the ego' and of 'structures in the superego.' This refers, in contrast to 'flexibility,' to a relative 'stability' of functions, as it is clearly observable, e.g., in the automatisms." Rapaport (1951a, p. 692f.), on the other hand, while talking of structural givens (existing from the beginning) such as the apparatuses that lay down memory traces, thresholds of tension tolerance, etc., and how these structures are later on embodied in the superorganization that we call the ego, states clearly that "These structures are also referred to as *ego-apparatuses.*"

This difference in the usage of or preference for certain terms is characteristic of other authors as well. Arlow and Brenner, for example, in their book *Psychoanalytic Concepts and the Structural Theory* (1964) mostly manage with the use of terms such as ego apparatus or functions where Rapaport would have used structure. The index of their book does not include the term structure (in Rapaport's more specific sense), though there are a large number of entries listed

6 The index of this book contains only two references, one to structure on page 26 and one to structural development on page 52. There are, nevertheless, throughout the book, two or three other places where it can be found.

under structural theory. It is quite interesting that Rapaport appears neither in the index nor in their bibliography. Spitz, in his book *A Genetic Field Theory of Ego Formation* (1959), uses the term structure in the more general sense implied by terms such as psychic structure, although there is no lack of the occasional references to structure in Rapaport's more concrete sense (as I shall show below).

It should also be noted that it is not clear how the term "structural theory" came to be coined and generally accepted. References to "structure" are rather sparse even in Freud's *The Ego and the Id* (1923), and the term "structural theory" does not appear there at all.[7]

With regard to structures Gill (1963, p. 113) says that once one "has been formed it constitutes a fixed organization, so that neither the structure nor the function it regulates undergoes any change." This rigidity of the structures was rightly questioned by Beres (1965, p. 58), but it seems as an unhappy form of expression, since Gill explained in a discussion with Beres that he really means to imply a "slow rate of change." Beres quotes Brierley (1944) whose formulation he prefers: "first, mental organization involves continual reorganization and second, . . . although mental life is conditioned by organization, it is also emergent or new from moment to moment." On this subject Colby (1955) remarks, "One of our great metapsychological problems is how to conceptualize this constancy of change within a constancy of order" (p. 86).

In his monograph Gill (1963) is careful in stating that he will not attempt to discuss what is meant by psychic structures as such (p. 3) and is similarly careful in maintaining a distinction between "mode of function" and "mode of organization." The former refers to a process, the latter to a structure (p. 2, n.).

He introduces two variations of the term structure when he designates id, ego, and superego as *macrostructures* while utilizing the term *microstructures* to refer to relatively stable organizations within the macrostructures, such as memories and ideas (p. 135).[8]

Gill describes what he calls *ad hoc* functioning, which may take place according to either primary or secondary process. He adds:

[7] Anna Freud has suggested to me that it was probably Ernst Kris who coined the term. Others commented that the term they heard Ernst Kris use most often was "structural hypothesis," and since such terms were generally used in discussions of "theory," they believe the two were wedded.

[8] The term microstructures was introduced by Glover in 1948.

"When a particular form of discharge becomes regular and habitual, a structure has been formed which regulates discharge of what was at first either primary- or secondary-process *ad hoc* discharge" (p. 113).[9] When a pattern is formed that repeats the pattern of the *ad hoc* primary- or secondary-process event, a structure has developed that can be referred to as primary- or secondary-process structure. He was explicit in stating that analysts fail to distinguish clearly between functioning regulated by a structure and the *ad hoc* psychic functioning (just mentioned) not thus regulated, a statement which Beres (1965, p. 57) took exception to because it implies, among other things, that function can take place without structure.[10] Beres asked "whether one can conceive of human psychic function without structure?" Although I believe Beres's objection to be valid, he seems to have overlooked that Gill retraced his steps on the next page of his monograph where the following appears: "It is conceivable that even *ad hoc* discharges are regulated by structures and that what we are accustomed to call the primary-process mechanisms are structures which regulate *ad hoc* primary-process functioning" (p. 114). A similar argument applies, he believes, to secondary-process functioning. Beres similarly objects to mechanisms and processes such as primary and secondary processes being conceptualized as structures because all they really are is a mode of discharge of psychic energy (p. 60).

Gill makes clear that by primary- and secondary-process structures he does not mean that the structures themselves are thus organized. He only means the structures that regulate such functioning.

Gill probably takes his lead from Rapaport who also referred to primary-process mechanisms as "structures." In his paper "Psychoanalysis as a Developmental Psychology" (1960b, p. 243), Rapaport, discussing how secondary processes integrate and use primary-process mechanisms, speaks of the difference existing between *structuralized and nonstructuralized* primary-process mechanisms. According to him, the essential difference between them is that the structuralized primary-process mechanisms can be integrated by secondary proc-

[9] As I shall discuss later, I regard *ad hoc* functioning a result of *ad hoc* structures, the further vicissitudes of which vary according to circumstances.

[10] This lack of clear distinction between the two possibilities is blamed for the failure to distinguish between a structure and the process or function it regulates.

esses, in which case they are energized by more neutralized cathexis than the nonstructuralized primary-process mechanism. Further, he stated: "The primary-process mechanisms (displacement, condensation, substitution) are basically means of immediate drive discharge. In this role they have a structural characteristic, since the discharge attained through them is slower than a discharge which can take place without them. Nevertheless, they are at best *ad hoc,* short-lived structures. When they appear in a form which is integrated into the secondary process, their lifetime is increased: they have become further structuralized" (1960b, p. 243, n. 24). One area in which Rapaport believed one can observe structured primary-process mechanisms is in the primitive thought processes of children (p. 245). He maintained to the end that primary-process mechanisms are structures (see, for example, 1960c, p. 128, n. 5).

Spitz (1959) makes a number of interesting links between structural development, the development of specific structures, and his concepts of developmental imbalance and mental organizers such as the smiling response in the third month, the anxiety response of the eighth month. He says: "When a developmental imbalance is firmly established at one level, then it will modify the pattern of the next major organizer, in conformity with the law of dependent development. Structures which now should emerge may remain absent or emerge in a distorted form. In either case the intrasystemic and the intersystemic relations will be severely impaired or at least modified. Ego apparatuses, ego functions, ego systems will be out of balance, some inhibited, some emphasized. . . . But the process does not end there. If each successive organizer is dependent on the establishment of the structures integrated under normal circumstances through the preceding organizer, then the distortion of the structure pattern of the preceding organizer must lead to a distortion of the subsequent organizing process, whether this distortion be one of delay in time or a compensatory reshuffling of the structures themselves" (p. 93f.).

In referring to the smiling response as the third month organizer he states: "It is as if a number of functions had been brought into relation with each other and linked into a coherent unit. A structural pattern emerges which did not exist before in the psyche. After the establishment of this integration, the response to experience will no longer be in terms of unrelated, discrete components, but in terms of the integrated operation of the unit as a whole" (p. 27). He further clarifies the organizer and its role in terms of psychic structures when he states: "The organizer is a modification of the psychic structure, be that from an undifferentiated to a structured state, or, at the next step, a restructuration of already existing structure on a higher level of complexity" (p. 75).

I have referred earlier to Spitz's more flexible use of the term structure. A good example of it is the following passage when he discusses the many changes in the ego that have taken place by the eighth month of life in relation to the second organizer (eight-month anxiety): "It [the ego] has developed a series of systems [Rapaport probably would have said structures controlling the functions of . . .], like memory, perception, the thought process, the faculty of judgment . . . and ego apparatuses [Rapaport might have used the term structure here too] like the understanding of space, the social gesture, a little later the capacity for locomotion, all of which make the ego a more effective, but also a more complex structure" (p. 42).

Lustman, in his paper on "Impulse Control, Structure, and the Synthetic Function" (1966), makes a number of interesting points concerning the acquisition or failure of acquiring appropriate *controlling structures* (impulse control) during development and, perhaps more important, in the course of therapy. He says: "There can . . . be no doubt that primitive identification processes played a dominant role in the failure of *controlling structures* to emerge . . . and that, in addition to insight, identification processes with the analyst likewise played a part in the subsequent emergence of such *structures* via internalization during the treatment" (p. 200; my italics). He makes clear that by structuralization of control he means the acquisition of a "stable function highly resistant to change via regression or reinstinctualization" (p. 201), a formulation that I believe can be extended and applied to all structures and not only to those in charge of impulse control. Lustman states that structuralization of a function is linked with stability: "as soon as a function becomes structuralized, i.e., as soon as it begins to function with a degree of stability, its further differentiation will tend to be modified by its own activity, in addition to other forces. . . . Further, this functional differentiation of one structure may very well act as an inducer to other structural development" (p. 203). (Cf. Spitz's views cited above.) In the case Lustman uses to illustrate his propositions, the deficiency in the child's ego structure "was apparent in little or no internalized delaying or controlling substructures, and a fragmentation of other ego functions such as thinking" (p. 202). He clearly suggests how deficient structures or substructures, such as those concerning impulse control, will affect the performance of many ego functions that are dependent on such structures or ego apparatuses.

Although the id is considered one of the "structures" of the personality, there are few references to be found to structures in its realm, unless one includes the primary-process mechanisms as structures (which were mentioned above). Schur (1966) is something of an exception when he says: "The application of the genetic point of view and of the concept of a continuum has also led me to the assumption that the id is structural and has 'content.' Moreover, as we saw earlier . . . , my discussion postulates the maturation and development of the id, a development which was described by Freud after his exposition of the various phases of psychosexual development" (p. 118).[11]

Naturally enough, the structural theory did not escape criticism. As Arlow and Brenner (1964, p. 2) point out, these criticisms may apply only to specific aspects of the structural formulations or, in some cases, may go as far as a preference for the "topographical theory"; and in still others, the need is felt for a completely new formulation that will take the place of both the topographical and structural models of the mind.

My own view is closer to that of Hartmann, Gill—and even that of Arlow and Brenner, without going as far as proposing a complete and total abandonment of the topographical theory as the last two authors do. To my mind there is much in that earlier model that can be retranslated into the structural one and thereby enrich it.

Among the more recent exponents of such criticisms are Apfelbaum (1962, 1965, 1966), Loewald (1952, 1960), Colby (1955),[12]

11 Colby (1955) too has argued against the idea of lack of structure in the id, as I have mentioned earlier.

12 Colby has in fact proposed an alternative model of the psychic apparatus that he has named a cyclic-circular model. He does not deny the usefulness of the structural theory in a clinical setting but considers it insufficient from the theorist point of view. According to the author, his model is particularly useful in terms of the interrelation of the basic postulates of psychic energy and structure.

Kubie (1958), White (1963), and even Glover (1961). A discussion of their criticism of the structural theory as a whole (such as that of Kubie) or of specific aspects of it, either in Freud's formulation or in those of Hartmann, Kris, Loewenstein, Gill, Brenner, Arlow, Anna Freud, Rapaport, and many others will be the subject of an independent essay.

If we speak in terms of structures rather than apparatuses or functions, it is necessary to postulate the existence from the very beginning of life of a number of ready-made primitive structures or organizations in charge of primitive mental processes that deal with the regulation of early perceptual activities, the laying down of memory traces, and certain motoric activities, etc. This is completely in line with Hartmann's assumptions of inborn ego apparatuses belonging to the conflict-free sphere. In fact, it is only another way of stating exactly the same set of problems. These structures exist at birth, while most other structures have to be created during development; that is, further structuralization is taking place all the time as development proceeds.

Some Implications for a Theory of Learning and Creativity

In these processes of further structuralization[13] a number of factors are involved. There is, first of all, the ongoing physical maturation of the physical structures or somatic apparatuses on the basis of which ego functions will become possible. In humans, however, an equally important role is played by experience and learning. Physical maturation per se will allow only a certain (unknown) level of performance in terms of the ego, a level that is then raised by the essential contribution made to the development of ego functions by the processes of learning and experiencing. Thus, for example, we have to learn to perceive or to organize percepts in a meaningful way before we are capable of exercising the function of perception (in the sense of apperception) as we know that function in the adult. "Experiments of nature" involving persons born blind with congenital cataracts or corneal lesions, later remedied by grafts of the cornea, have shown that when sight is restored, the reception of

[13] One could also say: acquisition of new apparatuses or functions.

visual stimuli coming from the different objects does not allow for the recognition (apperception) of such objects. The sensations produced by the objects are registered but remain meaningless until the person learns to perceive them, that is, to organize the perception according to a system that makes apperception possible. Clearly, this requires a multiplicity of interaction of ego functions and apparatuses in specific hierarchical orders, an ability that is normally acquired in the early years of life through experimentation, trial and error, experiencing and learning. What applies to perception presumably applies to most other complex ego functions. It is possible to assume that in the absence of experiencing and learning opportunities (a completely hypothetical situation) all that the somatic apparatuses would be able to do is to register the stimuli that reach them in ways that are not completely clear to us but that include in many cases an awareness of an impression or sensation and the laying down of a memory trace.

Learning, as used by me here, refers not only to learning facts about the environment and its objects, or learning about the subject; but, even more important, it includes learning to use the mental apparatus as it develops, learning to combine in an infinite number of ways the different functions of which it is capable. The combination of various functions in specific ways (that have to be learned) enables the mental apparatus to perform any number of new functions, suitable for the solution of ever more difficult problems confronting the organism. When such a combination of functions in a predetermined sequence or hierarchical functional order proves a suitable tool to deal with specific problems, or specific aspects of external or internal reality that frequently confront the human being, a new ego apparatus (to use Hartmann's term), a new psychological structure (to use Rapaport's term) has been acquired, one that is capable of dealing with the specific aspects of internal or external reality.[14] It is to be presumed that such processes of structuralization, of creating new ego apparatuses, are never-ending proc-

[14] Hartmann (1939) has expressed a similar view: "Ego development is a differentiation, in which these primitive regulating factors are increasingly replaced or supplemented by more effective ego regulations. . . . Differentiation progresses not only by the creation of new apparatuses to master new demands and new tasks but also and mainly by new apparatuses taking over, on a higher level, functions which were originally performed by more primitive means" (p. 49f.).

esses, although their rate of development is of course by far the greatest in the early years of life.

Three factors seem to be relevant as determinants of the rate and extent of structuralization that is acquired. First, there are innate limitations which account to some extent for interindividual differences in general, and for differences in the individual's abilities in certain specific areas. There can be little doubt that differences in the inborn qualities of the different somatic structures play some role. Secondly, human needs and human nature partly determine the degree of structuralization required. Our instinctual equipment is not such that we can satisfy our needs according to rigid "instinctual patterns"; rather, we are in most cases dependent on intelligent behavior for their satisfaction; moreover, our mental apparatus is itself sufficiently complex to allow for such learning and intelligent responses. For these reasons, our needs trigger us off in the path of structuralization and ego development. Thirdly, there is the question of the environment into which we happen to be born. The demands of a highly civilized society are much greater in these respects than those of a primitive one. The adaptation to a high degree of civilization demands a greater extent in ego structuralization.

In describing the performance of the mental apparatus of an adult or child, we ought to distinguish between *ad hoc* performances activated to deal with a single new problem just once and more automatized performances utilized to deal with problems which we encounter regularly and for the solution of which we have developed specific *ad hoc* psychological structures or *ad hoc* psychological ego apparatuses. This is not a purely academic question but seems to me to be relevant in terms of our conceptualization of structures, intelligence, learning processes, and preconscious automatisms.

Let us imagine the hypothetical situation of a child of three or four years who is for the first time confronted with the task of learning to add and who is presented, for example, with the problem that $1 + 1 = 2$. He has to master a new situation and faces for the first time the task of mastering a number of new conceptual propositions and abstractions (I am assuming that the child is not just memorizing the figures but attempting to master the conceptual problems involved and posed to him). The child at that age has available a large number of structures (or ego apparatuses) capable of performing a variety of functions. What he has to do to master the new situation is to combine the function of several such structures (or ego apparatuses) until he hits on a combination that produces the desired result in terms of insight, i.e., one allowing him to understand and master the conceptual problems involved. The combination of the structures thus selected (in whatever hierarchical functional order) constitutes a new and *ad hoc* structure. Before the right combination of structures is produced for the solution of the specific new problem, several unsuitable combinations presumably are tried out until partly through trial and error, partly perhaps through intelligent selection, the correct combination is produced.[15] In any case the scanning process performed by the ego for the selection of the most suitable of the available structures or ego apparatuses (and in what combinations) is one of the most important functions of which it is capable. I suggest to call it the *functional-coordinative function of the ego.*[16]

The situation I have described above applies whenever a human being, child or adult, is presented with a completely new task, with a new set of problems requiring solution. Further, since intelligence is frequently defined as the capacity to solve new problems, it follows that the quality of this special function of the ego is an essential aspect of it, as are the number and quality of structures available to this functional-coordinative function.

When the child has produced the suitable combination for the mastery of the new conceptual problems and their solution, he has

15 The older child has a greater variety of structures at his command. The more experience the child has acquired in the solution of problems, the more intelligent selection by the ego of the suitable structures becomes possible, but trial and error can always be resorted to when intelligent selection fails.

16 The *functional-coordinative function* of the ego must not be confused with Nunberg's synthetic function (1930) or with the *organizing function* of the ego, a term that Hartmann considers more appropriate (1947, p. 62). Hartmann has described the synthetic or organizing function as "the constant balancing of these three systems [id, ego, superego] against each other as well as the checking of demands of the outer world against those of the psychic systems" (p. 62f.). See also Hartmann (1948, p. 86; 1950, pp. 115 and 138; 1959, p. 329). The functional-coordinative function only scans for the right combination of *the resources available within the system ego,* in terms of the appropriate structures or ego apparatuses (and their possible combinations), so as to find the best combination for the solution of the problem posed. But this is a solution in ego terms only and need not have taken into consideration the demands of the other two systems, id and superego. It is conceivable that in many cases the synthetic function—whose task it is to take these demands into account—works over the results of the functional-coordinative function once they have been put forward, while in many others both functions operate simultaneously.

created, as I said above, a new and *ad hoc* structure. The fate of such *ad hoc* structures is variable. Once they have served their particular purpose they may never be required again, unless the same or related conceptual problems arise again. Thus, they can be transitory in nature, although the ego now has the potential ability to re-create such a structure if necessity arises; that is, the ego has enriched itself, its functional possibilities. If, as in the case of the mathematical problem referred to earlier, the conceptual problems involved are frequently met by the child's ego, the structure becomes perfected and a permanent feature of the ego organization.[17] Adding up, the solution of this and related types of mathematical problems is a task that confronts the ego frequently. The permanent structure that is thus established within the ego organization is the appropriate tool or instrument (in fact, a new ego apparatus) for the solution of a group of related problems. But the establishment of such a new structure or ego apparatus performs another important role, that is, its existence enables the ego to develop further and to solve problems of increasing complexity, since the newly acquired structure can be taken as a fresh point of departure and reference for other more sophisticated ones. A "permanent structure" of this type soon becomes, functionally speaking, automatized to a high degree insofar as it is constantly used for the solution of the specific problems it is meant to deal with. On the other hand, it can still be used when required to contribute to the building up of *ad hoc* structures for the solution of new specific problems presented to the ego in new *ad hoc* combinations. What I wish to highlight in all this is the sharp contrast between the ego's extreme flexibility and freedom to recombine the available structures to produce *ad hoc* solutions to new problems by means of *ad hoc* structures having only a temporary character, and the ego's simultaneous use of the same structures for its specific aims in more rigid, automatized fashion. Intelligent behavior and all learning processes are naturally highly dependent on the former ability.[18]

17 This is perhaps a good example of Rapaport's "stimulus nutriment" referred to above; that is, a case in which environmental stimulation of a sort contributes if not to the maintenance of a permanent psychological structure at least to its perfection and readiness.

18 I believe it is abundantly clear from the discussion so far that terms such as "psychological ego apparatus" and "psychological structures" can be, and frequently are, used synonymously in the psychoanalytic literature.

There are, speaking relatively, no limits to the number of new problems that can be presented to the human mind, especially if we take into account that the solution of a scientific problem or question simultaneously raises a number of other problems and questions that in turn require more answers. Just as there seems to be no limit (for all practical purposes) to the number of problems that can be presented to the ego, there seems to be no limit (again for all practical purposes) to the number of structures, or *functional combinations,* that the ego can produce in order to deal with them.

The role that the process of adaptation (of the individual and of the species) plays in this must not be underestimated. As I said, we are constantly confronted with new problems as we go along in the solution of old ones. Moreover, man is capable of modifying his environment, and these modifications frequently carry with them the need to adapt to new changed conditions and the solution of sometimes new and unsuspected problems. The modifications I have in mind here refer not only to the physical conditions of his milieu and their multiple derivations but to those in our social, political, philosophical, and even religious systems.

It is in the nature of physical conditions to change constantly and it is precisely the nature of the human mind (or mental apparatuses)—its flexibility and man's ability to produce adaptive solutions—that partly guarantee survival. Thus, there is no limit to the potential number of ego functions, just as there is no limit to the number of *psychological ego apparatuses*—or, if we prefer it, to the number of structures—that can be created within the ego organization to deal with new problems.

In the course of civilization the human species has developed a number of functional structures (psychological ego apparatuses) that were required to deal with the new changing conditions. As civilization progresses and is itself structured first by tradition, later by education and organized transmission of knowledge, the establishment of political, social, and religious institutions, in short, as civilization becomes more complex, it makes further demands on the ego's capabilities to deal with the ever-increasing complexity of propositions of the new order of things. (Freud's statement about the child having to achieve in a brief period of time what took civilization thousands of years to accomplish is relevant here.) From this point of view education as we know it today is, among other things, the system devised to teach children in a condensed and simplified manner the means by which they can build complex psychological ego apparatuses capable of dealing with the complexities created in our world. All education does is to exercise a number of mental capabilities in special directions and combinations until the ego learns to perform a number of complicated functions in interaction.

These multiple interacting functions that are required to achieve the ego's aims follow a logical system, an order, a sequence. There is a hierarchy in the functional order and interaction. Slowly, we teach the child how to establish a *functional structure,* which, once learned, has an independence of its own and enables him to deal with a particular aspect of reality in an economic and systematic fashion. In fact, we have by this means established a new *psychological ego apparatus* to deal with specific problems. This process is repeated *ad infinitum* by education (including formal schooling and informal general education of the young by society in general, and parents in particular) and covers a multiplicity of areas in human development. Nevertheless, it will be true to say that, in most cases and with respect to what I have referred to here as informal education, we have no explicit awareness of having such aims (of furthering the development of certain psychological ego apparatuses) since these aims are implicit in the social order we have developed.

If we take the training of a physicist, a mathematician, an engineer, etc., a similar process is in action. In fact, we are teaching him an abbreviated form of what took thousands of years to develop and required the minds of innumerable outstanding men. We are trying to develop in him specialized ego apparatuses capable of performing the complex activities required for the solution of a number of specific types of problems. This is, of course, a special case; but adaptation to the conditions of our special environment requires the development of a number of common ego apparatuses (with qualitative differences between individuals) if we are to function within normal limits in that environment.

The nature and the quality of such structures or ego apparatuses will vary greatly according to the level of civilization and the specific requirements of a given milieu. The ego function and apparatus of perception of a primitive savage living in the jungle will obviously be inadequate to cope with stimuli in the streets of London, while those of the Londoner will be similarly poorly adapted to the conditions of the jungle.

Finally, I want to call attention to a significant difference between human beings that is highlighted by my form of presentation. I refer now to the difference between those with highly creative minds and the ordinary members of the community, as well as to the significance of the creative process itself. Most educated men in the community are quite capable of assimilating and mastering the complexities involved in a new scientific advance, but few of them possess the capacity to unravel the secrets that have to be unraveled for scientific progress to take place. Only a limited number of people seem to have this ability developed to an exceptional degree, and they are the pioneers of scientific progress.

Thus, once a new and revolutionary step forward is taken, for example, in science, due to the efforts of a particular scientist, we are in a position to impart that new knowledge to many members of our community. We can teach them, so to say, the steps that are necessary to organize the different psychological structures in the right hierarchical functional order for the mastery of the new discovery. There is indeed little difficulty in doing this; and yet, as I pointed out, very few, if any of those able to learn it, would have been capable of solving the riddle themselves, however hard they may have tried. Thus it seems (leaving aside "chance discoveries," if such a thing does exist) that the creative capacity on a big scale is in part related to the special qualities and flexibility of that function of the ego that scans, combines, and recombines the functions of any number of psychological structures in the search for the solution of a problem, a capacity that presumably is associated with special sets of motivations.

BIBLIOGRAPHY

Apfelbaum, B. (1962), Some Problems in Contemporary Ego Psychology. *J. Amer. Psa. Assn.*, 10:526-537.

—— (1965), Ego Psychology, Psychic Energy, and the Hazards of the Quantitative Explanation in Psycho-Analytic Theory. *Int. J. Psa.*, 46:168-182.

—— (1966), On Ego Psychology: A Critique of the Structural Approach to Psycho-Analytic Theory. *Int. J. Psa.*, 47:451-475.

Arlow, J. A. & Brenner, C. (1964), *Psychoanalytic Concepts and the Structural Theory*. New York: International Universities Press.

Beres, D. (1965), Structure and Function in Psycho-Analysis. *Int. J. Psa.*, 46:53-63.

Colby, K. M. (1955), *Energy and Structure in Psychoanalysis.* New York: Ronald Press.

Freud, S. (1915), The Unconscious. *Standard Edition,* 14:159-215. London: Hogarth Press, 1957.

—— (1923), The Ego and the Id. *Standard Edition,* 19:3-66. London: Hogarth Press, 1961.

Gill, M. M. (1963), *Topography and Systems in Psychoanalytic Theory* [*Psychological Issues,* Monogr. 10]. New York: International Universities Press.

Glover, E. (1948), The Future Development of Psycho-Analysis. *On the Early Development of Mind.* New York: International Universities Press, 1956, pp. 333-351.

—— (1961), Some Recent Trends in Psychoanalytic Theory. *Psa. Quart.*, 30:86-107.

Hartmann, H. (1939), *Ego Psychology and the Problem of Adaptation.* New York: International Universities Press, 1958.

—— (1947), On Rational and Irrational Action. *Essays on Ego Psychology.* New York: International Universities Press, 1964, pp. 37-68.

—— (1948), Comments on the Psychoanalytic Theory of Instinctual Drives. *Essays on Ego Psychology.* New York: International Universities Press, 1964, pp. 69-89.

—— (1950), Comments on the Psychoanalytic Theory of the Ego. *Essays on Ego Psychology.* New York: International Universities Press, 1964, pp. 113-141.

—— (1959), Psychoanalysis as a Scientific Theory. *Essays on Ego Psychology.* New York: International Universities Press, 1964, pp. 318-350.

—— (1964), *Essays on Ego Psychology: Selected Problems in Psychoanalytic Theory.* New York: International Universities Press.

Holt, R. R. (1965), Ego Autonomy Re-Evaluated. *Int. J. Psa.*, 46:151-167.

Kubie, L. S. (1958), *Neurotic Distortion of the Creative Process.* Lawrence, Kansas: University of Kansas Press.

Lewis, W. C. (1965), Structural Aspects of the Psychoanalytic Theory of Instinctual Drives, Affects, and Time. In: *Psychoanalysis and Current Biological Thought,* ed. N. S. Greenfield & W. C. Lewis. Madison & Milwaukee: University of Wisconsin Press, pp. 151-180.

Loewald, H. W. (1952), The Problem of Defence and the Neurotic Interpretation of Reality. *Int. J. Psa.*, 33:444-449.

—— (1960), On the Therapeutic Action of Psycho-Analysis. *Int. J. Psa.*, 41:16-33.

Lustman, S. L. (1966), Impulse Control, Structure, and the Synthetic Function. In: *Psychoanalysis—A General Psychology: Essays in Honor of Heinz Hartmann,* ed. R. M. Loewenstein, L. M. Newman, M. Schur, & A. J. Solnit. New York: International Universities Press, pp. 190-221.

Miller, G. C. (1962), Ego-Autonomy in Sensory Deprivation, Isolation and Stress. *Int. J. Psa.*, 43:1-20.

Nunberg, H. (1930), The Synthetic Function of the Ego. In: *Practice and Theory of Psychoanalysis,* 1:120-136. New York: International Universities Press, 1960.

Rapaport, D. (1951a), *Organization and Pathology of Thought.* New York: Columbia University Press.

—— (1951b), The Autonomy of the Ego. *Bull. Menninger Clin.*, 15:113-123.

—— (1957), Cognitive Structures. In: *Contemporary Approaches to Cognition.* Cambridge: Harvard University Press, pp. 157-200.

—— (1958), The Theory of Ego Autonomy: A Generalization. *Bull. Menninger Clin.*, 22:13-25.

—— (1960a), On the Psychoanalytic Theory of Motivation. In: *Nebraska Symposium on Motivation,* ed. M. R. Jones. Lincoln: University of Nebraska Press, pp. 173-247.

—— (1960b), Psychoanalysis as a Developmental Psychology. In: *Perspectives in Psychological Theory,* ed. B. Kaplan & S. Wapner. New York: International Universities Press, pp. 210-256.

—— (1960c), *The Structure of Psychoanalytic Theory* [*Psychological Issues,* Monogr. 6]. New York: International Universities Press.

Schur, M. (1966), *The Id and the Regulatory Principles of Mental Functioning.* New York: International Universities Press.

Spitz, R. A. (1959), *A Genetic Field Theory of Ego Formation.* New York: International Universities Press.

White, R. W. (1963), *Ego and Reality in Psychoanalytic Theory* [*Psychological Issues,* Monogr. 11]. New York: International Universities Press.

A CONTRIBUTION TO THE METAPSYCHOLOGY OF THE PREANALYTIC PATIENT

IRVING SHUREN, M.A. (New York)

Within the frame of reference of psychoanalytic ego psychology, the term "analysand" may be understood to refer to someone whose ego structure is relatively intact, whose defenses operate largely selectively, and whose capacity to sustain object cathexes tends to be stable. The ego structure has reached a degree of secondary autonomy (Hartmann, 1939, 1950, 1952, 1955), in which the defense system remains stable, except for the partial failures that result in symptoms. In the analytic situation, when regression of drives and of ego functions occurs, the process is more or less in the service of the ego (Kris, 1934). Regression is mainly orderly, usually partial, and under rather flexible ego control; and, most important, the regression ordinarily is temporary and is readily reversible. The secondary autonomy of ego functions is maintained, the ego is relatively free of uncontrolled regression, and relatively independent of environmental pressures (Rapaport, 1958).

By contrast, a large number of prospective adult patients fail to fulfill these ego requirements for an analysand. This is evidenced by their entering treatment in a *partial* and *chronic* state of ego and instinctual regression. From among these patients, I have distinguished and selected a subgroup that exhibits a specific, identifiable structural and functional ego pathology. In this subgroup, traumatization during and just following the symbiotic phase (two to six months) and infantilization by the mother during the separation-individuation phase (six to thirty-six months) have led to fixation

---

I am very grateful to my colleagues Emily Anne Gargiulo and Armand Gargiulo for their valuable suggestions and criticisms. An earlier version of this paper was read at the Fourth Annual Scientific Conference on Psychoanalysis of The Council of Psychoanalytic Psychotherapists, February 20, 1966, in New York City.

tendencies of ego functions at these levels.[1] Since emotional separation from objects has never been adequately achieved, secondary ego autonomy has not been stabilized. Therefore, partial and somewhat uncontrolled regression of the ego is inevitable in the face of later difficulties. Subsequent chronic regression of ego functions has taken place to these earlier levels, from the ego organization of the oedipal and postoedipal periods, in response to both a push "from above" in the form of castration anxiety, guilt, and narcissistic mortification, and to a "pull from below" in the form of a wish for symbiotic union.

Poorly relinquished preoedipal wishes have colored oedipal wishes with acquisitive greed and envy. Moreover, because of displacement and generalization of oedipal wishes, all objects are viewed in oedipal terms. Inevitable and repeated disappointment in objects has led to a failure in adaptation. In turn, this failure has disturbed the intrapsychic balance between defense and impulse, and has led to failure of repression and to regression of ego and drives. Descriptively, regression to preoedipal levels represents a defensive retreat from unresolved oedipal conflicts that have been recathected, following failure in adaptation. In order to halt the course of regression and to retain a measure of autonomy, the ego has attempted to stabilize at the separation-individuation phase. At this level object relationships operate via the modes of introjective and projective identification. In line with the use of these mechanisms, objects toward whom libidinal and aggressive cathexes are directed are now experienced as neither completely symbiotic extensions, nor as completely separate objects, but as something in between. They also possess both these qualities simultaneously.

Partial and chronic regression of ego functions, such as defense, neutralization, and mode of object relationship to the ego structure of the separation-individuation phase, does not in itself constitute a separate clinical entity. It can be found as a more or less chronic condition in patients who are variously diagnosed as character disorders, borderlines, prepsychotics and psychopaths. Because modes of introjective and projective identification are frequently socially adaptive, their pathological quality often goes undetected, even by

[1] See Mahler and La Perriere (1965) for details of the developmental timetable used in this paper.

analysts, and may often be considered to be not only normal, but even preferable. In a less chronic form they also play a role in neuroses. In a nonpathological, flexible form, moreover, they are employed in the service of the ego, particularly in the operation of empathy. In their pathological form in the group of patients under discussion they constitute a specific ego pathology. They are accompanied by a cluster of identifiable ego deficiencies that result from a failure of secondary autonomy.

After the defense mechanism of repression has partially failed, the ego's defense function intensifies its use of reaction formation. After repression fails and, along with it, some of the capacity for neutralization, reaction formation is the only defense mechanism left that has the potential *selectively* to bind large quantities of specific instinctual derivatives and to stabilize the ego structure at the highest level of the separation-individuation phase. Were this defensive position successful, it is unlikely that the person would enter therapy. However, since failure in secondary ego autonomy in the type of patient under discussion is partly the result of a deficiency in the ego's function of integration, the binding capacity of the ego is unstable. Correspondingly, reaction formation does not produce sufficiently stable characterological changes. Reaction formation thus tends to fail and lead to the use of turning against the self, a defense mechanism that is more regressive and less selective. In using turning against the self, the ego attempts to ward off further regression of its functions and to protect the object from destruction by hostile wishes and impulses, by holding back and shunting drives in a global and somewhat less controlled fashion.

When free aggressive energy, resulting from partial loss of the capacity for neutralization following failure of secondary autonomy, is turned against the self representations under pressure from the superego, the suffering or defensive coldness it creates turns the person toward therapy. If the effect of turning aggression against the self disrupts the defensive balance that this maneuver has tried to sustain, other, more primitive defenses come to the ego's aid, such as introjective and projective identification, which are now used as defense mechanisms proper, in addition to being modes of object relationship. Turning against the self and introjective and projective identification are correlated with the earlier levels of the separation-individuation phase. Failure of these defenses leads to a regression to symbiosis and to the mechanisms of introjection, projection, and archaic forms of denial, all of which are characteristic of the symbiotic phase. Their appearance, which is common to this type of patient, is indicative of ego fragmentation; that is, of widespread splitting of the ego. Individual instances of regressive splitting follow the path of a prototypical massive cleavage between cognitive and experiencing functions, a cleavage that first occurred during or just following the original symbiotic phase in response to traumatic rupture of the stimulus barrier.

The ego deficiencies of this subgroup give rise to a cluster of clinical features, such as a labile sense of self-esteem, rapid vertical ego and instinctual fluctuations in regression and progression, mosaic pseudoidentities, emotional connectedness to objects, instinctualized ego functions, and a deficit and instability of object libido. The labile sense of self-esteem serves the therapist as an ongoing barometer of the intrapsychic balance of this patient. In normal development a sense of autonomy (separateness) forms the foundation for the phenomenological experience of selfhood, and thus is a precondition for true self-esteem. In this type of patient unstable emotional separateness leads to a defensive struggle to maintain autonomy at a level of the separation-individuation phase of development. Therefore, his self-esteem fluctuates with shifts in his capacity to sustain these defenses. Since perfectionistic standards, based on an unconscious sense of omnipotence and on a "purified pleasure ego," form an integral part of this defense system, the protection of narcissism is unstable. Narcissistic mortification is inevitable and repetitive.

The specific concept of an intrasystemic split between the cognitive and the experiencing functions of the ego, and the more general concept of an alteration in the structure of the ego, as they are used in this paper, are an outgrowth of Freud's ideas. We are familiar with his much-quoted statement: "it will be possible for the ego to avoid a rupture in any direction *by deforming itself,* by submitting to encroachments on its own unity and even perhaps by effecting *a cleavage or division of itself*" (1924, p. 152f., my italics). In this early statement Freud did not yet speak of a "splitting of the ego," but the subsequent direction of his ideas indicates that this is what he had in mind (1927, 1940a, 1940b).

The patients discussed in this paper are an identifiable subgroup of that larger group of patients who are properly termed "preanalytic." In this subgroup, before regression can be employed in the service of the ego, that is, for analysis proper, further emotional separation must be achieved in the course of therapy. As the chronic, regressed state of the ego is gradually reversed, the patient becomes more capable of observing himself, with appropriate affect, rather than be blindly immersed in his recathected infantile experiences and emotional attitudes. This is accomplished by combining a judicious use of parameters (Eissler, 1953), such as confrontation, a procedure that is directed more toward the intellect and to the structural features of the patient, and interpretation, the classical psychoanalytic procedure that is directed more toward the emotions and to the instinctual features of the patient.

This subgroup draws from the range of patients whose ego deformities, such as those described by Waelder (1958), constitute more than a symptom neurosis. Impulse disorders, perversions, and various rigid characters also contribute instances of patients who fall within this subgroup, as do, probably, many of the chronically labile emotional types described by Jacobson (1957). These patients exhibit disturbances in mental structure originating in the pregenital period of development. Stringent defensive operations, in response to trauma and severe conflict, have altered the basic structure of the ego, a process originally described by Freud (1924). The ego has been altered in its adaptive, controlling, and organizing functions, the central importance of which has more recently been re-emphasized by Hartmann (1956). The ego deficiencies of this subgroup are mainly found as structural features in a clinically heterogeneous variety of diagnostic categories, whose psychopathology falls between, and to a certain extent overlaps, neuroses and psychoses.

In the present paper, deficiencies in mental structure will be correlated with the aftereffects of traumatic rupture of the stimulus barrier, and deficiencies in emotional separation will be correlated with the aftereffects of disturbances in object relationship. Fear of trauma, on the one hand, and narcissistic defense, on the other, will form the pivotal concepts for developing the structural theory of the pregenital disturbances in the drive organization and in the structure of the ego of this type of patient. Hartmann's concept of secondary autonomy of the ego will be used as a basic reference point in this genetic schema. Disturbances in the maturation of drives and in the stability of mental structure will be related to the development of relative secondary autonomy, that is, to the various degrees of success and failure in approaching and sustaining this momentous achievement in mental development. I shall also draw liberally on the recently published book by Spitz (1965), which is a remarkable storehouse of important information about the first year of life.

No integrated psychoanalytic theory of technique as yet exists for the treatment of these ego deficiencies, although beginnings have been made in that direction, drawing heavily on the findings of psychoanalytic ego psychology. A recent example is a paper by Blanck (1966). The absence of a clearly drawn metapsychology has given rise to experimental techniques not solidly grounded in systematic psychoanalytic theory, although drawing on psychoanalytic concepts for their rationale. The present paper makes a contribution toward this metapsychology, and thus indirectly to a theory of technique. It demonstrates that these specific ego deficiencies and defenses are held in common by patients who evidence seemingly disparate clinical syndromes, and it delineates the metapsychology behind these structural features. In focusing on these patients it also makes a modest attempt to integrate the generally accepted laws depicted in the psychoanalytic theory of mental conflict with some of the hypotheses of psychoanalytic structural theory, and with some of the hypotheses of psychoanalytic ego psychology in general. In so doing, it also calls attention to a widespread structural syndrome that is often given insufficient direct attention in the process of therapy. In the more neurotic variants this oversight can lead to a "successful analysis" that leaves the patient feeling empty, and lacking a firm sense of identity, though his behavior is now more adaptive toward an "average expectable environment" (Hartmann, 1939) that currently often shares his pathology. In the more borderline variants this oversight can result in failure of therapy, usually by premature termination, all too often after years of treatment.

The metapsychology of these patients indicates that the separation-individuation phase, and its dilemma, may be as important in their case as the oedipal phase is in the case of neurotics. It is an impressive experience for the therapist, as he listens to the verbalizations of these patients, to think in terms of separation wishes and anxieties. What could not have been sufficiently understood, when viewed only in oedipal terms, becomes clear when viewed also as manifestations of unresolved separation-individuation conflicts. Even when these patients present seemingly blatant oedipal material, they unconsciously view it in preoedipal terms. For example, a dream in which a patient's mother appears naked, beckoning him toward her, may symbolically depict a fear of losing his separateness through intercourse (Handelsman, 1965). In the treatment of these cases, even if the patient cathects the oedipus complex in part, oedipal interpretations given early in treatment usually fall flat, or are accepted uncritically and without therapeutic effect. Even if the oedipus complex is considerably more strongly cathected, the ego is structurally not ready to face it. In this case oedipal interpretations tend to stir up intense anxiety and lead to a reactive reinforcement of the already too rigid defensive system. If this occurs, it is not to be seen as an instance of resistance, but is to be understood as resulting from "correct interpretations," given prematurely.

These patients have established a rigid equilibrium, from which they dare not budge, a situation that Fenichel so clearly depicts in his description of the difficulties encountered in the treatment of character disorders (1945, p. 537f.). The patients fear a regressive collapse of the ego. Only after the ego has been strengthened will separation anxieties be analyzable, and only then can the pathological defensive structure be reduced. In turn, loosening of reactive defenses leads to gradual emotional separation. As the ego reaches sufficient autonomy it can begin to deal with oedipal conflicts with objectivity and with controlled appropriate affect. And only then will oedipal conflicts proper be more fully cathected. Until then, conflicts which clinically appear to be oedipal conflicts are largely heightened and extended versions of unresolved preoedipal conflicts. The conflicts are more properly dealt with as preoedipal material. This phenomenon has also been described by Gitelson (1958).

Theory of Normal Infant Ego Development

Selected aspects of the psychoanalytic theory of normal infant development will serve as a background for the pathological variations encountered in these patients. In this section only the symbiotic phase will be discussed. This emphasis does not correspond to an evaluation of the relative importance of each phase in the pathology of these patients. There are several purposes served by this approach. One is to depict in detail the developmental aspects of the normal symbiotic phase which appear as regressive features in these patients, as a result of partial failures in their attempt to stabilize at the ego organization of the separation-individuation phase. Another is to delineate the relationship between trauma experienced during and just following the symbiotic phase, and the partial carry-over of its structural effects into the separation-individuation phase, such as an intensification of separation anxiety and difficulties in neutralization. In a subsequent section one feature of the normal separation-individuation phase will be stressed, namely, emotional separation, a process that is best understood through its pathological forms.

For developmental details of physical separation and of processes of ego individuation the reader is referred to the excellent papers by Mahler et al. A condensed presentation will be found in the recent paper by Mahler and La Perriere (1965) referred to earlier. The paper also offers a revised and refined version of Mahler's original developmental timetable. The theory of normal development of the oedipal phase will not be discussed in the present paper since it is well known, and since regression from this phase has produced patients who are essentially preoedipal. Their emotional life is an expression of a mixture of symbiotic and separation-individuation features. They give the clinical appearance of emotionally very immature and intellectually very precocious two-year-olds, who are trying to act as though they were adults.

In the structural development of the ego primitive projective and introjective processes serve as vehicles for developing initial distinctions between self and object, during the symbiotic phase of ego development. This sequence is well described in a recent paper by Brody and Mahoney (1964). The registration of these early distinctions between self and object is fluid. They come and go, very rapidly. In this process successive painful stimuli, from within and from without, are projected following their introjection. Memory traces form only gradually, leaving primitive global memory residues of a not-self. Similarly, pleasurable stimuli, experienced in contrast to painful stimuli, become the primitive global memory residues of a self. Only later, as frustration tolerance develops, will inner painful stimuli be also included in the self image. The symbiotic ego utilizes these memory traces to build primitive symbolic representations that become increasingly independent of the original stimuli.

The earliest form of self and object representations (Hartmann, 1950; Jacobson, 1964) are primitive symbolized experiences, which in turn are the precondition for the formation of class concepts during subsequent developmental phases of the ego. These early self representations form the basis for primitive identifications, that is, for a more stabilized mental structure (M. Klein, 1932, 1963). Adverse experiences during the symbiotic phase, such as physical pain experienced in an intensity sufficient to rupture the protective stimulus barrier, can lead to deficiencies in the ego functions of memory and symbolization, such as excessive fluidity or a narrowing and rigidification of these functions. The preanalytic patients described earlier evidence such disturbances.

Seen from a slightly different angle, during the symbiotic phase processes of internalization are utilized by the ego to develop a capacity for binding tension-producing stimuli, instead of having to discharge the tensions immediately. Binding reduces the fluidity of registered experience. The binding capacity makes it possible to lay down memory traces (Spitz, 1965, p. 41), which can then be used by the ego to anticipate danger. When memory becomes stabilized, it leads to a sustained capacity to anticipate danger, marking the advent of the signal function of the ego (Spitz, 1965, p. 115). The signal function helps protect the ego from traumatic anxiety (Freud, 1926), at first by alerting primitive defensive operations such as denial, and later by physical avoidance behavior, when physical maturation makes directed motor behavior possible. Furthermore, by making mental trial action possible the signal function helps the ego develop frustration tolerance, a process akin to the physiological dynamics of immunization.

The reality principle is thereby gradually established and added to the pleasure principle, and now contributes to the evaluation of situations for pleasure gain and for pleasure danger. The structural maturation of the infant's ego is given a strong impetus when the ego can draw on both the pleasure principle and the reality principle, and on their transitional forms, in the beginning development of a hierarchical organization of modes of tension and discharge. In the subgroup of preanalytic patients described earlier, the signal function is defective. A process akin to the physiological dynamics of hypersensitization has resulted from early traumatic experience, creating a chronic emergency state in which signal anxiety readily changes to traumatic anxiety.

The structural developments of the normal symbiotic phase are greatly enhanced when the autonomous synthetic function of the ego, a function believed to be congenital by Glover (1943) and by Spitz (1965, p. 104), develops sufficiently to combine the memory traces deriving from the operation of analogous units of mental function. These units of function, consisting of clusters of drive, stimulus, object, and discharge mode, at first lay down corresponding clusters of memory traces, which Glover (1933, 1943) has termed ego nuclei. The synthetic function of the ego now combines groups of ego nuclei and erects boundaries around them, thus creating a more unified structural ego. Spitz (1965, p. 104f.) dates this process at three months, whereas Glover dates it much later.

The combining of ego nuclei also makes possible, for the first time, a true experience of emotion as distinct from an experience of sensation. Emotion is a conscious phenomenological ego experience at the boundary of the ego, where the id impulse comes into contact with the boundary, a process that has been carefully depicted by Federn (1952). Affective experience develops from the matrix of physical sensations. Affects are aim-inhibited variations of sensation and are correlated with the maturational capacity of the ego to bind and partly to neutralize the drives. Before the advent of emotional reactions, when excessive stimulation threatens to break through the stimulus barrier (Spitz, 1965, p. 105f.), the infant responds with rapid visceral and neuromotor discharges. The discharges may be accompanied by intense visceral sensations, but not by true emotions. In turn, the advent of a capacity for emotional reactions plays an important role in the operation of the signal function of the ego, by providing the ego with a sensory apparatus that warns of impending mental trauma or of bodily danger (Freud, 1926). The capacity for aim inhibition and the formation of a structural ego also make possible the constitution of the primary libidinal object in contradistinction to the more primitive need-gratifying object (A. Freud, 1953). Gradual internalization of the libidinal object during the first three years of life leads eventually to internal object constancy.

Hartmann (1950) believes that both neutralization and synthesis are autonomous ego functions that are present at birth in rudimentary form. It is my view that these two ego functions, acting in an endless variety of combinations, are the fundaments of all other ego functions. It is also my view that *variegated* emotional experience represents the highest level of differentiation of the experiencing functions of the ego, and that a complete sense of emotional separateness of self from objects is its precondition. Since the preanalytic patients under discussion are deficient in the functions of neutralization and synthesis, and in emotional separation, we can expect to find pathological ego functions of various kinds. As an example, their emotional life is primitive and narrow and readily regresses to impulsive behavior, in which the capacity for aim inhibition has been lost. The regressive sequence leads from failure of the capacity to experience emotion consciously, through failure of the capacity to experience physical sensations consciously, to the partial failure to inhibit physical action. Impulses bypass these functions and are acted out. Instances of these various decreasing levels of neutralization and synthesis are typical of this type of preanalytic patient. Primitive acting out fluctuates with outbursts of raw emotion, or the search for physical sensations becomes the ego's desperate attempt to reinstate instinctual cathexes that have been withdrawn from the representations of the bodily self, and thus an attempt to ward off psychotic regression to ego dedifferentiation.

The synthetic function of the ego is present, and begins to develop, during the early oral phase of the drive organization, which corresponds with the symbiotic phase (two to six months) in the development of the ego. Accordingly, the synthetic function is concurrent with the mode of introjection. Drive derivatives and primitive object representations are internalized by the ego, and are then linked together by its synthetic function. Unlike the customary views, I do not consider integration either as one of the properties of synthesis or as being synonymous with synthesis. Integration appears to be a separate ego function. Synthesis can be likened to a chemical mixture, where the properties are simply additive and the ingredients are in juxtaposition with one another. Further, there is no endogenous reason why these particular ingredients are together. Integration is more like a chemical compound, whose properties are different and more complex than those of its original ingredients, and whose ingredients are interlocked in an arrangement that is specific to the properties of these ingredients.

It is my belief that the integrative function of the ego begins to develop during the separation-individuation phase (six to thirty-six months) in the development of the ego, that is, concurrent with the late oral and with the anal phases of drive organization. Accordingly, the integrative function is concurrent, first, with the mode of introjective identification, then with turning against the self, then with reaction formation, and finally with repression. I believe that the integrative function does not reach its full development until the oedipal period, when the mode of identification proper becomes possible. Even then the function of synthesis overlaps with, and by far outstrips, that of integration. The personality structure of the oedipal phase still consists of a loosely knit union of introjects. The identifications of this phase may give way under stress. The combined operation of the synthetic and integrative functions is therefore a precondition for the achievement of secondary autonomy. This combination would probably be close to Hartmann's concept of an organizing function (1947, 1950), although he often uses these terms interchangeably. The function of differentiation, which Hartmann includes under the organizing function, would correlate with temporary decreases in the cathexes of the synthetic function, which correspondingly allows the ego to reorganize and restructure the internal building blocks that have been temporarily loosened.

Synthesis and integration are of prime importance in coordinating the cognitive functions of the ego with the experiencing functions of the ego, two sets of functions that for genetic reasons are structurally separate from each other from their inception. The experiencing functions of the ego derive from the id and remain in close proximity to the id. They stem from the primitive body ego that *passively* registers visceromotor sensations. The experiencing functions join the cognitive functions of the ego, thus acquiring the status of ego functions proper, probably only when the synthetic function of the ego has matured sufficiently to erect boundaries around the ego nuclei. Spitz (1965, pp. 104-107) dates this at three months and correlates it with a shift from passive ego experiences to actively directed ego functions. He further correlates this with the appearance of the object-*directed* smiling response. Once the experiencing functions have been incorporated into the ego, the organizing functions of the ego can then *actively* bind the drives. In contrast to the origin of the experiencing functions in the id, the cognitive functions are largely autonomous to the ego (Hartmann, 1950). From the outset they stand closer to the control systems of the ego, those of defense and neutralization, than to the drive systems of the id. The pathological use of synthesis and an unstable capacity for integration, which are characteristic of the type of preanalytic patient under discussion, create a proneness toward regression of experiencing functions back to their origin in the id. This produces the pathological intermittent split between these two sets of functions that was referred to earlier. It accounts for the impulsive and irrational behavior that occurs whenever the defenses that maintain separation-individuation fail.

Economically, the ego directs two basic types of object cathexes that derive from the cognitive and experiencing functions. The energy that derives from the cognitive structure of the ego draws mainly on neutral and neutralized energy (Hartmann, 1955). It is perceptual and conceptual in quality. The energy that derives from the experiencing structure originates in the id and retains its instinctual quality, both libidinal and aggressive. Functionally, instinctual and cognitive cathexes may both be operative at any one time, or any combination of the three forms of energy may be withdrawn for defensive purposes, either temporarily or permanently. Massive withdrawal of any one or more of these leads to pathological attitudes and behavior that represent side effects in the use of these stringent, psychoticlike defenses. These phenomena are characteristic of the type of patient under discussion. For example, withdrawal of cognitive object cathexis constitutes perceptual denial and leads to a completely instinctual experiencing of objects, with lack of judgment. Correspondingly, withdrawal of libidinal object cathexis constitutes a special instance of instinct defusion and may lead to behavioral outbursts of direct aggression. Since absence of libido removes the capacity for emotional compassion, the aggression is held in check only to the extent that judgment, derived from cognitive cathexes, still holds, and that ego controls still remain intact.

Success in maintaining defense against drives has thus resulted in a failure of adaptation. In turn, failure in adaptation leads indirectly to subsequent failure in the defense against drives. Regression of ego structure and drives results. This sequence of intrapsychic dynamics is characteristic of the type of preanalytic patient under discussion. They attempt to augment their defensive position by withdrawing both libidinal and aggressive object cathexes, turning them against the self and then trying to neutralize them, and by relating to objects in an affectless, intellectual fashion. Ultimately, this defensive operation also fails and leads to regression, because of the basic instability of their capacity for neutralization, which has made these autistic defenses necessary to begin with.

In summary, this short depiction of infantile development has been used to point out the sequential origins of the deficiencies in ego structure of the type of preanalytic patient under discussion. These include binding capacity, conceptual memory, signal function, anticipatory anxiety, frustration tolerance, reality principle, integrative capacity, emotional capacity, and object-cathecting capacity. These deficiencies have been presented as though all of them appeared in each case and in equal degree. Actually, for didactic purposes, this portrayal has been schematic. Any or all of these deficiencies may appear, either initially or as therapy continues, and in varying degrees. The variance falls along a continuum, from instances of actual arrested development of specific ego functions in the more borderline type of patient, to regressive loss of function in the more neurotic type. Loss of function may be more readily restored following resolution of pathological defenses and anxieties. Further stimulation of arrested functional capacities depends upon the extent to which a particular function has a developmental critical phase, and the extent to which partial aspects of a particular function have developed under subsequently more favorable conditions. The partially developed aspects may serve as platforms on which lesser developed aspects may evolve under therapeutic stimulation. In general, the less adaptive the deficiency, the easier it is to detect. Sometimes the deficiencies appear suddenly, when analysis of defense has been overly systematic, a phenomenon reminiscent of a pseudoneurotic psychosis. Finally, it is hoped that this schematic presentation will help alert therapists to the more adaptive forms of this pathology.

Ego Pathology Derived from the Symbiotic Phase

The ego of this type of preanalytic patient has been traumatized by excessive stimulation during infancy and early childhood. The infantile ego could not adequately bind the tensions because primitive mechanisms of defense were still unreliable (Spitz, 1965, p. 5). Furthermore, because of the maturational insufficiency of the ego's directed discharge function, and perhaps also because of an innate deficiency of the stimulus barrier, a backlog of chronic pressure develops on the stimulus barrier. This bound-up state makes the stimulus barrier susceptible to rupture, and rupture of the stimulus barrier disrupts the protective symbiotic state. The excessive stimulation derived, variously, from prolonged crying, from strong physical pain, from the shocks of primal-scene experiences, and from the shocks accompanying the mother's narcissistic alternating between object cathexes and detachment. Although the causes in any individual case vary, all cases seem to have experienced narcissistic mothers and thus constant disruption of the symbiotic state. Detachment of libido by the infant and child, in defensive reaction to mother's detachment, compounds the difficulty by adding to the defects in object relationship. This appears as a defensive process in each adult patient of this group.

When the infant's ego is suddenly confronted with excessive stimulation, the cognitive functions of the ego are forced into a premature wakefulness. This creates the artificial, partial separation of cognitive functions and experiencing functions. It also disrupts the budding libidinal object cathexes of the ego by prematurely confronting the infant with an *emotional* awareness of mother's separateness from him, and thus of his own separateness. The state of protective primary narcissism is disrupted. Therefore, the ego experiences both stimulus trauma and sudden object loss. The sudden experience of loss of the anaclitic object interferes with the gradual formation of stable unconscious representations of this object. This is the forerunner of the defective object constancy that can be observed in these preanalytic patients as ego deficiencies in object relationship, such as an unstable capacity for libidinal object cathexes.

The ego deficiency is largely in terms of libidinal object cathexes. Cognitive object cathexes are more stable. This fact is of practical significance for the analyst, since the capacity to form stable cognitive object cathexes provides these patients with an intellectual base on which to develop a sustained relationship with the analyst, provided that the analyst takes full advantage of this by enlisting the ego interests of these patients. As the patients experience, primarily intellectually and secondarily emotionally, that what the analyst says makes sense, their relationship to the analyst gradually becomes more libidinal and leads to the gradual development of a transference neurosis. Whether or not a full transference neurosis develops will depend upon the degree of intensity of object libido that can be stimulated. Until then the transference situation is largely based on neutral energy and on partly neutralized aggressive energy. This is a workable situation that serves the analyst as a substitute for the positive transference found in neurotic patients, until a more libidinal positive transference develops.

Returning now to the rupture of the symbiosis, this experience suddenly confronts the ego not only with excessive anxiety brought on by stimulation from without but also with excessive anxiety brought on by stimulation from within, in the form of primitive rage. Aggressive energy, mobilized in reaction to the traumatic state, threatens to overwhelm the ego. The ego attempts to reduce the multiple anxieties by trying to repair the rupture. It reinstates the temporarily lost object internally, via processes of internalization. However, since the integrative capacity of the ego has not yet developed, the ego cannot undergo the process of mourning, and thus cannot assimilate the introjected object into the core of its structure. It cannot replace the lost object with a characterological identification.

The normal infant and child is able to build a stable mental structure because he and mother have been sufficiently successful in adapting to and gratifying each other's needs. In addition to having experienced any of the other sources of excessive stimulation, the infant and child who develops the ego deficiencies depicted above has experienced repeated failures in his capacity to adapt to mother's repeated narcissistic detachment. Failure to stimulate the mother sufficiently so that she can relinquish her detachment results in inadequate gratification of his basic needs, such as the need for *gradual* stimulation, and the need for feeding conditions that are sensitive to his varying oral and gastrointestinal demands. The lack of a mothering experience in infancy and early childhood, an experience that should be constant and need-specific, has prevented these patients from developing *stable* object constancy (M. Klein, 1934, 1940; Jacobson, 1964), that is, firm and continuous internal representations of whole objects. Although partial object constancy has developed, it is prone to regressive dissolution whenever disappointments are experienced with current objects. Withdrawal of cathexes from object representations then leads to a hunger for current external objects, a phenomenon that is reminiscent of the "love addicts" described by Fenichel (1945, p. 382); but their strong dependency makes them overly suspicious of these objects.[2] Their suspiciousness is increased by the fact that all disappointments are interpreted as an impending re-experiencing of the original infantile traumas.

Early trauma also seems to interfere with the development of the integrative function, probably by delaying its maturation. When the integrative function does finally develop, it is unstable. It is my view that a capacity for integration is also the basis for the ego's developing a higher-order capacity for neutralizing drive energy. Delayed development of the integrative function in early childhood seems to account for the unstable quality of neutralization in these adult patients, which in turn seems to account for the excessive rage following disappointment in current objects. Since choice of objects is based on infantile and childhood fixations and subject to the repetition compulsion, these experiences are unconsciously directed blind ventures which are frequently devastatingly disappointing.

These patients try to ward off this entire sequence by keeping their libidinal and aggressive object cathexes to a minimum, and relating to people largely through their cognitive functions. Since neutralization is inadequate, this is accomplished by turning the drive energy toward the self. This mechanism also defends them

2 For a discussion of issues that are related to these problems in interpersonal adaptation, see Hartmann (1939, pp. 22-48) and Erikson (1950, pp. 219-224).

against their tendency to experience heightened stimulation as impending trauma. Although this allows them to retain object cathexes, and thus helps keep them oriented to external reality, it leads to a shallow, feelingless view of people and things. Whatever object-libidinal feelings remain, are very muted. Life is devoid of joy. These characterological features, centered around the excessive fear of excitation, seem to correspond to W. Reich's description of the masochistic character (1933, pp. 234-245). However, whereas Reich then stressed only the unpleasure resulting from bound-up libidinal drives, we would now equally stress the aggressive components of unpleasure. Because of turning the drives against the self, the ego is subject to pathological shifts in mood (Jacobson, 1957), between libidinized and aggressivized paranoid self-aggrandizement and self-destructive masochistic attitudes. If their aggression cannot be completely contained by defensive turning against the self short of self-destruction, the boundaries between self and object representations may break down. Aggression then "spills over" and spoils the unconscious representations of good objects (M. Klein, 1934), turning good internal objects into bad internal objects. It manifests itself clinically either directly as a pervasive depressive quality or, following the use of projective defenses, as paranoid attitudes.

Disruption to the development of a stable image of the primary libidinal object during symbiosis also forms an early root for the subsequent pathology of the separation-individuation phase. In his inordinate need to restore the lost, good libidinal object, this infant learns to drape himself to the physical and psychological contours of his mother (Mahler and La Perriere, 1965). Draping to mother's physical contours consists of molding reactions to the surface of mother's body. Draping to mother's psychological contours consists of adaptation to her attitudes and emotions. Therefore, when autonomous strivings for separateness arise during the separation-individuation phase, the fear of object loss gives rise to an inordinate fear of becoming a separate person. Pathological separation anxiety still represents a major problem in the adult preanalytic patient.

If this fear is overcome in therapy, separation is once more put into motion. With the advent of separation, the pull from the partially still-unresolved original symbiotic fixation then gives rise to the opposite fear, the fear of loss of self. Whereas formerly closeness to the object was the primary need, now it is replaced by a pathological need for distance,[3] which acts as a defense against symbiosis. The danger of symbiotic regression must be overcome in therapy if libidinal object cathexes are ever to develop to their full potential, since it is primarily libidinal needs that pull them toward symbiosis. On the one hand, the wish to regress to symbiosis must be fully analyzed, so that the wish can be relinquished. On the other hand, separation must be more firmly established. This is an exceedingly difficult task that involves a reconstruction of the infantile traumas and an analysis of the historical layering of defenses against these traumas which prevent further separation. It eventually also involves demonstration to the current ego that it no longer need fear a separation trauma, that although the patient has been too afraid to let himself know it, he has all along been a separate person. This step can be taken only when sufficient integration has been accomplished, so that the danger of *uncontrolled regression* has been greatly reduced. Only then can the patient fully consciously experience his underlying *wish to regress,* then augment his separateness, and finally face the oedipus conflict again and resolve it. The therapeutic work weaves back and forth among these issues, between wishes, anxieties, and defenses. Each strengthening of the ego slowly leads to upward developmental movement in the direction of the oedipus complex. The recathexes of the oedipus complex should remain largely untouched until the conflicts are sufficiently cathected to be interpreted with full therapeutic effect.

Since integration binds drive energy by stabilizing defenses and regulates the discharge of drives, the structural weakness of the ego's capacity for integration results in intermittent failure of defenses. When defenses fail, the ego cannot either hold back the drives or direct their discharge with adequate control. Further loss of integration in these preanalytic patients, which eventually leads to splitting, correlates with a sequence in defensive failures. First, repression fails, then reaction formation. Finally, turning against the self fails. At that point the integrity of the ego is at stake, since splitting begins to take place. This constitutes a chronic emergency state. As a result, defense becomes the major concern of this ego. Conflict-free

[3] For an excellent discussion of shifts in psychological distance and their implications for therapy, see Bouvet (1958).

autonomous ego functions are also drawn into the struggle against the drives, in an attempt to ward off regressive splitting. In the ego's attempt to seal the breaches in its defenses, the total personality may be energically impoverished, as mental structures become more rigid and less mental energy is available for the operation of conflict-free ego functions.

A major example of defense involving conflict-free functions is intellectualization. In an attempt to ward off regressive discharges, the cognitive ego siphons off the cathexes of the experiencing ego and hypercathects its own functions; i.e., the ego unconsciously offers its own functions as object for the drives. This appears clinically as a self-aggrandized valuation of intellectual prowess that is both highly sexualized and highly aggressivized. The level of superego functioning that corresponds with this narcissistic defense is intermittently placed in the service of instinctual drives. Its effectiveness then lasts only as long as the object complies with the ego's hyper-instinctualized narcissistic needs. These pathological modifications of ego and superego often produce a feelingless pseudoconcern for the object, a concern that is mechanical in quality and largely devoid of affective identification with the object's needs. These pathological ego attitudes can already be detected in the behavior of children who later develop the character structure of these preanalytic patients. The unconscious attitudes of these children toward objects are a pathological variant on the normal self-centeredness of childhood. In the adult patients this has led to a cold, intellectual understanding of people that is used for purposes of manipulation. When the therapist indirectly tampers with this defensive structure by not accommodating the patients' psychopathic maneuvers, he encounters a cold wall of unconscious, unverbalizable rage.

Failure of the defensive system of the ego is also the result of unconscious regressive wishes to return to the ego and drive organization of the symbiotic phase. The ego is unsuccessful in its attempt to ward off an inordinate, unconscious, inclination to give up all higher-level controls, which are already difficult to sustain without adequate cathexes being available to the conflict-free segment of the ego. A varying success in maintaining secondary autonomy is visible within the analytic situation. It appears as a simultaneous multiplicity of various developmental ego levels, defenses and drive states, as the depth of partial regressions rapidly fluctuates up and down, sometimes within a single session. The primitive discharges referred to earlier in this paper occur whenever turning against the self fails, and with it the capacity for integrating cognitive and experiencing functions. These patients are unusually blind to the existence of the behavioral disparities in themselves that result from unconscious splitting of the ego. As part of the emergency defense state of the ego, the synthetic combining function unconsciously includes the disparities within the self image, but without integration.

When the narcissistic defenses of the ego fail, the ego of these patients is rendered passive and thus helpless. Further ego control then becomes overly dependent upon the auxiliary control functions of a regressively reactived archaic superego system that operates with poorly neutralized aggressive energy. The surplus of aggressive energy turned on the ego by this archaic superego gives the defensive state a rigid and brittle quality. Aggression turned against the ego often also leads to the ego's reactive defenses against the superego commands and thus to acting out of impulses. The defective neutralizing capacity of the ego eventually also contributes to a subsequent failure in the internalizing efforts of the ego's defensive function of turning against the ego. The signal function, which operates with partly neutralized aggressive energy, breaks down when the aggressive energy becomes more instinctualized. The overaggressivized superego then indirectly fosters regression of the ego, instead of producing signal guilt and anxiety. It is when both the integrative function and the signal function fail that impulsive behavior alternates with rigid defensive counterreactions, in the ego's attempt first to discharge excessive drive tension and then to reinstate a defense equilibrium. As failure of defense alternates with reinstatement of defense, cathexes shift over both sides of the split in an unpredictable fashion. A rapid alternation of these cathexes constitutes the essentially artificial control system of these preanalytic patients and serves as a diagnostic sign for the therapist. The regressive discharges temporarily reduce the drive pressure on the ego, allowing the ego to reinstate higher-level defenses, such as turning against the self, reaction formation and repression, and making further splitting unnecessary. The regressive, split-off discharges of the preanalytic patients under discussion are to be understood as instances of temporary breakthroughs of an underlying global and chronic split, which originated in infancy and has only partially been sealed by subsequently developed reactive defenses.

The concept of a reduction of pressure on the ego that is made possible by splitting is an outgrowth of ideas expressed by Freud in his 1924 paper. For example, in postulating that the ego institutes a "cleavage or division of itself," Freud adds, "In this way the inconsistencies, eccentricities and follies of men would appear in a similar light to their sexual perversions, through the acceptance of which *they spare themselves repression*" (p. 153, my italics). Freud is here describing permanent pathological discharge modes, which appear as characterological peculiarities that compensate for the failure of higher-level defenses.

The original split between cognition and behavior that arose during the first year is reactivated because of the partial regressive loss of the unstable integrative function of the ego. Although in this paper I focus mainly on the failure of integration between cognitive and experiencing functions, this represents a major instance of a general deficiency of the integrative function. That is, failures in integration also occur within the cognitive and experiencing functions themselves. This results in defective coordination of separate motor functions, in disjointed emotional reactions, and in defective coordination of separate intellectual functions.

The treatment of these patients aims at a stabilization of object constancy and at the further development and stabilization of the capacities for integration and neutralization. As part of the therapeutic process the experience of loss of the original libidinal object must be made manifest once more, and the patients helped to work through a belated mourning. If successful, this will help the patients relinquish their pathological defenses against trauma and object loss, and help them to neutralize their infantile rage. In turn, a decrease in infantile rage will allow the ego functions of neutralization and integration to develop and to stabilize. This will also make it possible to assimilate the positive aspects of the original split-off introjected object. Additional introjects that have been associatively repressed and split off, following subsequent disappointment in other external objects, can then be released from the synthetic function that binds them to the original libidinal introject. They will then be subjected to the integrative function. In the process of integration all split-off introjects will become part of the structure of the adult ego and superego and provide a structural aid in achieving secondary ego autonomy.

Ego Pathology Derived from the Separation-Individuation Phase

Having first focused mainly on the normal and pathological conditions during the symbiotic phase of development, I shall now proceed more directly to the separation-individuation phase. The decisive fixation points in these preanalytic patients fall in the symbiotic and separation-individuation phases. They begin in infancy and extend to the onset of the oedipal phase, at about age three. Serious and unresolved conflicts in infancy and childhood involving the highly correlated developmental needs of the ego for object constancy and for separateness appear to account for the ego pathology of these patients. By contrast, proper gratification of these needs provides the basis for the capacity to love others as separate objects (Spitz, 1965). In the future preanalytic patients poor consistency in experiencing objects during the symbiotic phase results in a subsequent tendency toward regression to symbiosis, when the infant encounters conflicts during the separation-individuation phase.

The prime developmental hurdle of the experiencing functions of the ego during the normal separation-individuation phase is the achievement of an emotional sense of separateness. For the child who will later develop the ego deficiencies depicted here, this maturational hurdle presents a serious two-dimensional dilemma that heightens the "age-specific vulnerability" (Spitz, 1965, p. 109f.) of this transitional stage. One dimension is of intrapsychic origin and results from his symbiotic fixation. The original experience of a sudden rupture of the symbiosis has made the child fearful of re-experiencing trauma and object loss. The maturational push toward separation that ushers in and characterizes the separation-individuation phase once more raises up these fears. The child has used clingingness to ward off these fears. Now he feels an impelling urge toward relinquishing this hold. The need for symbiotic defense, on the one hand, and the response to a maturational drive toward separation, on the other, present the ego with a seemingly insoluble conflict.

The other dimension of the dilemma is interpersonal in origin and is a direct outgrowth of the child's relationship to his mother during the separation-individuation phase. It arises in reaction to a partially narcissistic and symbiotic mother, who responds to her aggressive and libidinal needs by unconsciously opposing her child's strivings for separateness. On one side of the dilemma stands the child's fear that, if he gives in to his autonomous, maturational need for separateness, he risks losing mother's love. This reflects not only a more primitive dread of abandonment but also a need for mother's love which is now autonomous and on which his basic self-esteem depends. On the other side of the dilemma is his fear that he will lose whatever newly founded ego capacities he has managed to develop in spite of his clingingness to mother, if he gives in to his need to be loved and submits to mother's pressures. This is an incorrect interpretation of mother's selective pressures which are oriented toward specific behavior threatening her own symbiotic defenses. The child's inability to make selective distinctions represents a failure in adaptation that is a product of the ego's relative immaturity and perhaps also of a congenital deficiency.

The mothers of these patients are very narcissistic and make their children's capacity to sustain object cathexes faulty. Moreover, because of their own symbiotic needs, they unconsciously experience their children as extensions of themselves. With the advent of the capacities for crawling, walking, and speech during the separation-individuation phase, the child's strivings for separateness often disturb either the mother's narcissistic state, her sense of autonomy, or both. She withdraws part of her object libido and directs aggression toward the child in the form of strong disapproval whenever she feels threatened by his behavior. When the behavior continues, she may temporarily and completely withdraw all object cathexes from him. When the child then anxiously becomes compliant, the mother recathects him as a libidinal extension of herself. Since the child's repeated use of his new, successively available autonomous ego capacities often upsets the mother's symbiotic orientation, he is subjected to a repeated re-experiencing of decathexis. Since at this early age the self image is normally very dependent on the mother, the child's emotional and attitudinal reactions alternate between feeling alive and lovable and feeling nonexistent and worthless. Primitive affects of anxiety, rage, and depression fluctuate with the sequence of mother's behavior. Since his poor adaptive capacity leads to faulty predictions of mother's behavior, the child is unable to ward off the traumatic effects resulting from repeated experiences of object loss. This may induce a deep depression or apathy, the concomitant to a sense of hopelessness.

These pathological vicissitudes of ego and id stand in sharp contrast to the corresponding situation in normal development, where symbiotic gratifications are gradually relinquished as the mother helps her child become aware of his independent ego capacities and encourages him to enjoy exercising these capacities. However, in spite of their dilemmas during the separation-individuation phase, children who later become preanalytic patients respond to their maturational push toward separation and achieve some measure of emotional separateness and individuation of their ego capacities. But when sexual maturation later ushers in the oedipal phase, insoluble oedipal conflicts lead to some ego regression and thus to partial loss of emotional separateness. However, for the most part, the gains in separation achieved during the separation-individuation phase hold fairly well, until the balance is once again upset with the onset of puberty. Here the ego loses some more ground. But it is usually not until they are more fully confronted by the fact of their separateness, such as when they have to earn their own living, that massive ego regressions occur.

The ego subsequently tries to strike up a balance between clingingness and separateness, to reach an equilibrium at a point between full symbiosis and full separateness. It attempts to stabilize at separation-individuation. This process appears clinically in the transference relationship of these patients as a preponderance of attitudes toward the analyst that are based on the modes of introjective and projective identification. In this way these patients try to prevent regression to symbiosis, by warding off the unbearable pressures of the oedipal conflicts that would appear following more complete separation. They try to reach an equilibrium through the use of denial, by holding on to the conscious illusion that they are completely independent of others, a self-containment that is a variant of the state of primary narcissism, and by clinging to a reassuring unconscious illusion that they are connected to objects, have omnipotent control of them, and cannot lose them. This double illusion constitutes the framework for the nuclear defense of this type of patient, aimed at restoring the experience of primary narcissism. Its normal developmental prototype occurs in the toddler who goes off by himself to play and periodically returns to mother. To the extent that the toddler has not yet achieved internal object constancy, he is still emotionally in need of something akin to primary narcissism. By reassuring himself that mother is still there, he unconsciously and temporarily restores primary narcissism in a symbolic fashion and can then venture forth again on his own.

The interference of these mothers with their children's strivings for separateness continues after the separation-individuation phase is past. When the superego proper forms during and following the oedipal phase, guilt becomes an additional obstacle to further separation. It acts largely in the service of maintaining preoedipal defenses. The mother's overconcern with his behavior leads the child to conclude that she cannot do without his continuous attention. He becomes fearful that further separation from her would cause her harm. Although this attitude derives in part from his own dependency on her and is a projection of his fear of not being able to manage without her, his conclusions about mother's needs are in part correct. However, this assessment is usually overblown by the narcissistic pleasure such thoughts afford him. He thus holds himself back more than even mother requires. The conflict between the need for autonomy and the need to be loved is thus augmented by a form of gratification akin to the process of secondary gain. His fears for mother's sake are in turn fed by his hostile wishes toward her, which arise from feelings of rage in reaction to her undermining of his autonomous strivings for independence. But under the impetus of maturational factors his assertive strivings continue, in spite of separation anxieties and guilt feelings. Although subsequently modified by favorable experiences (Hartmann, 1954), these conflicts and attitudes continue into adulthood. Although they begin in the relationship to mother, they gradually become generalized toward all potential and real love objects. The combination effect of fear of trauma, separation anxiety, castration anxiety, and guilt prevented full separation as a child, and continues to have this effect subsequently. When, as adults, they arrive as patients, their unconscious illusion of omnipotence is much in evidence. It has now become entrenched in a generalized character attitude of connectedness toward all objects.

When these patients' ability to manipulate others is threatened, their nuclear defense is temporarily shaken. As a result, they fluctuate between submission (symbiosis) and defiance (separation-individuation) as their defenses temporarily fail and are then reinstated. Defense is reinstated when submission succeeds in regaining the object's cathexes, since this allows them to reinstate their unconscious illusion of omnipotent control of the object. The fluctuation between submission and defiance is also an expression of their basic ambivalence, the result of partial instinct defusion. When libidinal drives are uppermost, passive submission results, and rage is turned against the self as partial ego regression occurs. When the need for autonomy is uppermost, aggression is directed against others as a distancing mechanism, in an attempt to maintain separateness. Fluctuation between submission and defiance becomes part of a lifelong pattern, since partial failures in separation-individuation defenses keep recurring. The clearest clinical examples are the compulsive-obsessive character disorders.

In order to sustain their illusion of omnipotence, these patients unconsciously insist that things go according to their wishes. Successful manipulation of objects also helps them maintain their conscious denial of their overdependence on others, since only unconsciously do objects then appear to exist solely for their wishes. Unless they can maintain this unconscious conviction, their symbiotic longings increase and upset the balance between defenses and drives. When the illusion of omnipotence fails, defenses fail and regression sets in. Manipulation is accomplished either through compulsive-driving behavior or by a nonregressive *active* submission. The compulsive activity forms part of a reactive defense against unconscious passive longings of symbiotic origin. The underlying passivity can be sensed behind the false bravado and frantic assertiveness that often appear in the clinical situation. The unconscious illusion of omnipotence can be maintained only when objects respond favorably to their wishes. Any lack of gratification may disrupt their unconscious sense of omnipotent connectedness, if they are unable to ward off this confrontation by denial or by some other defensive procedure.

Threatened disruptions result in renewed compulsive or submissive measures to force others to their will.

In its compulsive, paranoid form, the defense is similar in structure to the relation between a puppeteer and his puppets, where the movements of the puppets are controlled by the puppeteer, as he pulls on the strings connected to them. In its submissive, masochistic form, the defense takes a form similar to a parasite that attaches itself to, and lives off, its host. These modes of defense correspond to projective and introjective identification, which in these patients also constitutes a mode of relationship to objects. The ego has lost some of its capacity for identification proper, because of a partial regression to the ego organization of the separation-individuation phase.

To the extent that these patients' object relationships follow the modes of introjective and projective identification, their unconscious wish is to create an ideal self by taking in all the good qualities they see in others. But the regressively weakened integrative capacities of these patients are insufficient to modify these introjects selectively and to incorporate them organically into the basic ego structure. As a result, the introjects are only loosely tied to their character structure. Although the ego can utilize the introjects for adaptive purposes, it does not sufficiently accept them as aspects of the self. The phenomenological experience of the presence of introjects is acquisitive. The introjects are evaluated as interchangeable and replaceable possessions of varying usefulness, as mental objects for manipulative use. This is the counterpart of these patients' relatedness to outer objects, which they treat in a similar fashion.

This primitive identificatory orientation also forms the core of these patients' defensive system. It produces pathological ego attitudes, whose overall aim is to construct a perfect mosaic self, a conglomerate personality that is free of anxiety by virtue of its imagined omnipotence. In reality, the synthetic function of the ego succeeds only in producing a nonintegrated, artificial personality. The synthetic function in these patients is often precocious and overly developed. This can be viewed as a compensatory attempt by the ego to deal with its faulty integrative and neutralizing capacities. It is my view that this is an important factor that makes it possible for further structural development to take place. It helps account for the fact that these patients have generally been able to ward off psychotic episodes, which their egos, weakened in their neutralizing and integrative capacities, might otherwise be prone to. Mosaic introjection, combined with a hyperactive synthetic function, makes possible an adaptation to an "average expectable environment" (Hartmann, 1939). This adaptive mode may have worked reasonably well for years, prior to entering treatment. However, eventually the inability to integrate experience adequately, coupled with demands by the environment to assume the responsibilities of adulthood, and not just the vocabulary of an adult, has led to a failure of the defense structure. Omnipotent self-expectations, derived from their defense structure, indirectly result in failure of defense by leading them to undertake unrealistic ventures, in which wishes substitute for planned and sustained action. Repeated experiences of failure eventually lead to partial symbiotic regression.

To the extent that separation-individuation defenses have begun to fail, the ego loses some of its directed *active* quality. That is, it returns to the *passive* state it was in prior to the combining of ego nuclei. In addition to further loss of integration, the synthetic function has now also begun to lose some of its capacity. The passive ego has now become the object of the introjects, instead of the subject. Impulsive behavior results whenever the introjects become hypercathected. To the extent that a substantial segment of the ego maintains its active orientation, these experiences are frightening. The ego tries to ward off anxiety by splitting off these experiences and projecting them onto others.

To the extent that the synthetic function is intact when such a patient begins treatment, the therapist may mistake the patient's capacity to adapt to the requirements of the therapeutic situation as being indicative of a flexible, "strong" ego. The ego is not flexible. It is rather accomodating, and is indicative of multiple splits in the ego structure. Interpretations do not lead to therapeutic gains until the ego structure mends itself somewhat. Reduction in the use of denial and splitting, made possible by confrontation and by a careful reconstruction of early traumas and separation conflicts, paves the way for the successful use of interpretations by fostering further emotional separation. As a reduction of splitting and an increase in separation take place, these preanalytic patients gradually become more analytic patients.

During the preanalytic period of therapy the patients restrict their lives in order to maintain the unconscious illusion of omnipotence on which the defense of their autonomy rests. Since failure of defense leads to symbiotic regression, they are terrified whenever the behavior of others cannot be fitted into this illusion. In the course of therapy, as symbiotic regressions are reduced, the illusion of omnipotence begins to be relinquished. This leads to further separation. As this occurs, castration anxiety once again makes its appearance, partly replacing separation anxiety. At that point, a temporary shift in conscious attitudes and in unconscious defenses takes place. Since more complete separateness now ushers in oedipal fears, they ward off, via denial, a recognition of their accomplishments. If denials fail, and they are forced to confront their individuality, temporary regression to separation-individuation may take place once more, as a defense against castration anxiety. With it comes a temporary return of the old separation anxiety. It is a striking phenomenon to see some of these patients accomplish complex feats of the ego, both professionally and personally, while at the same time not valuing their accomplishments, and crediting others instead, such as the attitude that their high salary is a gift from a generous boss. In this way they re-establish the unconscious sense of connection to others that is characteristic of their separation-individuation defense. Repeated working through of their separation anxieties consolidates separation and gradually encourages the ego to face the oedipal anxieties.

Summary

I have described a specific structural ego pathology that appears in a wide grouping of varied clinical syndromes. The ego deficiencies are found in patients who fall within "the widening scope of psychoanalysis" (Stone et al., 1954). They begin treatment in a chronic state of partial ego regression. The ego has attempted to stabilize at the ego organization of the separation-individuation phase and has failed, in part, to do so. Although the paper limits itself to a metapsychological study of this specific mental structure, some inferences are drawn which also contribute to a theory of technique. The technique of therapy involves "preparation for analysis," in which adequate emotional separateness must first be laboriously achieved before controlled regression can occur "in the service of the ego." The ego pathology is correlated with an inability to sustain secondary autonomy, so that the ego is prone to regression and is overly dependent on environmental stimuli. It is theorized that paramount among these ego deficiencies are an unstable capacity for neutralization and for integration and a special sensitivity toward traumatic anxiety. Also depicted as defective are memory, signal function, frustration tolerance, emotional capacity, and the capacity to cathect objects. Genetic and dynamic distinctions are drawn between integration and synthesis, in presenting them as two separate ego functions.

The failure in secondary autonomy is correlated with the clinical fact that defense has become the prime concern of this ego, thus creating an impoverished personality. The defenses are depicted as rigid and brittle and as continually failing under increase in pressure from the drives, the superego, and the external world. When this occurs, the ego structure eventually splits between its cognitive functions and its experiencing functions. Splitting is seen as following along lines of an earlier split derived from a rupture of the stimulus barrier during the first year of life. The earlier split is understood as having been covered over by reactive defenses, such as turning against the self. Poorly controlled behavioral discharges are ascribed to a loss of the ego's capacity to integrate these two sets of functions when defenses fail. Under conditions of splitting, the ego is depicted as being passive and helpless, because of a regressive loss of its control functions.

These ego deficiencies appear in an identifiable subcategory of a large grouping of patients referred to as "preanalytic." This designation encompasses a clinically heterogeneous variety of patients, whose psychopathology falls between, and to a certain extent overlaps, neuroses and psychoses. This paper also contributes some of the foundation for a theory of technique of these patients, by delineating the metapsychology of the ego deficiencies and defenses held in common by this subcategory. The decisive fixation points of the subcategory appear to fall in the symbiotic and separation-individuation phases. They begin in infancy and extend to the onset of the oedipal phase, at about age three. The ego pathology seems best understood as the effect of serious and unresolved conflicts around the developmental needs of the ego for object constancy and emotional separateness.

The differential factors that determine the severity of individual cases are the developmental age when fixations occurred, the intensity of these fixations, and the quantitative ratio between fixation and regression. Those patients who tend more in a psychotic direction, the borderline states, are understood as cases of actual arrested development, in which libidinal resources and some early ego functions failed to develop further. Those patients who tend more in a neurotic direction are seen as illustrating the loss of functions through regression. The level of differentiation of individual ego functions and the capacity of the ego to sustain these functions without regression define the strength of the ego in an individual case and also appear to determine the prognosis.

All of these patients appear to be in a chronic state of impoverished libidinal object cathexes. This applies mainly to representations of current external objects and to representations of the current self. This phenomenology is a major factor behind the generalized complaints that bring them into treatment. There also appears to be a deficit of cognitive object cathexes that is correlated with the widespread use of denial. The explanation is offered that cathexes have been withdrawn from objects, bit by bit, whenever disappointments were experienced in the past. The energies that have been withdrawn are understood to have been reinvested in an unconscious nuclear defense that is based on an illusion of symbiotic connectedness and on an omnipotent self image. Since objects are still decathected whenever these illusions are threatened in the present, it is concluded that this defense is still current and that these energies are also used to reinforce the defense.

Clinically, the illusory omnipotence is removed gradually in the course of therapy as self-esteem is increased along realistic lines. This occurs within the context of a basically positive transference, which helps the patient rebuild a sustained capacity for libidinal object cathexis, through a sense of trust. Only the achievement of secondary ego autonomy will sufficiently protect the patient from regression and finally permit him to relinquish his pathological illusions. The nuclear defense that consists of omnipotent expectations, characterological passivity, and separation-individuation attitudes of connectedness to objects will remain a major focus throughout the course of therapy. These factors will appear intermittently, even to the end of an analysis itself. As their gradual resolution slowly completes the process of preparation for analysis, this simultaneously makes further analysis proper possible.

BIBLIOGRAPHY

Blanck, G. (1966), Some Technical Implications of Ego Psychology. *Int. J. Psa.*, 47:6-13.

Bouvet, M. (1958), Technical Variation and the Concept of Distance, *Int. J. Psa.*, 39:211-221.

Brody, M. W. & Mahoney, V. P. (1964), Introjection, Identification and Incorporation. *Int. J. Psa.*, 45:57-63.

Eissler, K. R. (1953), The Effect of the Structure of the Ego on Psychoanalytic Technique. *J. Amer. Psa. Assn.*, 1:104-143.

Erikson, E. H. (1950), *Childhood and Society*. New York: Norton.

Federn, P. (1952), *Ego Psychology and the Psychoses*. New York: Basic Books.

Fenichel, O. (1945), *The Psychoanalytic Theory of Neurosis*. New York: Norton.

Freud, A. (1953), Some Remarks on Infant Observation. *This Annual*, 8:9-19.

—— (1965), *Normality and Pathology in Childhood: Assessments of Development*. New York: International Universities Press.

Freud, S. (1924 [1923]), Neurosis and Psychosis. *Standard Edition*, 19:147-153. London: Hogarth Press, 1961.

—— (1926 [1925]), Inhibitions, Symptoms and Anxiety. *Standard Edition*, 20:75-175. London: Hogarth Press, 1959.

—— (1927), Fetishism. *Standard Edition*, 21:147-157. London: Hogarth Press, 1961.

—— (1940a [1938]), An Outline of Psycho-Analysis. *Standard Edition*, 23:139-207. London: Hogarth Press, 1964.

—— (1940b, [1938]), Splitting of the Ego in the Process of Defence. *Standard Edition*, 23:271-278. London: Hogarth Press, 1964.

Gitelson, M. (1958), On Ego Distortion. *Int. J. Psa.*, 39:245-257.

Glover, E. (1933), The Relation of Perversion-Formation to the Development of Reality-Sense. *Int. J. Psa.*, 14:486-504.

—— (1943), The Concept of Dissociation. *On the Early Development of Mind*. New York: International Universities Press, 1956, pp. 307-323.

Handelsman, I. (1965), The Effects of Early Object Relationships on Sexual Development: Autistic and Symbiotic Modes of Adaptation. *This Annual*, 20:367-383.

Hartmann, H. (1939), *Ego Psychology and the Problem of Adaptation*. New York: International Universities Press, 1958.

—— (1947), On Rational and Irrational Action. *Essays on Ego Psychology: Selected Problems in Psychoanalytic Theory*. New York: International Universities Press, 1964, pp. 37-68.

—— (1950), Comments on the Psychoanalytic Theory of the Ego. *This Annual*, 5:74-96.

—— (1952), The Mutual Influences in the Development of Ego and Id. *This Annual*, 7:9-30.

—— (1954), Problems of Infantile Neurosis. *Essays on Ego Psychology: Selected Problems in Psychoanalytic Theory*. New York: International Universities Press, 1964, pp. 207-214.

—— (1955), Notes on the Theory of Sublimation. *This Annual,* 10:9-29.
—— (1956), The Development of the Ego Concept in Freud's Work. *Essays on Ego Psychology: Selected Problems in Psychoanalytic Theory.* New York: International Universities Press, 1964, pp. 268-296.
Jacobson, E. (1957), On Normal and Pathological Moods: Their Nature and Functions. *This Annual,* 12:73-113.
—— (1964), *The Self and the Object World.* New York: International Universities Press.
Klein, M. (1932), *The Psycho-Analysis of Children.* London: Hogarth Press, 3rd ed., 1949.
—— (1934), A Contribution to the Psychogenesis of Manic-Depressive States. *Contributions to Psycho-Analysis 1921-1945.* London: Hogarth Press, 1948, pp. 282-310.
—— (1940), Mourning and Its Relation to Manic-Depressive States. *Contributions to Psycho-Analysis 1921-1945.* London: Hogarth Press, 1948, pp. 311-338.
—— (1963), *Our Adult World, and Other Essays.* New York: Basic Books.
Kris, E. (1934), The Psychology of Caricature. *Psychoanalytic Explorations in Art.* New York: International Universities Press, 1952, pp. 173-188.
Mahler, M. S. & La Perriere, K. (1965), Mother-Child Interaction during Separation-Individuation. *Psa. Quart.,* 34:483-498.
Rapaport, D. (1958), The Theory of Ego Autonomy: A Generalization. *Bull. Menninger Clin.,* 22:13-35.
Reich, W. (1933), *Character Analysis.* New York: Orgone Institute Press, 3rd ed., 1949.
Spitz, R. A. (1965), *The First Year of Life: A Psychoanalytic Study of Normal and Deviant Development of Object Relations.* New York: International Universities Press.
Stone, L. et al. (1954), The Widening Scope of Indications for Psychoanalysis. *J. Amer. Psa. Assn.,* 2:567-620.
Waelder, R. (1958), Neurotic Ego Distortion: Opening Remarks to the Panel Discussion. *Int. J. Psa.,* 39:243-244.

CONTRIBUTIONS TO NORMAL AND PATHOLOGICAL DEVELOPMENT

PRENURSERY PROJECT

Indications and Counterindications for Therapeutic Intervention in the Prenursery via the Mother

AUGUSTA ALPERT, Ph.D. (New York)

This paper is an extension of a series of papers on "The Treatment of the Under-Five by Way of His Mother" presented at the first national meeting of the American Association of Child Psychoanalysis in April, 1966, by Erna Furman and discussed by Elizabeth Daunton and Lois Archer. Our experience in the Child Development Center with "under-threes" leads us to raise several diagnostic and therapeutic questions *specific for the age* and therefore not touched on last year.

My own efforts at earlier *localization of pathology* reported in several papers on "corrective object relations" (Alpert, 1957, 1959, 1963) have been facilitated and illuminated by the work of Anna Freud, Mahler, and others. As a result, it has made the guidance of mothers in the prenursery more specific and effective. But as is often the case, clarification frequently leads to the recognition of new problems. When therapeutic intervention for the children was indicated, it soon became clear that the *treatment of choice* for *under-threes* is *not based on diagnosis alone.* Their treatment via the mother is age syntonic and so culturally entrenched as to influence therapeutic choice. The *diagnostic selection of mothers* becomes even more essential than was made clear last year by the Cleveland papers. Certain problems implicit in such a choice for *under-threes* seem to me to need further study. I am grateful to the Program Committee for including this topic again. I have selected for this paper two mother-child pairs, one of which demonstrates positive and the other negative indications for therapeutic intervention via the mother.

Presented at the second annual meeting of the American Association for Child Psychoanalysis, Cleveland (Aurora), Ohio, June 1967.

Dr. Alpert is Associate Director, Child Development Center, New York, N.Y.

Aims and Description of Project

In setting up our prenursery project for two- to three-year-olds and their mothers we were motivated by two aims: one, to get an earlier start in our study of development and diagnosis; two, to create a setting for therapeutic intervention via guidance of the mother as indicated.

Anna Freud's Foreword to *Early Childhood Disturbances* by Humberto Nagera (1966) is so admirable a statement of the first aim that I can do no better than to quote it here at length.

> What the author of this monograph does . . . is a careful apportioning of pathogenic impact to external and internal interferences at any time of the child's life; the location of the internal influences in any part of the psychic structure or in the interaction between any of the inner agencies; and the building up, step by step, of an orderly sequence of childhood disorders, of which the infantile neurosis is not the base, but the final, complex apex.
>
> What satisfies the student of analysis in an exposition of this nature is the fact that on the one hand it is rooted in the notion of a hypothetical norm of childhood development, while on the other hand it establishes a hierarchy of disturbances which is valid for the period of immaturity and meaningful as a forerunner of adult psychopathology.

In our prenursery there are two groups of five children each, in a nursery room equipped for the age. One teacher and a teacher-fellow are in charge. The groups meet biweekly, for one hour. During each nursery session, the mothers meet in an alcove off the nursery with their group therapist, informally, over coffee. They are encouraged to bring in current problems with their children, which is an important source of supplementary developmental data. The physical setup is such as to facilitate easy access between mothers and children. The extent to which children avail themselves of this as they feel the need to "refuel" (Furer) or seek "rapprochement" (Mahler) is an indicator of the level they have reached in separation-individuation (Mahler), especially in object constancy. It also reflects the child's anxiety proneness and tolerance for anxiety. We frequently see important confirmation of subphase-related behavior, normal and deviant.

Our setup also offers natural observations of the mother's emotional availability to her child, the subphase on which she can best relate and least relate, an assessment project in its own right. In this connection it seems to me that it is not generally recognized that the selection of mother-child pairs implies a diagnostic assessment of mother and child *during* the intake study, a goal rarely fulfilled. In fact, such assessments in our project are the cumulative product of team discussions which follow each nursery session. At these conferences each team member contributes current findings and impressions for the family.[1] Such data are repeatedly checked among us for inconsistencies and implications. The cumulative data are then integrated and abstracted by myself and form the basis for a treatment plan. Thus we are as likely to have formulated criteria for therapeutic intervention *after* the prenursery experience as before. As Anna Freud's guidelines for assessment of normality and pathology (1965) are extended to cover the gamut of development and become more familiar tools, our diagnostic skills will become more scientific and more sensitive.

Description of Cases

The cases of Debby E. and Sally K. illustrate well the line of divergence between pairs, favorable and unfavorable, for therapeutic intervention via the mother. In both bases the mothers were aware or became aware early of the difficulties with their children and sought help. They were ready to participate in the full prenursery program and showed the same regularity in attendance. Debby E. was two years, five months at the start of the program and Sally K. was two and a half. Debby's presenting symptom was motion sickness (cars, buses), making travel disagreeable and sometimes impossible. Although Mrs. K. brought Sally to us as a "no-problem" child, after some reduction of her anxiety, she presented Sally's symptoms as fear of noises, such as bells and sirens, and excessive masturbation. It was apparent that both were showing intensification due to parental mishandling. The two significant differences between the cases, bearing

1 The prenursery team consists of Dr. Alpert, Consultant, Mrs. Virginia Bach, teacher, Mrs. Hilda Fischman, group therapist, Miss Annie Hermann, Educational Director, Mrs. Rosalind Sands, group therapist, Dr. Nina Lief and Dr. Rachel Milano, psychiatric and psychologic consultants, respectively.

on diagnostic and therapeutic criteria, were the *onset of the symptoms* and the *personality structure of the mothers.*

Case 1. Debby and Her Mother

Anamnesis: Debby was the younger of two siblings. Her brother Leon was eighteen months when she was born. Pregnancy, birth, and delivery were normal. Debby's developmental landmarks were within normal range. No difficulties were reported in weaning or toilet training. She was experienced as an easy infant. However, these facts are subject to question in the light of the family crisis which occurred when Debby was three months old, and which has colored the life of this family ever since. Debby's father died suddenly of cardiac failure while roughhousing with her brother, Leon, then twenty-one months of age. We have reason to believe that the marriage was a good one for both partners, with perhaps an unusual degree of containment as a couple. To this terrible shock Mrs. E. responded with unusual self-control and competence—doing alone what had to be done, including moving from one city to another. She recalls crying, but "not in the presence of the children." In fact, the father's death was never referred to at home, until Leon, age three and a half, pointed to a picture of his father and called him by his uncle's name. By this time, Mrs. E. could explain that the father had died and would not come back.

Mrs. E. continued to nurse Debby until she was nine months of age—a rather protracted period in our culture. (Leon was nursed for four months.) We speculated whether this was not an unconscious response to her sense of loss, and by what signals this communicated itself to Debby. The mother reported Debby's tendency to *gag* on new solid foods (four months), to put four fingers in her mouth while eating, describing this as "strange and crazy-looking." I am told by Dr. Annemarie Weil that Debby may have used this as an aid to swallowing, in which case it may have been the first sign of sluggish reflexes, to be referred to again. Dr. Mahler, on the other hand, sees this as suggestive of rumination. In that case it can be seen as a physiological predictor of the vomiting to come. Another possibility occurred to me: that Debby was reproducing in this way the sensation of a stuffed mouth, as breast feeding was experienced by her. The constant thumb sucking since sixteen months of age, reported by the mother, coincides with the beginning of walking alone, seemingly a regression to the oral hold on the object, when confronted by the challenge of autonomous separation. Anxiety at separation from the object was seen again in prolonged periods of wakefulness before falling asleep from age two to two and a half years, when phase-related sleep disturbances are common. Debby did *not* have a "transitional object" (Winnicott, 1953). Stranger anxiety was not reported during infancy, but during the study Mrs. E. described Debby as not "thawing out" when in the presence of strangers. From eighteen months on, she approached strange men in the park for physical contact. This active seeking indicates that the absence of the father figure was already felt, probably communicated by mother and brother. Somewhat later an unusually *strong* attachment to her brother was formed.

The team's first impression that Debby's motion sickness was *reactive* to a family crisis was borne out by the continuing study. We agreed that the mother was basically unambivalent about her maternal role and that she desperately needed help and wanted it.

During the first prenursery session, the mother presented a forced smile and ingratiating manner. Both mother and child were awkward and self-conscious, more striking in the child. Debby's "Groucho Marx walk," as the mother described it, was more like an anthropoid infant's posture, legs apart, and arms extended at elbows as if she just detached from clinging to mother. Her mouth was open, with tongue hanging out. The mother led her, heavy-footed, into the nursery on the first day, and Debby made no protest when her mother entered the alcove. In fact, she did not even seek reunion with her mother, as the other children did, causing Mrs. E. to comment that she felt "sort of left out," reminiscent of the fear of being "cast off" expressed by Catherine's mother in Annie Katan's paper (1959). Debby stood around expectantly until the teacher chanted the "putting-away-time" tune, whereupon she uttered some vehement "no's" and ran out to mother's lap. Responding to the group therapist's suggestion that Mrs. E. go back with Debby into the nursery, the mother picked Debby up and enfolded her in her arms like an infant. This was group refreshment time. Debby agreed to take a cracker *only if she could have one for Leon, too* ("rapprochement" with sibling). This refrain continued for the rest of the year. The next three sessions were very much the same: Debby's "ambitendent" (Mahler) stance between mother and nursery continued. As for Mrs. E., her need to hold on to her child physically and her wish to be with the mothers' group raised conflictual emotions with anger barely held in check. Her smiling grimace expressed the conflict. In the meantime a detailed picture of the antivomiting preparations for the prenursery trip also became clear. These consisted of admonitions, diapers as bibs, picture books and toys as distractors in the cab, instructions to the cab driver for the shortest route to anticipate Debby's "six-minute tolerance"! The team was impressed by the huddled closeness of the three members of the family—an "incarceration" which the mother attributed to Debby's car sickness and the frequent colds of the entire family. Mother's and Debby's dependence on Leon as the father surrogate was another detail in the emerging picture of a family caught in the mother's sadomasochistic personality, reactively intensified since the death of her husband.

The Prenursery Team agreed on a working hypothesis: that Mrs. E. reacted to the shock of her husband's death with increased symbiotic-parasitic needs and intensification of the masochistic component in her personality. Toward Debby it took the form of protracted nursing and holding, and toward Leon using him as a surrogate for the missing husband, thus placing an unbearable burden on him. A three-pronged intervention was worked out on the basis of this hypothesis.

1. A "transitional object" was "experimentally prescribed" for Debby, not in the true Winnicott sense but as a bridge between home and nursery.

2. Intensified guidance treatment of the mother, who was given an individual session each week in addition to the prenursery group session. This was intended as a symbolic anaclitic need satisfaction to help loosen her hold on Debby. Suggestions were made to help her reduce the anticipatory drama of every trip which acted as a suggestion to vomit and as a secondary gain for Debby. It was hoped that by slowly lifting the affect of anger surrounding her husband's death from repression, she could be helped to face her accusation of being abandoned by her husband. She blamed his death on his professional ambition and overwork. She thus implied that she felt "abandoned" by him even while he was alive. Our aid was indirectly to reduce the

displaced rage against her children and the sadomasochistic containments in her relation with them.

3. Coordination of Leon's therapy (he was in psychoanalytic therapy here three times weekly) with the program of the rest of the family, through regular integration meetings with the *family team,* at which the treatment plan is evolved or modified for the entire family. Leon had already been included in the Child Development Center nursery five-year-old group, which provided another vantage point for our study of the family dynamics. The nursery would help reinforce Leon's deficient identity, especially in relation to peers.

The prenursery teachers adopted a watchful, guarded readiness to facilitate achievement of Debby's steps in separation-individuation, not yet accomplished on entry. Debby stopped vomiting very soon. One day when they had difficulty getting a cab to the nursery and Mrs. E. was ready to return home, Debby insisted on going by bus. The trip was without incident. She began to bring two transitional objects to the nursery, ceremonially giving one to the teacher for safekeeping. She showed in this way her readiness to accept the teacher as a "transitional" substitute for mother. She made her first overture to her mother's therapist by showing her the transitional object. It seemed to help her lose much of her self-consciousness. One is reminded of the adolescent's dependence on a cigarette to hide social anxiety. The first time she joined the group at the snack table, she called out to her mother to observe and share in her daring. For a while she still had difficulty leaving her mother and joining the group at the beginning of the session. She would stand teetering on the threshold between the mothers' alcove and the nursery, a picture of ambivalence. The day she showed only a token indecision and moved smoothly into the nursery, the other mothers applauded and shed some tears. For them it was a dramatic demonstration of a child's struggle to master her separation anxiety; for us, a demonstration of the child's struggle between symbiosis and autonomy.

There was one regressive period after an absence of two sessions during which period the family bird died. The teacher reports, "Debby stood outside unable to enter, shook her head, 'no.' " With some persuasion, teacher was able to engage her in building a simple enclosure for her kitten, the "transitional" object, which represented the bridge between home and school. "However, her mood that day remained sober and sad." But Debby soon recovered her former gains and became a happy member of the small group. At home she often repeated the songs and play in the prenursery, identifying with the teacher. She thus showed her capacity for identification and a beginning readiness to include others into the orbit of need-satisfying objects.

Nevertheless, we predicted that the protracted mother-child symbiosis, which necessarily delayed separation-individuation and differentiation, would leave its imprint on Debby and that her brother Leon would be the next "symbiotic object." Both predictions proved to be true throughout the following year in the three-year-old nursery. Leon was an ever-present presence in the nursery, which Debby expressed by repeatedly injecting such phrases as "me and Leon," "Leon, too," "like Leon." The mother's fostering of this "togetherness" was dealt with in her therapy. Leon, fortunately, did not continue to need this. In fact, he began to try to shake off his sister's heavy attachment. This attachment to her brother did not interfere with her growing relationship with the new teacher (Lockwood). But her struggle in mastering the "loyalty conflict" presented by the two relationships with mother and with teacher was almost as dramatic in the three-year-old group as the separation had been in the two-year-old group.

Let us now see how the prenursery experience of Debby and her mother bears on the topic of this paper which focuses on two aspects: what are the indications for therapeutic intervention as early as the *third year of life;* and for such intervention *via the mother.*

It seemed to me that the interference with Debby's development was already pronounced at two and a half years and that time was not on her side. The prolonged symbiosis clearly delayed differentiation of self from others and the autonomy of the ego. It also raised the level of anxiety. Although we judged Debby to have a potentially strong ego, I doubt that she could have been helped to overcome this regressive pull exerted by her own unresolved separation-individuation conflict, as well as her mother's, *without our extending help to her mother* and Leon as well. (Our judgment was based in part on an initial conference with Mrs. E. and Debby held by Miss Eva Landauer,[2] in which she found Debby "friendly, appropriate,

[2] Miss Eva Landauer, Child Therapist.

speech adequate, good capacity for object relations.") We assumed, therefore, that Debby's behavior in the prenursery was a regression induced specifically by the threat of separation and a reaction to the *strange*. The secondary gain from the neuroticlike symptom of motion sickness and the growing sadomasochistic relationship of mother and child would have masked the *original locus of pathology* on which the symptoms were superimposed. This would have made therapeutic intervention at a later age much more difficult. Infantile amnesia, often an unyielding obstacle in analytic work, is, as we know, most massive for the prepictorial (B. D. Lewin) and *preverbal period*. This is in my estimation the most eloquent argument in favor of therapeutic intervention as close to the phase when the fixation occurred, via the mother *when possible*. The child's greater plasticity during the third year of life is a clear asset; her dependence on the object renders her more susceptible to change as the object changes. But the real advantage in this case derived from the *simultaneity* of our approach.

To the extent to which we have succeeded in correcting the disturbance during the separation-individuation phase and improving the basis of the relationship between mother and child, to that extent we have laid a healthier foundation for the child—and for the family. The rest depends on the vicissitudes of reality and on the unfolding of endogenous pathology unpredictable at this time, i.e., in the prenursery.

It should be noted, however, that our intervention addressed itself to the presumed *reactivity* of the protracted and ambivalent symbiosis. We did not close our eyes to certain features in Debby which are suggestive of organic ego deviancy, such as her bizarre posture and appearance. While the anthropoid posture and protruding tongue disappeared in prenursery, the posture and gait remained heavy and awkward. The following year sluggish protective reflex reaction, e.g., eye-blink, was reported by her teacher, Miss Lockwood. Her speech showed marked deviancy from that of her mother, brother, and relatives. She spoke with something like a heavy East European accent. So far we have not been able to trace the accent. I am inclined to ascribe it to a mild organic impairment of the speech apparatus. Recently, Mrs. E. described her husband's articulation as "lazy." Debby's pattern of communication went from long silences to long obsessional reports, with endless details, uttered in a deep monotone, not unlike the speech of the severe adult obsessional. This, too, has no model in the family. These may be endogenous pathological signs which are not yet understood well enough to fit them into "an orderly sequence of childhood disorders" (A. Freud, 1966a). Thus the *reactive* features of the dyadic pathology and the *mother's strong maternal feeling* for her children discernible as such under the pathological contaminants were the signs favoring intervention via the mother. Yet it is misleading to speak of this as therapeutic intervention via the mother. Strictly speaking it was concomitant therapy of mother and child, with the prenursery as a therapeutic or reinforcing corrective agent for the child.

It should be at least briefly noted here that the prenursery, which meets only biweekly for one hour, leaves a remarkably strong imprint on the children, beyond our anticipation. The implications of this for the maturational level of such ego functions as retention of mental representations, reality testing, transfer of learning, object constancy, identification with adults and peers have bearing on assessment studies.

Case 2. Sally and Her Mother

Certainly one of the distinguishing differences between Mrs. E. and Mrs. K., the mother of Sally, is the capacity for mothering. Already during the intake study, Mrs. K. was seen as a career-bound woman, strikingly unfeminine in appearance and unmaternal, though not rejecting toward Sally. The mother's narcissistic fixation, her incapacity for even "ordinary good mothering" (Winnicott, 1953), her identification with her child as her "illusory penis" unfolded in the course of the prenursery period.

On the basis of neither the mother's qualifications nor Sally's history did this pair meet the criteria for treatment via the mother. But the environment was so grossly disadvantageous to Sally that we decided nevertheles to try to influence it through guidance of the mother, while Sally was in the prenursery. We did not achieve this short-range goal, in the prenursery. In the long run, i.e., seen now, when Sally is four and a half in our middle group, I believe we did help both mother and child *separately,* in a limited way. Such help will need to be continued indefinitely.

But first a few diagnostic remarks about mother and father limited to their bearing on Sally's development. Mrs. K. is of superior intelligence and creative. She has been able to make use of her endowment to *sublimate her competitive exhibitionistic* impulses at least partially. Her conflict about sexual identification which extends to a denial of biological and social differences between male and female is central and derives from similar conflicts in her mother, who was an international sports champion and continues in a career chosen in our culture only by men.

Mrs. K. referred to Sally during the intake study as "my social crutch," revealing thus not only her social anxiety but also the passing on of the sexual conflict to the third generation. She was anxious and defensive about her role as a mother ("I was suicidal when I thought I had a 'problem child' ").

On the psychodiagnostic examination the father, too, showed superior intelligence and "subtle paranoid tendencies well contained"; he appeared "egocentric and immature, competitive with both his wife and daughter." He is the passive partner in the marriage and is one of the baby sitters for Sally. He is strikingly unspontaneous with her. Both parents are proud of Sally. They are undemonstrative in their affection, but have outbursts of rage toward Sally and use physical punishment. With both, their careers come first and Sally is expected to fit into the many changes brought on by the mother's professional tours and the father's academic requirements. Both parents are in their late twenties and well-mated.

Anamnesis: Sally is an only child. She was a "blue baby" at birth with malformed skull probably due to forceps delivery and needed to be kept in a warmer for two days. She was breast-fed for four and a half months. Colic and vomiting continued until three and a half months, but she was described as a smiling and ebullient baby during that period. From six to eighteen months she suffered from severe diarrhea with temperature rise and was "convulsive." At eleven months she was hospitalized for ten days and fed intravenously. The diagnosis was "structural difficulty in the colon." We were unable to get hospital reports. She was on a liquid diet after discharge due to dehydration. By eighteen months the diarrhea ceased, but periodic complaints of stomachache continue to the present. In the hospital the parents took turns to be with Sally during her *waking* time (recently proven untrue). Weaning from the bottle was inflexible: Sally cried for four days and subsequently refused milk. Toilet training was characterized by the mother's punitive attitude toward accidents. Urine and feces were differentiated by Mrs. K. as "yellow and brown wee-wee," which was only one indication of her resistance to sexual differentiation. No stranger anxiety was reported, but some fear of dark-skinned people. I am not sure of the skin color of her baby sitters, who attended her from the first week, when the father or neighbors were not available. Like Debby, Sally had no transitional object, but for unlike reasons. Developmental landmarks appeared rather early, especially speech.

This fragile infant coping with *internal* sensations of pain and distress was from earliest infancy subjected to excessive *external* stimulation: not only because of the shifting caretakers and the parents' "bohemian" way of life, but also "on prescription" as it were. A psychologist friend urged them to place the crib in such a way that sun and street lights could make patterns for Sally. What a pity that this psychologist did not furnish observational data for this period! The absence of reliable observations during the first two years of life in clinical setups such as ours leads to too much reliance on parents' reports. This is of necessity a qualifying factor in our diagnostic assessments.

As a matter of policy Sally's curiosity, sexual and otherwise, was encouraged, and long, stimulating explanations were given which led to repeated questioning. The parents made no attempt to shield her from their private lives or from exciting and sometimes frightening family events, as though this, too, was part of their child-rearing policy: that a child must fit into the world of adults and the earlier she starts the better, and the burden of flexibility lies on the child. This is such a typical adult expectation that it is seldom seen from the child's point of view. Her environment provided no structure, no sense of sequence, and no basic trust. It could only have heightened anticipatory anxiety.

At intake, Mrs. K. described Sally as a "souped-up engine!" In the prenursery Sally did not appear like the ego-disturbed or brain-damaged child we were led to expect from the history, nor did she act like a "souped-up engine." It should be recalled that Mrs. K. brought Sally to our prenursery as a "no-problem" child. She was hyperalert and distractible. What was most conspicuous to participant and nonparticipant observers was the precocious and persistent penis envy and later castration anxiety. She corresponded to the clinical picture described in the literature: severe penis envy and castration anxiety associated with early and extensive medical manipulation. This left the child first with the sense of a damaged body, which then crystallized as penis envy under the impact of internal and external events and in identification with a "phallic mother." This was first expressed in the theme of "me-too." Whatever she was doing would be dropped in favor of what someone else, usually a boy, was doing. The same would be true of possessions, so that she appeared distractible, constantly on the move, reaching out for someone else or something else. As I look back over our notes, including those of the nonparticipant observer, I can easily allow that the "me-too" also expressed poor differentiation between herself and others. Later, I began to hear another theme: "I fell because I was *sick*," "I sit like this [on her legs] because *I'm a girl*," "I am a *sick* girl, I have accidents and *get hurt*." Penis envy and castration anxiety continued to be the dominant theme throughout prenursery and in the three-year-old nursery. In the mothers' group, Mrs. K. revealed her fury when Sally masturbated and pretended she was a boy. The mother's own masculine identification and use of the child as her phallus or "crutch" and the child's sense of a damaged body served to exacerbate the castration anxiety of both. The confluence of internal and external pressures exerting their "pathological impact" on the fragile unfolding ego is especially clear here. Anxiety when sirens sounded was more marked than with some other children, but within "normal" limits. A hyperalertness was also observed, probably a specific reaction to a sensed hearing deficiency, discovered by the mother in the fourth year. Echoing became more noticeable toward the end of the year but was limited to her teacher with whom Sally had formed a close relationship. Primary-process talk as recorded by nonparticipant observer was within normal limits in the prenursery[3] but became prolific in the three-year-old group. In this group, too,

3 In his paper "Premature Ego Development" (1960), M. James speaks of a "traumatic access of images threatening to organize into thought . . . at a time when the secondary process is not phase-adequate." Indeed Sally's verbalization seemed to be made up of such an "access of images" from the past when they could not be assimilated.

the distractibility noted in the prenursery showed up as a remarkable intake of stimuli, central and peripheral. This hyperreceptivity went along with a related deficiency in organizing stimuli into meaningful and familiar patterns, as speculated by Leitch and Escalona (1949): "prolonged or severe tension states may interfere with orderly developmental progress, causing in some instances unusual alertness and sensitivity in some areas but interfering with adequate integration of functioning." In short, Sally in the three-year-old group looked like an ego-deviant child. But in the prenursery this diagnosis could not be made. This reflects our present difficulty in defining developmental norms in the third year of life, but perhaps it also bears on the *time table of the endogenous pathological process.* Both series of data are essential to arrive at an "orderly sequence of childhood disorders" aimed at by A. Freud and Nagera (1966). I wonder whether one can say that the *overdetermined and precocious castration anxiety, internally and externally stimulated, pre-empted, and overtaxed the organizing function of the ego unduly strained by external events and unassisted by the mother as auxiliary ego.*

Here we see how fine is the line which divides *"internal* and *external* interferences." Natal and neonatal events contributed to the "predisposition to anxiety" (Greenacre, 1945)—cyanosis, malformed skull, followed by "organismic distress" (Mahler, 1965)—colic, vomiting for three and a half months, followed by severe diarrhea, six to eighteen months, necessitating hospitalization and painful medical intervention. These physiological events surely influenced the nascent ego, stamping the body-ego image specifically and delaying differentiation between *inside* and *outside.* The effect of separation from the mother during hospitalization is hard to assess in view of the mother's inconstancy. It must be assumed that the drives, too, were adversely affected with respect to fusion, differentiation, and neutralization. This sequence, mainly internally determined, might have had a quite different effect on Sally's development if her mother had been capable of providing the maternal supplies to mitigate the noxious stimulation from within and without during the twelve months of illness. This incapacity of the mother and of the father was and is Sally's milieu. The father remained insufficiently differentiated from the mother through each phase of her life, due primarily to his own pathological and incomplete development. If a child's three requirements are, as Anna Freud lists them, affection, continuity, and stimulation, Sally had only an abundance of stimulation, but it was unpredictable and not phase-related.

As already stated, Sally and her mother as a *dyad* do not meet any established criteria for *therapeutic intervention in prenursery via the mother.* They do illustrate the importance of the prenursery as a medium of data collection on mother and child, during a period infrequently seen in private analytic practice. The prenursery may also be seen as a slow introduction to individual guidance for a mother as anxious and as resistant as Mrs. K. was. Moreover, it was instrumental in interrupting the grossly inappropriate handling of the child. But the *counterindications for therapeutic intervention for the child via the mother,* already clear in the prenursery, were confirmed during the subsequent years. The mother's inability to correct the damage of the first two years of life was established. Assignment of the task to a therapeutic object who would provide the auxiliary ego which was deficient throughout Sally's infancy was held up by parental resistance. In the three-year-old nursery one of her teachers, Miss Anne Lockwood, undertook this "repair job," as she called it, in the group, with good results for that year. She was ably assisted in this by her co-teacher, Miss Paige Epps. However, this should not distract us from the fact that such measures, i.e., "ego repair" for under-threes, are still largely *improvisational.* Therapeutic intervention for under-threes has not yet found its legitimate place on our professional agenda.

Summary

In this short paper I have raised more questions than can be answered in our present state of competence. This has led me to make some suggestions for further study:

1. How to assess the mother's potentialities as an instrument in the treatment of her two- to three-year-old. This involves an assessment of her own developmental progression,[4] of the rigidity of her fixation, especially with respect to her sexual identification; her ability to tolerate therapeutic intervention. Some of these are also referred to by Annie Katan (1959). At the present time we are still

[4] See Benedek (1959) and also D. M. Levy (1942).

guided mostly by clinical intuition. Mahler's charting of the separation-individuation process for the child has also shed light on the *mother's fixation points.* These need to be studied specifically before an informed selection of a mother for therapeutic purposes—her own and her young child's—can be made.

2. How to recognize and localize the nature of interference with the child's developmental progression, and gauge such interference in its short- and long-range implications. We need an extension of Mahler's subphases together with Anna Freud's Profile of "developmental lines" for the third year of life, as well as a "timetable," if there is one, of the unfolding of constitutional, endogenous pathology before we can have the "orderly sequence of childhood disorders" aimed at by A. Freud and Nagera (1966). Additional clinical sensitivity is required to differentiate between pathological behavior which reflects *imitation of the mother, and/or identification with the mother, and/or reaction to the mother and her handling.* To quote Anna Freud (1966b): "We agree wholeheartedly with him [Hartmann] that the whole subject of diagnostic categorization needs reformulation so far as childhood pathology is concerned." I should like to add only that this reformulation should go hand in hand with the inextricably related topic of therapeutic choice.

3. The need to develop plastic therapeutic interventions for under-threes related to deficits in mothering during the separation-individuation phase, such intervention to be applied as close to the subphase affected as possible. It is questionable whether such early, preverbal deficits can be made up when the child is old enough to be analyzed. While it is also questionable, at this time, whether they can be made up by earlier intervention, my experience with corrective object relations prejudices me in favor trying.

BIBLIOGRAPHY

Alpert, A. (1957), A Special Therapeutic Technique for Certain Developmental Disorders in Prelatency Children. *Amer. J. Orthopsychiat.,* 27:256-270.

—— (1959), Reversibility of Pathological Fixations Associated with Maternal Deprivation in Infancy. *This Annual,* 14:169-185.

—— (1963), A Special Therapeutic Technique for Prelatency Children with a History of Deficiency in Maternal Care. *Amer. J. Orthopsychiat.,* 33:161-182.

Benedek, T. (1959), Parenthood as a Developmental Phase. *J. Amer. Psa. Assn.,* 7:389-417.

Freud, A. (1965), *Normality and Pathology in Childhood: Assessments of Development.* New York: International Universities Press.

—— (1966a), Foreword to H. Nagera, *Early Childhood Disturbances, the Infantile Neurosis, and the Adulthood Disturbances: Problems of a Developmental Psychoanalytic Psychology* [*The Psychoanalytic Study of the Child,* Monogr. 2]. New York: International Universities Press, pp. 9-10.

—— (1966b), Links between Hartmann's Ego Psychology and the Child Analyst's Thinking. In: *Psychoanalysis—A General Psychology: Essays in Honor of Heinz Hartmann,* ed. R. M. Loewenstein, L. M. Newman, M. Schur, & A. J. Solnit. New York: International Universities Press, pp. 16-27.

Furman, E. (1957), Treatment of Under-Fives by Way of Parents. *This Annual,* 12:250-262.

—— (1966),Treatment of the Under-five by Way of His Mother: Assessment of Mother. Paper presented at Meeting of American Association of Child Psychoanalysis, Topeka, Kansas.

Greenacre, P. (1945), The Biologic Economy of Birth. *This Annual,* 1:31-51.

Hartmann, H. (1939), *Ego Psychology and the Problem of Adaptation.* New York: International Universities Press, 1958.

James, M. (1960), Premature Ego Development: Some Observations upon Disturbances in the First Three Years of Life. *Int. J. Psa.,* 41:288-294.

Katan, A. (1959), The Nursery School as a Diagnostic Help to the Child Guidance Clinic. *This Annual,* 14:250-264.

Leitch, M. & Escalona, S. K. (1949), The Reaction of Infants to Stress: A Report of Clinical Findings. *This Annual,* 3/4:461-488.

Levy, D. M. (1942), Psychosomatic Studies of Some Aspects of Maternal Behavior. *Psychosom. Med.,* 4:223-227.

Mahler, M. S. (1965), On the Significance of the Normal Separation-Individuation Phase: With Reference to Research in Symbiotic Child Psychosis. In: *Drives, Affects, Behavior,* ed. M. Schur. New York: International Universities Press, 2:161-169.

—— & La Perriere, K. (1965), Mother-Child Interaction during Separation-Individuation. *Psa. Quart.,* 34:483-498.

Nagera, H. (1966), *Early Childhood Disturbances, the Infantile Neurosis, and the Adulthood Disturbances: Problems of a Developmental Psychoanalytic Psychology* [*The Psychoanalytic Study of the Child,* Monogr. 2]. New York: International Universities Press.

Winnicott, D. W. (1953), Transitional Objects and Transitional Phenomena: A Study of the First Not-Me Possession. *Int. J. Psa.,* 34:89-97.

THE RECOVERY OF A MEMORY FROM THREE MONTHS OF AGE

ANNE E. H. BERNSTEIN, M.D. and
RICHARD S. BLACHER, M.D. (New York)

The very young infant is generally considered to live in a rather amorphous undifferentiated state. Perceptions, sensations, and experiences are fleeting and not integrated; for this reason most authors assume that discrete memories from the earliest months are not recoverable as such but rather emerge as sensations of a more general type (Anthony, 1961; Isakower, 1938; Lewin, 1953).

Kris (1956) has pointed out that childhood experiences become layered with experiences and fantasies of later developmental periods and therefore are often not retrievable. If memories from an even earlier time, from the preverbal state, are registered, they would be even more difficult to recover. Indeed, most analysts would doubt their existence. Thus, in the case of the Wolf Man, Freud (1918), in dating the time of the traumatic primal scene to one and a half years, dismisses the possibility of the episode having occurred at six months as "scarcely tenable."

The following case report would seem to raise questions concerning the accuracy of some commonly held views on mentation in early infancy, especially on the laying down of precise and integrated memory traces. It is a report of a mother's observation of a two-year-old child's recollection of a traumatic episode that had occurred when the infant was three months of age. While this observation

---

We would like to express our thanks to Dr. Edith Jacobson for her helpful suggestions in the preparation of this report.

Presented at the Fall Meetings of the American Psychoanalyitc Association, New York, on December 16, 1966.

From the Department of Psychiatry, The Mount Sinai School of Medicine and The Mount Sinai Hospital of New York, where Dr. Bernstein is an Instructor in Psychiatry, Clinical Assistant Psychiatrist, and Dr. Blacher is Associate Clinical Professor, Associate Attending Psychiatrist.

was not made in an analytic setting, it was carried out by a trained psychiatrist with an analytic background. We therefore venture this report, keeping in mind the limitations that may be inherent in such situations.

Laura's mother was a psychiatric resident at the time of the child's birth and her father was an engineer. After an uncomplicated pregnancy there was a spontaneous full-term delivery. The newborn weighed 7 pounds, 14 ounces and had a head circumference of 39 centimeters. At birth, a diagnosis of hydrocephalus of unknown etiology was made, but no other abnormalities were noted.

At three months of age the head circumference had grown to 46 centimeters, but neurological findings were within normal limits. Laura ate well and slept through the night. Because of the rapidly increasing head circumference she was hospitalized for neurological investigation. This included X-rays and subdural taps. A pneumoencephalogram via the lumbar route was performed, with the spinal needle in place for two hours; during this time she screamed continuously.

During the hospitalization, construction work was carried on in the hospital. There was much hammering in a nearby room and Laura seemed disturbed by this. After the pneumoencephalogram she awoke frequently, screaming and unamenable to comforting.

A diagnosis of communicating hydrocephalus was made and she was treated with Diamox, an oral diuretic medication taken twice a day. Further growth and development seemed normal except for occasional waking at night. She would awake screaming, in apparent terror, soaked with perspiration and rubbing her head. Mrs. L. realized that Laura was not fully awake, and only upon fully awakening her, could the mother console the child.

At three-month intervals Laura was evaluated by the neurosurgeon in his office at the hospital. On these occasions her head circumference was measured and a complete neurological examination was performed. She was reminded by her parents that she had once been in this hospital as a baby when she was ill, but the nature of the illness and the hospital procedures were never discussed. Both parents are certain of this. Routine pediatric care was carried out by the family pediatrician, and routine immunizations were done at home.

Despite the hydrocephalus, the pediatrician felt that the child was precocious when he noted a persistent smiling response from the tenth day on. At five months Laura said "Dada" and "Mama" and at nine months added her sister's name. By seventeen months she had a vocabulary of twenty-four words. At ten months she could sit up without falling, and she took her first steps at seventeen months. From three months on, that is, after the pneumoencephalogram, she began to scream whenever a man except her father approached, although she could tolerate the presence of women. (To this day she shows some distrust of strange adults of either sex, although she gets along well with other children.) At thirty months she was able to play the card game Casino with her sister and play correctly. Thus we see a child of obvious precocity handicapped minimally by the hydrocephalus in her motor development.

At age twenty-seven months, Laura had an echoencephalogram in the outpatient department of the same hospital. This was a painless procedure which was developed only after her first examination. It required the application of conductive fluid to the scalp and the placing of electrodes. She was accompanied by both parents, and her initial anxiety was overcome by making the test into a game. This diagnostic procedure indicated an arrest of the hydrocephalus, and clinical examination showed a well-developed two-year-old with a wide forehead, but with a normal neurological status.

When Laura was twenty-eight months old a new neighbor moved next door. There were several days when much hammering was heard, the result of some construction work and the hanging of pictures. Laura seemed terrified and did not respond to explanations or demonstrations of how pictures were hung by hammering nails. Again she woke up screaming from afternoon naps. She complained, "My dolly is not sleeping all night." When asked why, she responded: "Man is knocking—might knock her head off." To the query, "What man?" she answered, "In the hospital the man knocked my head off." Her mother then recalled the hammering that had taken place during the construction work at the time of Laura's hospitalization for the pneumoencephalogram. The next time Laura brought up the matter of the knocking, she was asked, "What happened in the hospital?" She replied, pointing to her backside, "Man stuck me in the tushie and knocked my head off." She went on to explain that this meant it hurt her head.

She was then for the first time given the explanation that when she was a baby she had been in the hospital and had received an injection which had caused the headache. She was also told that at that time the hospital was being built and that there had been a great deal of hammering. Night terrors continued and during one she was heard to call out, "Don't hurt me! My daddy loves me." She was told, "You are a big girl now and no one is going to hurt you. The headache happened a long time ago when you were a baby." The night terrors ceased for a week and then recurred. When the explanation was repeated, Laura said, "But the man brushed my hair." At this point the echoencephalographic procedure was reviewed and Laura was told that this did not hurt her, nor would anything further be done to hurt her head. The night terrors again subsided, although she still whined while rubbing her head during sleep. Interestingly, Laura, at three and a half years, is still upset by noises, but holds her head instead of her ears as would most children.

Since this observation is so unusual and, to our knowledge, without precedent in the literature of child development, we have hesitated in presenting it. We began as skeptics in attempting to explain what happened, but found the evidence too compelling to ignore. We would not, of course, claim this evidence to be absolute proof, and we recognize the possibility of the entire episode being simply explained by factors unknown to us. The possibility even exists that Laura's memory was a fantasy which coincided with reality. While we think the various explanations are unsatisfactory, we cannot easily dismiss any reasonable objection to such an unusual observation.

We do not suggest that the memory was as discrete as presented by Laura; she connected the lumbar injection with the headache, and these with the hammering on the walls. But she went further and identified the hospital. It is hardly conceivable that she could have known the locale of her experience; rather, this must represent her connection between her visits to what she came to know as "the hospital" and an intense interest in her head on the part of "the man."

The key question, of course, remains the problem of parental memory. Although Laura's head was naturally much in focus because of the ongoing procedures, and although, in keeping with current thought, as much as was felt appropriate was explained to and discussed with her, nothing was ever said of the lumbar puncture, pneumoencephalogram, or hammering on the walls in the hospital. This is felt by both parents with certainty. Nor would this be unlikely—these aspects of her illness would not seem to have a high priority in discussions with a child of this age, nor for that matter in discussions about her when she would be presumably out of earshot. The fact of the hammering indeed was only recalled by the parents after Laura became upset by the hammering next door.

Could Laura have been informed of the procedure by someone else? This too seems improbable. Certainly none of her medical attendants were with her without her mother's presence after the procedure; relatives would hardly discuss the procedure in detail, and such information was not available to her two-and-a-half-year-old sister. Further, knowledge that a headache follows a pneumoencephalogram would be generally available only to physicians and those who have undergone such a procedure.

What other possibilities exist? Perhaps Laura's connecting her backside and the headache and the hammering was not a memory but a conglomeration of impressions linked with hospitals—and temperature taking, for example—and early sensations on the order of the Isakower phenomenon. This may well be; as we have stated, we would not insist on this as such a discrete memory. However, Laura's associations do suggest a higher order of actual recall. Finally, we note Laura's reaction to the clarification concerning the current anxiety symptoms and their relationship to the past. The symptoms subsided, much as they might in response to a correct analytic interpretation. This may perhaps be an added confirmation—but a response which can of course be explained on other grounds.

If this really was a memory and not a description by the child of something she had heard more recently, how does one account for the absence of similar observations? While it does not seem likely that other observers with much experience would miss making similar observations, it may be that the special circumstances in this case allowed just such an observation to be made. An extremely precocious child (who spoke at five months) was exposed to an extremely severe trauma, the pneumoencephalogram; the continued focus on her head would tend to keep such a memory constantly reinforced. The stimulus of the neighbor's hammering was certainly the fortuitous circumstance that allowed the memory to be revealed. This case must make us wonder whether such early memory traces are not more common than we assume, but not noted, and then lost, in the process of further development.

BIBLIOGRAPHY

Anthony, E. J. (1961), A Study of "Screen Sensations." *This Annual,* 16:211-245.

Freud, S. (1918), From the History of an Infantile Neurosis. *Standard Edition,* 17:3-123. London: Hogarth Press, 1955.

Isakower, O. (1938), A Contribution to the Patho-Psychology of Phenomena Associated with Falling Asleep. *Int. J. Psa.,* 19:331-345.

Kris, E. (1956), The Recovery of Childhood Memories in Psychoanalysis. *This Annual,* 11:54-88.

Lewin, B. D. (1953), Reconsideration of the Dream Screen. *Psa. Quart.,* 22:174-199.

THE SECOND INDIVIDUATION PROCESS OF ADOLESCENCE

PETER BLOS, Ph.D. (New York)

The biological processes of growth and differentiation during puberty effect changes in the structure and in the functioning of the organism. These changes occur in a typical and sequential order, called maturation. The same applies to the psychological changes of adolescence. These, too, follow a developmental pattern but of a different order, since these changes draw content, stimulation, aim, and direction from a complex interplay of inner and outer impingements. What we, eventually, observe are new stabilizing processes and alterations of psychic structures, both of which are the result of adolescent accommodations.

At the points where both the pubertal maturation and the adolescent accommodation intersect in order to become integrated, there we find the critical stations of adolescent development. I have described these stations, clinically and theoretically, in terms of adolescent phases (Blos, 1962). They are the milestones of progressive development, each marked by a phase-specific conflict, a maturational task, and a resolution that is preconditional for the advance to higher levels of differentiation. Beyond these typical aspects of the adolescent phases, we can recognize a component in psychic restructuring that winds, like a scarlet thread, through the entire fabric of adolescence. This unrelenting component is manifest with equal pertinacity in preadolescence as in late adolescence. It is conceptualized here as the second individuation process of adolescence. In my previous studies of adolescence I have continuously emphasized the heterogeneity of phases in terms of the positions and movements of

The first draft of this paper was presented at Georgetown University Hospital, Washington, D.C., April 5, 1965; the second draft at the University Hospital, Ann Arbor, Michigan, February 15, 1966; the final draft at the Cleveland Psychoanalytic Society, February 17, 1967, and at the Michigan Association for Psychoanalysis, February 18, 1967.

drive and ego. My attention turns now to a process of a more pervasive order whose sameness in direction and in aim extends without letup through the entire period of adolescence.

I propose to view adolescence in its totality as the second individuation process, the first one having been completed toward the end of the third year of life with the attainment of object constancy. Both periods have in common a heightened vulnerability of the personality organization. Both periods have in common the urgency for changes in psychic structure in consonance with the maturational forward surge. Last but not least, both periods—should they miscarry—are followed by a specific deviant development (psychopathology) that embodies the respective failures of individuation. What is in infancy a "hatching from the symbiotic membrane to become an individuated toddler" (Mahler, 1963), becomes in adolescence the shedding of family dependencies, the loosening of infantile object ties in order to become a member of society at large or, simply, of the adult world. In metapsychological terms, we would say that not until the termination of adolescence do self and object representations acquire stability and firm boundaries, i.e., they become resistant to cathectic shifts. The oedipal superego—in contrast to the archaic superego—loses in the process some of its rigidity and power, while the narcissistic institution of the ego ideal acquires more pervasive prominence and influence. The maintenance of the narcissistic balance is thus further internalized. These structural changes establish constancy of self-esteem and of mood as increasingly independent from external sources or, at best, dependent on the external sources of one's own choosing.

The disengagement from internalized objects—love and hate objects—opens the way in adolescence to the finding of external and extrafamilial love and hate objects. The reverse was true in early childhood during the separation-individuation phase, when the child gained psychological separateness from a concrete object, the mother. This was achieved through the process of internalization that gradually facilitated the child's growing independence from the mother's presence, her ministrations, and her emotional supplies as the chief and sole regulators of psychophysiological homeostasis. The progress from the symbiotic oneness of child and mother to that of separateness from her is marked by the formation of internal regulatory capacities which are assisted and promoted by maturational—especially motor, perceptual, verbal, and cognitive—advances. This process is at best a pendular one, as we observe again in the second individuation process of adolescence. Regressive and progressive movements alternate in shorter or longer intervals, easily giving the casual observer of the child a lopsided maturational impression. Only observation over a period of time enables us to judge the behavior of the average toddler or of the average adolescent as to its normal or deviant nature.

Adolescent individuation is the reflection of those structural changes that accompany the emotional disengagement from internalized infantile objects. The complexity of this process has been, for some time, in the center of analytic attention. In fact, it is by now axiomatic that without a successful disengagement from infantile internalized objects, the finding of new, namely, extrafamilial, love objects in the outside world either is precluded, hindered, or remains restricted to simple replication and substitution. The ego is intrinsically involved in this process because, up to adolescence, the parental ego is selectively available to the child and, indeed, is his legitimate ego extension. This condition is an integral aspect of childhood dependency in the service of anxiety control and self-esteem regulation. With the disengagement from infantile libidinal dependencies in adolescence, the accustomed ego dependencies of the latency period are repudiated as well. Therefore, the ego weakness of adolescence is not only due to the increasing strength of the drives but, in large measure, to the disengagement from the parental ego support. Up to adolescence this support constitutes an essential component of the child's ego. Relative ego weakness due to the intensification of the drives, as well as absolute ego weakness due to the reduction of parental ego support are both enmeshed in our clinical observations. The recognition of these disparate elements of adolescent ego weakness is of theoretical interest but also of practical usefulness in our analytic work. A case illustration will clarify this point.

A young adolescent boy, tormented by castration anxiety, had borrowed his mother's magical defense that says: "nothing bad will ever happen as long as you don't think about it." The boy's use of thought control in the service of anxiety management revealed two components, inextricably linked together. The drive component resided in the boy's masochistic submission to his mother's will and advice, while his ego had borrowed the mother's magic in order to free itself from intense anxiety. The child's ego had identified with the mother's anxiety-control system. With the advent of puberty the renewed and, indeed, frantic employment of the mother's magic only increased his dependency on her, thus indicating the only course his sexual drive could take, namely, infantile, sadomasochistic dependency. In freeing himself from the dependency on his mother by using her magic device, he made himself the victim of her omnipotence by sharing her falsification of reality. The libidinization of submission obstructed progressive development. The magic device could become ego alien only after the ego had gained in critical self-observation and in reality testing. To say it differently: only after the castration anxiety in relation to the archaic mother was recognized, could the phallic modality assert itself and counteract the passive submissive trend. On the ego level, this shift in drive orientation appeared as a repudiation of the magical fallacy whose prototype was the omnipotent mother of infancy. A growing capacity of reality testing went parallel with the repudiation of infantile ego positions, thus enlarging the scope of the autonomous ego.

The disengagement from the infantile object is always paralleled by ego maturation. The reverse is equally true, namely, that adolescent inadequacy or impairment of ego functions is symptomatic of drive fixations and infantile object dependencies. The accumulative ego alterations that parallel drive progression in each adolescent phase accrue in a structural innovation that is identified here as the second individuation.

Without doubt, there appear during adolescence unique and new ego capacities or faculties, such as, for instance, the spectacular advances in the cognitive sphere (Inhelder and Piaget, 1958). However, observation has left us wondering as to their nature of primary autonomy and, furthermore, as to their independence from drive maturation. Experience teaches us that, whenever drive development lags critically behind adolescent ego differentiation, the newly acquired ego functions are, without fail, drawn into defensive employment and lose their autonomous character. Reversely, an advance in drive maturation affects ego differentiation and functioning favorably. The interacting stimulation between drive and ego proceeds most vigorously and effectively if both operate and progress within an optional proximity of each other. Both drive and ego development exert a continuous influence on each other. The loosening of the infantile object ties not only makes way for more mature or age-adequate relationships, but simultaneously the ego in turn becomes increasingly antagonistic to the re-establishment of outmoded and partly abandoned ego states and drive gratifications of childhood.

Analysts, familiar with adolescents, have always been impressed by the central concern which relationships occupy in the life of the adolescent. The intensity and extent of object-directed drive manifestations or the intensity and extent of object-directed drive inhibition should, however, not obscure the radical alterations in ego structure that take place during this time. The sum total of these structural changes survives adolescence as enduring personality attributes.

What I endeavor to convey is the particular character of psychic restructuring in adolescence when shifts in object libido bring about ego alterations, which in turn give the process of object losing and object finding ("pushing away" and "holding on") not only a greater urgency but also a broader adaptive scope. This circular response has normally diminished by the close of adolescence with the result that the ego has acquired its distinct and definitive organization. Within this organization there remains a wide scope open for elaborations during adult life. The ego ideal affects these elaborations decisively.

We are now eager to trace the steps of individuation during adolescence. In studying this process we have learned much from those adolescents who sidestep the transformation of psychic structure and replace the disengagement from internal objects by a polarization to them in the form of idiosyncratic behavior and social role. Ego disturbances, apparent in acting out, in learning disorders, in lack of purpose, in procrastination, in moodiness and negativism, are frequently the symptomatic signs of a failure in the disengagement from infantile objects and, consequently, they represent a failure of individuation itself. As clinicians we recognize in the adolescent's wholesale rejection of his family and of his own past the frantic circumvention of the painful disengagement process. Such avoidances are usually transient and the delays are self-liquidating. They might, however, assume extreme forms. We are familiar with the adolescent who runs away, drives off in a stolen car, leaves school, "bums" his way to nowhere, takes to promiscuity and to drugs. These adolescents have usually removed themselves, emphatically and with finality, from their families, convinced that no useful communication is possible between the generations. In the assessment of such cases one often arrives at the conclusion that the adolescent is "doing the wrong thing for the right reasons." One cannot fail but recognize in the emergency measures of a violent rupture with childhood and family continuities the escape from an overwhelming regressive pull to infantile dependencies, grandiosities, safeties, and gratifications. The effort to separate from infantile dependencies is in consonance with the adolescent task: the means employed, however, are bound to abort the maturational momentum.

For many adolescents this violent rupture constitutes a respite, a holding position, until progressive development is rekindled again. For many, however, it becomes a way of life which sooner or later leads back to what, at the outset, was to be avoided, namely, regression. By forcing a physical, geographic, moral, and ideational distance from the family or the locale of childhood, this type of adolescent renders an internal separation dispensable. In his actual separateness and independence he experiences an intoxicating sense of triumph over his past and slowly becomes addicted to his state of apparent liberation. The countercathectic energy employed in upholding this state of life accounts for the often striking inefficacy, emotional shallowness, procrastination, and expectant suspense which characterize the various forms of individuation avoidance. True enough, the physical separateness from the parent or the polarization with the past through change in social role, style of dress and grooming, special interests, and moral choices often represent the only means by which the adolescent can maintain his psychological integrity during some critical stages of the individuation process. The degree of maturity, ultimately attained, depends on how far the individuation process advanced or where it came to an impasse and was left incomplete. It follows from the above that the second individuation is a relative concept: on the one hand, it depends on drive maturation and, on the other hand, it acquires durability in ego structure. The second individuation, therefore, connotes those ego changes that are the accompaniment and the consequence of the adolescent disengagement from infantile objects.

Individuation implies that the growing person takes increasing responsibility for what he does and what he is, rather than depositing this responsibility onto the shoulders of those under whose influence and tutelage he has grown up. In our times it has become a pervasive attitude of the more sophisticated adolescent to blame the parent for the shortcomings and disappointments of his youth or, on a transcendental scale, to see in the uncontrollable powers of various designations the ultimate and absolute forces that govern life. It appears senseless to the adolescent who has taken such a position to rise against these forces, but he rather declares a resigned purposelessness of such an effort the true hallmark of maturity. It is the Camusian stance of the protagonist in *The Stranger*. The incapacity to separate from internal objects except by detachment, rejection, and debasement is subjectively experienced as a sense of alienation. We recognize in it the endemic mood of a considerable segment of present-day adolescents, promising and gifted sons and daughters, having grown up in ambitious, yet indulgent, usually middle-class, often progressive and liberal, families. In studying the morphology of adolescent individuation in historical perspective we come to realize that each epoch evolves predominant roles and styles through which this adolescent task is implemented and socialized. Such epiphenomena of the individuation process always stand in opposition to the established order, in one way or another.[1] It remains a crucial difference whether this new way of life becomes the displaced battleground of liberation from childhood dependencies, thus leading to individuation, or whether the new forms become permanent substitutions of childhood states, thus precluding progressive development. The pathognomic valence of a physical separation like "running away," "leaving school" or rushing into all sorts of adultomorphic, especially sexual, forms of life can be determined only

[1] As example, one might think of the ostentatiously simple and comfortable clothes, introduced by a faction of educated German male youth during the second half of the eighteenth century as a reaction to the French refinement and daintiness of men's clothing. Tearing off the delicate laces from their shirtfronts was complemented by an affectation of exuberant emotionality between male youths (tears, embraces), and a replacement of the wig by free-flowing natural hair. The influence of Rousseau as well as a reaction to the "Phoniness of the Establishment" is traceable in that segment of youth that created its own unconventional and natural style and, beyond that, furnished its part to the political ferment of the times.

if viewed in relation to the individual life history, to the total milieu and its traditional sanctions of the behavioral forms that give expression to pubertal needs. Pubertal drive intensification reactivates primary object relations within the context of certain preferential, pregenital drive modalities. However, libido and aggression do not simply shift in a turnabout-face move from primary love objects to nonincestuous ones during adolescence. All along, the ego is intrinsically involved in these cathectic shifts and it acquires in the process the structure by which the postadolescent personality is defined. Adolescent individuation, then, reflects a process and an achievement, both of which constitute integral components of the total adolescent process.

I shall now leave the description of familiar adolescent accommodations and turn to a discussion of their theoretical implications. The process of disengagement from infantile objects, so essential for progressive development, renews the ego's contact with infantile drive and infantile ego positions. The postlatency ego is, so to say, prepared for this regressive encounter and capable of different, more stable and age-adequate solutions of infantile predilections. The reinstatement of infantile positions, ego and drive positions, is an essential component of the adolescent disengagement process. Relatively stable ego functions, for example, memory or motor control, and, furthermore, relatively stable psychic institutions, for example, the superego, will undergo remarkable fluctuations and changes in their executive functions. The trained observer can recognize in the transient breakdown and in the final reconstitution of these functions and institutions their ontogenetic history. One is tempted to speak, mechanistically, of an adolescent reassemblage of the psychic components within the framework of a fixed psychic apparatus. The superego, once considered an inflexible postoedipal institution, undergoes considerable reorganization during adolescence (A. Freud, 1952). The analytic observation of superego changes has been most instructive for studying the mutability of psychic structure. We shall now look closer at the changeability of this postoedipal institution. The regressive personification of the superego appears in great clarity during the analysis of adolescents. This permits us to glance at its origin in object relations. The unraveling of the process that led to superego formation is like a film played backward. Excerpts from the analysis of two adolescents will illustrate this. Both of them were unable to conform with any routine requirements of daily life; both of them were failures in work of any kind, and, also, in love of any kind.

1. An older adolescent boy became puzzled by the fact that he is equally neglectful of what he likes to do as of what he dislikes to do. The latter he could easily understand, but the former made no sense to him. He became aware of a preconscious thought that accompanied his activity or the choice of it. He asked himself: "Would my mother consider what I do a good thing; would she want me to do it?" The affirmative thought automatically spoiled the activity, even if it was one of a pleasurable nature. At this impasse he became totally inactive. He continued the recounting of this dilemma by saying: "When I know that my mother wants me to do what I want to do—namely, if we both want the same—then I get embarrassed and I stop whatever I am doing."

2. An older adolescent girl, who all through childhood had guided her actions to win the praise and admiration of those close to her, embarked in her late adolescence on a way of life that stood in stark opposition to family standards and style. She had stopped to be what she thought others wanted her to be. To her distress, her self-chosen independence afforded her no sense of self-determination because, at every turn, the thought of her parents' approval or disapproval intervened. Her decisions, so she felt, were not her own, because they were guided by doing the obverse of what would please her parents. A total stalemate of action and decision making was the result. She drifted hither and yon in the fickle breeze of circumstances. All she could do was to delegate parental guidance to her friends of both sexes, living vicariously by their expectancies and gratifications, while being tormented by the constant fear of succumbing to their influence or, on a deeper level, of merging and losing her sense of self.

In both cases the enmeshment of the superego with infantile object relations resulted in a developmental impasse. What, normally, is accomplished during latency, namely, the reduction of infantile object dependency through identification and through the organization of the superego, had failed to succeed in both cases I have mentioned. Instead, primitive identifications, as those laid down in the archaic superego and in precursory stages of the superego, had left their powerful imprint on these two adolescents. Uniqueness fantasies and grandiose self-expectations, once realized through identification with the omnipotent mother, made all goal-directed action painfully insignificant and disappointing. The adolescent task of superego reorganization threw these two adolescents back onto the archaic level of primitive identifications (A. Reich, 1954). The origin of the superego in oedipal and in preoedipal object relations renders this institution the subject for a radical revision in adolescence. It is no wonder that superego disturbances constitute a uniquely adolescent deviancy. Whenever the secondary autonomy of ego functions has only tenuously been achieved in childhood, object libido continues to gain gratification in their exercise. This heritage will throw superego functions into a disastrous disarray with the advance of pubertal maturation. Should adolescent behavior be dictated, massively and lastingly, by a defense against infantile object gratification, then the adolescent reorganization of the superego is precluded or, in other words, adolescent individuation remains incomplete.

Analytic work with adolescents demonstrates, almost monotonously, the reinvolvment of ego and superego functions with infantile object relations. The study of this subject has convinced me that the danger to ego integrity does not derive alone from the strength of the pubertal drives, but comes, in equal measure, from the strength of the regressive pull. Discounting the assumption of a fundamental enmity between ego and id, I came to the conclusion that the task of psychic restructuring by regression represents the most formidable psychic work of adolescence. Just as Hamlet who longs for the comforts of sleep but fears the dreams that sleep might bring, so the adolescent longs for the comforts of drive gratification but fears the reinvolvements in infantile object relations. Paradoxically, only through regression, drive and ego regression, can the adolescent task be fulfilled. This is made feasible through the ego differentiation or ego maturation that is the normal heritage of the latency period. The reality-bound and self-observing part of the ego is normally kept, at least marginally, intact during the regressive movements of adolescence. Thus the dangers of regression are reduced or regulated, averting the catastrophic danger of the regressive loss of self, of a return to the undifferentiated stage, or of merger. However, only through regression at adolescence can the residues of infantile trauma, conflict or fixation be modified by bringing to bear on them the ego's extended resources that draw, at this age, support from the developmental momentum of growth and maturation.

Geleerd (1961) has suggested that "in adolescence a partial regression to the undifferentiated phase of object relationship occurs." In a later paper, based on this earlier study, Geleerd (1964) has broadened her view and stated that "the growing individual passes through many regressive stages in which all three structures participate." This last-mentioned formulation has been affirmed by clinical work and is by now an integral part of the psychoanalytic theory of adolescence. Hartmann (1939) had laid the foundation for these developmental considerations in his formulation of "regressive adaptation." This adaptive modality plays a role throughout life in all kinds of situations.

What I emphasize here is the fact that adolescence is the only period in human life during which ego regression and drive regression constitute an obligatory component of normal development. Adolescent regression operates, therefore, in the service of development. Furthermore, the subject of my investigation is the mutual influence of, or the interaction between, ego and drive regression as they effect changes in psychic structure. The process and the achievement of those structural changes are conceptualized here as adolescent individuation, emphasizing the prominent role of the decathexis of infantile object representations in adolescent psychic restructuring. The phase-specific regression initiates transient, maladaptive hazards and maintains a state of high psychic volatility in youth (Blos, 1963). This condition accounts for much of the perplexing behavior and of the unique emotional turbulence of this age.

In order to expound further the function of adolescent regression it might be useful to compare it with the regressive movements of early childhood. States of stress that overtax the child's adaptive capacity are in early childhood normally responded to by drive and ego regression. Regressions of this nature do not, however, constitute developmental steps that are preconditional to ego and drive maturation. In contrast, adolescent regression, which is not defensive in nature, constitutes an integral part of development at puberty. This regression, nevertheless, induces anxiety more often than not. Should this anxiety become unmanageable, then, secondarily, defensive measures become mobilized. Regression in adolescence is not, in and by itself, a defense, but it constitutes an essential psychic process that, despite the anxiety it engenders, must take its course. Only then can the task be fulfilled that is implicit in adolescent development. It cannot be emphasized enough that what, initially, in this process serves a defensive or restitutive function turns, normally, into an adaptive one and contributes decisively to the uniqueness of a given personality.

In the process of psychic restructuring we observe not only drive regression but also ego regression as a universal byplay of the adolescent individuation process. Ego regression connotes the re-experiencing of abandoned or partly abandoned ego states which had been either citadels of safety and security, or which once had constituted special ways of coping with stress. Ego regression is always in evidence in the adolescent process, but only as far as it operates purely defensively does it work against the evolvement of individuation. We cannot but recognize, retrospectively, in many an adolescent's vagary, that a strategic retreat was the surest road to victory. *Reculer pour mieux sauter.* Only when drive and ego regression reach the immobility of an adolescent fixation does progressive development come to a standstill.

Ego regression is, for example, to be found in the re-experiencing of traumatic states of which no childhood was ever wanting. In self-contrived confrontations with miniature editions or proxy representations of the original trauma in real life situations, the ego gradually acquires mastery over prototypical danger situations. Adolescent play-acting and experimentation as well as much of delinquent pathology belong into this, often maladaptive, ego activity. Normally, a broadened ego autonomy ensues from the struggle against and with the remnants of childhood trauma. From this point of view, adolescence can be contemplated as offering a second chance for coming to terms with overwhelming danger situations (in relation to id, superego, and reality) that have survived the periods of infancy and childhood.

Adolescent ego states of a regressed nature can be recognized in a return to "action language" as distinguished from verbal, i.e., symbolic communication, and, furthermore, in a return to "body language," to somatization of affects, conflicts, and drives. This latter condition is responsible for the many typical physical complaints and conditions of adolescence, which are epitomized in anorexia nervosa and in psychogenic obesity. This is particularly evident in girls, in contrast to boys; it is part of that libidinal diffusion that effects in the female the erotization of the body, especially its surface. Object libido deflected on body parts or organ systems facilitates the formation of "hypochondriacal sensations and feelings of body changes that are well known clinically from initial stages of psychotic illness" (A. Freud, 1958).

Contemplating the "action language" of adolescent behavior, one cannot fail but recognize in it the problem of active versus passive. This antithesis constitutes the earliest one in individual life. It is not surprising that with the onset of puberty, with the bewildering crescendo of instinctual tension, the adolescent falls back on old and familiar modes of tension reduction. Drive regression, in search of one of these modes, leads ultimately to primal passivity. This stands in fatal opposition to the maturing body, to its emerging physical competencies as well as to newly unfolding mental capabilities. Progressive development points to an increasing degree of self-reliance, to an ever greater mastery of the environment, indeed, to its transformation, thus bringing the realization of desires and aspirations within reach.

Regressed ego states are identifiable also in the well-known adolescent idolization and adoration of famous men and women. In our contemporary world they are, predominantly, chosen from show business and sports. These figures are the collective great ones. We are reminded of the idealized parent of the child's younger years. Their glorified images constituted an indispensable regulator of the child's narcissistic balance. It should not surprise us that the bedroom walls, plastered with the collective idols, become bare as soon as object libido is engaged in genuine relationships. Then, the pictorial flock of transient gods and goddesses is rendered dispensable almost overnight.

Infantile ego states are, furthermore, recognizable in the emotional state that is akin to merger. Such states are frequently experienced, e.g., in relation to abstractions such as Truth, Nature, Beauty or in the involvement with ideas or ideals of a political, philosophical, aesthetic, or religious nature. Such ego states of quasi-merger in the realm of symbolic representations are sought as temporary respite and serve as safeguards against total merger with the infantile, internalized objects. Religious conversions or merger states induced by drugs belong to this realm of ego regression.

Ego regression to the stage where self and inner object merge is a pathognomic phenomenon because, normally, the ego component to which we refer as the critical and observing ego continues to exercise its function, even if conspicuously diminished, and thus prevents ego regression from deteriorating into an infantile state of merger. Limited ego regression, typical as well as obligatory in adolescence, can occur only within a relatively intact ego. There is no doubt that adolescent ego regression puts the ego to a severe test. It has been pointed out earlier that, up to adolescence, the parental ego makes itself available to the child and lends structure and organization to its ego as a functional entity. Adolescence disrupts this alliance, and ego regression lays bare the intactness or defectiveness of the early ego organization, which derived decisive positive and negative qualities from the passage through the first separation-individuation phase in the second and third year of life. Adolescent ego regression within a defective ego structure engulfs the regressed ego in its early abnormal condition. The distinction between the pathognomic and normal nature of ego regression lies precisely in the alternative whether ego regression to the undifferentiated stage is approximated or consummated. This distinction is comparable to that between a dream and a hallucination. The regression to a seriously defective ego of early childhood will turn a developmental impasse, so typical of adolescence, into a temporary or permanent psychotic illness. The degree of early ego inadequacy often does not become apparent until adolescence, when regression fails to serve progressive development, precludes individuation, and closes the door to drive and ego maturation.

In following the development of schizophrenic children whom I had treated successfully in early and middle childhood, I became aware of the fact that they encountered a more or less serious recurrence of their early pathology in late adolescence. This usually occurred at the time of their leaving home after they had made in the intervening years remarkable strides in their psychological development. The developmental function of adolescent ego regression came to naught when early ego states, from which the second individuation process must draw its strength, were reactivated in these children. The nuclear pathology flared up once more. The failure of the emotional disengagement from the family during adolescence demonstrated how extensively these children had lived on borrowed ego strength in the intervening years. Therapy had enabled them to derive emotional nurture from the environment. This capacity stood them in good stead during their second acute illness; indeed, it carried them through and made their recovery possible. When the psychological navel cord has to be cut in adolescence, children with early ego damage fall back on a defective psychic structure that is totally inadequate to the task of the adolescent individuation process. While these cases throw light on the structural problems of a certain adolescent psychopathology, they also hint at a treatment continuum of childhood psychosis or childhood schizophrenia, reaching into or having to be resumed again in the adolescent, usually the late adolescent years.

A characteristic of adolescence that cannot escape our notice lies in a frantic effort to keep reality bound, i.e., to be active, to move about, and to keep doing things. Furthermore, it appears in the need for group experiences or individual relationships of vivid and acute excitement and affectivity. The frequent and often abrupt change of these relationships with either sex highlights their ungenuine character. What is sought is not the personal bond but the sharpness of affect and the emotional agitation evoked by it. Into this realm belongs the pressing need to do things "for kicks," thus escaping affective loneliness, dullness, and boredom. This picture would be incomplete without mentioning the adolescent who seeks solitude and splendid isolation where he conjures up in his mind affective states of extraordinary intensity. These propensities are best designated as affect and object hunger. What all these adolescents have in common is the need for sharp, intense, affective states, be they marked by exuberance and elation, pain and anguish. We can look at this affective condition as a restitutive phenomenon that follows in the wake of internal object loss and the concomitant ego impoverishment.[2] The subjective experience of the adolescent, expressed in the quandary of "Who am I?" contains multitudinous perplexities and reflects what is conceptualized as ego loss and ego impoverishment. Ego loss, then, remains throughout adolescence a constant threat to psychological integrity and gives rise to forms of behavior that appear deviant but need to be assessed as efforts to keep the adolescent process in motion by a frantic—event if maladaptive—turn to reality. The clinical picture of many a delinquent, if viewed within this perspective, reveals often more of a healthy component than he is usually credited with.

I shall, once more, consider adolescent object hunger and ego impoverishment. Both these developmental transient conditions find compensatory relief in the group, the gang, the coterie, the contemporaries generally. This social formation is a substitute, often literally, of the adolescent's family. Within the society of the contemporaries lies stimulation, belongingness, loyalty, devotion, empathy, and resonance. I am here reminded of the healthy toddler in Mahler's study (1963) who shows during the separation-individuation crisis an amazing capacity to "extract contact supplies and participation from the mother." This contact supply in adolescence is obtained from the group of contemporaries. The toddler requires the help of the mother to reach autonomy, while the adolescent turns to the contemporary horde, of whatever type it may be, to extract those contact supplies without which individuation cannot be realized. The group permits identifications as role tryouts without any permanent commitment, as well as interactional experimentation as severance actions from childhood dependencies, rather than as preludes to any new and permanent, personal and intimate relationship. Furthermore, the group shares and thus alleviates individual guilt feelings that accompany the emancipation from childhood dependencies, prohibitions, and loyalties. We can summarize and say that, by and large, the contemporaries ease the way to member-

2 It seems, at first sight, a contradiction to speak of "ego impoverishment" when object libido is deflected on the self. However, a healthy ego cannot tolerate well and for long being cut off from object relations. The flooding of the self with narcissistic libido becomes ego syntonic only in the psychotic adolescent; for him, the real world is dull and colorless. The "normal" adolescent experiences a sense of frightening unreality in mounting narcissistic isolation from the object world. Masturbation, therefore, can never offer a permanent form of gratification because, eventually, it lowers self-esteem.

ship in the new generation within which the adolescent has to establish his social, personal, and sexual identity. Whenever peer relationships simply replace childhood dependencies, then the group has miscarried its function. In such cases, the adolescent process has been short-circuited with the result that unresolved emotional dependencies are made permanent personality attributes. Under these circumstances life within the new generation unfolds strangely like a shadow play of the individual past: What was to be avoided most repeats itself with fateful accuracy.

An older adolescent girl, stalemated in a massive anticonformity position that served as a protection against an unusually strong regressive pull, put so well into words what I have endeavored to convey, that I shall let her speak. In contemplating an instance of nonconformity, she said: "If you act in opposition to what is expected, you bump right and left into regulations and rules. Today, when I ignored school—just didn't go—it made me feel very good. It gave me a sense of being a person, not just an automaton. If you continue to rebel and bump into the world around you often enough, then an outline of yourself gets drawn in your mind. You need that. Maybe, when you know who you are, you don't have to be different from those who know, or think they know, who you should be."

I shall now turn to the broader consequences of the fact that regression in adolescence is the precondition for progressive development. I inferred from clinical observations that the adolescent has to come into emotional contact with the passions of his infancy and early childhood, in order for them to surrender their original cathexes; only then can the past fade into conscious and unconscious memories, and only then will the forward movement of the libido give youth that unique emotional intensity and power of purpose.

The profoundest and most unique quality of adolescence lies in its capacity to move between regressive and progressive consciousness with an ease that has no equal at any other period in human life. This might account for the remarkable creative achievements of this particular age. The adolescent experimentation with self and reality, with feeling states and thoughts will accrue, if all goes well, in giving a lasting and precise content and form to individuation in terms of its actualization on the environment. The choice of a vocation, for example, represents one such crucial form of actualization.

In the process of disengagement from primary love and hate objects, a quality of early object relations appears in the form of ambivalence. The clinical picture of adolescence demonstrates the defusion of instinctual drives. Acts of raw aggression are typical of adolescence in general and of male adolescence in particular. The analysis of these aggressive manifestations leads ultimately to elements of infantile rage and sadism, in essence, to infantile ambivalence. Infantile object relations, when revived at adolescence, are bound to appear in their original form, which is to say, in an ambivalent state. Indeed, it remains the ultimate task of adolescence to strengthen postambivalent object relations. The emotional instability of relationships and, above and beyond that, the inundation of autonomous ego functions by ambivalence generally creates in the adolescent a state of precarious lability and incomprehensible contradictions in affect, drive, thought, and behavior. The emotional fluctuations between the extremes of love and hate, of activity and passivity, of fascination and disinterest, represent a characteristic of adolescence so well known that it requires no elaboration. However, this phenomenon is worth exploring in relation to the subject of this investigation, namely, individuation. A state of ambivalence confronts the ego with a condition that—due to the ego's relatively mature state—is felt as intolerable, yet it remains temporarily, at least, beyond the ego's synthesizing capacity to deal with this condition constructively. Much that appears to be a defensive operation, such as negativism, oppositionalism, indifference, etc., is but a manifestation of an ambivalent state that has pervaded the total personality.

Before pursuing these thoughts any further, I shall illustrate them with an excerpt from the analysis of a seventeen-year-old boy. I shall concentrate in what follows on those aspects of the analytic material that reflect the disengagement from the archaic mother and that have a direct bearing on the topic of ambivalence and individuation. The boy, able and intelligent, related on an intellectualizing level to people, better to adults than to peers. A passive aggressive attitude pervaded his contact with people, especially within the family. One became aware of a tumultuous inner life that had found no expression in affective behavior. The boy was given to moodiness, secretiveness, uneven work performance in school, periodic stubbornness and negativism coupled with a cold demandingness at home. Within this fluctuating picture one could discern an all-pervasive haughty, impenetrable superciliousness that bordered on arrogance. This abnormal state was well fortified by compulsive-obsessional defenses. The choice of this defense in and by itself hints at the dominant role of ambivalence in the pathogenesis of this case.

Not until the boy's fantasies became accessible was it possible to appreciate his need for a rigid and unassailable defense organization. His every act and thought was accompanied by a, heretofore unconscious, involvement with the mother and her fantasied complicity, good or bad, in his daily life. He had possessed an insatiable need for closeness to his mother, who had left him from early life on in the care of a well-meaning relative. The boy had always admired, envied, and praised his mother. The analysis helped him experience his hate, contempt, and fear in relation to her whenever his intense wishes for her material generosity were thwarted. It became clear that his actions and moods were determined by the ebb and flow of love and hate that he felt toward his mother or that he imagined his mother felt toward him. In consequence, for example, he would not do his homework when the thought prevailed that his academic achievement would please his mother. At other times it was the reverse. When he received a reward at school, he kept it a secret from his mother so she could not use his achievement as a "feather in her own cap" or, in other words, take it away from him. When he went for a walk he did so in secret, because his mother preferred an outdoor boy and, to put her in the wrong, he would then let her scold him for not getting any fresh air. Should he enjoy a show or invite a friend, it ruined the pleasure of the event when the mother showed delight and approval. In retaliation, he practiced the piano, as he was supposed to do, but played the pieces fortissimo, knowing well that the loud sound would get on his mother's nerves. Playing loud substituted for shouting at her. The realization of his aggression made him anxious.

At this point, the analysis of the boy's ambivalence became blocked by a narcissistic defense. He experienced himself as being an outsider to the drama of life, of being uninvolved in the events of the day, and of seeing his surroundings in blurred and fuzzy outlines. The usual compulsive-obsessional defenses (like cataloguing, filing, repairing) failed in coping with this emergency. He found this state of depersonalization quite unpleasant and disconcerting. The analytic work began to flow again when he became aware of the sadistic aspect of his ambivalence. Then, the strange ego state left him. He felt and verbalized his impulse toward violence, namely, to strike out and hurt his mother physically whenever she frustrated him. The sense of frustration was not dependent on her objective actions but rather on the ebb and flow of his needs. The replication of infantile ambivalence was apparent. He was now able to differentiate between the mother of the infantile period and the mother of the present situation. This enabled us to trace the involvement of ego functions in his adolescent ambivalence conflict and bring about the restoration of their autonomy.

It was interesting to observe how in the resolution of the ambivalence conflict certain selected attributes of the mother's personality became attributes of the boy's ego, such as her capacity to work, her use of intelligence, and her able sociability, which all had been the objects of the son's envy. On the other hand, some of her values, standards, and character traits were rejected by him as undesirable or repugnant. They were no longer perceived as the mother's arbitrary unwillingness to be whatever would please and comfort her child. A secondary object constancy in relation to the mother of the adolescent period became established. The omnipotent mother of the infantitle period was superseded by the son's realization of her fallibilities and virtues. In short, she became humanized. Only through regression was it possible for the boy to re-experience the maternal image and institute those corrections and differentiations that effected a neutralization of preoedipal, ambivalent object relations. The psychic reorganization, as described in his case, was subjectively experienced by the boy as a sharp realization of a sense of self, of that awareness, and conviction, best summarized in the phrase of "this is me." The state of consciousness and the subjective feeling, just paraphrased, reflect an emerging differentiation within the ego that is here conceptualized as the second individuation process.

The first exhilaration that comes with the independence from the internalized parent or, more precisely, from the parental object representations is complemented by a depressed affect that accompanies and follows the loss of the internal object. The affect accompanying this object loss has been likened to the state of mourning and to the work of mourning. There remains, normally, a continuity in the relationship to the actual parent after the infantile character of the relationship is given up. The work of the adolescent individuation is related to both these aspects, infantile and contemporary. Both these parental object representations are derived from the same person but at different stages of development. This tends to confuse the relationship of the adolescent to his parent who is experienced partly or wholly as the one of the infantile period. This confusion is worsened whenever the parent participates in the shifting positions of the adolescent and proves unable to maintain his fixed place as an adult vis-à-vis the maturing child. The adolescent disengagement from infantile objects necessitates first their decathexis before libido can again be turned outward in the search of phase-specific object gratifications. We observe in adolescence that object libido—in various degrees, to be sure—is withdrawn from outer and inner objects and is converted into narcissistic libido by being deflected onto the self. This shift from object to self results in the proverbial self-centeredness and self-absorption of the adolescent who fancies himself to be independent from the love and hate objects of his childhood. The flooding of the self with narcissistic libido has the effect of self-aggrandizement and an overestimation of the powers of body and mind. This condition affects reality testing adversely. To cite a familiar consequence of this state, I remind you of the frequent automobile accidents of adolescents which occur despite their expert skill and technical knowledge. Should the process of individuation stop at this stage, then we encounter all sorts of narcissistic pathology of which the withdrawal from the object world, the psychotic disorder, represents the gravest impasse.

The internal changes accompanying individuation can be described from the side of the ego as a psychic restructuring during which the decathexis of the parental object representations in the ego brings about a general instability, a sense of insufficiency, and of estrangement. In the effort to protect the integrity of the ego organization, a familiar variety of defensive, restitutive, adaptive and maladaptive maneuvers are set into motion before a new psychic equilibrium is established. We recognize its attainment in a personal and autonomous life style.

At the time when the adolescent process of individuation is in its most vigorous season, deviant, i.e., irrational, erratic, turbulent behavior is most prominent. Such extreme measures are employed by the adolescent to safeguard psychic structure against regressive dissolution. The adolescent in this state presents the clinician with a most delicate task of discrimination as to the transient or permanent or, simply, as to the pathognomic or normal nature of the respective regressive phenomena. The perplexing ambiguity that clinical assessment has to cope with derives from the fact that a resistance against regression is as much a sign of normal as of abnormal development. It is a sign of abnormal development if resistance against regression precludes a modicum of regression that is essential for the disengagement from early object relations and infantile ego states or, in short, is preconditional for the reorganization of psychic structure. The problem of regression, both ego and drive regression, reverberates through adolescence without letup. These regressive movements make the attainment of adulthood possible and they have to be understood in these terms. They also represent the nuclei or the adolescent fixation points around which the failures of the adolescent process become organized. Adolescent disturbances have drawn our attention, almost exclusively, to the regressive symptomatology within the context of drive gratification or to the defensive operations and their sequelae. I submit that resistance against regression is, in equal measure, a cause for concern, when it presents a persistent and unsurmountable roadblock in the course of progressive development.

Resistance against regression can take many forms. One is exemplified in the adolescent's forceful turn toward the outside world, to action and bodily motion. Paradoxically, independence and self-determination in action and in thought tend to become most violent and reckless whenever the regressive pull possesses an inordinate strength. I have observed that children who were extremely clinging and dependent during childhood often resort in adolescence to the reverse attitude, namely, detached distance from the parent at any cost. In doing so they achieve an apparent but illusory victory. In such cases, action and thought are simply determined by the fact that they represent the obverse of expectations, wishes, and opinions of the parent or of their substitutes and representatives in society, such as teacher, policeman, and adults generally or, more abstractly, such as law, tradition, convention, and order anywhere, in any form, and regardless of their social purpose and meaning. Here again, transient disturbances in the interaction between the adolescent and his environment render them qualitatively different from those that acquire permanency, mold in a definitive fashion the ego's relation to the outside world, and bring the adolescent process to a premature standstill.

Based on our experience with the neurotic child and adult we grew accustomed to concentrate on defenses as the major obstacles in the path of normal development. Furthermore, we grew accustomed to think of regression as a psychic process that stands in opposition to progressive development, to drive maturation and to ego differentiation. Adolescence can teach us well that these connotations are limited and limiting. It is true that we are ill prepared to say what, in a regressed state during adolescence, is simply the static resuscitation of the past and what represents the heralding prelude to psychic restructuring. It is reasonable to assume that the adolescent, who surrounds himself with pictures of idolized persons, not only repeats a childhood pattern that once gratified narcissistic needs, but that he simultaneously takes part in a collective experience that makes him an empathic member of his peer group. Sharing the same idols is tantamount to being part of the same family; however, a crucial difference cannot escape us, namely, that the new social matrix at this stage of life promotes the adolescent process through participation in a symbolic, stylized, exclusive, tribal ritual. Regression under these auspices seeks not simply to re-establish the past but to reach the new, the future, via the detour along familiar pathways. A sentence by John Dewey comes to mind here. "The present," he says, "is not just something which comes after the past. . . . It is what life is in leaving the past behind."

The thoughts assembled in this paper have drifted toward a converging goal with the common objective of elucidating the changes in ego organization as they are brought about by drive maturation. It has become convincingly clear from clinical investigations of the adolescent process that both, the task of disengagement from primary objects and the abandonment of infantile ego states, necessitate a return to early phases of development. Only through the reanimation of the infantile emotional involvements and of the concomitant ego positions (fantasies, coping patterns, defensive organization) can the disengagement from internal objects be achieved. This achievement, then, hinges on regression, drive and ego regression, both ushering in, along their course, a multitude of, pragmatically speaking, maladaptive measures. In a paradoxical fashion one might say that progressive development is precluded if regression does not take its proper course at the proper time within the sequential pattern of the adolescent process.

In defining the individuation process as the ego aspect of the regressive task in adolescence, it becomes apparent that the adolescent process constitutes, in essence, a dialectic tension between primitivization and differentiation, between regressive and progressive positions, each drawing its impetus from the other, as well as each rendering the other workable and feasible. The ensuing tension, implicit in this dialectic process, puts an inordinate strain on both ego and drive organization or, rather, on their interaction. This strain is responsible for the many and varied distortions of as well as failures in individuation—clinical and subclinical—that we encounter at this age. Much of what appears, at first glance, as defensive in adolescence might, more correctly, be identified as a precondition of progressive development to get under way and to be kept in flux.

It is my hope that the concept of the second individuation will shed light on the structural problems of the adolescent process, because it relates, even synthesizes, such antagonistic trends as regressive primitivization and progressive differentiation, viewing both within their reciprocal influence. In short, what I have endeavored in this presentation is to make the adolescent paradox explicit and intelligible.

BIBLIOGRAPHY

Blos, P. (1962), *On Adolescence: A Psychoanalytic Interpretation.* New York: Free Press of Glencoe.

—— (1963), The Concept of Acting Out in Relation to the Adolescent Process. *J. Amer. Acad. Child Psychiat.,* 2:118-143.

Freud, A. (1952), The Mutual Influences in the Development of Ego and Id: Introduction to the Discussion. *This Annual,* 7:42-50.
—— (1958), Adolescence. *This Annual,* 13:255-278.
Geleerd, E. R. (1961), Some Aspects of Ego Vicissitudes in Adolescence. *J. Amer. Psa. Assn.,* 9:394-405.
—— (1964), Adolescence and Adaptive Regression. *Bull. Menninger Clin.,* 28:302-308.
Hartmann, H. (1939), *Ego Psychology and the Problem of Adaptation.* New York: International Universities Press, 1958.
Inhelder, B. & Piaget, J. (1958), *The Growth of Logical Thinking from Childhood to Adolescence.* New York: Basic Books.
Mahler, M. S. (1963), Thoughts about Development and Individuation. *This Annual,* 8:307-324.
Reich, A. (1954), Early Identifications as Archaic Elements in the Superego. *J. Amer. Psa. Assn.,* 2:218-238.

DEVELOPMENTAL CONSIDERATIONS IN THE OCCUPATIONS OF THE BLIND

DOROTHY BURLINGHAM (London)

One of the problems that occurs in the care of young blind children is how to find suitable occupations and appropriate toys for them. Both mothers and nursery school teachers of such children are continually at a loss as to how to interest them. The children seem to lack any desire for the objects surrounding them and consequently show no sign of a wish to play.

This differs significantly from our experience with sighted children and their inevitable curiosity, where it is as difficult to keep objects from them as it is to interest the blind in the same items. Toys for the sighted child are everywhere and in such numbers that the problem that arises is one of eliminating toys which are unsuitable or even harmful.

Much has been written about the toys and occupations of sighted infants, and a sequence has been established of the interrelation between the various stages of sensory and instinctual development and its expression in play. To quote only a few examples: putting objects into each other, next to each other, on top of each other; each of these belongs to a certain stage of development, with libidinal interest derived from notions and experimentations about the inside of the body, its dimensions, etc. To build up and then knock down a tower gives expression to both constructive and destructive urges. Pleasure in mastery is expressed by the successful handling of small copies of life-size objects.

Children are motivated to climb steps and try to attain heights on the jungle gym by the wish to be tall; both muscular and exhibi-

---

The work with blind children is part of the Education Unit of the Hampstead Child-Therapy Course and Clinic and as such is maintained by the Grant Foundation, Inc., New York. The research work with the blind is assisted further by the National Institute of Mental Health, Bethesda, Maryland.

tionistic pleasure is gained from gymnastics, acrobatics, and so on. Play with dolls fosters and expresses the identification with mother in girls; interest in mechanics, trains, engines, and both toy and real cars are certain signs of the boy's phallic interests. Copying games serve as a training ground for later achievements; many mechanical toys introduce the child to very real technical and scientific preoccupations of the future.

In studying these occupations and the toys and tools which serve them, we do not ask ourselves sufficiently through which sensory channel they make their appeal to the child,[1] i.e., whether they are primarily seen, heard, or felt. It is this latter problem with which we are confronted in full force when we are dealing with the blind.

There is, of course, the possibility that we are wrong in judging the development of the blind child on the basis of comparisons with the sighted. What in this light appears as backwardness or a slowing up may turn out to be a matter of much greater basic difference in kind. To deal with visual representations of things, as the seeing do, is probably a much easier process than to deal with the verbal abstractions to which the blind are confined and for which they depend wholly on the progressive development of verbalization and its ramifications—inevitably later occurrences.

Even before speech, seeing infants can relate directly to the objects around them. The blind, at the same age, have to fall back on guessing, association, concluding, and will only too frequently come up with the wrong answer. It seems to me that there is an expenditure of energy and intellect here which is quite formidable but often undervalued.

The question arises how these differences in development relate to the choice of toys and occupations.

The Mother's Body as the First Toy

With regard to play, the blind are nearest the seeing in infancy, when all children have the mother's body as their plaything. The difference begins when the seeing child exchanges the mother's body for transitional objects and cuddly toys, while the blind infant is

[1] With the exception of Maria Montessori.

less attracted to the inanimate world and consequently remains for a long time in this first stage.

It is difficult to say where, for the blind, play ends and learning begins or vice versa, or whether it is impossible to distinguish between the two at this stage. Touching the mother's hair, nose, mouth, eyes, etc., gives the child knowledge of her face, as looking does, while at the same time the pleasure associated with touching turns this activity into play.

Mothers will need to be taught a great deal in order to alert them to the necessity of lending their bodies to the child to play with, a necessity which is much greater in the case of the blind than it is in seeing infants. Left to themselves, the mothers of blind infants will at this time tend to ignore the child's pleasure in touch; instead they express their concern over his vision by holding things near the child's eyes to test his vision or by engaging his attention for the purpose of testing his intelligence in a variety of ways. These actions are at best meaningless to the child; at worst they are distressing because, as far as vision is concerned, he cannot fulfill the mother's hopes and expectations and may easily react to her discouragement.

It may be equally important to assure the mothers that infants, and especially blind infants, not only like to play with the mother's body but also enjoy having their own bodies played with. This comes natural to the normal mother, but may be absent when a mother is depressed, and disappointed in her child, as the mothers of blind children are. Nevertheless, her play with the infant's fingers, toes, and the surface of his skin is needed to libidinize his body. When this is missing, blind children often do not develop a relationship to their own bodies until a much later age.

Contrary to the mother's concern, neither the child's play with her body nor her play with the child's overstimulates him. In fact, we believe that the opposite is the case and that the well-known blindisms, i.e., the rhythmical rocking, swaying, and eye rubbing, are the result of too little stimulation through mutual body play in infancy. According to our experience, the mother's body retains its role as a toy for the blind child far beyond infancy and certainly until nursery school age. We may, of course, be influenced in this opinion by the fact that the children we deal with have been deprived of this first "toy" by their mother's depression, withdrawal, lack of knowledge and empathy with the child.

Playing with the Feet and Other Body Games

We have observed that, in play, a blind infant prefers to use his legs and feet rather than his arms and hands. We assume that the latter are inactive since there is no visual stimulation to reaching, grasping, and holding. An additional reason for preferring the legs appears to be their greater strength and efficiency. Accordingly, to kick and push against the bars of the cot becomes a favorite game, which is endlessly repeated. The fact that this produces noise as well as muscular tension naturally serves to heighten the enjoyment.

It would be easy, at this stage, to meet the child on his own ground and to enlarge on and vary this spontaneous play. A knowledgeable mother would therefore offer the child her own hands to push against, instead of the bars; this would lead to enjoyable baby gymnastics, etc. The main point is that the infant has made a spontaneous choice to play and should be encouraged rather than discouraged in his occupation. Instead, what usually happens to him at this stage is the experience of being offered a variety of objects which he is expected to reach for and handle—a play activity appropriate for his sighted contemporaries.

In fact, the blind children's potential enjoyment of their musculature and of body play in general is much greater than one would expect from seeing them arrive at nursery school or elementary school, where they appear almost immobile, clumsy, and often apathetic. It seems that these attitudes are the consequence of the many obstacles, dangers, and accidents which occurred so often when they moved spontaneously, as well as of their mothers' efforts to keep them "safe," which, in their case, means inactive. The picture changes quickly if steps are taken to safeguard them while at the same time providing the ultimate in movement for them. Walking frames and bouncers for the toddler would enable him much earlier to follow his mother at home as she moves about the room, thereby providing him with the enjoyment of all the exciting sensations which the sighted child enjoys in crawling and taking his first steps. In the larger space provided by the nursery school, a trampoline offers unrivaled opportunity for jumping, which is otherwise denied the blind. Children delight in the abandon of the movement while they are safe, and the rhythmical quality of the activity probably also adds to the pleasure. Children can be seen to improve further if one adds all sorts of noise-making devices on the trampoline as they jump. Jumping on the trampoline, jumping down steps or ladders while holding the teacher's hand, running while holding on to her hand, or even freely running toward her hand clapping are the next stages in play. From there the children find an easy transition to climbing frames and jungle gyms, tricycles, etc., on which they become amazingly proficient.

An interesting game which is not beyond the scope of blind children is the obstacle race or its equivalent. The same pieces of furniture which frighten and hurt the child who meets them accidentally become "toys" when they are piled in an orderly fashion by the teacher, to be circumnavigated by the child. They are felt, handled, pushed into place, climbed over carefully, jumped off, and thoroughly enjoyed as props in an exciting game.

To draw the comparison with the sighted: all children, whether normal or handicapped, love body games. The difference lies in the fact that, for the blind, they play a predominant part at an age when sighted children simultaneously build, construct, explore, draw, paint, etc.

Playing with Sound

In the absence of vision, sound cannot fail to play an overwhelming part in the lives of blind children. Touching and feeling the mother's body, as described, go side by side of course with listening to her. The mother's handling of things in preparation for his bottle, her picking up and putting down of objects, her footsteps, the rattle of dishes in the kitchen, the rustling of clothes, all these become familiar noises that the child soon learns to interpret correctly. This is of course crowned by her keeping contact with him through her voice which, in the case of blind children, has to take the place of the mother's glance.

There is an obvious and convenient path here from hearing the familiar sounds to touching and handling the objects that produce them, i.e., playing with them. Unluckily, children at this early stage are unable to make their wishes in this respect known, and for this reason many mothers miss the opportunity of offering these familiar objects as playthings instead of specially constructed toys, when the pots and pans and other household articles which have announced themselves by means of sound would mean so much more to the child.

Blind children are not only attracted to playthings by sounds, they also play by producing additional sounds. This results, of course, in their handling various objects in a different manner from the seeing. Whatever they are given is pushed, scraped, dropped, hit, and banged on different surfaces, and the various noises thus produced are listened to eagerly. An impasse between mother and child frequently arises in this respect, with the mother attempting to make her child use the object purposefully, as it "should be used," while the child continues to play wtih it for the purpose of creating and experimenting with accoustic pleasure.

Playing with sounds soon becomes a favorite occupation and underlies many other purposes. While normal children copy what they see, the copying games of the blind consist of reproducing whatever they hear: the noises made by mother as described, as well as the noises of the street, the coming and going, and honking of cars; the noise of the gramophone, the wireless, and the television, including the squeaks, the vacuum cleaners; the sounds heard at a fair; etc. It may be this play with sounds that not infrequently interferes with the language development of the blind children. The normal infant's babbling, which produces pleasure without serving communication, is in the blind enormously prolonged and overlaps with verbalization proper. Blind children are often found to "parrot" or use babble talk even though they are perfectly able to talk properly. There is no doubt that they play with words. They copy everything, from different accents heard to snatches of sounds and to poetry which is not understood. It seems to me that it would be advantageous rather than the opposite if the children were not only permitted but even encouraged and joined in extending this activity in a playful manner, by means of which many verbal copying games could be developed. This might be more helpful in the long run than placing all emphasis on offering the usual books and stories for children, which are, after all, full of visual descriptions and innumerable items without relevance for the blind. It would be a different matter if special books were devised specifically for the blind, with the content based on their own sense experience and geared to the specific stage of their intellectual and emotional development.

What extends far beyond the area of play is the blind child's interest in music. They may begin with musical toys of all kinds, such as cymbals, drums, mouth organ, xylophone, and musical games such as percussion bands, dancing to music, etc., and may well lead on to the playing of real instruments such as the flute, the piano, the violin, etc. It is not difficult to illustrate with examples that music meets a very real and deep need in the blind child and seems to be the nearest substitute for vision that can be found as far as emotional expression and involvement are concerned.

Many blind children invest an immeasurably greater libidinal cathexis in this activity than in any other, and at least one child proved to be very proficient in this area while she was seemingly backward in all other respects.

A Common Toy for the Blind: The Door

The following is an example of how widely the child's own spontaneous choice of occupations diverges from the official idea of what a toy should be. If not unduly restricted, blind children of nursery school age are fascinated by playing with the doors of the room, ignoring many proper toys which are offered to them. They are inseparable from the door, which they open, shut, bang, swing on, go through, leave and find again, open and shut again, repeating single actions many times over. It takes prolonged observation of the child before one can puzzle out the appeal that this game has. What the door offers is obviously a combined exercise in muscular control, mastery, touch, and noise. In addition to the use of the senses, there is also the turning from passive into active, since the child is here leaving and returning instead of being left and returned to. There is, furthermore, the fascination of the moving object, of special interest in the phallic phase, as well as the enjoyment of controlling it.

From this door game branches off a more detached interest in the vibration felt, the meaning of space, the impact of the swing. All this makes it more understandable that blind children will leave a roomful of playthings in order to devote themselves to a door.

Unluckily, what is fascinating to the children is often discouraged by the adults, who consider this occupation not only dangerous but also annoying and exasperating in the extreme.

Mastery of Tasks through Play and Occupations

As observers of play we have to turn from the sighted to the blind to appreciate how many of our common toys appeal to the child only or mainly on the basis of vision. I take as an example the so-called "little world," which has become more or less a stand-by in every nursery whether at home or at school. By way of the miniature replica of the people and things of everyday life, children not only are acquainted with the world at large, they are simultaneously allowed to feel that this world is under their control and can be arranged, directed, redirected—in short, mastered by them. This is an experience on which the blind children miss out altogether. Houses, churches, fences, lampposts, human figures, domestic and wild animals, which are all part of the little world, may look like the real thing changed only in dimensions, but they certainly neither feel, sound, nor smell like it.

For the blind child, there is not the slightest similarity between a real church and its steeple (of which he has no personal experience) and the toy which represents it. Still, blind children, when given playthings of this kind, learn by rote that this particular shape is called by the adults "church" or "fence" and therefore learn to call it by that name. Since there is, for the blind, no real personal association betwen such toys and the real thing, they certainly do not experience the corresponding pleasure in handling them; such toys, therefore, do not open up a path to the mastery of the real world.

What is true of the "little world" applies to a lesser degree to dolls and teddy bears. These toys have a double appeal, one of them being through touch because they are cuddly; and this pleasure is shared by the blind and the sighted alike. By both sighted and blind children these toys are not only loved but also thrown around, picked up, cuddled, banged, smacked, etc.; i.e., they are mastered and controlled and offer a channel of expression for the child's loving and aggressive feelings toward human objects. But secondly, dolls and teddy bears are also skillfully fashioned to resemble human beings and animals, a fact that heightens their usefulness for the sighted; where vision is lacking, however, this attribute remains unnoticed and detracts from their value. We only need to watch a blind child holding her doll upside down, trying to feed its legs instead of its mouth, to realize the extent to which doll play is an imperfectly maintained, learned occupation for the blind.

I should like to take as the next example the occupations offered to normal children in a Montessori nursery school, where they experience immense pleasure through the simple means of being allowed to carry out everyday tasks that are usually reserved for the adults, such as setting the table for meals, carrying dishes filled with food, filling tumblers from pitchers, washing dishes, handling hot and cold water faucets, washing clothes, etc. Not only do the children quickly show proficiency at these tasks through copying what the adults do, but their self-respect is heightened and their fantasies of being big are nourished. According to the Montessori method, the pleasure gained thereby is sufficient to make a child persevere; praise and recognition by the teacher become superfluous.

It is an interesting problem to try and see how far these particular occupations suit the blind or in what respect they have to be varied to serve the same purpose. The overriding consideration is to leave out any part of the program which pleases the child only because it is pleasing to the eyes, and which therefore offers no enjoyment to the blind. A good example is setting the table, an activity which is most sought after by sighted children in the nursery school, where they survey the results of their efforts with great pride. In contrast, this is a chore which one should not impose on the blind child, who does not see what he is doing and cannot gauge the effect of what he has done. By this I do not mean to say that blind children cannot be taught to set the table, but only that they cannot be taught to enjoy doing it. An occupation of this kind, immensely boring to them, is maintained only artificially by the teacher substituting continual encouragement and praise for the missing pleasure.

Matters are quite different with regard to filling and emptying, carrying and fetching, especially washing dishes or clothes, i.e., occupations which either activate the child's instinctual pleasure in playing with water or in which success and failure can be felt (not seen) directly, as is the case with spilling or its opposite. Carefully selected, these occupations give the blind the same feeling of successful mastery and pride as they give to the seeing. Of special value are those activities where not only one but two senses and at least one sublimated drive derivative can come into play.

Since blind children usually are permitted to do even less at home than the sighted (to prevent damage to themselves and to the objects), the scope of "adult occupations" allowed to them at school can be correspondingly greater. Even such simple activities as turning light switches, ringing the door bell, putting the record on the gramophone can give the child a sense of mastery. We must not forget that the blind, even more than sighted children, need constant support of their self-esteem; moreover, to do what the sighted children do is a powerful incentive for them.

Where the last two purposes are not promoted by the occupation, we find it much more difficult to engage the children's interest. I mean by this that they are much more willing to master the world around them than to cope with the difficulties they encounter in the common learning tasks. For the later instruction in Braille, a highly developed sense of touch is necessary, and many of the preschool-age games and occupations for the blind are devised with this aim in mind. Separating materials of all kinds according to texture, shape, and size, and sorting shells and marbles require much effort and give comparatively little pleasure.

Intelligent blind children in the phallic phase show the same needs for mechanical and construction toys with which we are familiar in the sighted. The wish to know how things work, what makes things move, and how they are put together is derived from sexual curiosity and interest in the difference between the sexes; these are fed by the phallic sensations which are phase-adequate. With the seeing, curiosity is constantly fed by observation, just as their pride in mastery is constantly transformed into exhibiting their functioning. Even though these incentives are missing in the blind, the blind share many interests with the sighted. When some of our blind boys were at this stage taken into the front seat of a car and allowed to move knobs, switches, levers, pedals, etc., they showed all the excitement and pleasure of the seeing, the same identification with the omnipotent driver; they asked the same questions and acquired a similar level of knowledge as the sighted. They even understood traffic lights through the impact of stop and go.

On the other hand, it should not be forgotten that much of the knowledge acquired by the blind child may be less sound than it appears to be. Carried away by their excitement about car and driver, they inevitably gloss over many details and fiil the gaps with undigested verbal information. In order to turn this "hearsay" knowledge into real knowledge "by acquaintance," they need, as a complement, the opportunity to play freely with large-sized wheels, cars, carts, any kind of moving vehicle which is theirs and which they can take apart and put together again, and which, in this way, can become real to them. Such toys for blind children do not yet exist, but once the need for them is recognized, there is no reason why they should not be constructed.

Building is another activity that plays a large part in both sighted and blind children, but there is a significant difference in the way in which the blind carry out this activity. The building of the seeing child is normally guided by some inner image which the child attempts to reproduce in the outside world. Such an image may be retained from actual experience or may be wholly or in part the product of the child's imagination. The more faithfully this inner image has been reproduced, the more will the builder be pleased with the result of his efforts.

Apart from very exceptional cases, the imagination of the blind does not seem to work on the same level, nor are there any visual images to be retained. Accordingly, with many such children, building may proceed aimlessly and consist essentially of knocking or throwing blocks about rather than be an organized activity. This is remedied in part by the teacher's verbal explanations. The child is taught what is high or low, underneath or on top, etc., and if he is willing to follow instructions, the result can be a pretense of spontaneous building, which in turn is praised and encouraged by the sighted adult. There is no doubt that the child "learns" a good deal about space in this manner and that this is a necessary prop for the orientation of the blind.

What I have in mind is that this can hardly be classed as play in the first instance, since it does not give expression to any of the child's instinctual needs. It is acquired rather than spontaneous, a learning activity rather than a play activity. Once learned, it can be used in the service of play.

On the other hand, building can be a spontaneous activity if we allow it to proceed in the opposite direction, i.e., from the finished product to the idea of it instead of from the imagination to the finished product. I would suggest giving the blind children the opportunity to dismantle familiar objects in their surroundings such as vehicles, trucks, pieces of furniture, etc. This activity is easily understood by them because it gives scope to their instinctual strivings. Once the thing is dismantled, there should be a chance to put it together again; this gratifies constructive wishes of the ego and demands no effort of the imagination because this type of building is guided by the very recent experience of a whole familiar object.

Conclusion

The more interested we become in this subject of toys and activities for the blind, the less easily do we understand why so many children with this handicap spend hours of boredom, inactivity, and waiting; or why so many mothers despair of occupying them and of "keeping them happy." It seems that, so far, we have tapped only a minimum of the energies which lie dormant and ready to be employed pleasurably.

LIBIDINAL PHASES IN THE ANALYTIC TREATMENT OF A PRESCHOOL CHILD

MARIE EDWARDS, M.S.S. (New York)

Ellen was referred to the Child Development Center[1] by her family physician who felt that she could benefit from a therapeutic nursery. Her parents had had difficulties for some time and finally separated about four months before referral when Ellen was just under three years of age.

Diagnostic Study

Presenting Symptoms

Ellen began having nightmares just before the parents' separation. During these, she would cry out, "Don't do it—don't hit me." She feared loud noises such as thunder, a doorbell or parades. After the previous Christmas when her nurse had taken her to a Catholic church, she developed a fear of the crucifix. She called the crucifix "the man with the boo-boo," referring to the wounds in the hands of Jesus, and would ask, "When is he coming? Can he hurt me?" Seemingly in an attempt to master her anxiety, whenever she was in a stationery store, she would seek out the religious cards in order to look at the crucifix.

Ellen was extremely jealous of her younger sister, Jane, who was born when Ellen was twenty months old. At the same time Ellen showed clear signs of guilt in relation to Jane. For example, when Jane was physically hurt or punished by the parents, Ellen would

---

I am indebted to Dr. Augusta Alpert for her invaluable help throughout this child's treatment, with problems of both theory and technique, as well as for the suggestions she contributed to this paper.

[1] The Child Development Center, a division of the Jewish Board of Guardians, is a research and treatment center for prelatency children and their families. The children attend a therapeutic nursery school daily and, when clinically indicated, treatment is available for both children and parents.

begin to cry. When Jane fell down, Ellen sometimes ran away and hid in a corner, and once when Jane's nose began to bleed, Ellen became hysterical.

As is commonly seen in little girls during the phallic phase, Ellen stated openly that she wanted to be a boy. However, the degree of her insistence was unusual. She would urinate standing up, "like daddy," and would try to hold her genitals as if she had a penis. When her father told her, "One advantage of being a girl is to be able to sit on the toilet," she compromised by sitting backward. She often played being a boy by going around with a banana and two oranges in her pants. She sought out older children in her play, apparently enjoying the challenge of trying to keep up with them. She took advantage of younger children by hitting them or taking from them whatever she wanted. She also hit and belittled adults whenever she could get away with it, and was very manipulative especially in relation to her mother.

Developmental History

A retrospective examination of Ellen's libidinal phase development discloses signs that clearly foreshadow later pathology.

Oral Phase: Ellen was bottle-fed and always held. The father had his business in the home and did a large amount of the feeding and nurturing during Ellen's early life. She was described as a slow eater, sometimes taking about one hour to feed: "She just didn't seem to be interested." When Ellen was thirteen months of age, the parents took her to Europe for a three-month vacation. They were often out at night, leaving her in the care of various baby sitters. Both parents stated that the child adapted well, except in eating: "Food was her enemy." Her stomach was almost constantly upset, and she was taken to the hospital many times, but each time the parents were reassured by the doctors that she was all right. She did not lose weight because she drank "tons of milk." She ate only solids that she could hold in her hands; that is, nothing from a plate or spoon. She was weaned suddenly at eighteen months. The mother reported that she had been advised by a physician to wean Ellen in this manner. After the weaning Ellen cried constantly for two days. Before this, she had sucked her thumb occasionally, but after weaning began to do so more and more. When Ellen was twenty months old, two months after the sudden weaning, her younger sister Jane was born. Thus at this crucial time Ellen was exposed to another deprivation.

The events occurring in this phase indicate the basis for oral fixation, namely: the anxiety around separation from the parents while they were in Europe, accented by the many sudden changes in parent substitutes who were total strangers; the constant disturbance of the gastrointestinal tract which was probably related to this tension and anxiety; the sudden weaning which must have been seen by the child as a deliberate deprivation on the part of the mother; and then the birth of Jane who displaced Ellen as the baby in the family, thus increasing Ellen's feeling of being rejected by her mother.

Anal Phase: Toilet training began at about fifteen months of age, after the family's return from Europe. Mrs. E. described herself as being sometimes firm and sometimes permissive. Ellen was partially trained by the time Jane was born, but thereafter she reverted to complete lack of control and refused to cooperate with any of the mother's attempts to train her—until she trained herself overnight at age three. Four months after Jane was born, Ellen began to bite whoever annoyed her in any minor way, an oral-sadistic expression of anger. The parents disagreed on how to handle the biting, the mother feeling that Ellen should be punished, and the father saying that the bitten children would learn to stand up for themselves in time. At age two, Ellen began to bite her fingernails and toenails, evidently turning some of her aggression toward herself. (The toenail biting had stopped two months before the referral.) Also at age two, when Ellen was ignored by strangers, she would seek them out. However, when they approached her first, she would say angrily, "Don't speak to me—don't look at me." At the time of the referral she often said to strangers, "Hello, I'm not being fresh."

In this phase we see, first, the mother's inconsistency in handling the training, an inconsistency that would make self-control more difficult for the child. Secondly, there was disagreement between the parents on handling Ellen's aggression toward others, another inconsistency that would add to the child's confusion. These factors undoubtedly played a part in Ellen's insistence on taking over complete control of her training, and probably contributed, in part, to Ellen's later intense need for independence and control. In addition,

Jane's birth seems to have reactivated the early oral conflicts, so that the biting became an expression of both oral and anal aggression. Even speaking to someone and being spoken to became confused with direct aggression. Her greeting people with "Hello, I'm not being fresh" suggested a possible ego deviation in object relations which needed exploration.

Phallic Phase: Ellen's parents did not believe in privacy in dressing and toileting. One time Ellen asked to touch her father's penis and, although he refused to let her, he continued undressing before her. When Ellen saw her mother undressed, she would tease her mother by pretending she was going to tickle the mother's breasts or genital area. About the time of referral she saw her mother undressed during a menstrual period, and the mother told her she was wearing "a bandage." Ellen had always been fond of long hair and desperately longed for a ponytail. Her favorite play was to have a switch of hair fastened around her head, or put on her father's tie. Once she asked her mother whether, if she pulled on her clitoris, she could make it grow bigger.

Seeing the genitals of both parents and comparing them with her own as an undeveloped little girl may have left her feeling angry and cheated. There was also ample opportunity to compare mother with father, and the mother's explanation that she was "bandaged" must have fed into the child's conception of women being castrated. Although penis envy regularly occurs in the normal development of little girls, the strength of Ellen's need to have both penis and testicles was pathological and overdetermined.

Oedipal Phase: Oedipal features began to emerge around age three. The parents separated when Ellen was at the height of the oedipal period, an event that gave impetus to Ellen's fantasies that there was a possibility of winning the father for herself. The fact that he had been a major nurturing figure in her early infancy served to intensify these wishes by renewing the unresolved preoedipal longings. Ellen was very seductive with her father, and this quite often became mutual. She saw his visits after the parents' separation as his coming to see primarily her. When he came to visit the home, Ellen threw herself on the floor, squirming in a frenzy of delight. Jealousy shown toward the mother also seemed to be, at least partially, on an oedipal level.

Diagnostic Statement

Psychological testing showed Ellen to be of superior intelligence. In her emotional development phallic and oedipal features were evident. At the time of the initial diagnostic conference her problems seemed to be reactive to her life's experiences. However, she was enrolled in the therapeutic nursery school for a period of observation and further diagnostic clarification.

Ellen entered the nursery in January and was in the three-year group until June. She was seen during this period as a child who had an insatiable desire for food, and flitted restlessly from activity to activity. She seemed to find very little satisfaction in play and was almost constantly angry. She remained inconsistent in her relationship to both children and adults. She often rejected overtures of friendship or, after having been friendly, easily rejected the same child. She was extremely ambivalent toward male adults who visited the nursery, vacillating between outright seduction and violent anger. By the end of the school year there was no improvement, and it became clearer that there were internalized neurotic conflicts. Treatment was then recommended, to begin in the fall on a four-times-a-week basis.

Treatment

Both parents were in treatment outside the agency. However, they were also seen by another agency worker who guided them in problems concerning their relationship to Ellen.

In the first few sessions Ellen tried very hard to conform and please, but this was short-lived. A negative transference soon developed, and the therapist became the threatening, depriving phallic mother whom Ellen envied and resented but for whose approval she longed. Throughout this period, the theme was dissatisfaction with what she had and a constant search for something more satisfying. When it was time for her appointment, she wanted to stay in the nursery. When she did not have an appointment, she demanded to know why her "appointment lady" had not come for her. She did not want to go to her treatment sessions and would greet the therapist with: "I don't like you; I don't like your face; I don't like your dress." When she was given some special toy, she was delighted, but the newness soon wore off and she returned to her old complaint, i.e., "What have you done for me lately?" This left her flitting from place to place, each time suffering disappointment and anger that the elusive "something" could not be found or bestowed. At this point, she was usually unable to stay in the therapy room for more than a brief period of time. This was due partly to her restless search and partly to the anxiety generated by anything approaching exposure of her real feelings and wishes. An example of this was most clearly seen in her wish for, and simultaneous fear of, oral regression. At the beginning of treatment, she asked for milk, and a carton was available for her whenever she wanted it. After much doll play with the milk, she began one day to drink some from the bottle, but was so conflicted about this that she ran out of the room immediately afterward. She then was able to stay in the room if I turned my face to the wall and did not look at Ellen, and many other sessions were spent in this manner. She often stored food in her drawer, bringing it with her from the nursery. She adamantly projected her own predatory wishes onto me. For instance, after Ellen had confiscated some jewelry from the nursery school's jewelry box, she stated with conviction that she was sure I would try to take her jewelry away from her if she was not careful. Her reaction to seeing something pretty that belonged to me, such as a paperweight, was a peevish demand, "Where did you get that?" Ellen apparently felt that the phallic mother had deliberately deprived her of something she herself wanted.

During this time Ellen often had difficulties with memory and showed confusion in her object relations. For instance, she could never report correctly where she had been on weekends, and she often confused relatives, calling her grandmother her aunt, etc. It seems that her anger and anxiety were intense enough to flood her ego functioning, especially in object relations.

Ellen demonstrated in the treatment how very much she feared that her angry aggressive feelings would get out of hand. She often drew monsters and an angry dog on the blackboard, and then put them in a cage where they "could not get out and hurt people." She was not quite satisfied with this situation either, however. On one occasion, she erased the dog so that he would no longer be dangerous, but then drew two girls, one being happy because the dog was gone and the other being angry because he had been taken away. Although at times she seemed to flaunt authority and test limits that had been set, she also revealed her struggle to conform and win approval. For example, one day after a silent struggle with herself, she gave up the impulse to take candy from another therapist's office next door. She said repeatedly, "I didn't take it—I didn't take it." At another time, when she accidentally broke a dish, she froze in her tracks and looked up fearfully at the therapist. When I commented that she seemed to think I would be furious with her, Ellen studied my face carefully and said: "I thought you were, but I guess you're not." The transference at this point was marked by ambivalence; she saw me, on the one hand, as someone she at times could trust and love and, on the other hand, as someone she feared and resented.

Soon after therapy began the parents reported a considerable change in Ellen's behavior to adults, including her mother. She became less oppositional and the constant dissatisfaction with everything the mother did for her abated. This was evidently due to Ellen's splitting objects into good and bad, and transferring the negative feelings to the therapist, who did not see the change of behavior in treatment.

The sessions began to shift from predominantly oral to predominantly anal and phallic material. For example, Ellen no longer needed to have milk during the treatment sessions, and the bottle began to serve another purpose. At one point, she took the bottle, filled it with water, and, placing it near her genital area, proceeded to squirt water around the room. She called the water "poison." Thus, she associated the urethral discharge with hostility, an anal concomitant. At another time she insisted that her mother was the one who "had the water squirter." From her associations I surmised that Ellen needed to maintain the fantasy that breast and penis were the same and that in the absence of the father her mother was endowed with the life-sustaining breast-penis.

Ellen increasingly verbalized her hostile, aggressive feelings, and as these were worked through in treatment, her fear of monsters began to diminish. She expressed anal aggression by throwing things around the room, and in her drawings she often added crosses of paper which she then hung on the wall. Her fear of the crucifix, which had begun around age three, clearly became a fear of the consequences of her own aggression. She saw Jesus as a hostile, angry man who was killed because he "said bad things," i.e., as a result of his hostility. "He said bad things and they killed him." At this point she still had to keep her own feelings removed from herself. For example, using her wooden replica of Superman, which she had made in the school workshop and which she had painted a lovely pale blue with silver shoes, she would have what she called a "discuss" between the therapist and Superman about his "murd feelings" and what set these off. She reminded me several times that she was describing Superman and his mother and not herself. Very soon afterward, however, she was able to talk about her own rage when mother did not do what Ellen wanted.

She indicated her feeling that her own aggression had played a part in her parents' separation. For example, in a sequence of doll play she clearly announced that the father was "out of the game"; she then pronounced him dead and declared that he was in heaven where he was discontented because it was so quiet there. He wanted his children to make noise so that he could "come alive again," and although it was fully in their power to do so, they flatly refused to cooperate, tiptoeing around instead. The same theme appeared in relation to the mother, when Ellen saw her anger leading to her mother's death and herself as being punished by God. Her sadness about the separation became more open, with less denial of her feelings about it. For example, on several occasions she drew or played out the family being divided and living in two houses; acknowledging her dislike of the situation, she then merged the two in a wishful solution of being one family in one house.

Oedipal conflicts emerging in this period indicated that Ellen was seeking a solution by identifying with her father. At this time Ellen showed some of the earmarks of the one-parent child that have been described by Neubauer (1960). At home, she became very seductive with her mother and openly played the role of father. As Ellen saw it, this solution had several advantages: (1) she could retain the absent father by becoming the father; (2) she could reassure herself about the fear of loss of the mother by becoming the mother's love object; (3) she could hold on to and play out her own strong phallic wishes. An example of this was shown in treatment when she jumped into a pair of heavy shoes under my desk, announcing that she was a man named Joe and that she was going to marry me. Ellen was still conflicted about settling for this identification, however, and occasionally would declare: "It really is all right if the girl has short, fluffy hair instead of a ponytail." This was an attempt to identify with the therapist.

In this period there was a further change in the transference. Although it was still characterized by ambivalence, there now were more extended periods of strong, positive feelings. One day Ellen revealed her fearful secret that at times she wished "You were my mommy and my mommy my appointment lady." After expressing this wish, she was able to work on her fear of losing one love object if she acknowledged positive feelings for another, a fear that seemed to be determined by several factors: (1) Ellen's experiencing the separation of her parents—the primary love objects—as forcing her to choose between one or the other; (2) a feeling of disloyalty to the mother if Ellen loved another woman as well; (3) a fear that she would not have enough positive feelings left within herself if she gave them to another, thus again necessitating a choice; (4) a fear of being dependent on the therapist, thus depriving her of her own sense of power.

As the positive feelings for me became less threatening to Ellen, her attitude toward treatment changed considerably: she joined me in trying to gain understanding of herself. She left the nursery much more easily for her appointments and began to stay through the whole session. She also took pride in making sure that I would stick to the rules of the game, so to speak. The following incidents illustrate Ellen's attitude toward treatment during this period.

As Ellen once charged up the steps after an appointment, yelling, "I'm the leader," I commented that perhaps one of these days we would get to understand why it was so important for her *always* to be the leader. Ellen reprimanded me, saying that this was not the place to talk about these things; it belonged in the office. I acknowledged that she was right. Ellen mumbled as she walked up the steps that she did hope she would remember to discuss this in the office. A few steps later, she turned and said doubtfully, "I've already forgotten—now what was it I was going to discuss in the office?"

Another time I made an interpretation, adding that this seemed to fit into the puzzle of our understanding her feelings. Ellen declared adamantly, "It does *not* fit!" over and over. However, when I waited her out, she later said wistfully, "It does fit, but I wish it didn't." On another occasion Ellen said that she had a secret that she would not talk about; but then said she could not remember what the secret was. I wondered aloud why she could not remember this secret even if she would not talk about it. Ellen commented thoughtfully, "Because I don't want to want to remember." With this acknowledgment we could then discuss her wish to keep herself from looking at these uncomfortable feelings, thus preparing the way for her to bring them into treatment at a later time.

During this period Ellen continued to have a positive relationship with her mother and was less demanding during the daytime. However, at night, she began to have nightmares, calling out to her mother in fear; but then she was very angry when her mother went in to comfort her. It seemed that during the day she was exercising a great deal of control over her anger, but the conflicts then came out at night. In the nursery school she became an overly good little girl. She not only was careful to do the right thing at the right time, but she tried to see to it that everyone else did the same. She was much more accepting of affection and closeness from the teachers, and the restless flitting from one activity to another almost disappeared.

When Ellen returned to treatment after a summer vacation, her anger at her sister Jane was much more in the open. For several reasons it had become much harder for Ellen to repress it. In the first place, Jane had blossomed into a real charmer capturing everyone's attention, which had previously been given primarily to Ellen. Jane was also beginning to catch up on some of the skills that Ellen had prized as belonging only to herself. To top it off, Jane had invaded Ellen's private territory—the daily nursery school. When the mother now brought Ellen for the therapy appointments, she also brought Jane to the nursery school. Ellen's anger was so intense that, in the beginning, she could not acknowledge it openly; but this too was short-lived. In the treatment sessions she soon found many ingenious ways of getting rid of the bane of her existence. The baby in the doll family who at first was being cared for tenderly would suddenly be left to freeze in the cold. The bottle which at first held milk for the baby would suddenly be filled with poison, a brew of black and green paint which Ellen mixed with witchlike glee for the baby. The small mop in the office became a stake to which the Jane doll was elaborately tied and then used to clean up the floor. By this time, Ellen was able to acknowledge that it made her furious when people commented on how cute Jane was. On a day when Ellen found Jane particularly hard to take, Ellen vehemently said that she would kill Jane. She openly expressed resentment when her mother took Jane to the nursery before bringing Ellen to her appointment; but when this procedure was reversed, Ellen was of course equally dissatisfied. She began to demand equal time, and more, from her mother by running out of the therapy room and back to the elevator after Jane had been delivered to the nursery. This made her mother angry and brought little satisfaction to Ellen.

The self-defeating aspects of handling her anger toward Jane in this way were pointed out again and again. It also became evident that Ellen's need to keep the anger at Jane at fever pitch seemed to serve another purpose; namely, it kept Ellen from looking at her even more intense anger at her mother, which for several reasons had been revived at this time. Ellen's mother was on a hectic schedule: she had a new job, went back to school, and had a new male friend who occupied a great deal of her time.

Suddenly, at school, Ellen became tired to the point of exhaustion. She was diagnosed as having an allergy and, for a brief period, was put on a small dose of Benadryl by the pediatrician. Immediately after this she was found to have two infected teeth which needed to be pulled. It was also discovered that Jane, with whom Ellen shared a room, was waking up during the night and that Ellen was getting too little sleep. When some of the environmental factors were changed, such as the sleeping arrangements, the dynamics of treatment became clearer. At this point in her treatment there was considerable acting out of her anger, which actually was a resistance to working it out in treatment. I commented that I thought Ellen did not want to hear anything I had to say. Ellen replied gaily, "You're right! You fit the piece in the puzzle that time!" When this attitude persisted for several sessions, I commented on several occasions that I believed this staying angry was not working as well for Ellen as she wanted to pretend. One day Ellen arrived for her session and announced, "There will be no more fooling around. This is talk day, and I'm going to talk about my angry feelings."

It was of course not so simple, but in the following weeks Ellen began to express what was building up her cumulative anger at her mother. The dominant factors, in Ellen's words, were: Why did she deprive me of daddy? Why did she make Jane? Why does she have a boyfriend when I can't have one? Above all, why did she make me a girl? This concern in particular became a major theme. Ellen announced that I must never again mention the word "boy" in the office. However, she herself could not suppress playing out her envy of a boy's power. Once in her play, after turning a boy scout into a killer who killed the whole family, she looked at me and announced defiantly: "And I don't care if he did—*I like him!*" She then proceeded to portray herself as a powerhouse of a girl. For a period of time she again became Superman, adding even more powerful characteristics to him. For instance, she described with pride her Superman costume as having "bullets on the chest that will slide down if you need to shoot a bad guy." She acted out this description, starting the "bullets" in the breast area and going down to the genital area, from where she would "shoot."

During this time, everything that she made of paper or painted was adorned with a "decoration." Ellen's identification with Superman was followed by "Space-girl," and finally by "Pooper-girl," when she decided that "Superman can only fly to the moon where it is cold and he would freeze, but Pooper-girl can fly to all the planets unharmed." Ellen spent many of her treatment sessions on an improvised throne so that she could be "higher than anyone." From there, she surveyed her "Pooper-girl" domain in queenlike fashion, or shot off rockets of crayons, carefully giving the count-down and announcing how many hundreds of miles in space she was at that time. Occasionally she invited me to join her in space (i.e., sit beside her on the shelf), but only for very brief moments, and I was soon banished to earth, with Ellen gloating over her superior position. At the end of these sessions, Ellen almost invariably left wearing a paper crown, a paper watch, an improvised bracelet or some other "decoration."

It was during this period that Ellen had to have two teeth pulled, an event that contributed to her anger. Beneath the anger and

"Pooper-girl" scenes, however, were her intense feelings of castration and loss. I had an opportunity to reach these feelings when, immediately after the teeth were pulled, Ellen sadly drew a little deer that had only two legs, the other two were missing. I wondered whether the missing teeth reminded Ellen of other things that she felt were missing. Moreover, when she showed intense jealousy of the boys in her class, I said that it must make her very angry that boys have a "decoration" which she does not have.

She became increasingly able to spell out the advantages of being a "Pooper-girl" in relation to her sister: "I will kill Jane, and then put her in jail, and then put her in a cage with a lion." At another time, she said that she would fight her mother and shoot her because she would then have a gun. She began to be more explicit in describing how she constantly tried to prove her strength in the nursery school. For instance, she told how she pinched and hit Jim, making him cry; but when Jim hit her, she would not cry because "I have steel in my head." She characterized her relationship with Robert by saying, "We are fighting friends." At home, she commented to her mother, "When I hate somebody, that means I love them." This again is a typical example of the ambivalence of anal love. When her anger was compounded by her penis envy, she began to tease or throw things around the room in her sessions.

One day she declared that she "hated" her teacher. Since she was also extremely fond of her teacher, it was fairly easy to get her to explore this. She said thoughtfully, "I hate her when she stops me from doing what I want to do." She also described how she hated Mildred, her maid at home, saying it was "when Mildred won't give me chewing gum when it isn't a gum day." She would then tease Mildred by not letting her dress her and Mildred would get angry. I pointed out to Ellen that her need to be Pooper-girl (omnipotent) all the time surely did get her in a mess. Not wanting to hear this, Ellen resorted to teasing me by calling me "Messy-Chusetts."

During one session, she calmly asked me to bring her something and then, when she looked up and saw how tall I was standing over her, she became annoyed. I commented resignedly: "You know, Ellen, you'll grow up to be a big girl some day, but you have a long time to be a little girl first. This way you sure will have a long time to stay angry." She did not say a word, but suddenly turned and looked at me as though she realized for the first time what I had been saying to her. It was interesting that following that session, when Ellen talked of loving someone, her mother thought Ellen was again confusing loving and hating. However, Ellen explained that she meant just what she said, adding, "love is love and hate is hate." Her tone of voice indicated that of course everyone knew that.

During this period of treatment there were brief accounts of real enjoyment at being a girl. For instance, at Thanksgiving, she looked forward to helping her grandmother cook a turkey. She was proud of an apron that she had made in school. On one occasion, when she was going out to play with Robert, she got all dressed up with obvious delight. She also played out getting married and taking care of her baby. Ellen's wish at that time seemed not to be either a boy or a girl, but to have all of the pleasurable aspects of both.

At this point in treatment Ellen was able to approach some of her anxiety concerning separation and loss of a maternal figure. These fears had of course motivated much of her behavior which earlier in treatment had appeared to be due primarily to anal or oedipal conflicts. As these fears came closer to a preconscious level, she had considerable difficulty in letting her mother leave her at my office and go to her job. There were repeated scenes in which Ellen, screaming and crying, clung to her mother. It was typical of this child that she was able to come to grips with what was happening more easily when I was understanding but did not take her outward behavior too seriously. After one of these scenes I remarked casually, "Ellen, you're acting as if there's no tomorrow," and walked into the office. Ellen followed me and immediately told me about the time she had been in Europe with her parents. She blithely told how she had gone through "the tunnel in London and I saw the Eiffel Tower in Paris." She spoke of this as if it had all been great fun. I reminded her that she also had often been left with strange baby sitters in strange hotels and asked whether this had not been frightening to her. At first she denied any fears; but as we spoke in more detail of how it must have been *then* when she was a baby, she could get closer to acknowledging that she must have felt frightened and helpless. We then talked about how such old fears can be revived. I told her I thought that she must have felt especially helpless because as an infant she had had no way of letting her mother know how she felt, whereas now she was quite able to talk about her feelings without going into a tantrum.

It also became clear that whenever her separation fears were revived, one of Ellen's defenses was to identify with the "rejector." During this period, due to a union-management disagreement, the Center was closed and therapy had to be discontinued for a period of time. When Ellen returned she announced that she was "calling a strike on appointments." She added that she was not striking against going to school (which had also been closed)—to make sure I would know that the rejection was directed at me. Another example of "identification with the rejector" as a defense occurred when the family maid, who was Negro, left to take another job. Ellen belligerently announced that she hated Mildred because she was colored and was glad she was leaving. When I waited, Ellen embarked on a speech about how she liked only "Caucasian people" and in an aside told me to note the big words she was able to use. However, after the session, as we walked down the hall, Ellen saw Mr. W., the maintenance man who also was Negro, whom Ellen fondly admired. As usual she became the seductive little female with him, and then she suddenly remembered what she had said about not liking anyone who was Negro. She looked at me, clamped her hand over her mouth, and burst into a big laugh. Thereafter she was able to talk about the fact that she was really angry at Mildred for leaving her, that it had nothing to do with color, and that she often reacted in the same way to other people when she felt rejected.

As a result of unavoidable factors it was necessary to end treatment at the end of this year and we began to work toward termination. As could be expected, there was a revival of the old conflicts on each libidinal level, but this revival also gave us a chance to work them through once more. Expressing her phallic concerns, for instance, she repeatedly demanded that I make her a paper crown before leaving the session, but she was always dissatisfied, complaining that the "points" were not high enough and did not show enough in the front. When she finally received a big enough crown, she looked at herself and announced with false bravado: "King Elizabeth—long live the King—dead live the Queen."

After a period in which the relationship with the father had improved, she declared: "Daddy hates me, he doesn't like my face."

There was a renewed outburst of teasing her sister during which it became obvious that Jane was the recipient of the anger that Ellen felt for me and her teacher who were deserting her. When I asked her why she had been giving Jane such a hard time, Ellen finally said, "I know so well that I don't want to say." Openly to acknowledge and tolerate sad feelings was very, very hard for Ellen.

During these sessions Ellen often ran to the bathroom at the very time when I thought she was about to cry. This pattern of behavior is suggestive of the correlation between urination and weeping to which Phyllis Greenacre (1945) has pointed. For Ellen, having to go to the bathroom meant no loss of pride, whereas weeping would have made her feel the helpless little girl, a feeling she could not tolerate. Finally, one day she asked me: "Would you laugh if I cried?" We were then able to work on her distortion of the meaning of crying and the feelings of sadness and missing someone. The impending termination provided frequent opportunities to work through her separation anxiety and sense of loss.

Treatment was terminated with the knowledge that Ellen's conflicts on each of the libidinal levels had not been completely resolved. However, progress had been made to the extent that it enabled growth in several important areas. As the need for constant oral gratification diminished, she was able to concentrate on an activity for an extended period of time and derive real satisfaction from these activities. She could now remember and report accurately on events and people in her life. This improved ego functioning seemed to be the result of having worked through some of the aggression and underlying anxiety. As a further consequence, there was considerable improvement in her learning ability. She no longer had nightmares, nor was she phobic. Perhaps the most striking improvement came in her object relations. Despite periods of envy and discontent with both the teacher and me, Ellen's relationship to us was basically trusting. Both parents reported that they enjoyed her more because she was more reasonable; moreover, they fortunately appreciated her new ability to tell them what she really felt.

On the other hand, much work remains to be done. Ellen's intense sibling rivalry with Jane is by no means settled. Her need to be either the biggest or the best still drives her in some instances to battle with her peers or to stand in self-righteous judgment over them. The anxiety related to her parents' separation and her fear of separation from her mother still emerge in different forms from time to time. One might anticipate that when she reaches adolescence, there may be a revival of her identity conflict as well as other aspects of the unresolved oedipal conflicts, and that further working through of these conflicts at that time might be indicated.

BIBLIOGRAPHY

Greenacre, P. (1945), Urination and Weeping. *Amer. J. Orthopsychiat.*, 15:81-88.

Neubauer, P. B. (1960), The One-Parent Child and His Oedipal Development. *This Annual,* 15:286-309.

ASSESSMENT OF EARLY INFANCY

Problems and Considerations

W. ERNEST FREUD (London)

History of the Project

The various departments and research projects of the Hampstead Child-Therapy Clinic have for some time been working with the diagnostic Profile developed by Anna Freud (1962) for the assessment of childhood disturbances. This original Profile has been expanded (A. Freud, 1963) and adapted for use with adolescents (Laufer, 1965) and adults (A. Freud, H. Nagera, and W. E. Freud, 1965).

It was therefore natural to venture into assessment of early infancy. My own interest in this was greatly enhanced last year when a five-and-a-half-year-old girl was referred for diagnostic assessment. This child had been known by our Well-Baby Clinic staff almost since birth, had then graduated to our toddler group and from there to our nursery school. It was most rewarding to make a Profile on the basis of these earlier observations contained in our records. For once, it was possible to perceive the whole range of development in detail. I was struck by features which had been evident from very early in life (e.g., the child's tension, on which all observers had commented) and by later features which seemed closely connected with those earlier ones (e.g., her constant state of anxiety). It was tempting to

This paper, presented in June, 1967, is part of a study, entitled "Assessment of Pathology in Childhood," which is financed by the National Institute of Mental Health, Bethesda, Maryland (N.I.M.H. Grant M-5683-0405). The Study is conducted at the Hampstead Child-Therapy Clinic, London, where Mr. Freud is a research psychoanalyst.

The views expressed in this paper are not necessarily those of the members of the Well-Baby Research Group of the Hampstead Child-Therapy Clinic. The members of this group are: Dorothy Burlingham, Liselotte Frankl, Anna Freud, Irene Freud, W. Ernest Freud, E. Model, Humberto Nagera, Marjorie Sprince, and the Well-Baby Clinic's pediatrician, Josefine Stross. I am greatly indebted to them for their enthusiastic support and interchange of ideas; without them the project could not have been launched.

regard one as the forerunner of the other and to establish causal links.[1]

The next step was to think of a Profile specifically designed for earliest infancy—a Baby Profile. I received further encouragement for such a project from Marianne Kris, who thought that a Baby Profile might be ideally suited to evaluate retrospectively the very early data obtained in longitudinal studies. For if it were possible to construct a Baby Profile on the same metapsychological principles as the existing Profiles, we would have a comparable instrument with which to assess psychological phenomena as they develop from their origins. We could trace them forward through the later vicissitudes and note their appearance, often in disguised forms, in sometimes unexpected places. Furthermore, we could trace backward apparently similar manifestations (e.g., "obsessionallike symptoms") to their dissimilar sources.

In early January, 1967, we formed the Well-Baby Research group to tackle this project. In this paper I want to describe some of our preliminary considerations.

The first question that needed to be solved was the choice of an infant suitable for a pilot study. We agreed that we wanted a healthy baby with a fairly well-adjusted mother, rather than a disturbed one. Moreover, we wanted a relatively "uncontaminated" mother who had no previous experience with children. Therefore, the baby had to be a firstborn. Our choice fell on a little boy, Danny, who had been known to the Well-Baby Clinic since the age of six weeks and whose home had, in connection with another project, been visited about once a week since he was nearly four months old.

After having chosen Danny, we found that through their excellence the Well-Baby Clinic reports and the home observations provided more than enough material for generations of researchers. In order to attempt a trial Profile I had to limit myself to reading the file only up to the time Danny was six months old. This had the added advantage of limiting discussion, so that it need not range along comparisons of forerunners of early manifestations with later ones—or so we thought.

Before going any further, let me say something about our Well-

[1] Sally Provence's paper (1966) is an example of a most impressive achievement in this direction.

Baby Clinic. We offer a medical service with psychological advice, where necessary. We explain to mothers that the Baby Clinic is part of the larger research clinic and that we are collecting data on the development of normal children. The service is free, but in order for the data to be useful we must see the children fairly regularly.

Most of our mothers, like Danny's, come on the recommendation of other mothers. When they are inexperienced, they might come weekly or fortnightly with the newborn baby and thereafter once a month or according to their needs. Parents can also telephone for advice or ask for an appointment when they are worried about a child.

While the orientation and training of our Well-Baby Clinic staff are psychoanalytic, we use no other formal and predetermined principles in the collection and evaluation of data. We merely keep our clinical impressions and the medical data on one and the same mother and child together in one and the same file. I was surprised to see that in fact the attitude of our Well-Baby Clinic is best characterized by Ernst Kris's description of the setup in Yale:

> [Here, as there,] Contact with the parents is kept spontaneous, i.e., a minimum of questions is asked. The topics of discussion are largely determined by their urgency to the parent. We start, therefore, with a limited set of data on the parent and watch the growth of these data over time. Hence presence or absence of data at any given time become significant in themselves. The contact with the parents is viewed as a dynamic and unfolding experience.
>
> The pediatrician's role with the family is essentially that of the authority on child care, and no advice or instruction is withheld which the doctor feels would enhance the health of the child and the parent-child relationship. That this advice is modified in accordance with the individual situation goes without saying. The pediatrician advises not in terms of what is theoretically optimal in child care, but in terms of what seems best for this mother and her child. It should be added that the physician-family relationship remains child centered. Perhaps the only important variation of the pediatrician's role in this study from that of the pediatrician in private practice is in the enlargement of his responsibilities for observation of the child's environment, and the efforts to distinguish as clearly as possible between subjective and objective data [Coleman, Kris, and Provence, 1953, p. 29].

Orientation and Approach

Just as any respectable psychoanalytic piece of work should do justice to the five metapsychological points of view (Rapaport and Gill, 1959), so any Profile design worth its salt should reflect the following five orientations:

1. It should be on all fours with *metapsychology* itself.

2. It should take account of *normal as well as abnormal* development (Anna Freud, 1965).

3. It should take account of the *literature*. In writing about the well-baby Profile I felt especially close to its major spiritual godparents: Ernst and Marianne Kris and their co-workers of the Yale Child Study Center, and D. W. Winnicott, with his *Ordinary Devoted Mother and Her Baby* (1949).[2]

4. *It should link up with existing metapsychological Profiles* (A. Freud, 1962; Laufer, 1965; A. Freud et al., 1965). The importance for longitudinal studies needs no comment.

Looking at it in a little more detail: the first five sections of the existing Profiles needed to be spread out. For this reason the hope that the sections of the Baby Profile would dovetail one by one with the corresponding sections in the other Profiles had to be abandoned. On the other hand, there are many similarities: e.g., we expect the baby to be full of *Drives*. The *Ego* section has to allow for emerging structures. *Superego* development seems a long way off; it will nevertheless merit very close scrutiny in view of Nagera's formulation (1966, p. 50f.). He holds the view that very early processes of identification imply the presence of introjects active as superego precursors and says that "some of the early introjections include not only a given prohibition or command but also the capacity to enforce them, that is, the necessary authority to see them through."

We hope to learn a lot about prototypes, precursors, antecedents, and forerunners in general, and especially about those concerning *object relations* and *defense mechanisms*.

[2] See Coleman et al. (1953), E. Kris (1950), M. Kris (1957), Winnicott (1960). Other sources of constant inspiration have been the formulations of Heinz Hartmann (1950), Hartmann and E. Kris (1945), Hartmann, E. Kris, and Loewenstein (1946), and the work of René A. Spitz (1951, 1959, 1964, 1965), Benjamin (1959, 1961), Escalona and Heider (1959), Brody (1956).

There is no reason either why we should not work out an entirely new set of *Lines of Development* which would take account of the very early formation of the personality, though it is also possible that we may need several sets. *Fixation points* will be linked with the idea of very early fixation potentials that are created through the mother's handling. *Conflicts* appear to be initially purely external for the baby, but here too we are ready to revise opinions.

In general, complete and unconventional freedom to look at every concept—even those that appear to be well established—with a doubtful and critical eye will remain the keystone of this promising new venture.

5. The Profile must be based on our own *clinical observations.* This goes without saying and yet deserves special mention because we have found from experience that the quality of a Profile, as well as the quality of its sections, depends upon the extent to which one works from the clinical material to the Profile, and not the other way around (Nagera, 1963).[3]

The five points of orientation mentioned above determine our *method of procedure;* that is to say, when we deal with any phenomenon or observation, we use them all the time without necessarily being aware of it. The Well-Baby Research Group discussions testify to this. On paper it looks a little forced when it is pointed out, but let me illustrate it from an occasion when the following observation, made on the fifth home visit, was discussed:

Danny, nearly five months old, was playing with his favorite toy (a rubber-suction object with three balls), sucking the rubber-suction pad and laughing happily. After a while he started to whimper and the mother lifted him to show the visitor his latest development: "He jumps in a standing position, pushing his body up and down by bending his legs; he loves this movement and does it repeatedly both against his mother and against the back of the couch." Mrs. Sprince added in brackets: "Is this a masturbatory movement—the obvious pleasure seemed greater than just from motility discharge?" Whenever he got at all whiny he had only to be lifted to this position to change his mood.
(Comment: approach 5—*clinical observation.*)

Like most discussions on rhythmic movement, this one was lively, enjoyable, and inconclusive. It ran along the following lines: the

[3] In another communication (1967) I have referred to this as "Nagera's dictum."

activity could be viewed either as phase-adequate or as regressive (approach 1—*metapsychological*). If it was predominantly in the service of muscular pleasure, the rhythm would reflect exercise necessary for normal development; if the pleasure was mainly in the rhythm and if the activity had a compulsive aspect, it might be taken to lean more toward abnormal development (approach 2—*normal and abnormal* development). Somewhere at the back of our minds were memories of weighty panel discussions on masturbation from which one might have quoted criteria for deciding the issue (approach 3—taking account of the *literature*), but no such specific attempt was made in the midst of the discussion. If the observation was more representative of normal development, it could remain in the Profile section called "Aggression—Enjoyment of Movement." If it was a predominantly autoerotic pleasure, it would be banned and relegated to some other section (approach 4—*link up with existing Profiles*).

Apart from the changing shift of emphasis from one approach to another, there is in addition a frequent switch of viewpoint, in that at one moment we may concentrate on evaluating (i) the *mother,* at the next moment (ii) the *baby;* or we may look (iii) at their *mutual interaction;* provided always that we are not just then (iv) focusing on any one of the *general problems of assessment* itself that continually come up. It can readily be seen how open-ended this project is.

Procedure

In attempting to design a new Baby Profile I started with existing relevant knowledge, in our case, the metapsychological assessment Profile used for children. Since early infancy obviously differs from later childhood, the various sections of the child Profile are not equally applicable and useful. However, they do provide a general framework which can then be elaborated or revised. This, as one would expect, proved easiest with the initial Profile sections, which deal mainly with environmental aspects.

The Baby Profile does not yet exist, but I can present some samples from the provisional draft of the first few sections, using the example of Danny B. as an illustration.

I. Reason and Circumstances for Approaching Well-Baby Clinic

Mrs. B. knew the mother of a child who attends the Well-Baby Clinic very regularly. This mother suggested to Mrs. B. that she should bring her baby to us. They were first seen by Dr. Stross when Danny was six weeks old.

II. Description of Parents or Parent Substitutes

The *mother* is in her middle twenties, the only child of a middle-class Jewish family who emigrated from the Continent in 1938/39. When she was born during the war, her father had a mental breakdown and has been hospitalized since. Her mother has had to work throughout Mrs. B.'s childhood.

Here I would like to digress. The fact of the maternal father's mental illness did not emerge until nearly three months after we first knew the mother and even then it emerged inaccurately (in terms of her father's breakdown having occurred a year after Mrs. B.'s birth). Whereas the inaccuracy need not concern us too much in this particular case, the knowledge of the maternal father's illness did, of course, affect our assessment and from then on we were prepared to find somewhere in the background of the mother's feelings an anxiety about the possibility that her father's illness might affect the child. When Danny was five and a half months old the Well-Baby Clinic staff observed that "the mother seems content, but somehow not to have fully invested this child and one wonders to what extent her fears about mental illness influence her handling."

Many other determinants may, of course, also have gone into this absence of full investment.

"We would describe Mrs. B. as of good average intelligence with considerable artistic gifts. She has high standards for herself within the home; she appears to be a rather superficial, thoughtless person, she is sociable and enjoys company. In her care of Danny in the first six months, most striking were her inexperience, lack of imagination, a tendency to assume that the baby would fit in with her life, and some boredom in being at home with the child." It was also thought that due to the circumstances of her father's absence, she had probably received inadequate mothering, which may account for her attitude to Danny.

Mrs. Sprince, on her first home visit (when Danny was nearly four months old), had this to say: "I had the impression of a very anxious, immature person, who feared being judged incompetent, who hoped for a motherly ally, but above all at that moment, who wanted me to be interested in her problems and not in the child. Almost immediately she introduced the main problem: did I know anyone who could baby-sit, so that she could take a job?" But this is another matter, and I shall come back to it.

The *father,* of West Indian descent (i.e., colored), is fourteen years older than the mother. He has been in England since his teens, has held several unskilled jobs, and now works as a messenger for a large firm. Mrs. B. describes him as intelligent, spontaneous, well liked by everyone, and very fond of children. He thinks Danny is marvelous. We have no information about his family.

III. Description of the Infant

This section fills pages in the actual Profile, because I wanted to give as many details as possible. For the present purposes, I have chosen the impression the Well-Baby Clinic staff had on the occasion of his first visit, at age *six weeks:*

Danny smiled and was relaxed and contented for most of the examination. He cried after a time, but was quiet when his position was changed. Mother says he began to smile at her at about three weeks. His birth weight was 7 lbs. 14 ozs., and he is "more or less" on demand feeding and has been from the beginning (five to six feedings daily). He now takes the breast well and mother had no complaints or anxieties about the feeding.

His mixed parentage showed only by the color of his hands and the darkness of his scrotum. (When he was seen at age three months the Well-Baby Clinic noted that his skin was losing the pinkness of the newborn and was becoming coffee-colored.)

We usually ascribe special importance to first impressions (Frankl, 1958). When Mrs. Sprince first visited the home (when Danny was *nearly four months* old), she found him lying on his tummy in the pram, gurgling and looking around him intelligently. For his age he seemed particularly strong and alert.

He was lying on his stomach facing the door which led to a garden patch outside, so that when Mrs. B. asked me to sit down behind the pram he had to crane his neck and turn backward to see us. He did this all the time, raising himself on his hands from within the depth so that his head came up and down like a jack-in-the-box. He looked mainly at me because my chair was slightly to the left-hand side, whereas his mother sat right behind him. Right through our initial conversation, which lasted for the first thirty minutes, she made no move toward him, except occasionally to tell him to give up and go to sleep. She said that she would have put him outside, but she thought it might rain.

The observation tells us as much about the mother as about the child. We form an impression about the child's ego, and we wonder whether he could possibly already distinguish between what is outside him and what is within.[4]

On the occasion of that first home visit of the observer the mother immediately introduced her main problem: they wanted a home of their own. For this she must earn. Before starting a job she would have to find someone to care for the child. "People say that it's bad for the child if you go out to work."

She rushes to Spock for everything; she's been getting terribly thin and tired, so she started to wean Danny—he's taken the bottle well, but didn't sleep last night—usually he sleeps right through.

Mrs. B. then asked whether Mrs. Sprince really believed that children of under a year notice things and are affected by things. She thought mothers should go out to work while the children were under two and didn't notice—after two they needed their mother—surely what happens in the first year doesn't matter that much?

It was not easy to decide whether the mother began weaning from the breast (at four months three days) because she wanted to go out to work or whether, as she said, it was because she was getting terribly thin and tired. I found it most interesting that, under the pressure of her anxiety, she developed a theory to support her rationalizations: that children under a year "don't notice things and are not affected by them," that what happens in the first year doesn't matter much, and that it is not until after two that they need their mothers.

[4] This was just one of the many other topics that beckoned to us en route and to which we hope to return at a later date (Hoffer, 1952).

IV. Family Background (Past and Present)

Their present accommodation is a furnished flat consisting of living room, bedroom, and bathroom, at 9 guineas a week. It was neat and tidy. At the father's insistence Danny sleeps in the bedroom with the parents. (This section should really contain more detailed information about the parents and their background.)

What may merit comment is first the mixed marriage, which sheds light on the kind of resolution of the mother's oedipus complex and incest taboo (Lehrman, 1967), and secondly the age difference between the parents.

It is interesting that so far the mother has shown no overt reaction to the infant's color. Nor does she seem to regard the complex setup of a mixed marriage as different from any other. (We would have expected reactions to both.)

V. Before Birth—Mother

This section is subdivided into "Physical" and "Psychological." The *Physical* section deals with conception and pregnancy. The *Psychological* section covers: the mother's anxieties, her expectations (e.g., of the kind of labor she would have), and what aspirations she has for a child (whether she wants a boy or a girl and what they should be when they grow up, from handyman to prime minister; from typist to ballerina, or housewife with a large family of children).

In our case, the mother, on her first visit to the Well-Baby Clinic, mentioned the following:

She explained that they married when she was two months pregnant. She said this very easily, as if it had not caused great family upheaval or distress.

When Mrs. Sprince made her first home visit the mother told her that from the beginning she had not wanted to give up work at all; she was never the sort of girl who wanted children—most girls admire babies in the street—she did not. When he came, of course she loved him, but she does not think she wants more because of the pain and "your life is so different."

Three weeks later, on the occasion of the fourth home visit, the mother told Mrs. Sprince that a year ago this time he was not even thought of—she described how she had two "ghost periods" so that she did not realize she was pregnant until three months and then she did everything possible to get rid of the child—now, of course, she is glad she has him, but she would not want another. The husband wanted her to have the child from the beginning, but she wanted a home before they married (which they acquired four months before he was due).

For the purpose of assessment we simultaneously look at these three different statements made on three different occasions. Our first reaction might be that here is a mother whose negative attitude to conception and having children is significant in that it will color her whole outlook to Danny and his future development. Our second reaction might be: "Is it not possible that her attitude is qualitatively a different one once the child is born, and especially when it is a boy?" Such considerations point up the need for cautiousness. On the other hand, we realize that we have had a glimpse of one of the mother's areas of conflict. We would, I think, suspect that somehow her original attitude to children would somewhere affect the handling of the child. And once such an idea has been formed, it is very difficult to dismiss it entirely.

VI. History of Birth (physical and emotional)—The Newborn Period up to Six Weeks (pediatrician's impression)

Details of labor and birth: The mother told the pediatrician on her first visit to the clinic that it had been an easy birth, "no stitches."

As an aside I would say that in this area we usually find that the most important details are not known and impossible to get, even from the maternity hospital. Yet, this is an area that offers immense possibilities for lavishly endowed research projects to initiate and collect observations on some factors which are often crucial to the whole of the infant's later development.[5]

In this section we also look at such items as the *separation of the baby from the mother after delivery* (whether he is brought to her only for feedings or whether there is a rooming-in arrangement); the separation of mothers from their premature babies; maternity hospital visiting facilities; the mother's affective state (e.g., postpuerperal depression); the support she gets from the *father.*

[5] See, e.g., the pilot studies by Bibring (1959) and Bibring et al. (1961).

It seems to us that the father has not been accorded the place he deserves since the days when it was fashionable to mention couvade (the practice in some primitive societies of the father retiring to bed during the time the mother has the child) (Reik, 1919) and when Ruth Mack Brunswick (1940) described the little boy's wish for a baby. Directly and indirectly he complements (sometimes negatively) the mother's handling of the child.[6] We are therefore interested in the differences in fathers: from the father who dissociates himself physically or emotionally on learning that the mother has become pregnant (to the extent of deserting her or instituting a divorce) to the father who eagerly attends all prenatal lectures with the mother in the maternity hospital and is even prepared to substitute for her by attending the lecture on his own if she is unable to go.

We all know fathers who tend to become a second mother to the baby and other fathers who become more of a second baby to the mother, adding to the strain on her. In between there are fathers who remain relatively neutral, neither burdening the mother nor helping her very much.

We would like to know what the father did during the mother's stay in the hospital—a period in which his behavior can range from sprucing up the home to rushing into an affair with another woman.

When it comes to caring for the child, does the father help the mother, does he take over the child's care completely, or does he have no part in it; e.g., does *he* get up in the night and walk up and down with the baby over his shoulder until the infant falls asleep, or does he keep strictly to his bed on such occasions? Does he play with the baby in the daytime, does he pram him, is he proud of him, or is he ashamed? There are great variations and each tells us something about the marital relationship and about an important part of the baby's environment.

In the final Baby Profile we shall list many other factors which, in this preliminary paper, must be omitted.[7]

[6] I focus here only on the father's role as it directly bears on the mother's handling of the child. It is of course obvious that the relationship which the parents have to each other is of tremendous importance and also has an impact on the child.

[7] Although the Well-Baby Research Group has met only five times since its inception, so many interesting issues have arisen in our discussions that only a limited number of them can be included here.

VII. Present Environmental Circumstances and Management[8]

It was against the background of formulations by Nagera (1964, p. 248ff.) and Spitz (1965, p. 42) that it seemed legitimate to explore the quality of mothering in vital areas of the infant's functioning. (We are leaving aside for the moment which areas will remain after a search for the least number of mutually independent necessary and sufficient assumptions.)

1. Auxiliary Ego—Assessment of the Mother's Manifest Responses to the Baby

My first approach resulted in the scheme for assessment that is presented in the diagram entitled *Auxiliary Ego.* As regards the *efficiency* of the infant's auxiliary ego, my approach was to assess how much the mother can and does help the baby to maintain pleasure-unpleasure equilibrium, in the vital areas of sleep, feeding (intake, processing, output), cleanliness, comfort, motility.

AUXILIARY EGO

Diagram illustrating the range of possibilities at the disposal of the Auxiliary Ego for influencing pleasure-unpleasure equilibrium in the infant.

UNPLEASURE ⟵ ⟶ PLEASURE

creating	maintaining	removing	Passively tolerating either. (Mother incapacitated, e.g., by illness, withdrawal or depression.)	maintaining and supporting (following the infant's need)	actively fostering and eliciting (by stimulation and encouragement)

Unpleasure Pleasure

This diagram is not meant to be a rating scale, nor does the space allocated to the various sections reflect their relative importance.

[8] For lively descriptions of such situations see Joyce Robertson (1962, 1965).

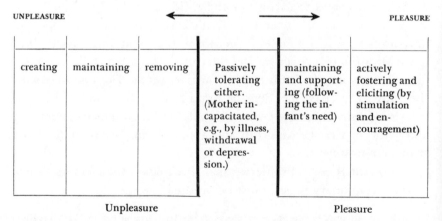

Unpleasure

The spectrum ranges (center to left) from *removing* of unpleasure (e.g., removal of tension, later leading to binding of free-floating anxiety by simple ministrations)—to *maintaining* unpleasure (e.g., through misinterpreting the baby's needs, or the baby's sounds and signals)—to *creating* unpleasure and pain (e.g., through applying age-inadequate frustrations, untimely or unsmooth weaning; through being out of tune or lacking "empathy"; through ignorance or inexperience; through her own pathology such as sadomasochistic involvement).

Pleasure

At the other end of the spectrum (center to right) one would find: *maintaining* pleasure—*creating* pleasure (actively fostering and eliciting pleasure by stimulation and encouragement; e.g., how the mother positions herself in relation to the child, how she holds him, what kind of general contact she has with him, what kind of body, skin, sound, and speech contact; what is the quality of her presence or absence, her smiling contact, her furthering of his motility, her provision of age-adequate stimulation). Going to extremes, *overstimulation* leads right back to the other end of the spectrum, i.e., creating unpleasure.

In the middle range (center) the mother *passively tolerates either* pleasure or unpleasure in the child when she is incapacitated, e.g., by illness, withdrawal, depression.

In the case of Danny's mother, something could be said about many of the above-mentioned aspects.

In the area of *feeding* the mother seemed to function efficiently ("more or less on demand") and she had no complaints or anxieties about it (when Danny was six weeks old).

Similarly, the mother scored above average in the areas of *cleanliness, comfort,* and (as Mrs. Sprince stressed) especially in furthering the child's *motility*.

Looking at the spectrum of the *pleasure-unpleasure* series, there is evidence (though from later reports) that the mother *maintains unpleasure* through misinterpreting the baby's sounds and therefore some of his needs. As regards *creating unpleasure,* it seemed to me that the weaning had not been uninfluenced by the mother's intention to become more independent, i.e., to take up work and leave Danny in the care of another woman.

At the far end of the spectrum, she failed in maintaining pleasure by *positioning* herself in such a way that the baby could see *neither* her *nor* the visitor (first home visit when Danny was nearly four months old). At the same time this very fact highlighted the outgoing, progressive tendencies in the baby, who raised himself, craned his neck, and turned backward for quite some time. On this occasion the mother scored poorly on the point of *general contact with the child* (throughout the initial thirty-minute conversation she made no move toward Danny—in fact, she sat right behind him—except occasionally to tell him to give up and go to sleep). The *sound contact* has already been commented upon. In general, she was thought to be adequate in stimulating the child with words or songs. In her intention to go out to work she would fail in maintaining age-adequate pleasure.

Smiling contact with the infant seemed very adequate (see Well-Baby Clinic report at the age of three months: "Smiles when one leans over him; the smile was quick and he seemed thoroughly delighted with the attention he got here").

As to *motility,* this requires a comment: Dr. Stross rightly drew attention to the fact that the mother restricts Danny's hands during feeding. (She restricts movement only when it might lead to messiness.) It was also felt that the mother cannot tolerate Danny's independent motility, though this needs further qualification. What was obvious was the child's pleasure in movement.

Wherever aspects of the mother's makeup were found wanting and where she failed him, Danny seemed to respond with positively oriented moves. He has an excellent *ego* and *functions* very efficiently (perception, memory, voluntary movement). He sustains interest in an object for a very long time. For a child of four months he seemed particularly strong and alert (first home visit).

Incidentally, on our prognostic pointers (*General Characteristics* in A. Freud's Profile [1962]) he scores very high: (1) He shows a high *frustration tolerance.* (2) Little free-floating *anxiety* has been noted so far (the Well-Baby Clinic reports repeatedly mention his relaxed and contented state, certainly up to three months). (3) *"Sublimation* potential" seems high—he is very ready to accept substitute gratifications. (4) He chooses *progressive* moves in situations where he might be expected to show regressive tendencies (e.g., in response to being left with the baby sitter).

What complicates prognostic assessments is that some of the relatively stable features in a mother may nevertheless be subjected to change, apart from those variations that occur in response to the child's ongoing development (Coleman, Kris, and Provence, 1953). For instance, drastic and traumatic life experiences, such as the death of a grandparent, change of residence to another continent, war, emigration, or other "psychic traumatization through social catastrophe" may trigger off changes in mothering.

Such unpredictable influences on the mother are more than matched by the unpredictability of development in the child. One crucial but often neglected factor that should make us cautious is: development need not necessarily be straightforward, but can just as well take place in somewhat "unexpected" directions. One and the same stimulus (e.g., separation from the mother) may become a trauma, causing regression, or it may become a spur to further development. The two trends can sometimes also be observed in the same child concurrently, e.g., when there is ego development alongside libidinal regression. Another possibility is that the child may develop an unduly strong attitude of self-mothering (we have seen several such children for diagnostic assessment).

In our group, opinions about the effect of the separation on Danny were divided.

[The mother had told Mrs. Sprince at the third visit (when Danny was four months nine days) that she had found] a baby sitter —a working-class woman, mum of four, registered foster parent, nuts on children, clean but poor. Mrs. B. will let Danny go for half a day tomorrow and half a day on Wednesday to see how it works. She does believe that children should get used to other people, but she would like to know more about the person. She plans to take him there before the feeding and let her get on with it. Then she became very anxious: Do I think he will eat? Do children ever refuse their food if a stranger feeds them? She thinks he will eat if he is hungry; could he starve? At this point he had two thirds finished his bottle and she lifted him to burp him, sitting him up and rubbing him. She passed him to me while she fetched his solid food and he began to cry. She said she could not understand this—he had never minded other people until recently. He did this when her mother lifted him and her mother had said he was ill.

[At her next visit (when Danny was four months nineteen days) Mrs. Sprince learned how, according to the mother, the baby sitting had worked out:] She had taken him three times the previous week and when she fetched him, he had been surrounded by three toddlers (two-year-olds) and he was laughing and giggling. Mrs. B. repeated how much Danny loves children; she thinks he has become more sociable since the three visits. There, and on Sunday when her mother came, he did not cry (which he usually does when Mrs. B.'s mother visits). He ate happily there too.

This was all the more surprising in view of the mother's concern about it the previous week. The Well-Baby Clinic record at the visit when Danny was four months four days old contained the statement: "All these things reinforce the mother's difficulties in handling Danny, which at present do not show in any gross way, but instead appear, e.g., in her rather inept way of comforting him. When he fusses and whimpers and struggles on her lap, she will change his position and say, 'Oh, shut up!' This is not said with any great aggression but with impatience. She does not really observe the baby and is not really in tune with his feelings and needs."

Wherever we found that Danny chose the alternative of *un*expected development—in this instance apparently thriving in response to being boarded out—we tended to put it down to innate endowment, having previously seen similar positive reactions in other children of colored descent. On the other hand, there remained misgivings. Solnit and Marianne Kris (1967) quote Ernst Kris's statement: "the relative importance of a current experience for the child may become clear only in the future, when prospective and retrospective data can be combined" (p. 218).

2. AUXILIARY EGO—ASSESSMENT OF THE MOTHER'S LATENT ATTITUDES

After a while the first scheme seemed no longer satisfactory to me and I proceeded from the surface to the depths. This involved a metapsychological appraisal of the mother. It is probably no coincidence that, in order to arrive at a Profile for the baby, we first had to go into the opposite direction, via the Profile of the adult. The simplest explanation of this apparent paradox would seem to be that in the assessment of the adult personality we can draw on a wealth of metapsychological formulations, whereas in evaluating the small infant we may have to develop formulations as we go along.

Be that as it may, it seemed easy enough to spot certain features in the mother which could not fail to affect her handling of the child.[9]

A *working hypothesis* now suggested itself which could easily be tested by comparing later events with earlier ones. It states:

Ideally, mothering should occur solely according to the actual needs of the child (e.g., a cry for hunger leading to provision of food). It is the mother's task to observe and assess the child's signals correctly and to carry out her ministrations with appropriate, i.e., optimal cathexis.

When, however, the mother's objective observation and assessment of the child are interfered with by contributions from her inner psychic reality, it is more than likely, first, that undue delay occurs from the time the infant communicates a need to the time it is met; and, secondly, that ministrations will no longer be applied solely according to the child's needs.

In other words, the infant is then handled with inappropriate cathexis (undercathexis, or overcathexis, or cathexis of a different quality). Where such "inappropriate" ministrations by the mother impinge on a particular vital area in the child (e.g., feeding, sleep, motility) mothering goes beyond the child's need or falls short of it. A special kind of cathexis is then created in that vital area of the child. It need be no more than something like a greater readiness or sensitivity or potential for vulnerability, but it is thought that such

[9] The following formulation by Marianne Kris (1957) is pertinent: "Knowing that neurotic behavior is repetitive and relatively immune to outside events, we tend to select as having predictive value those characteristics of the mother's personality which reflect the greatest inflexibility. We assume that her behavior with the child is then dominated by her own inner conflicts which make her less aware of the child's needs and therefore less responsive to clues from the child—in other words, that she will, with her pathology, disturb the natural rhythm of the child's evolving endowment and narrow its potentialities" (p. 186). See also Augusta Bonnard's formulation: The mother's psychic reality is the external reality of the child.

specially sensitized areas may become potentially particularly fertile grounds for later fixations.[10]

We now want to know which aspects of the mother's personality are likely to lend themselves to interference with the child's needs or demands. The factors that were thought likely to contribute their share are, in ascending order of importance, the following: defenses, fixation points, unresolved conflicts, anxieties.

Observations from the case material will serve to illustrate what is meant. It can be seen how in one vital area—*feeding*—each of the four aspects of the mother's personality makes its contribution.

Age four months two days (second home visit)

Mrs. B. has fed Danny on solids since he was five weeks; he likes fruit, but is less interested in other foods. The mother explained that he must have the bottle first, but that his attitude to the bottle is different from that to the breast—*bottle feeding is much quicker*—he used to stop and laugh or look round every few minutes on the breast. [Mrs. Sprince continues:] Mrs. B. tells me that he resists for the first few spoons and then *puts his head back* and complies. To avoid his messing, she puts his arm under her armpit and holds the other arm. In fact, he becomes somewhat rigid, while she shovels in one spoon after the other so that he barely has time to swallow. I found this most difficult to watch and felt like saying: "Slow down."

Comment: The whole activity takes place under the sway of the *conflict* about wanting to go out to work, which in turn required early weaning. The emphasis on speed also seems to be connected with this. We see how the mother's conflicts around messing (anal) necessitate restriction of Danny's arm movements. The reaction formation (*defense*) points to an *anal fixation* point.

The two following examples from a week later show the *anxiety* behind the feeding. Apparently Mrs. B. is concerned that Danny learn to eat reliably so that she need not worry about his getting enough food from the baby sitter:

[10] It is interesting to recall that in 1958 Anna Freud said: "I agree with Ernst Kris that we cannot predict from outside observations, and at the time of occurrence, which events will prove important for future pathology. I should like to add that we do not know either which aspect or element of a given experience will be selected for cathexis and emotional involvement" (p. 114). Perhaps we are now a step nearer to pinpointing the relative impact of the quality of the mother's handling.

Age four months nine days (third home visit)

During this conversation Mrs. B. was feeding Danny solids. He took the first spoons happily, then lay back with his head back. She pointed to this and became anxious.

She said that she did not know how much he should eat—sometimes he wants the whole bottle, but often he does not, and she feels that she ought to force him. Danny had eaten half and now refused the rest, though Mrs. B. repeatedly tried to persuade him. Unwillingly, she gave him the remainder of the bottle and said repeatedly that she did not know what to do.

The next example seems to show how the mother has to deny the importance of the breast because of her need to get Danny weaned as quickly as possible, so that she does not have to worry and need not feel so guilty about boarding him out (*defense* and *conflict*):

Nearly five months (fifth home visit)

Mrs. B. put Danny in a lying position and offered him her fingers to pull himself up. He did this and immediately grasped hold of her dress at the point of the breasts and tried to suck. She doubted that this was connected with the breasts, but I noticed that he did it twice or three times—and equally purposefully clutched her beads.

The following example shows the reaction formation (*defense*) against disgust (*anal fixation* point):

Age five months five days (sixth home visit)

The mother withdrew the bottle partially for a brief second (twice) and then withdrew it fully when he had taken two thirds of the bottle. His solid food was too hot, so she played with Danny while I cooled his food. He was pulling at her necklace (a metal one) and when he burped, she said it was a lovely one.

[On the same occasion Mrs. Sprince noticed that] Mrs. B. was feeding Danny rather slowly and that he was mouthing the food and, it seemed to me, enjoying it. The mother said, however, she felt that he wanted it more quickly—that he expected it to come as quickly as the bottle and she increased the speed. Danny responded by spitting some of the food out until finally he started to cry and Mrs. B. gave him the bottle, which he drank avidly. She returned to the food and Danny's hands were loose, but he did not impede the feeding. After a short time the mother said that he really likes to eat sitting up, but then all the food falls out. [*Comment:* Her inability to let him sit up is dictated by *conflicts* around messing—*anal fixation.*]

At this point Danny threw his head right back and stared at the ceiling. He stayed like this while the mother continued to fill his mouth; he swallowed, but showed no pleasure in the food. Finally, he objected and was given the last bit of bottle.

[*Comment:* All examples seem to point to the mother's own *conflicts* around feeding—*oral fixation* points.]

It should be remembered that so far only the environmental sections of the Profile have been considered. They are usually thought to be the easiest. When it comes to drives, ego, superego, and conflicts, the implications of the differences between the relatively fully structured personality of the older child and the essentially unstructured personality of the baby will present a further variety of fascinating and challenging problems (which will be taken up in a future publication).

I shall end this paper with a statement made by Anna Freud: "Investigations into the first year of life and the consequences of the earliest mother-child relationship had revealed that much may be acquired by the infant that had been considered as innate before" (1958, p. 96). It is my hope that through the development and application of the Baby Profile the frontiers of what is regarded as innate may become delineated more clearly and in greater detail.

BIBLIOGRAPHY

Benjamin, J. D. (1959), Prediction and Psychopathological Theory. In: *Dynamic Psychopathology in Childhood,* ed. L. Jessner & E. Pavenstedt. New York: Grune & Stratton, pp. 6-77.

—— (1961), The Innate and the Experiential in Development. In: *Lectures in Experimental Psychiatry,* ed. H. W. Brosin. Pittsburgh: Pittsburgh University Press, pp. 19-42.

Bibring, G. L. (1959), Some Considerations of the Psychological Processes in Pregnancy. *This Annual,* 14:113-121.

—— Dwyer, T. F., Huntington, D. S., & Valenstein, A. F. (1961), A Study of the Psychological Processes in Pregnancy and of the Earliest Mother-Child Relationship. *This Annual,* 16:9-72.

Brody, S. (1956), *Patterns of Mothering.* New York: International Universities Press.

Brunswick, R. M. (1940), The Preoedipal Phase of the Libido Development. In: *The Psychoanalytic Reader,* ed. R. Fliess. New York: International Universities Press, 1948, 1:261-283.

Burlingham, D. (1965), Some Problems of Ego Development in Blind Children. *This Annual,* 20:194-208.

Coleman, R. W., Kris, E., & Provence, S. (1953), The Study of Variations of Early Parental Attitudes: A Preliminary Report. *This Annual,* 8:20-47.

Escalona, S. K. & Heider, G. M. (1959), *Prediction and Outcome.* New York: Basic Books.

Frankl, L. (1958), Enquiry into the Difficulty of Diagnosis by Comparing the Impressions in the Diagnostic Interviews with the Material Elicited in the Course of the Child's Analysis. *Proc. Royal Soc. Med.,* 51(11):945-946.

—— (1961), Some Observations on the Development and Disturbances of Integration in Childhood. *This Annual,* 16:146-163.

Freud, A. (1958), Child Observation and Prediction of Development: A Memorial Lecture in Honor of Ernst Kris. *This Annual,* 13:92-124.

—— (1962), Assessment of Childhood Disturbances. *This Annual,* 17:149-158.

—— (1963), The Concept of Developmental Lines. *This Annual,* 18:245-265.

—— (1965), *Normality and Pathology in Childhood: Assessments of Development.* New York: International Universities Press.

—— Nagera, H., & Freud, W. E. (1965), Metapsychological Assessment of the Adult Personality: The Adult Profile. *This Annual,* 20:9-41.

Freud, W. E. (1967), Some General Reflections on the Metapsychological Profile. *Int. J. Psa.* (in press).

Hartmann, H. (1950), Psychoanalysis and Developmental Psychology. *This Annual,* 5:7-17.

—— & Kris, E. (1945), The Genetic Approach in Psychoanalysis. *This Annual,* 1:11-30.

—— —— & Loewenstein, R. M. (1946), Comments on the Formation of Psychic Structure. *This Annual,* 2:11-38.

Hoffer, W. (1952), The Mutual Influences in the Development of Ego and Id: Earliest Stages. *This Annual,* 7:31-41.

Kris, E. (1950), Notes on the Development and on Some Current Problems of Psychoanalytic Child Psychology. *This Annual,* 5:24-46.

Kris, M. (1957), The Use of Prediction in a Longitudinal Study. *This Annual,* 12:175-189.

Laufer, M. (1965), Assessment of Adolescent Disturbances: The Application of Anna Freud's Diagnostic Profile. *This Annual,* 20:99-123.

Lehrman, S. R. (1967), Psychopathology in Mixed Marriages. *Psa. Quart.,* 36:67-82.

Nagera, H. (1963), The Developmental Profile: Notes on Some Practical Considerations Regarding Its Use. *This Annual,* 18:511-540.

—— (1964), Autoerotism, Autoerotic Activities, and Ego Development. *This Annual,* 19:240-255.

—— (1966), *Early Childhood Disturbances, the Infantile Neurosis, and the Adulthood Disturbances: Problems of a Developmental Psychoanalytic Psychology* [The Psychoanalytic Study of the Child, Monogr. 2]. New York: International Universities Press.

Provence, S. (1966), Some Aspects of Early Ego Development: Data from a Longitudinal Study. In: *Psychoanalysis—A General Psychology: Essays in Honor of Heinz Hartmann,* ed. R. M. Loewenstein, L. M. Newman, M. Schur, & A. J. Solnit. New York: International Universities Press, pp. 107-122.

Rapaport, D. & Gill, M. M. (1959), The Points of View and Assumptions of Metapsychology. *Int. J. Psa.,* 40:153-162.

Reik, T. (1919), *Ritual: Psychoanalytic Studies.* New York: International Universities Press, 1958.

Robertson, Joyce (1962), Mothering as an Influence on Early Development: A Study of Well-Baby Clinic Records. *This Annual,* 17:245-264.

—— (1965), Mother-Infant Interaction from Birth to Twelve Months. In: *Determinants of Infant Behaviour III,* ed. B. M. Foss. London: Methuen; New York: John Wiley, pp. 111-127.

Solnit, A. J. & Kris, M. (1967), Trauma and Infantile Experiences: A Longitudinal Perspective. In: *Psychic Trauma,* ed. S. S. Furst. New York: Basic Books, pp. 175-220.

Spitz, R. A. (1951), The Psychogenic Diseases in Infancy: An Attempt at Their Etiologic Classification. *This Annual,* 6:255-275.
—— (1959), *A Genetic Field Theory of Ego Formation.* New York: International Universities Press.
—— (1964), The Derailment of Dialogue: Stimulus Overload, Action Cycles, and the Completion Gradient. *J. Amer. Psa. Assn.,* 12:752-775.
—— (1965), *The First Year of Life.* New York: International Universities Press.
Winnicott, D. W. (1949), *The Ordinary Devoted Mother and Her Baby.* London: Tavistock Publications.
—— (1960), The Theory of the Parent-Infant Relationship. *Int. J. Psa.,* 41:585-595.

THE PEEK-A-BOO GAME

Part I: Its Origins, Meanings, and Related Phenomena in the First Year

JAMES A. KLEEMAN, M.D. (New Haven)

Despite the universality of the peek-a-boo game, no paper has been devoted to it in the psychoanalytic literature. In neither of two extensive indices of psychoanalytic writing (Grinstein, Hart[1]) is there a single title. The following study includes longitudinal observations of three children and cross-sectional data from others. The observations reported here are largely of one child who displayed the phenomena most eloquently. Heloise is chosen not because her peek-a-boo activities are typical of all children but rather because the interaction between her innate endowment and her experience resulted in a wide range of behavior illuminating the peek-a-boo game. I shall explore both peek-a-boo itself and a variety of important behaviors with which it becomes associated. I shall limit myself to the first year.

Observations

Heloise S. was a mature, strong, healthy baby at birth and weighed 7 pounds 12 ounces. She was her mother's first child, delivered without anesthesia after a prolonged and difficult labor. She exhibited a high level of activity and vitality. After leaving the hospital, she gradually showed above-average sensitivity to various external and internal stimuli. Starting at twelve days and lasting somewhat beyond three months, she had colic. At five weeks she smiled, laughed, gurgled, and "talked" with a wide variation of

1 Henry H. Hart kindly sent me six items culled from over 1,400 page references to "play and games." These were papers which contained some material related to peek-a-boo but were not applicable to the peek-a-boo game in the first year of life. His is an index of clinical observations and ideas, not titles.

facial expressions and closed her eyes tightly in bright sunshine. When her pediatrician saw her at five weeks, and then again at eleven weeks, he characterized her as very acute visually, alert and active and unusually responsive to touch and sound.

Mrs. S. experienced life deeply and wanted to allow her daughter to "feel" openly, on both emotional and sensory levels. However, her observation led her to feel Heloise had a below-average stimulus barrier which, because of her perceptive acuteness, made her overly vulnerable to stimuli. Mrs. S. tried to modify the environment to protect the baby. In the seven- to eight-week period the mother would sometimes cover Heloise's head with a cotton blanket to cut down outside stimuli and help the infant go to sleep while nursing or sucking a pacifier. The above factors are important in understanding the peek-a-boo manifestations in this child.[2]

By twenty weeks Heloise enjoyed being taken to a mirror and responded to the images with a smile. She demonstrated many other responses indicating an increasing awareness of external objects: she cuddled a doll with enjoyment, watched her mother moving about a room, showed recognition of her mother's breast (she nursed until she was ten and a half months), and soon distinguished her father as different from her mother.

Observation 1 (22 weeks):[3] For some time Heloise's mother had kept at the head end in her crib a diaper. Heloise often pressed the diaper against her face in a lulling endeavor. On this day when the mother entered the child's room after naptime, she found Heloise lying on her back with the diaper covering her face including her eyes. As her mother approached, the child began to kick her feet and laugh under the diaper.

I label this a peek-a-boo precursor. It is not yet the on-and-off alternation of the peek-a-boo game but illustrates the progress of ego functions (control of motility, memory, differentiation, and use of auditory perception) which now permit the child excited anticipation and recognition of the mother despite momentary controlled

[2] Heloise's early experience and data about her parents are detailed elsewhere (Kleeman, 1964).

[3] These observations represent a selected fraction of the total number recorded which pertained to the peek-a-boo game and in turn are part of a larger total directed at other topics.

restriction of vision. It is specially noteworthy that the child spontaneously initiated this play.

Observation 2 (23 weeks): Frequently now Heloise, on her back, pulled pillows, blankets, towels, or diapers over her face and kicked and laughed under her face covering. Her mother wondered if this could be associated with the much earlier passive experience of having a blanket over her head while she nursed or sucked a pacifier.[4]

This peek-a-boo precursor coincided in time with another forestage of awareness of a self separate from objects: looking over the edge of her jumper chair at objects that had dropped (and soon that *she* had dropped) to the floor. This recalls Freud's famous description of an eighteen-month-old and the bobbin (1920) and raises the interesting issue of the relationship between the dropping or tossing of objects and the peek-a-boo game (see Discussion).

Observation 3 (24 weeks): The parents had put Heloise in her crib to nap. After a short while she was "calling." When the parents entered the room, she was on her back, had pulled a diaper over her face, and was chortling and gleefully kicking her feet. Playfully they said, "Where is Heloise?" She seemed delighted, kept the diaper on her face, kicked, and squealed. Then the parents were completely quiet. She lay there, waiting for a response. Again she tried to kick and call. Seconds passed as she remained still, her face covered. Then as if the silence were too much, she removed the diaper from her eyes, still leaving it over the rest of her face. She looked a little startled. Then her face suddenly lit up with a big smile.

The significance of peek-a-boo in communicating with a love object and in an early form of joking is suggested by this example. The timing of it corresponded to many evidences of beginning *intention* in other behavioral areas.

Observation 4 ($24\frac{1}{2}$ weeks): On this occasion Heloise lay next to her mother on her parents' bed with a diaper drawn over her face. The mother got under the diaper with the baby. Mrs. S. noted that Heloise was sniffing the diaper, suggesting it had an appealing odor. Another time that week Heloise repeatedly put the diaper over

4 It could be a "collective alternate" (Greenacre, 1957, 1962) of the previous primary experience at two months and later, but probably is best explained as a maturational behavioral manifestation common about this age, perhaps augmented by the earlier experience.

her face and removed it in a playful way, laughing with the mother as she carried out the alternating act.

With the advent of this alternating covering and uncovering Heloise (before the age of six months) presents the full early form of the active peek-a-boo game.

At twenty-six weeks peek-a-boo was being joined by other social games, involving excitement, fun, and stimulation with the parents. Heloise delighted in pat-a-cake and the West Wind Game. In the latter Heloise would watch passively and then emit shouts of glee and laughter as her father, with serious face and a deep voice, would mimic the wind close to his daughter's face.

Imitation of facial expression and other body movements was a prominent feature of Heloise's behavior at this time.

The intentional dropping of toys from her jumper chair was also frequent and vigorous and was now accompanied by looking over the edge at them, often for a prolonged period.

The following seemed important in comprehending this behavior: On several occasions instead of just dropping her doll on the floor, she lowered it to the floor (she was close to the floor in the jumper seat) by holding its arm and then would draw it back up to herself. At other times she would drop it, or she would let it fall and try to pick it up again.

This activity is included because of the close tie existing between peek-a-boo and the dropping of objects. The contention is that object dropping is the predecessor of tossing and that the child's tossing of objects from the crib or high chair often represents the first half of a double act (illustrated by Freud's example of the child with the bobbin), the last half of which, the retrieving, is not seen because the object has no string. (It seems reasonable to suppose that object tossing and the hiding aspect of peek-a-boo make a significant contribution to the emergence of the self. The removal of "part of oneself" through tossing or hiding seems to illustrate a testing of the stability of the early self image. The second half—the effort to retrieve the object or the re-establishment of visual contact in peek-a-boo—further tests the boundaries of the budding self.)

Observation 5 (27½ weeks): On vacation she slept in a crib in the same motel room with her parents. It was clear that she discerned the strangeness of her surroundings and did much intent looking all around. Before sleep she repeatedly covered and uncovered her eyes with her diaper in play with her father.

It was speculated that the instigation of the peek-a-boo activity on this occasion was the anxiety aroused by the strangeness of the motel room and having her crib in the parents' bedroom for the first time.

During the next month Heloise acquired great skill in playing peek-a-boo. For seven or eight minutes at a time, lying on her back, frequently after nursing, she would cover either her whole face or often just her eyes with a diaper as her father would say "Where is Heloise?" or ask the mother, "Have you seen Heloise?" Heloise would then jerk the diaper off her face to her father's accompaniment, "There she is!" Over and over again she would repeat this sequence with him with delight, smiles, squeals, and limb thrashing.

This behavior I call the prototype of the peek-a-boo game in its active form. She is actively carrying it out in conjunction with a loved person. Her capacity for this sensorimotor activity coincided with a greater eye-hand coordination and mastery in general at this age.

Sometimes when Heloise was tired, she would suck her thumb and shut out visual intake by closing her eyes or covering them with the back of her hand or a diaper.

Throughout the paper it will be evident how this stimulation-sensitive child devised ways to limit her sensory intake, in this case creating her own sensory deprivation to foster regression to sleep. Limitation of visual intake became entwined with peek-a-boo activities, and peek-a-boo behavior often served that purpose.

Relatively new was Heloise's pleasure in watching her father or mother cover and uncover their faces as a playful activity. The child showed her joy with laughs, smiles, and gurgles.

This I would term a passive form of peek-a-boo, which would also characterize the adult's covering the child's face to play the game. In many cases a passive form precedes the active one, which I believe is one reason some authors have stressed that the peek-a-boo game is an example of imitation. One of the three children I followed longitudinally, by eight months, was participating in the peek-a-boo game only to the extent of showing interest in a parent's or a sibling's covering or uncovering the face, or disappearing and reappearing, but did not carry out or initiate the active form himself. Interestingly, Heloise demonstrated the active form considerably before experiencing the passive kind. This suggests that imitation did not play a major role in her starting to play peek-a-boo actively. One could argue that the mother's coming and going was an instigating predecessor, but even in this case Heloise's peek-a-boo would be better termed a response to that than an imitation.

Observation 6 (30 weeks): At a morning nursing, Heloise nursed hungrily on one breast and then wanted to play rather than complete the feeding on the other breast. The play was a stall and included pulling a blanket over her face and playing peek-a-boo. The mother, feeling sure the baby was still hungry, did not encourage this and insisted on completing the feeding.

On this occasion the baby used the peek-a-boo game in the middle of a nursing as a playful stall to engage the mother. It was entirely instituted by Heloise without mutual participation by the mother who wanted her to nurse. This came at a time when Heloise in other ways was more capable of actively communicating her wishes.

Observation 7 (32½ weeks): The father had come home at noon. The infant and mother were on a bed partly through a nursing. Heloise was playfully rocking on her hands and knees and put her face down in a soft blanket. Father asked, "Where is Heloise?" She raised her head with a smile and vocalized, "Ah, ah" (as though to answer, "There she is"). This form of peek-a-boo was repeated five or six times.

This occurred when there was evidence of Heloise's increasing comprehension of words. It illustrates how the peek-a-boo game was further becoming involved with language development. Furthermore, it is a suggestive example of how imitation *did* contribute to the peek-a-boo game in Heloise, since part of the repetitive play had included the adult's saying, "There she is!" which she seemed to try to imitate here.

Observation 8 (32½ weeks): At one suppertime Heloise was sitting in her high chair, which was near the refrigerator. When the refrigerator door was opened, the child grabbed the dish towel which had been hanging from the handle and initiated the peek-a-boo game. Then she dropped the towel to the floor, looked prolongedly at it, and vocalized in a way clearly suggesting she wished to have it back.

This example demonstrates the complexity of motor skills, thought, and early language surrounding the peek-a-boo game and an occasion when peek-a-boo and object dropping were contiguous.

Several days previously Heloise (possibly related to anxiety) spontaneously began playing peek-a-boo at her pediatrician's office at the time of a routine examination and inoculation.

Observation 9 (33½ weeks): In her playpen Heloise utilized an empty cracker carton available to her to cover her face and start a peek-a-boo game with her father who was in the room.

The selection of a variety of materials and uses (previously the dish towel and the stalling during nursing) which Heloise introduced into her peek-a-boo play could be called the beginnings of creative imagination which became even more evident in later observations.

Observation 10 (34 weeks): Heloise's mother experimented with a large paper supermarket sack, instituting a game of peek-a-boo by playfully putting it over Heloise's head. The baby joined in and would remove the sack as her father would say, "There you are." Mother tried putting the sack over Heloise's legs and playing a game of "getting a package at the grocery." Heloise did not yet have a very good concept that these were her legs in the sack. The mother tore a small hole in the bag so that one foot could emerge. The child looked at her foot and reached for it. Mother provided a hole for the other foot. Heloise looked from one foot to the other. She did not yet comprehend that these were her feet, nor did she seem to think this game was a lot of fun. She did, however, delight in tearing the sack up and putting the pieces in her mouth.

Language development was proceeding. Not only was her word comprehension greater, but when her father would play peek-a-boo with her, she would use her "tonal" vocabulary. Each time he would reappear, she would give a shout, always with the same intensity and tonal quality, much as he would previously say, "Here I am."

Other cognitive functions in addition to language were now

emerging in association with peek-a-boo play such as a beginning awareness of space and body image. She had only a faint idea of a body part like the foot inside a closed and unseen space, and a slightly better concept of her head enclosed.

By thirty-four weeks it was clear that Heloise had distinct feelings for her father. There was an increasingly differentiated response to her father compared with her response to her mother. She laughed and played with him; she "knew" his voice, recognizing it from a distance. He played peek-a-boo with her perhaps more than the mother, and Heloise was more apt to begin peek-a-boo on her own with him than with the mother. In fact, her overall relationship with the father had a peek-a-boo quality to it: she was much concerned when he was not there; when he was in her presence, she would often turn away and peek back coyly.

Observation 11 (34 weeks): Heloise was holding and mouthing a teething ring. Her father sat close to her high chair and encouraged her to offer it to his mouth. She would bring it close to his mouth, pull it away, and put it in her mouth. She repeated this six or seven times, and it was fairly clear that she was tempting or teasing her father; she would laugh if he would touch it with his mouth, and she would withdraw it to her own.

This play contained the peek-a-boo rhythm, illustrated the process of self-differentiation, and possibly was a forerunner of certain later character qualities, i.e., teasing and coyness.

During the eighth month Heloise appeared to be striving within herself to effect greater separateness from the mother. She took a more active role in approaching or dismissing the breast in feeding, reflecting a greater awareness that it was part of "mommy." (A partial weaning followed this behavior.) She indicated to her mother not to linger at bedtimes and began to settle herself to sleep. With her increased sense of separateness she seemed to seek more actively a transitional object. Patting, holding, smelling, and burying her face in it, she showed increased interest in a soft orlon blanket. The same cloths she had utilized, and still used, for peek-a-boo play increasingly were treasured as transitional objects (Winnicott, 1953), which she often dragged with her when she crept.

She continued to play peek-a-boo spontaneously but less frequently than earlier. She still greatly enjoyed her mother's face disappearing and appearing in passive peek-a-boo play. When alone, she would be seen covering her eyes, apparently experimenting with making inanimate objects disappear (and reappear). She would squeal with delight in being reunited with her mother (after a nap or mother's short absence from home). Often now Heloise imitated her mother's mouth and jaw movements.

Observation 12 (36 weeks 5 days): At a developmental examination Heloise uncovered a toy hidden by a diaper and removed a cube from the cup.

At thirty-nine weeks Heloise, in voluntarily dropping objects from her high chair, would close her eyes as she released them, anticipating the noise as they hit the floor.

These responses reflect advancing cognitive development, equally applicable to her conception and infrequent practice of peek-a-boo. Her rather mild "stranger reaction," which lasted only a few weeks, seemed past now. Flirtatiousness with her father was often observed.

Observation 13 (40 weeks): The mother had taken off her blouse and left it momentarily on her bed. Heloise, who was creeping on the floor, pulled herself to standing, appropriated the blouse, smelled it, covered her face with it, and then buried her face in it.

Here by chance we see elements of peek-a-boo cover, attachment to mother, and transitional object formation associated together.

At forty-one weeks Heloise, using a blanket, would happily play peek-a-boo with her father while her mother changed her diaper. It originated with either him or her. She was skilled at and delighted in doing it.

Play alone in her crib now included some similar behavior. Before or after naps in her crib she would "talk," squeal, jump, pull the shade from the window (her crib was close to the window), and look out, suck her thumb, or cover her face with a cotton blanket. Tossing her blanket, diaper, dolls, and soft animals out of her crib was rapidly becoming an active and usual project.

Various observations soon made it clear that one aspect of throwing objects from the crib was a wish for an adult to retrieve them. Other aspects surely were the practice of release (part of the broader social modality of letting go) (Erikson, 1948), the pleasure in exercising a new motor skill, and the exploration of spatial relations (Piaget, 1937).

Also apparent at this time was the capacity to locate a missing object without looking at it, such as reaching for a plastic nipple cover behind her without fixing her gaze on it. This suggested new advance in memory for hidden objects and spatial relations.

At forty-three and one half weeks Heloise would often cover her face with a diaper and then move it to uncover one eye. She would peek out at her father. It was reminiscent of a Spanish girl flirting behind a fan.

In the tenth month Heloise still liked peek-a-boo a lot. In addition to gaining attention, it was used in the mastery of vision, as an active control causing objects to disappear and reappear, and to shut out light (in apparent regression). It would seem it assisted in the formation of early fantasies and illusions. The cover material doubled as a now highly invested transitional object.

Increased evidence of separation anxiety was now seen when the mother absented herself from home for several hours; on one occasion it was overnight. Heloise would more significantly cry as she saw her mother prepare to leave and after she left.

Observation 14 (45 weeks): The mother gave Heloise an apple, but she did not seem interested in eating it. Encouraging her, the mother held the apple to her own mouth, pretending to eat it, making the "mmm" sounds Heloise uttered when she was enjoying food. The baby then picked up the apple, making movements with her mouth and saying "mmm" as though she were eating it. The mother then ate a bite of the apple, and Heloise responded by continuing to simulate eating. Mother thought this was very funny, and Heloise joined in smiling.

This observation is included because it seemed an initial example of pretend at a time when fantasy was beginning to be involved with peek-a-boo, which was now rarely instigated by Heloise but which she was happy to play if her father started it.

In the ten days preceding this observation Heloise became interested in swinging doors open and closed, was completely weaned from the breast, and was practicing release of objects from her hand.

Observation 15 (46 weeks): After the water had drained from Heloise's bath, she became interested in the rubber mat on which she had been sitting. It was a little heavy and awkward for her to handle, but she became totally absorbed in experimenting with and manipulating it. She held it in front of her face, draped it around her shoulders, then over her legs. She tried to push the mat away. As it was rubbery, it would spring back and fall on her knee or press against her side or back. Then she was restimulated to explore its texture or motion and again would drape it around her shoulders, etc. It was as though the mat were animate and actively making movements toward her. It kept engaging her attention even after she had decided she had had enough.

This was a very charming scene to watch. She became so wrapped up in the activity that she was oblivious of onlookers. It was apparent from her reactions that there was still tremendous magic in her world. Play with the mat, like peek-a-boo at this time, became an opportunity for all kinds of experimentation and curious exploring.

Observation 16 (46½ weeks): As mother came into her room after nighttime sleep, Heloise was quite excited to see her and momentarily covered her face with a diaper.

Heloise's action seemed a cutting down of the intense stimulation aroused by seeing her mother. Although this observation is not conclusive, there were many observations indicating that the peek-a-boo gesture or activity served as stimulus barrier at times. Heloise would close her eyes behind the cover. She would then sometimes open her mouth and sniff, as though at these times shutting out light increased other sensory intake.

By forty-seven weeks the mother and infant were playing a game of "chase," originated by the mother in response to the unfolding of new activities of the baby. The mother would say, "I am coming after you," and Heloise would creep away. The mother pretended to be moving fast, making more noise than movement with her feet. This gave Heloise a chance to "win." Heloise would creep rapidly from the mother, stop, sit up, look back to "check" the mother, and then go on or turn, with outstretched arms to be picked up. Her mother would pick her up and cuddle her. By now there was no visible evidence of anxiety, but considerable pleasure in being chased. The game reached the point where the baby would begin to laugh and "run" away as soon as she saw a familiar facial expression on the mother which conveyed, "I am going to catch you."

About a month earlier when this game was begun, Heloise would quiver and tremble when she stopped to look back, suggesting some anxiety about being overtaken by the big person coming after her. The stopping often suggested the wish to "stop the game" before she was caught. The mother felt that by responding to clues she felt were indicative of the baby's feelings she helped Heloise to master the feelings of anxiety and turn the game into one of excited pleasure.

The link between this game and peek-a-boo is evident in the alternation between "disappearing" and checking for mother. Without the mother's presence, controlled by the baby's creeping or looking back, the game is destroyed. This game also serves as a bridge between peek-a-boo, in its simplest form, and "hide and seek" versions later.

One can speculate that this chase game, especially at its inception with the evidence of some anxiety, might be one prototypical experience contributing to the common adult dream where the dreamer is frozen in his tracks in the face of some huge dangerous object getting ever closer.

Heloise at this time often cruised around the house out of sight of her mother. She often was willing to leave the adult but did not wish to be left.

By forty-seven and a half weeks it was often routine for Heloise to drag a diaper with her as she crept around the house. She showed a lot of attachment to diapers and a soft flannel blanket. In her crib she would finger them, rub them, hold them against her face or bury her face in them, or use them as a facial cover, alternately put on and taken off. She did not suck her thumb a great deal, but when she did, the activity was often accompanied by pressing the diaper against her face. Waking from a nap, she would play alone in her crib, vocalizing, covering and uncovering her face with delight with her diaper or cotton blanket, and dropping objects onto the floor.

Such observations made with Heloise's unawareness of an adult's presence reveal the face covering and uncovering in close association with the object dropping. Both represent a rhythmical motor activity, in this case practiced alone in her crib (cf. Greenacre, 1960). They occur at a time when the modalities of retaining and releasing were in increasing prominence in many ways (Erikson, 1950). Heloise showed a greater awareness of containers, much more retentiveness, and a new skill in releasing objects, to her mother's hand, for example.

The peek-a-boo game was not as frequently initiated by her as previously but still occurred about every other day on her instigation and quite freely any time her father suggested it. If he handed her a diaper and said, "Where is Heloise?" she would cover her face with the diaper and play the game with him, smiling each time she pulled it aside. She still enjoyed covering one eye, coyly watching him with the other. Both types of play were carried out most often during diaper changing (while she was supine). The diaper was also used to cut out light. (One day in this month Heloise displayed a mild photophobia associated with a respiratory illness and seemed to use her diaper more than usual to protect her eyes from light.)

She exhibited, in a number of ways, an ability to limit the intensity of her experience, and the peek-a-boo maneuvers sometimes served this end. She always closed her eyes as she dropped an object in anticipation of the noise of its impact.

Observation 17 (49 weeks): Heloise sat on the floor of her room. Her father stood outside the room. Heloise closed the door between her and him. She reopened it to check for his continued presence. He encouraged the play by asking, "Where is Heloise?" the next time she shut him out, and "There she is" when she appeared in full view by opening it again.

The mastery of this and other new techniques for playing peek-a-boo involved more aggressive energy than when she played the game with a diaper while lying on her back. In the above instance she had crept to the door, put her fingers around the edge, and moved this large object aside. The essential peek-a-boo elements of alternating appearance and disappearance of the other person, all controlled by her, were unchanged.

Closing the door "in daddy's face" and reopening it had a flirtatious or teasing quality. This flirtatiousness was also expressed in her alternately looking at her father and turning her face away, and by "batting" her eyes, closing them deliberately, and fluttering them open. (She seemed to be saying, "Now you have me; now you do not.")

At one year the peek-a-boo game was still fairly frequently played, initiated either by Heloise or her parents. It was associated with language development to the extent that the comments "Put the diaper over your eyes" or "Where is Heloise?" (as she was handed a diaper) were sufficient to start her playing peek-a-boo. She showed intense participation, and it was fully a game: she thought the activity funny and would laugh behind the diaper. The same face covering used for peek-a-boo, for shutting out stimuli when she was fatigued, and for a transitional object itself, was used during thumb sucking: she would hold the diaper over one eye and against that cheek with one hand and suck the thumb of the other hand. While playing peek-a-boo, she might begin to suck her thumb after removing the diaper from her face.

Heloise showed considerable individuation and separateness. She had a capacity for imaginative or pretend play, as evident in peek-a-boo when she would carry it on with herself as an apparent fantasy activity. One day the father settled her for her nap and watched a minute through a crack in the door. With her own blanket Heloise covered her face, kicked her feet while she was thus draped, waited a moment, and pulled it away, repeating this sequence many times. There was also a greater awareness of what was happening outside the diaper and greater tolerance of delay, which were reflected in her permitting the diaper to remain over her eyes for prolonged periods rather than needing to remove it at once in the peek-a-boo play.

Shortly after one year Heloise began shaking her head from side to side in the no-no gesture. Her increased capacity to let go both animate and inanimate objects paralleled her release of the mother from view in the no gesture and her willingness to keep the diaper over her eyes for more prolonged periods in the peek-a-boo activities.

Discussion

In this paper "peek-a-boo" or "the peek-a-boo game" refers to controlled, alternating interruption and re-establishment of visual contact with a human object. The terms "peek-a-boo manifestations," "peek-a-boo play," "peek-a-boo activities," and "peek-a-boo behavior" are less precisely defined and include not only the peek-a-boo game but also peek-a-boo precursor behavior, alternating interruption of visual contact with inanimate objects, derivative behavior, behavior which resembles the form of the peek-a-boo game but is entwined with other activities, such as lulling with a transitional object, etc.

I differentiate two forms of the peek-a-boo game: (1) a passive one where the human object covers or uncovers the infant's face or appears to and disappears from the child's gaze, i.e., where the controlling of the alternation is by the human object; (2) an active type where the infant controls the on-and-off visual contact. The active form can be further subdivided according to whether the other person provides the stimulus for the instigation of the play or whether the play is self-initiated by the child.

COMPARISON OF PEEK-A-BOO IN THREE INFANTS

In this section I wish to demonstrate the great variation of the age of onset, form utilized, and degree of investment of interest in peek-a-boo by the three infants followed longitudinally.

In Heloise active peek-a-boo appeared before six months (Observation 4) when Heloise, on her own initiative, repeatedly covered and uncovered her face with a diaper in a game with her mother, after precursors were evident from twenty-two weeks. By six and a half months Heloise displayed great skill manipulating a diaper in performing an active peek-a-boo game with either parent. Passive peek-a-boo, i.e., her pleasure in the disappearance and reappearance of a parent's face, was preceded by the active form. Burying her face in a cloth when she was lying prone became an additional method of peek-a-boo, followed by use of an empty cracker carton and a paper sack. At eight months she began covering and uncovering her eyes in solitary play in her crib. A game of "chase" was added at forty-seven weeks. At forty-nine weeks she opened and closed doors in active peek-a-boo play. Peek-a-boo for her was greatly influenced by her sensitivity to stimuli and transitional object formation, and became an avenue of flirtatious and coy play with her father. Use of a cloth (diaper or blanket) to cover or uncover her face in active peek-a-boo remained her preferred peek-a-boo method throughout the first year.

In contrast, Bob did not show a clear-cut passive peek-a-boo response until he was six and a half months old, and not until eight months was unquestionable delight in passive peek-a-boo registered. He played an active peek-a-boo game, initiated by a parent, at eight months four days. At eight months and three weeks, still initiated by another, he played active peek-a-boo by burying his face in a towel while he was prone, or occasionally by covering his face with a diaper, or by standing at his crib side and alternately dropping down out of sight and standing again. At nine and a half months his preferred form of peek-a-boo was turning his head laterally so that he could not see the person, and then resuming visual contact as he returned his face to the midline. This was both active and initiated by him. That he clearly grasped the essence of peek-a-boo at this time was evident in his being able to interrupt and regain visual contact in ways other than the favorite horizontal head turning. If his relative position to the other demanded it, he would initiate vertical head bowing and raising. By ten and a half months his use of lateral head turning to play peek-a-boo had waned, and other methods were used. For example, at eleven months his most frequent means was an exciting game with his mother where he flopped to a prone position on his crib mattress, buried his face, and kicked his feet, followed by raising his head and looking at her with a laugh. The whole was repeated many times.

The third child, Carl, enjoyed passive peek-a-boo at five months (twenty-two weeks) when his mother would either duck out of sight and reappear or cover her face with a cloth and remove it. At six months, in his playpen, he would pull a diaper over his face and leave it there but was not really playing peek-a-boo. From thirty-two to thirty-four weeks he was showing some separation anxiety (when his mother left the room), was actively searching for a hidden object, was dropping and tossing objects from his crib, and continued to enjoy passive peek-a-boo. At nine months peek-a-boo was not especially important to him, but he still enjoyed the passive form. At forty-three weeks he would play "chase," creeping away from his mother with great excitement. At ten months he would play active peek-a-boo by vertical head movements or behind a door, but both initiated by another. Finally, at forty-six and a half weeks he displayed active peek-a-boo, self-initiated, by opening and closing a door with his parent just beyond the door. He evinced several other forms of self-initiated peek-a-boo during the first year, but peek-a-boo was never a highly invested activity. The relation to language was evident. Shortly before one year the following occurred: the mother furnished the verbal stimulus by asking, "Where is Carl?" and he began covering and uncovering his face; she then suggested playing "Where is mommy?" and he spontaneously covered her face with a diaper.

REVIEW OF RELEVANT LITERATURE

Although there are many statements about peek-a-boo in the literature, there is no single paper devoted to it or any attempt at comprehensive treatment of the behavior. The following headings illustrate the range of the statements about peek-a-boo: (1) age of onset (Rosenblith and Allinsmith, 1962; Bühler, 1930; Escalona, 1963; Stone and Church, 1957; Mahler and Furer, 1963; Murphy, Murphy, and Newcomb, 1937; Provence and Lipton, 1962; Mahler, 1965); (2) frequency (Thorpe, 1946); (3) frequency of eliciting smiles (Murphy, Murphy, and Newcomb, 1937); (4) age when no longer played (Phillips, 1960); (5) in chimpanzees (Cruikshank, 1946); (6) linked to pat-a-cake or bye-bye as social games (Ritvo and Provence, 1953; Brenner, 1955; Provence and Lipton, 1962; Omwake, 1963); (7) dependence on orientation to the human face (Ritvo and Provence, 1953); (8) as imitation (Hendrick, 1951; Ritvo and Provence, 1953; Brenner, 1955; Provence and Lipton, 1962; Omwake, 1963; Call and Marschak, 1966) (9) initiated by the mother but picked up by the infant (Hendrick, 1951; Peller, 1955; Mahler and Furer, 1963; Mahler, 1965); (10) nuances reflective of style of parent-infant interaction (Call and Marschak, 1966); (11) mastery of anxiety of separation or object loss) Freud, 1926; Fraiberg, 1959; Phillips, 1960, Schur, 1962; Mahler and Furer, 1963; Ross, 1965; Call and Marschak, 1966); (12) building secondary autonomy structure (Call and Marschak, 1966); (13) characteristic of first subphase of the individuation process (Mahler, 1965); (14) tentative experimentation at separation-individuation (Mahler and Furer, 1963); (15) affected by institutional care (Provence and Lipton, 1962); (16) included in classification of play activities (Peller, 1954); (17) illustrating a primitive, even rhythm (Greenacre, 1954, 1960); (18) repetition as basis of simple mastery (Greenacre, 1954, 1960; Schur, 1966); (19) turning of passive experience into an active one (Peller, 1955; Schur, 1962; Mahler and Furer, 1963); (20) transforming potentially painful experience into pleasurable one (Freud, 1926; Fraiberg, 1959); (21) baby learns order and stability (trust) (Rosenblith and Allinsmith, 1962); (22) develops attitude of confidence and assurance in repetition (Greenacre, 1960); (23) acquires "competence" in vision (Call and Marschak, 1966); in effective dealing with the environment (White, 1960); (24) fosters development of apparatus of primary autonomy (Call and Marschak, 1966); (25) contributes to reality testing (Greenacre, 1954, 1960); (26) provides method for using cathexis and decathexis of ego boundaries in the service of perception of other people (Federn); (27) practices ability to withdraw (Schur, 1962).

Age of Onset

The literature on age of onset deserves further comment. The issue is complicated by failure to distinguish between what I call passive peek-a-boo and active peek-a-boo. Some authors consider the mother's covering and uncovering her face for the infant the peek-a-boo game. This is implied by Rosenblith and Allinsmith (1962) who set four months as the age when babies begin to like the game. Other writers include only the infant's controlling the appearance and disappearance as the peek-a-boo game, while still others consider both possibilities in their discussion of peek-a-boo. The latter is inherent in Bühler's (1930) distinction between the diaper test (where the infant can remove a diaper laid on his face) at five months, the child's getting pleasure from "hide and seek" (passive peek-a-boo) at eight months, and actually playing the (active) peek-a-boo at eleven months.

Greenacre (1960) and others set about five months as the point marking the first clear separation of the infant from the mother under the infant's control, and this stage is followed by the definite emergence of the beginning mental ego. This approximate age, then, would be the earliest we would expect to see any form of active peek-a-boo, and in fact, it is usually somewhat later before the infant has the motor skills and executive capacity to carry it out. Heloise demonstrated this timetable. Other children (e.g., Carl) do not carry out active peek-a-boo until later.

Escalona (1963) states: "Many six-month-olds perform simple

feats of imitation, and all can actively participate in the universal game of peek-a-boo."[5]

Stone and Church (1957) declare children may begin to play peek-a-boo during the seventh month. Provence and Lipton (1962) say: "The baby first responds to, later imitates, and finally initiates such social games as peek-a-boo, pat-a-cake, and bye-bye. The response to peek-a-boo is usually seen at around eight months, the pat-a-cake and bye-bye about a month later." This designates a progression in peek-a-boo, as does the detailing of peek-a-boo by Mahler and Furer (1963) in a specific child who responded to (passive) peek-a-boo at five to six months, later practiced it himself, and carried it out ecstatically at eleven months. Mahler (1965) expresses a view that is especially concordant with my own, namely, that the peek-a-boo games initiated by the mother and then taken over by the infant are characteristic of the first subphase of the individuation process—i.e., *the phase of differentiation,* with the suggested range of five or six months to nine or eleven months, associated with all the maturational growth typical of that period.

Piaget's Contribution

Of those who have contributed to our understanding of the peek-a-boo phenomena one of the most important is Piaget (1936, 1937). Although he did not specifically study peek-a-boo, his investigations of the mechanism of intelligence including the elaboration of objects (inanimate) and the development of the conceptualization of space, causality, and time significantly add to our knowledge of peek-a-boo. Because Piaget essentially omits reference to needs, motivations, and the role of specific interpersonal relationships and specific endowment differences in the child and because my psychoanalytically oriented observations of Heloise and the other children in this study particularly focus on these very areas, his studies and

[5] Escalona does not here mean the same as I when I speak of active peek-a-boo. Two of the three normal infants (Bob and Carl) I am reporting in this paper were not playing active peek-a-boo at six months. By "active participation" Escalona meant "that the child must do more than merely smile or laugh as mother removes the cloth . . . some children actively pull down a screen held by the mother; others remove the cloth that has been placed over their own head; and yet others move their bodies so as to alternate between hiding and looking at the mother" (personal communication). Only the third condition mentioned is active peek-a-boo by my definition. The other two are either passive peek-a-boo or transitional between passive and active.

this one complement each other in illuminating peek-a-boo. None of the observations of Heloise clash in any essential way with Piaget's findings. A comparison of the two sets of data illustrates very well Klein's (1966) contention that clinical investigations utilizing psychoanalytic concepts with special focus on meanings and motivations produce data quite different from those Piaget obtained in his study, which is more an ontogenetic history of intelligence in the first eighteen months. Each can contribute to a total knowledge from its limited focus. Wolff (1960) has stressed the extent to which Piaget's work can enrich psychoanalytic child psychology.

I shall briefly summarize Piaget's conclusions which clarify peek-a-boo, restricting the summary largely to his elaboration of the gradual acquisition of the concept of the inanimate object. In the second stage (second to sixth month) of Piaget's six stages of sensorimotor development, the child becomes able to coordinate grasping with his hand with looking. There is progress toward objectification in the sense that a thing which can be simultaneously grasped, looked at, and sucked becomes externalized in relation to the subject in a way that differs from the situation in which the response is only with one modality. This is still far from a conceptualization of an object separate from the self. Piaget's study of the child's response to a disappearing object revealed that the infant responds to an object only as long as it is directly available to one or more of his coordinated sensorimotor activities; the infant makes no effort to recover it after it has disappeared from his sphere of action; i.e., the baby will not try to find a toy if it is placed under a cover.

Piaget (1937, p. 33) states: "From the age of five to seven months the child becomes capable of practicing a sort of game of hide-and-seek which consists in removing from in front of his face the screen obstructing his view." During the third stage (fifth to eighth month) a beginning of permanence is conferred on things, but no systematic search for absent objects is yet observable (Piaget, 1937, p. 4). When an object disappears from his field of vision, the infant searches for it persistently and undertakes action in order to rediscover it. But the child initiates no search for the object unless he was already making an effort to grasp it before it disappeared; he does not look for the lost object in new and different directions when the search in progress does not produce it (Wolff, 1960). There is a beginning experience of *before* and *after*. Intentionality is limited to repeating events presented to the child while he is active. Clear-cut conditions which determine intention for Piaget—goal-directedness and self-initiation—are not fully present.

In the fourth stage of sensorimotor development (eighth to twelfth month), there is significant progress in the child's capacity to search persistently first for a partially hidden object and finally for a completely hidden one. Advances include new motor procedures developed while the child pursues a *familiar* goal in *unfamiliar* circumstances, the capacity for delay between the first perception of a goal and final action, and the use of detours as a means toward an intended goal. This signifies a certain degree of object permanence in the child's mind and true intention. Sustained intention to recover a hidden object is now possible as the object continues to "exist" for the child after he discontinues action on it. However, the object's permanence is still a function of the child's previous experiences with it, not based on awareness of the object's own properties or displacements. The spatial concepts of "in front of" and "behind" are established.

Since I have defined the essence of peek-a-boo as an alternating and controlled breaking of visual contact with a human object and reinstating of that contact, it is clear that Piaget's researches furnish basic data for comprehending aspects of peek-a-boo phenomena at any given developmental level. Thus he establishes the approximate ages for the occurrence of (1) the child's progressive conceptualization of an object external to and separate from himself; (2) levels of means for re-establishing contact with that object when it disappears; (3) the emergence of object permanence; (4) intention (goal-directedness and self-initiation); (5) capacity for delay and use of detours as means to a goal; and (6) the conceptualization of space, time, and causality.

Whereas Piaget is not concerned with individual variations or deviations from normal development, Provence and Ritvo (1961) contribute to our understanding by demonstrating how the concept of the existence of the inanimate object is markedly delayed in institutionalized babies deprived of adequate maternal care.

It is of great interest that quite divergent studies establish five to six months as the point of appearance of peek-a-boo: (1) Bühler's diaper test (1930); (2) Greenacre's onset of separation from the mother and beginning mental ego (1960); (3) Escalona (1963); (4) Mahler's (1965) onset of the phase of differentiation; (5) Piaget's (1937) timing of the "sort of game of hide-and-seek" and of the third stage of sensorimotor development with its beginnings of object permanence, of *before* and *after,* and of intentionality; (6) the observations of Heloise, Bob, and Carl in this study.

I believe there is a second critical time in the first year (between eight and eleven months), which is toward the end of Mahler's phase of differentiation, coincides with Spitz's eight-month anxiety (1950) or Benjamin's peak of stranger anxiety[6] (1963) and with Piaget's fourth stage where the child first knows of the existence of a hidden object (1937). Changes in peek-a-boo behavior signifying these maturational advances may include: (1) more evidence of self-initiation of the game; (2) versatility in the child's inventing his own means to carry out the essence of the play; (3) the child's self-imposed, increased capacity to prolong the phase of not seeing the loved person; (4) more clear-cut evidence that peek-a-boo behavior may be used to master stranger anxiety and separation anxiety. In Heloise, self-initiation occurred much earlier and prolongation of the "hiding" phase was not striking until she was almost twelve months, but a clue to the cited maturational events was her ability at thirty-nine weeks to close her eyes in anticipation as she dropped objects from her high chair. In Bob, especially, the following appeared coincidentally, at nine and a half months: the ability to locate a hidden object, the self-initiation of active peek-a-boo, the capacity to prolong the "hiding" phase, and the invention of new means to carry out the essence of peek-a-boo.

MEANINGS AND SIGNIFICANCE OF PEEK-A-BOO

In enumerating the meanings of peek-a-boo in the first year I would like to stress that not all these meanings will be present in a given child on a particular day, that usually one or two meanings predominate in any specific occurrence, and that our knowledge of

[6] Lois Murphy (1964) cites six to eight months as the age when differentiated recognition of mother in contrast to strangers has emerged or is emerging, although some infants show this much earlier. Heloise was one of the latter. Peek-a-boo is one of the coping devices for dealing with stranger anxiety through the triple mechanism of dosing the strangeness, turning passive into active, and self-protective withdrawal.

maturation and development makes it clear that passive peek-a-boo in a five-month-old, for example, usually has a different significance than self-initiated, active peek-a-boo in a ten-month-old.

The anlage of peek-a-boo is inherent in the anatomy and physiology of the eye with the lid's function of permitting, limiting, or shutting off vision. Also important as background for peek-a-boo is the fundamental, primitive, even biological rhythm, characteristic of various functions in the human organism (Greenacre, 1954, 1960). Vision is of great importance in the development of the ego in the first year.

For ease of presentation I have arbitrarily divided the meanings into four groups, *object relations, mastery, exploration and reality testing,* and *other ego functions.* The groups are overlapping and have themselves no great significance.

Object relations: Peek-a-boo both reflects and contributes to object relations in a number of ways. It is a form of interaction, play, a social game pleasurable to infant and adult. It represents a mutually responsive communication with a love object, whose attention the infant thus gains or whom the child may wish to please by playing the game. Thus one id aspect is expression of libidinal drive. Observation suggests that at times the child experiences a peculiar tension-pleasure during the "disappearance" phase (cf. Schur, 1962). Greenacre (1959) remarks how anxiety contributes to fun and excitement of play. At different times peek-a-boo serves to master anxiety of separate functioning (Mahler and Furer, 1963), separation anxiety, or anxiety of strangeness. The game turns what would be a painful experience into a pleasurable one. On the other hand, the play fosters separateness and individuation (bodily and social autonomy). In its passive form the mother doses frustration to create optimal frustration which leads to mental structure building (Kohut, 1966). The imitation aspect of peek-a-boo is another way in which learning takes place. Although in active peek-a-boo the child's own body and muscular skills play an indispensable role and the executive functions are exerted on body mechanisms (vision, motility, perception), it is an activity which is predominantly a reaction to and on the environment rather than primarily focused on pleasure from the body or its functions. The early stages of peek-a-boo could be called a "transitional" game, halfway between an autoerotic activity and true object relations.

For Heloise, peek-a-boo had particular significance in establishing a special playful relationship with her father with an element of display for her future oedipal object, and the game acted as oracle for the later character qualities of coyness, teasing, and flirting (tamed aggression as well as libido).

Mastery: In addition to aspects of mastery already mentioned, there is the ego's repetitive mastery of sensorimotor skills, which also can be viewed in id terms of canalization of aggressive drive into coordinated actions with associated libidinal gratification. In other ego terms, there is a change from passivity to activity (in active peek-a-boo), with increased mastery of the object and lessened danger of helplessness. There is pleasure of initiation and of accomplishment as well as the pleasure inherent in functioning or in rhythmic backward and forward motions. Proficiency may contribute to a sense of competence or an attitude of confidence.

Exploration and reality testing: Peek-a-boo represents a form of exploration and a means to a number of beginning differentiations crucial to early reality testing: internal from external, *me* from *not me, me* from *animate not me* (boundary setting of Federn[7]), distinctions which in turn contribute to the concept of body image and to ego structure building including the concept of self. Also involved are a perfection of visual perception, the mastery of making an object go and come, as well as the *magical* manipulation suggested by *now it is here* and *now it is gone* and I can control its going and coming.

For stimuli-sensitive Heloise peek-a-boo also became an avenue for controlling and limiting her sensory intake, one facet of an elaborate stimulus barrier she erected for herself.

Other ego functions: Besides imitation, peek-a-boo contains other aspects of *identification* (for example, the incorporation of the com-

[7] Of historical note, Lili Peller informed me that Paul Federn was quite interested in peek-a-boo. Ernst Federn, his son, told me in a personal communication that Federn included dropping and regaining objects and peek-a-boo in his conception of the sequence of the cathexis and decathexis involved in normal development. He stressed that a vigorous and pleasurable playing of peek-a-boo was a sign of a healthy ego development in the young child. These thoughts were not published but were discussed fully in a seminar, the predecessor of the Paul Federn Study Group.

ing and going of the parent into the behavior); Spitz (1957) considers the mechanism of identification the most conspicuous adaptive device near the end of the first and throughout the second year.

There is an element of *regression* in peek-a-boo behavior, and Heloise often used peek-a-boo as a regressive maneuver. Piaget (1937) and Provence and Ritvo (1961) contribute that finding a toy behind a screen requires a *thought process* in which the infant sustains an image of the toy. This suggests that after eight to nine months peek-a-boo involves problem solving which requires linking of the past (memory) with *anticipation* of the future typical of *secondary-process thinking.* The child's capacity to delay removal of the screen, i.e., prolongation of the hiding phase, suggests such a mental process.

Besides mastering conflict and reducing anxiety, peek-a-boo sometimes expresses conflict. It is possible to see in it a prototype of ambivalence, i.e., Heloise's closing and opening the door in her father's face. In shutting out the unpleasant (cf. Cameron, 1963, p. 46), mastering dosage, and channeling aggressive energy, it exercises a primitive defense function, a forerunner of denial and repression. Schur's statement (1962) is pertinent: "the turning of the head which makes the object disappear [is] . . . not only . . . [an] important stepping stone for the separation of 'I' and the 'Not-I' and for the development of the concept of NO, but more generally speaking for the development of the crucial biophysiological function of withdrawal, which also is the model of defence." Schur sees two sets of biogenetic polar tendencies that contribute to the development of object relations and structure building, namely, the need to approach and the necessity to withdraw. Of course, peek-a-boo practices both alternately.

The data from Heloise were also suggestive of behavior expressing early fantasy and illusion, precursors of creative imagination (cf. Fineman, 1962), and early forms of joking or humor.

PHENOMENOLOGICALLY SIMILAR BEHAVIORS

Heloise showed various types of behavior which on the surface resembled peek-a-boo or became blended with peek-a-boo at times. I shall list these and elaborate on one in particular: (1) application of a transitional object to the face; (2) a variety of actions expressing the social modalities (Erikson, 1948) of *holding on* and *letting go;*

(3) other forms of imitation and early identification; (4) maneuvers used for regression, especially to limit visual sensory intake; (5) phenomena in the first year leading to the development of the no concept: for example, Bob at ten months would turn his head laterally to indicate negation when he was being fed solids and did not want any more; at the same age lateral head turning was his preferred peek-a-boo method. If his father was present when his mother was feeding him, Bob might begin lateral head turning, thus expressing his desire to play peek-a-boo with his father *and* his lack of interest in the food; (6) manifestations of and coping devices for separation anxiety and stranger anxiety: for example, Spitz's (1957) description of the eight-month-old's response to the stranger has striking connections with peek-a-boo: "it can go from an expression of awe, or lowering the eyes as if embarrassed, or covering the eyes with the hands, or lifting the clothing before the eyes, to hiding the face in the blankets, etc. With the exception of the first and mildest form, all these actions serve to exclude the perception of the stranger's face. . . . The best proof that the child is fully conscious of what he is doing, but still tries in a wishful way to make the stranger disappear, is that the child looks back at the stranger again and again. He peeks between his fingers, he lifts his face from the blanket—and hides its again" (p. 55). (7) dropping and tossing and sometimes retrieving objects.

TOSSING OBJECTS AND PEEK-A-BOO

The infant's intentional dropping or tossing objects (which are sometimes retrieved) has little outer resemblance to peek-a-boo but much metapsychological similarity. Of course, many writers have cited Freud's example of the child with the bobbin (1920) to draw a parallel between toy throwing and peek-a-boo, showing the effort to master anxiety of object loss in both; a wish to get back what is lost is apparent in each. The time of onset of object dropping with some intention and active peek-a-boo is related (in Heloise abouty twenty-six weeks for both). In my experience, the *tossing* of objects,[8] which

[8] Bühler (1930) clarifies the relation between object dropping and tossing in the following timetable: 0;4 an object is lifted and lowered; 0;6 an object is permitted to fall; 0;9 an object is lifted up and permitted to fall; 0;10 an object is lifted with one hand, grasped with the other hand and permitted to fall; 0;11 an object is lifted up and thrown forward.

produces the familiar scene where a parent enters the child's room and finds all the child's crib companions and objects on the floor (Heloise at forty-one weeks), makes its appearance later than the infant's ability to carry out active peek-a-boo; but, in general, the two behaviors, object tossing and active peek-a-boo, express some of the same motivation, require somewhat similar skills, and appear during approximately the same developmental period. Carl, who did not play active, self-initiated peek-a-boo until forty-six and a half weeks: (1) looked at fallen objects, not purposely dropped at seven months; (2) from thirty-two weeks intentionally dropped objects from his crib and carriage; (3) at thirty-eight to forty-one weeks actively engaged in and enjoyed dropping objects; (4) at forty-seven weeks tossed stuffed animals from the crib for his mother to retrieve.

Winnicott (1957) dates the game of throwing things away at seven to nine months and associates it with a possible readiness to wean. Stone and Church (1957) list the seventh month for both the onset of toy dropping and peek-a-boo. Bühler (1930) chronicles the child's attempt to reach a fallen object by throwing a second at the first at nine months; throwing objects is a striking characteristic of the ten-month-old, and the eleven-month-old throws a plaything away in order to grasp toward a comrade who is in this way brought nearer.[9] Gesell and Amatruda (1941) list releasing a cube into the cup as a twelve-month accomplishment and letting a ball go somewhat toward an examiner at fifty-six weeks. Spock (1946) has a heading of dropping and throwing things as one of the one-year-old's attributes.

Piaget (1937) describes how at eight months (fourth stage) the child systematically searches on the floor for everything he happens to drop. At ten months the child experiments with the perception of bringing an object in his hand close to his face and then away in a repeated back-and-forth movement. Piaget (1945) documents that the child discovers free fall at about one year and "amuses himself by throwing everything to the ground." He characterizes as the chief advance in the fifth stage (twelve to sixteen months) the child's experimental study of visible displacements, the geometric relations

[9] Bühler's age levels stated here are slightly at variance with those she uses elsewhere in her book in describing the development of lifting up and throwing away objects (see footnote 8).

among objects, including moving objects away and bringing them near, letting them drop or throwing them down to pick them up and begin again (1937). Thus, in the same way that experimentation with muscular control, spatial relations, and visual perception of a human object is involved in peek-a-boo, in Piaget's view the main significance of dropping and tossing objects is that they are part of "conducting every possible experiment with distant space as well as near space." Both Furer (1964) and Burlingham and Barron (1963) have noted the differentiation of self and object inherent in object throwing. Other meanings which object tossing shares with peek-a-boo include: (1) social interaction (the desire for mother to retrieve the tossed object); (2) functional pleasure; (3) rhythmical motor skill; (4) activity replacing passivity; and (5) an expression of the social modalities of holding on and letting go.

Sometimes object dropping merely reflects the child's discontinued interest in the object; at other times object dropping or tossing seems to be a testing to see if the object will come back (which can be understood in terms of either Piaget's geometric relations or Freud's mastery of object loss or Mahler's stage of differentiation).

Conclusions

1. The developmental line (A. Freud, 1963, 1965) approach applied to the study of peek-a-boo permits a comprehensive view of its origins and evolution, allows correlation with other behavior in the first year, and suggests links between forms of peek-a-boo, being chased, hide-and-seek, and other hiding behavior in later years.

2. Differences in constitution, maturational unfolding of capacities, the progress of libidinal and aggressive drive organizations and ego development, and learning processes including identifications and other environmental influences contribute to variations of time of onset, frequency, forms utilized, degree of investment in the activity, and which of the possible meanings are expressed in a given child's peek-a-boo behavior.

3. There is a need for definition of peek-a-boo phenomena. The essence of the peek-a-boo game is the controlled, alternating interruption of visual contact with another person, primarily a love object, and the re-establishment of the contact. The term passive

peek-a-boo is applied when the controlling is by the other person. Active peek-a-boo involves the child's controlling the off-and-on contact. The active form can be initiated by the other person or can be self-initiated by the child. These definitions imposed on descriptions of peek-a-boo in the literature add considerable clarity to chronology, ego apparatuses used, and functions and processes involved in peek-a-boo at different age and developmental levels.

4. The anlage of the peek-a-boo game, contributing to the importance of peek-a-boo among first year behaviors, is found in the anatomy and physiology of the eye, where lid action permits, limits, or shuts off visual intake and stimulation and in the significance of vision for ego development in the first year. This aspect of the eye and peek-a-boo serves the important mechanism of withdrawal and is a forerunner of primitive defense, especially denial and repression. The rhythmical nature of peek-a-boo reflects an even, primitive, biological rhythmicity inherent in the organism.

5. The data from this study and a review of the relevant literature point to a great variability in the onset of the peek-a-boo game in individual children. The range for having the necessary faculties for the occurrence of passive peek-a-boo is four to nine months with five to six months being most usual. The range for having the necessary capacities for carrying out active peek-a-boo is six to eleven months. Another meaningful way of approaching the age of onset of passive and active peek-a-boo is to emphasize their association with the first subphase of the individuation process, the phase of differentiation (Mahler, 1965), in conjunction with all the emerging capacities of that period.

6. Another conception of the early form of active peek-a-boo is as a "transitional" game. It originates in the same developmental period as transitional object formation; it is a bridge between an autoerotic activity and an expression of true object relations.

7. A necessary condition for the occurrence of active peek-a-boo is the maturation of the ego apparatuses involved in memory, anticipation, visual and auditory perception, beginning differentiation of self from nonself, and control of motility including hand-eye coordination. The work of Provence and Lipton (1962) shows that adequate maternal care is an added necessary condition for peek-a-boo to emerge. Passive peek-a-boo usually precedes the active form, with

the usual sequence in the child being: response to the adult, imitation, and finally initiation. An exception to this pattern was evident in Heloise, who displayed active peek-a-boo without passive peek-a-boo as predecessor.

8. Passive peek-a-boo offers a striking illustration of how the mother doses frustration to attain an optimum frustration which fosters separation-individuation and ego structure building.

9. Piaget's studies of the development of intelligence, especially his elaboration of the gradual acquisition of the concept of the inanimate object and the timing of awareness of a hidden object, help clarify the cognitive foundation for the type of peek-a-boo seen at different developmental levels.

10. Two critical periods associated with peek-a-boo in the first year can roughly be discerned. The first is about five to six months,[10] which is mostly a passive peek-a-boo stage. It is associated with beginning mental ego, the onset of Mahler's phase of differentiation and the early separation of self and object, the child's ability to remove a screen before its face, and the start of Piaget's third stage, with its beginnings of object permanence, of *before* and *after,* and of intentionality. Only the *start* of active peek-a-boo is occasionally seen.

11. A second critical time, the active peek-a-boo stage, is approximately eight to eleven months. This is toward the end of Mahler's phase of differentiation, and coincides with Spitz's eight-month anxiety, the peak of stranger anxiety (Benjamin), and Piaget's fourth stage, where knowledge of the existence of the hidden object is attained, and persistent search, a certain degree of object permanence, true intentionality, and the capacity for delay and detours are all appearing. In addition to the perfection of *active* peek-a-boo, the new acquirements may be reflected in: (1) more self-initiation; (2) inventing new forms; (3) self-imposed prolongation of hiding phase;

[10] The findings of Bühler (1930) vary some from my suggested critical times. Her developmental tests contain three peek-a-boo items: (1) the diaper test at five months, where the child can remove or extricate himself from a diaper laid on his face; (2) at nine months playing "cuckoo" (passive peek-a-boo): the child's face is covered with a diaper as the examiner says "cuckoo"; ten seconds later the diaper is lifted by the examiner who says "dada," and the child looks and smiles; (3) at eleven months, the "cuckoo" game is repeated, but at this age the child himself lifts the diaper and replaces it after it is first done by the examiner (active peek-a-boo, initiated by the object). Bühler also describes pleasure from "hide and seek" (passive peek-a-boo) at eight months.

(4) the use of peek-a-boo as means of mastery of stranger and separation anxiety.

12. The literature and data from this study suggest many meanings in the peek-a-boo phenomena, not all present on a given occurrence, nor in one child, nor at the same developmental level:

Peek-a-boo reflects and contributes to object relations; it is a social interaction and play, a mutually responsive communication which is pleasurable, often attention-seeking or carried out to please the love object, an expression of libidinal drive. In it can be seen imitation, identification, and other aspects of learning.

The game fosters separateness and individuation as well as a sense of twoness, enhancing awareness of another person separate from the self. There are thus many ways in which mental structure (both ego and id) building is spurred by peek-a-boo, including development of the self. An additional aspect of id organizing is the canalization of aggressive drive into coordinated action. Activity replaces passivity. Differentiations crucial to reality testing—internal and external, *me* and *not-me*—are encouraged. Body-image awareness is enhanced. Visual perception is perfected as well as a feeling of magic manipulation and control.

Tension-reduction aspects of the peek-a-boo game include: mastery of anxiety of strangeness and of separation, and practicing regression and the function of withdrawal, models of primitive defense.

Other positive aspects of peek-a-boo are: experimentation, including exploration of spatial relations; holding on and letting go; repetitive mastery of sensorimotor skills; functional pleasure and pleasure from an even rhythm; mastery of the environment; and developing a sense of competence and an attitude of assurance. A controlled, early form of ambivalence is expressed.

Additionally, for Heloise, the main subject of the observations above, peek-a-boo offered a special play with her father, the forerunner of oedipal themes and hints of later character qualities of coyness, teasing, and flirtatiousness, representing both tamed aggression and libidinal expression. For this stimulus-sensitive child the game was one way of dosing sensory intake, part of an elaborate stimulus barrier. It also seemed an avenue for fantasy elaboration and illusion, precursors to creative imagination, and possibly an early medium for joking and humor.

13. At one time peek-a-boo activity can predominantly be used for sensory withdrawal, at another time for seeking stimulation in the object world, or to master anxiety, or to practice newly discovered means of spatial exploration, at other times to test the reality of the external world or be used to communicate or be dropped when other communication takes precedence.

14. There is a progression of peek-a-boo during the first year, gradually becoming a more complex activity, expressing more meanings as new maturational capacities are acquired. For example, the tendency for self-imposed prolongation of the hiding phase, late in the first year, reflects greater differentiation of self and object, memory for the lost object, and tolerance of delay. There is a tendency to shift from passive to active peek-a-boo, though with overlapping.

15. Peek-a-boo becomes associated with other behaviors which either are phenomenologically similar or at times blend with peek-a-boo. Among the most important are: transitional object formation, the development of the concept of no, reality testing through visual perception, manifestations of and coping devices for stranger anxiety and separation anxiety, regressive maneuvers, especially those limiting visual sensory intake, and dropping and tossing of objects. Particularly the last-named has a number of metapsychological similarities to peek-a-boo. Two general tendencies of life are the need to approach and the necessity for withdrawal. Both are practiced in peek-a-boo.

16. Meanings shared in common by object tossing and peek-a-boo behavior include: social interaction, functional pleasure, rhythmical motor skill, holding on and letting go, mastery of object loss, separation of self and object, activity replacing passivity, and experimentation with spatial relations. The early forms of object tossing including dropping are, like peek-a-boo, associated with the phase of differentiation.

17. In the course of first year peek-a-boo, a number of key ego apparatuses, serving a variety of ego functions, part functions, and mechanisms, are both utilized and fostered. Involved in peek-a-boo are: memory; purposive control of motility, including control of rhythm; perception; anticipation; communicatory behavior including early language and sometimes speech; reality testing; emergence

of self; intention; object relations; positive cathexis of the body and evolvement of body image; intelligence including problem solving, spatial relations, and understanding cause and effect; synthesis and integration; thought (secondary process and fantasy); forerunners of character; primitive defense; positive employment of controlled aggression; turning of passive into active as adaptation; capacity for delay and detours; identification; and regression.

18. Because it is a behavior capable of utilizing and developing such a variety of ego apparatuses, of exercising many ego functions and mechanisms, and of expressing so many meanings, peek-a-boo has more importance than other infantile games in the first year and represents a landmark in first year development.

Summary

Data about the peek-a-boo game are presented from the longitudinal observations of one child in particular, during her first year, with additional related material from longitudinal studies of two other children, also in the first year. A variety of statements about peek-a-boo from the psychoanalytic literature and the studies of Piaget on the development of the concept of an object are compared with the findings of this study to clarify the origins, onset, meanings, and significance of peek-a-boo phenomena and their evolution and progression. This evolution is related to innate factors, maturational unfolding of capacities, and environmental influence and learning. Associated behavioral phenomena are traced. The essence of the peek-a-boo game is defined, and a distinction between passive and active peek-a-boo is suggested to illuminate the behavior more precisely. Active peek-a-boo is further subdivided according to whether initiation is from the child or the other person. The relation of object dropping and tossing to peek-a-boo is discussed. The complexity of meanings and functions expressed in peek-a-boo and the importance of the ego apparatuses it utilizes and develops make peek-a-boo a landmark in development of the first year.

BIBLIOGRAPHY

Benjamin, J. D. (1963), Further Comments on Some Developmental Aspects of Anxiety. In: *Counterpoint: Libidinal Object and Subject,* ed. H. S. Gaskill. New York: International Universities Press, pp. 121-153.

Brenner, C. (1955), *An Elementary Textbook of Psychoanalysis*. New York: International Universities Press.

Bühler, C. (1930), *The First Year of Life*. New York: John Day.

Burlingham, D. & Barron, A. T. (1963), A Study of Identical Twins: Their Analytic Material Compared with Existing Observation Data of Their Early Childhood. *This Annual,* 18:367-423.

Call, J. D. & Marschak, M. (1966), Styles and Games in Infancy. *J. Amer. Acad. Child Psychiat.,* 5:193-210.

Cameron, N. (1963), *Personality Development and Psychopathology*. Boston: Houghton Mifflin.

Cruikshank, R. M. (1946), Animal Infancy. In: *Manual of Child Psychology,* ed. L. Carmichael. New York: Wiley, 2nd ed., 1954, pp. 167-189.

Erikson, E. H. (1948), Growth and Crises of the Healthy Personality. In: *Identity and the Life Cycle* [*Psychological Issues,* Monogr. 1]. New York: International Universities Press, 1959, pp. 50-100.

—— (1950), *Childhood and Society*. New York: Norton.

Escalona, S. K. (1963), Patterns of Infantile Experience and the Developmental Process. *This Annual,* 18:197-244.

Federn, P. Personal communication from his son, Ernst Federn, 1966.

Fineman, J. (1962), Observations on the Development of Imaginative Play in Early Childhood. *J. Amer. Acad. Child Psychiat.,* 1:167-181.

Fraiberg, S. (1959), *The Magic Years*. New York: Scribner.

Freud, A. (1963), The Concept of Developmental Lines. *This Annual,* 18:245-265.

—— (1965), *Normality and Pathology in Childhood: Assessments of Development*. New York: International Universities Press.

Freud, S. (1920), Beyond the Pleasure Principle. *Standard Edition,* 18:7-64. London: Hogarth Press, 1955.

—— (1926), Inhibitions, Symptoms and Anxiety. *Standard Edition,* 20:87-172. London: Hogarth Press, 1959.

Furer, M. (1964), The Development of a Preschool Symbiotic Psychotic Boy. *This Annual,* 19:448-469.

Gesell, A. & Amatruda, C. S. (1941), *Developmental Diagnosis*. New York: Hoeber.

Greenacre, P. (1954), In: Problems of Infantile Neurosis: A Discussion. *This Annual,* 9:16-71.

—— (1957), The Childhood of the Artist: Libidinal Phase Development and Giftedness. *This Annual,* 12:47-72.

—— (1959), Play in Relation to Creative Imagination. *This Annual,* 14:61-80.

—— (1960), Considerations Regarding the Parent-Infant Relationship. *Int. J. Psa.,* 41:571-584.

—— (1962), Discussion and Comments on the Psychology of Creativity. *J. Amer. Acad. Child Psychiat.,* 1:129-137.

Grinstein, A. (1956-1965), *The Index of Psychoanalytic Writings,* 8 Vols. New York: International Universities Press.

Hendrick, I. (1951), Early Development of the Ego: Identification in Infancy. *Psa. Quart.,* 20:44-61.

Kleeman, J. A. (1964), Optimal Sensory Opportunity in Infancy: A Review and a Case Report from a Longitudinal Study. Unpublished.

Klein, G. S. (1966), Perspectives to Change in Psychoanalytic Theory. Presented at a meeting of the Western New England Psychoanalytic Society, New Haven, Conn.

Kohut, H. (1966), Discussion in a postgraduate seminar on Internalization, Western New England Institute for Psychoanalysis.

Mahler, M. S. (1965), On the Significance of the Normal Separation-Individuation Phase: With Reference to Research in Symbiotic Child Psychosis. In: *Drives, Affects, Behavior,* ed. M. Schur. New York: International Universities Press, 2:161-169.

—— & Furer, M. (1963), Certain Aspects of the Separation-Individuation Phase. *Psa. Quart.,* 32:1-14.
Murphy, G., Murphy, L. E., & Newcomb, T. M., eds. (1937), *Experimental Social Psychology.* New York: Harper.
Murphy, L. (1964), Adaptational Tasks in Childhood in Our Culture. *Bull. Menninger Clin.,* 28:309-322.
Omwake, E. (1963), The Child's Estate. In: *Modern Perspectives in Child Development: In Honor of Milton J. E. Senn,* ed. A. J. Solnit & S. A. Provence. New York: International Universities Press, pp. 577-594.
Peller, L. E. (1954), Libidinal Phases, Ego Development, and Play. *This Annual,* 9:178-198.
—— (1955), Libidinal Development as Reflected in Play. *Psychoanalysis,* 3(3):3-11.
Phillips, R. H. (1960), The Nature and Function of Children's Formal Games. *Psa. Quart.,* 29:200-207.
Piaget, J. (1936), *The Origins of Intelligence in Children.* New York: International Universities Press, 1952.
—— (1937), *The Construction of Reality in the Child.* New York: Basic Books, 1954.
—— (1945), *Play, Dreams and Imitation in Childhood.* New York: Norton, 1951.
Provence, S. A. & Lipton, R. C. (1962), *Infants in Institutions.* New York: International Universities Press.
—— & Ritvo, S. (1961), Effects of Deprivation on Institutionalized Infants: Disturbances in Development of Relationships to Inanimate Objects. *This Annual,* 16:189-205.
Ritvo, S. & Provence, S. A. (1953), Form Perception and Imitation in Some Autistic Children: Diagnostic Findings and Their Contextual Interpretation. *This Annual,* 8:155-161.
Rosenblith, J. F. & Allinsmith, W., eds. (1962), *The Causes of Behavior: Readings in Child Development and Educational Psychology.* Boston: Allyn & Bacon.
Ross, H. (1965), The Teacher Game. *This Annual,* 20:288-297.
Schur, M. (1962), The Theory of Parent-Infant Relationship. *Int. J. Psa.,* 43:243-245.
—— (1966), *The Id and the Regulatory Principles of Mental Functioning.* New York: International Universities Press.
Spitz, R. A. (1950), Anxiety in Infancy: A Study of Its Manifestations in the First Year of Life. *Int. J. Psa.,* 31:138-143.
—— (1957), *No and Yes: On the Genesis of Human Communication.* New York: International Universities Press.
Spock, B. (1946), *The Pocket Book of Baby and Child Care.* New York: Pocket Books.
Stone, L. J. & Church, J. (1957), *Childhood and Adolescence.* New York: Random House.
Thorpe, L. P. (1946), *Child Psychology and Development.* New York: Ronald Press.
White, R. W. (1960), Competence and the Psychosexual Stages of Development. In: *The Causes of Behavior: Readings in Child Development and Educational Psychology,* ed. J. F. Rosenblith & W. Allinsmith. Boston: Allyn & Bacon, 1962, pp. 213-221.
Winnicott, D. W. (1953), Transitional Objects and Transitional Phenomena: A Study of the First Not-Me Possession. *Int. J. Psa.,* 34:89-97.
—— (1957), *Mother and Child: A Primer of First Relationships.* New York: Basic Books.
Wolff, P. H. (1960), *The Developmental Psychologies of Jean Piaget and Psychoanalysis* [*Psychological Issues,* Monogr. 5]. New York: International Universities Press.

SOME PSYCHOANALYTIC CONSIDERATIONS ON SPEECH IN NORMAL DEVELOPMENT AND PSYCHOPATHOLOGY

HAROLD KOLANSKY, M.D. (Philadelphia)

Speech is necessary in virtually all human endeavors, though some professions or occupations depend more on speech than do others. The clinical practice of psychoanalysis makes very special use of speech. The analyst depends on the patient's speech to obtain a history of the present illness, to make a differential diagnosis, to assess levels of development and indications of ego and libidinal regression. Psychoanalytic treatment itself is conducted primarily by verbal means, on the part of both patient and analyst.

For this reason, the analyst must have an awareness of how to use his own speech as an effective therapeutic tool. In addition, he should know how speech develops and how it influences other aspects of personality development. Moreover, as an aid to diagnosis, he must have a working knowledge of the characteristic speech patterns in a variety of clinical conditions.

I shall present some clinical material and thoughts on the psychological aspects of normal speech and on some aspects of pathology related to speech. In this, I shall adopt a developmental framework. Given a normal central nervous system, each phase of psychosexual and ego development leaves its own imprint on speech development and pathology.

The Oral Phase

Initially during the primary narcissistic phase, the infant cannot distinguish between himself and external objects; he reacts to stress

Director, Section of Child Psychiatry at Albert Einstein Medical Center, Philadelphia, Pennsylvania, and member of the Child Analysis Study Group and faculty of the Institute of the Philadelphia Association for Psychoanalysis.

by crying rather than by words or other signals. Ferenczi (1913), in his classic paper on "Stages in the Development of the Sense of Reality," delineated the gradual transitions to the ability to use words as signals. Freud (1911) indicated that at first the infant's activities are governed by the pleasure principle. When "psychical rest was originally disturbed" by demands of internal wishes, "whatever was thought of (wished for) was simply presented in a hallucinatory manner, just as still happens to-day with our dream-thoughts every night. It was only the non-occurrence of the expected satisfaction, the disappointment experienced, that led to the abandonment of this attempt at satisfaction by means of hallucination." He stated that a new principle of mental functioning was introduced and this dealt with what was real, not simply with what was agreeable. This was the establishment of the reality principle. The reality principle leads the infant into socialization, education, interpersonal relationships, and the rapid expansion of appropriate ego functions, especially thinking, memory, judgment, control of motility, reality testing, and the synthetic function. All of this is, in no small measure, dependent upon the development of speech, for, as Freud stated, "thinking was originally unconscious, in so far as it went beyond mere ideational presentations and was directed to the relations between impressions of objects, and that it did not acquire further qualities, perceptible to consciousness until it became connected with verbal residues." If the infant's relationship to the mother is poor—either because of the mother's inability to provide psychological nurture for her offspring or because of a biological deficiency in the infant's central nervous system—then pleasure-principle functioning may continue, a delay in the self-object differentiation becomes evident, and the infant does not show the social precursors of differentiation and speech, such as smiling, cooing, and recognition of the part object. Development of speech may then be long delayed, or absent as in the autistic child. When speech develops in such a youngster, it is frequently echolalic and demonstrates a poor differentation from the mother, as can be seen by misuse of pronouns. Ekstein (1965), in an extensive review of psychoanalytic concepts on early development of language, presents some material on Nanny, a three-and-a-half-year-old autistic girl, who showed this type of pathology: she repeated the therapist's description of her activities in the third person, saying,

"Here, Nanny go." It appeared to Ekstein that eventually Nanny followed the commands of the therapist as if following a primitive (and I might add, incorporated) voice of conscience. The child's mother later noted Nanny repeating certain of the therapist's statements verbatim, and this "seemed to be an attempt to introject the therapist, to incorporate her voice, and to become the therapist. The therapist's communication, repeated later by the child, has now become a quasi organizer of the patient's inner life." He added that echolalia was "the auditory substitute for the transitional object." Ekstein stated, "The appeal of the psychotherapist has not yet become a permanent part of the child's inner life, but must constantly be restored through echolalia, a form of self-appeal, a *forerunner of internal language* and internal thought of silent inner speech." This example demonstrates not simply the pathology of undifferentiation, and a therapeutic effort to aid the child toward the step of differentiation; it also indicates the process by which the mother and her commands are incorporated (silently) by the healthy child whose differentiation from -the mother has proceeded well. Ekstein's example is reminiscent of an autistic boy of five whom I saw periodically over a period of several years (while primarily aiding his parents and teachers in providing a therapeutic environment for him). On one occasion, after his speech began to be evident, I gave him a red airplane which he had admired in my playroom. He responded to the gift with obvious pleasure and much excitement, but with only a partial ability to verbalize his own pleasure; he said what he had frequently heard his mother say, but it had not yet become fully part of himself: "Oh Jackie, say how glad you are, say how happy; Tell Dr. Kolansky, what a nice red airplane it is! Say thank you!"

Significantly, Anna Freud (1965) states, "In the beginning of life . . . the infant seems to concentrate on the development along those lines which call forth most ostensibly the mother's love and approval . . . and, in comparison, to neglect others where such approval is not given." The activities approved by the mother become libidinized, thereby receiving stimulation for further growth. Regarding speech, she said, it makes "a difference to the timing of speech development and the quality of early verbalization if a mother, for reasons of her own personality structure, makes contact with her infant not through bodily channels but through talking" (p. 86). Children of such mothers may speak quite precociously, but they may remain physically awkward for years because the mother does not appear to place libidinal interest in such activities.

To return to the theme of the importance of speech in the developmental processes of acquiring a sense of reality, secondary-process thinking, differentiation of self and external objects, and in furthering ego development, A. Katan (1961) particularly emphasized the importance of the young child's ability to verbalize feeling. She said, "1. Verbalization of perceptions of the outer world precedes verbalization of feelings. 2. Verbalization leads to an increase of the controlling function of the ego over affects and drives. 3. Verbalization increases for the ego the possibility of distinguishing between wishes and fantasies on the one hand, and reality on the other. In short, verbalization leads to the integrating process, which in turn results in reality testing and thus helps to establish the secondary process" (p. 185).

A woman with a severe character disorder manifesting itself especially in sadistic outbursts against her children demonstrated that pathology results not only from arrests in ego development before speech is acquired but also from ego regressions occurring after the acquisition of speech. When this woman was able to begin to be conscious of her feelings, through speech in the analytic sessions, the sadistic actions began to stop. A. Katan's emphasis on the acquisition of ego control through verbalization is noteworthy in regard to this vignette. Actually the process of psychoanalysis is in a sense entirely dependent on this very point—that speech replaces action. Ultimately, when neurotically induced regressions become understandable and pathological actions cease, integration occurs.

A. Freud (1965) complements A. Katan's remarks when she states, "*A temper tantrum* . . . may be no more than the direct motor-affective outlet for chaotic drive derivatives in a young child; in this case, there is every chance that it will disappear as a symptom, without any form of treatment, as soon as speech and other more ego-syntonic channels of discharge have been established" (p. 111). Again one must consider those cases in which, through regression, we become aware of the same process. A boy of eight had such temper tantrums unexpectedly whenever he had a brief holiday from school.

Finally, with the ability to discuss his feelings of anxiety about his acceptability to his peers, the regressive tantrums ceased and he was able to make age-appropriate plans.

The Anal-sadistic Phase

As we consider the vicissitudes of speech during the anal-sadistic phase of development, we are struck by speech taking on the characteristics and vicissitudes of that stage itself; thus, early in this phase of development, we see a strong element of negativism, and with it verbal refusals. This development is not in itself pathological; it appears to be related to the pleasure the toddler feels in having achieved a certain amount of autonomy through the development of speech and walking. Thus, he is now less dependent on his mother, having begun to pass through a separation-individuation phase. Mahler, Furer, and Settlage (1959) link speech and locomotion to separation-individuation. They state, "This primitive, initial phase of individuation occurring at the height of the symbiotic phase, advances toward the separation-individuation and consolidation of such autonomous functions of the ego as locomotion, the beginning of language, and ideation." One of my patients suffered from a symbiotic infantile psychosis, as described by Mahler (1952). His illness was characterized in part by a speech disorder in which at any moment one could recognize his partial identification with others. This was especially evident in relation to his mother, but was also seen in relation to his father, brother, teacher, and me. He appeared not to be a person in his own right, but to be composed of sharply segmented bits and pieces of all significant people who served the purpose of his symbiotic needs, in his massive effort to ward off overwhelming panic at times when he tried to separate himself from his mother. He showed no trace of negativism at any stage of his development, and this in itself is pathological.

Negativism and a negative verbal reaction have other important functions in the anal-sadistic phase. They assist in retaining the autonomy of newly acquired sphincter control. The child says in effect, through his negativism, "I will now control myself and my BM's, any way I please, and you cannot make me do it your way." We know the frequency with which we see the regressive components of the anal-sadistic stage of development in our obsessional patients, who are so prone to negativism, doubting, ambivalence, and obstinacy in their speech and action in the analysis. Freud made clear the relationship between the obsessional neurosis and the anal-sadistic stage as early as 1913.

An obsessional woman in analysis with me struggled with a form of thinking that could be understood as a type of thought equivalent of what she originally experienced during the actual control of her bowel movements in a physical way at ages two to three. It was as if the physical process of moving a mass (the bowel movement) from one location (her body) to another (her panties, the rug, or the toilet), while actively and verbally opposing her mother's commands, was now displaced to her thinking, in which one could sense her struggle over moving a thought to a new location, or in displacing one thought with another, accompanied by much doubting and obstinacy, in what she characterized as her "checks and balances." One day she arrived a minute late for her psychoanalytic session, an unheard-of transgression for her! While she told the story of her one-minute lateness her speech was characterized by the confusion so indicative of this laborious form of thought movement; it epitomized her struggle over autonomy or compliance in childhood. It was the last day of the month, a day when she always brought a check to pay for her analytic sessions. She left the house exactly on time, as was her custom, but she had forgotten the check! She was torn with conflict; she had never been late for a session, nor had she ever forgotten her check. She had to choose a course which would inevitably make her guilty. She returned for the check, and in the process was late, and then her speech was ununderstandable, in her ego's efforts to cover over the transgression of lateness.

There are numerous other vicissitudes of speech in the anal-sadistic phase; however, I shall refer to only one, stammering.

Spring (1935) gave a classic description of the relationship of stammering to conflicts over anal-sadistic wishes, demonstrating the upward displacement of the conflict from anus to mouth. Pearson (1949) described a thirteen-year-old boy with severe stammering, fears, nightmares, and asthma. The stuttering, in part, represented his desire to kiss and suck his mother's breasts. These ideas caused him horrible embarrassment. Contained in the symptom were marked anal-sadomasochistic attitudes as well. His fantasies were of murderous and cruel attacks on girls and women, particularly attacks on their buttocks. He had strong exhibitionistic drives; but through regression to the anal-sadistic stage and through upward displacement to the mouth, the exhibitionism was represented by the equivalent of passing flatus. His stutter thus conveyed the attacking, sucking, flatus-passing elements, satisfying his unconscious libidinal wishes, while simultaneously causing him great embarrassment, which in turn satisfied his superego's demand for punishment.

In an earlier report (1960) of the treatment of a three-year-old stammerer, I described at least two major components in the symptom: one was a wish to continue soiling, which had been curtailed when twin sisters were born. "Later, the conflict over this wish led to the formation of defenses: the anal preoccupation was displaced upward (to the mouth), and concurrently marked reaction formations against soiling developed. The other component . . . was a regression to oral sadism, activated by the absence of her mother . . . when the twins were born, by the severity of the grandmother's final measures to establish bowel training, and especially by the attention paid to her twin sisters" (p. 281f.). Biting wishes were repressed and there was a return of the repressed through the speech mechanism. Ann, the three-year-old, also turned much aggression against herself. The speech problem represented the wish to soil, bite, and to incorporate her mother; simultaneously it represented punishment because the mutilation of speech embarrassed her and did not allow her to receive the approval she wanted. Thus in Ann, and in Spring's and Pearson's cases, the speech disturbance was overdetermined, as neurotic symptoms are in general, and embodied wish and punishment components. In all three cases, anal-sadistic components were prominent aspects of the regressive nature of the stammering.

It is important to note that for similar reasons, normal children in the anal-sadistic stage of development may have very brief periods of stammering, from which they recover without treatment. These cases are of course variants of the infantile neurosis.

Wentworth and Flexner (1960) call attention to the way in which words describing bathroom activities, in the anal phase, reflect the actual sounds of the anal and urethral excretory activity through the use of onomatopoeia. Thus, we hear "cis," "boom-boom," "ah ah," "poo poo," "tinkle," and "wee." Moreover, they point to the adult's needs to become a child (regression) through the use of the terms "little boy's room" and "little girl's room."

The Phallic and Oedipal Phases

As we have seen so far, many psychological factors play their part in shaping speech in the oral and anal-sadistic phases of development, but speech itself is also a most important ego function serving to consolidate other aspects of the ego's development. In the phallic and oedipal phases of development, speech has many different purposes, one of which is its use to consolidate masculine and feminine identification. The boy, under the impact of his biological development, values the penis, masturbates, and exhibits the characteristics of aggressiveness, competition, noisy vocal dominance, and exhibitionism. If the parents are not threatened by this, due to their own unconscious conflicts, and if the father is both masculine and unworried about his son's advancements, the boy's phallic position is secured, and his voice reflects his father's. The girl is at first also under the dominance of the phallic drives, and her position and voice may be similar to the boy's, until the crushing acceptance of castration at the beginning of her oedipal phase ultimately turns her in the direction of femininity and thus also brings in its wake attempts to modify her voice. In children whose identification with the parent of the same sex is impaired, one of the first signs of severe emotional disorder apparent to us is the use of the voice in a way reminding us of the opposite sex. We also know of instances in children and adults in whom ego regressions occur in the face of severe castration threats, a first sign of such threat and regression often being infantile speech.

A boy of twelve, who suffered most intensely from phobias related to severe castration anxiety, talked in a high-pitched, babyish voice whenever boys in his class threatened him verbally or physically. His behavior soon matched his voice, so that he was in effect communicating the idea to the boys, "Don't pick on me. I am no threat to you. I am only a baby, and babies can't hurt anyone and shouldn't be hurt." This boy's ego was mildly impaired, and it was difficult for him to defend against his impulses; thus, at an earlier time, he expressed the fantasy and terrifying fear that he would become a "penis murderer," and as a consequence would lose his penis himself and die. In his analysis we were able to learn that he had had fantasies of cutting off his father's large penis and sewing it onto his own, thus making himself superattractive to his mother. The fantasied result was his father's death and, as a punishment, his own untimely death, by castration.

This boy's play sought to deny his smallness, which meant an inability to attract his mother, and so at an early age, he became proficient in the care of his father's cameras, projectors, tape recorders, and other items. However, this proficiency reintroduced castration anxiety and the ensuing verbal and play regression, since being big meant being a "penis murderer." In many ways his speech and play obeyed in caricature the normal speech and play of this stage, so well characterized by Peller (1954) in the following way: "The *anxiety* which this play [which has a high visibility and uses the trappings and costume and speech of the adult world] undertakes to deny may be put into these words: 'I am small, I am left out of the pleasures of the grownups,' and the *compensatory* fantasy: 'I am big, I can do what the adults are doing' " (p. 188). Peller describes the vividness of the play and speech of the oedipal phase in which "aspirations and disappointments strike hard." The child thus obtains libidinal and destructive satisfactions. We also know, however, that the anxiety engendered by his satisfactions are reflected in his phobias, nightmares, and pavor nocturnus—all components of the universal infantile neurosis.

We also know (Freud, 1923) that both boys and girls react to the perception of the fact that girls do not have penises, with denial. This is a normal mechanism of defense in the phallic phase; but if it is used excessively in later stages of development, it may indicate neurotic difficulty. The normal use of such denial in words was heard in the reaction of a three-year-old girl who saw her new baby brother being diapered for a first time: for several nights while being bathed by her mother, she asked a series of questions, which were derivatives of her penis envy and castration anxiety and generally dealt with concerns about the nature of the growth of trees, plants, and flowers. Finally, she embarked on a series of direct questions about the presence or absence of a penis in members of her family, acknowledging the presence of a penis on her grandfather, father, and brother, and the absence in her grandmother, aunts, and mother, but her final question was, "Do I have a penis?" To this her mother barely had time to answer *no,* when the little girl said, "Yes, I have a penis! Here it is," while pulling actively at her recessed umbilicus.

It is important to note that in prelatency children, speech ultimately aids us in understanding their masturbation struggles. Thus Blanchard (1953) said, in quoting Eichholtz and A. Freud, "It is impossible to guess from the behavior of children what their masturbation fantasies may be." She described a three-year-old who suffered intensely whenever his mother was away from him. At those times he sucked his thumb and with the other hand rubbed his penis. One day, in play he substituted a mother doll for his thumb, biting and sucking it vigorously; then he became very anxious, cried, and asked for his mother. She continued, "His anxiety subsided only after he was told repeatedly that he had not really eaten his mother but had only wished to eat her. Until he tried to eat the doll and then cried for his mother, the probable content of his masturbation fantasy could not be deduced from his behavior."

Similarly, in a young man who had treated women very cruelly and attempted suicide prior to coming into analysis, relative silence in the analytic sessions made it impossible to comprehend his behavior, until one day, two and one half years after the analysis began, and after a desperately anxious struggle, he told me that whenever he was silent he was struggling over the wish and the fear to tell me about his masturbation, which was practiced many times daily for ten years. His penis had become swollen, in its normal resting state, now greatly increasing his fears. His masturbation fantasies dealt with injuring, torturing, and killing, and in that sense he also reminds me of what Blanchard said of the usual cause of guilt and anxiety about masturbation in children: "It is not strange that children usually are anxious and guilty about masturbating, in view of the fact that the fantasies so often are concerned with injuring, torturing or killing people whom they love as well as hate." They then feel punishment is deserved.

It would appear that our language often reflects the adult's difficulties in resolving his sexual masturbatory guilts. One regressive avenue sought for solution is the commonplace use of oral terms for sexuality. Wentworth and Flexner (1960) list sixty-four such terms, including banana, cherry, chick, cold fish, dish, eat, fruit, honey, meat, nuts, sweetie, tart, tomato, and weenie.

The Latency Phase

The latency period also presents us with certain developmental and potentially pathological features that bear upon speech, and to consider these properly, we must ask ourselves what psychological purposes latency serves.

Among the developmental tasks of the latency period are: (1) The absolute need to keep in repression the prelatent oedipal impulses, which, if unrepressed, lead to continuing states of very marked castration anxiety. There is therefore the need to ward off masturbation. (2) Related to this aim and aiding its continuation is the continuing development of the superego. Through this development pregenital impulses are kept in check, and a portion of the superego is utilized in ego-ideal formation. (3) The ego's ability to utilize sublimation in learning experiences. Traditionally, the child begins school, learns sports, and learns many things from peers during this period. To a large extent, the psychic energy for these activities is derived from the repressed sexual impulses, including the incestuous wishes, in addition to sexual curiosity, exhibitionism, and voyeurism. (4) The learning experiences developed through peer relationships, which form a solid basis for later friendships and heterosexual relationships.

The latency child has three main routes available to accomplish these developmental tasks. These are: (1) Regression to preoedipal and anal-sadistic impulses, and obsessional defenses erected against the regressed derivatives, as described in Bornstein's (1951) fundamental paper on latency. (2) Development of increased motor activities, which also aid in keeping oedipal fantasies in repression. Kaplan (1965) has presented convincing material on this aspect of development. (3) Development of peer relationships, which take the child outside the home and away from the parental objects of his oedipal wishes. Pearson (1966) has described the importance of this often overlooked normal phase of latency development.

Madow and Silverman (1956) described aspects of cortical development and electroencephalographic tracings, which appear to confirm, from a biological standpoint, the psychological factors described by Bornstein (1951) to account for the different appearance of the child in the first and second phase of latency, especially in regard to the hyperactivity of the child from six to ten. They stated that myelinization of the corticothalamic tracts is not complete till about eight, and that around the same age the alpha-wave patterns in the electroencephalogram stabilize. It appears to me that, as the child enters latency, and must keep his oedipal fantasies and masturbation impulses in check to avoid the fear of castration, his motor activities in games based on oedipal fantasies must stop and that there is then a psychological and neurological factor responsible for the types of motor activities seen. A discharge phenomenon occurs partly because fantasy material is repressed and the buildup of tension calls for an outlet in the form of these more indiscriminate, rather than fantasy-directed, motor activities. As a consequence, the typical behavior of the latency child includes climbing, sliding, swinging, jumping, skipping, hopscotch, and laughing—all accompanied by the psychological factor of obliviousness to the adults around the child. Kaplan (1965) stressed these motor activities and also called attention to the lip sucking, nail and cuticle biting, and nose picking in the six- to eight-year-old. She stressed that rhythmical motor activities which are ego syntonic are the hallmark of latency; they not only aid in learning new skills, but also consolidate the body image and help the child's object relationships with peers. Children who do not move, jump, hop, skip, and bounce are not part of the group.

It is of interest to note that in the rhymes and games of children of this age, there is an occasional breakthrough of fantasy material in the service of continuing the motor activities. This can be seen in the tendency to jump over cracks in the sidewalk while singing, "If you step on a crack, you'll break your mother's back."

Similarly of interest is the fact that the ego ideals of children in this age group are primarily people of action—firemen and policemen for boys and dancers for girls. These direct motor activities are outside the sphere of conflict. As myelinization increases in the eight-year-old, all movements become more purposeful and smoother. A ball can be tossed more directly, and motor strength can be sustained.

If the parent insists on the child talking about his activities, denies the child this motoric freedom, and restricts his peer activities, marked ego inhibitions can result; the child then has great difficulty in keeping his oedipal impulses in repression, suffers terribly from castration anxiety, and shows impaired development of skills and peer relationships. The child may then be forced into neurotic solutions.

A girl of seven had parents who insisted on a close and intimate relationship with her and who were openly exhibitionistic with her. She was repeating second grade, had severe phobias and nightmares, poor relationships with peers, and her speech was intensely confused all the time. She gave the appearance of having a weak ego; in her analysis, however, we found that the anal and oral-sadistic impulses toward her younger sister which had become associated with her masturbation made her so guilty that unconsciously she had to fail in school and appear dumb and confused. She could thus appear less adequate than her sister. This satisfied her harsh superego.

Pearson's (1966) warnings in this context are relevant. He says, "there is an increasing tendency in American society to insure that children in the latency period have great cultural advantages. Children are encouraged to take art lessons on Saturday morning, to attend the children's orchestra concerts, etc. Here again there is adult supervision which restricts the rough-and-tumble free play of a child with his peers which he needs so much as part of his development during the late prelatent and latency periods."

We know how frequently obsessional disorders appear during this phase of development, partly as a consequence of this parental tendency to enforce the intellectual and to ignore the child's struggle to keep oedipal impulses repressed. That these impulses are never far removed from consciousness is evident enough if one hears the stories the latency child makes up. A representative normal story in a third grade class was the following: "Five girls were in a school yard and one fell. Her mouth fell on a snake's head or tail. The girl didn't have a mouth then, she died and became a ghost in heaven, after the snake bit off her head, the ghost said, 'Mommy I can't see.' " Another story was: "A girl had a pet dog and one day the dog saw her patting a bear. The dog got very angry and bit the bear. One bear ate him up and then began to pat the girl. They got married and were very happy, and lived happily ever after."

We must also keep in mind that if adults are sadistic and restrict children's motor, speech, and peer activities, at least temporary pathological consequences follow. The child is under those circumstances forced back to primary-process thinking, which undoes repression and increases apprehension. At a summer day camp, a group of six- and seven-year-old boys were observed at archery. The instructor was a teenager who understood neither archery nor how to handle children and was himself sadistic and uncomfortable. The children did not know the skills needed in archery. The instructor had large numbers of children waiting on a bench, restricting motor activity and discussion until their turn with the bow came up. Soon the children lost interest in what was happening; when finally it was their turn at the bow, they violated all rules of safety. The counselor then began to nudge with an arrowpoint, to get the child up to take his turn. His comments increased their apprehension while restricting their needed activities: "Be careful with the tips, they are dangerous and can kill you." Anxiety and restlessness increased in the group. Finally, the boys, unable to handle their anxiety and restricted in speech and motor activity, began holding and kissing each other. The counselor did not object to this as long as they remained silent and seated. Eventually, the group turned on him, clutching and leaning against him, which irritated him further.

It was obvious that the boys who could not release their energies in direct talk and physical activities, and in whom heterosexual fantasies of an incestuous type were also restricted because of repressive forces, finally found relief of tension through homosexual activities.

The Adolescent Phase

Many writers have stressed the biological impact of adolescence on the temporary strength of the ego. Pearson (1958) also re-emphasized the effect which the parents' own conflicts due to a reawakening of repressed oedipal wishes has on the adolescent's ego. In the face of the pressure from the parents (due to their own conflicts), the pressure of increased and often disparate growth rates which interfere with narcissistic valuation of the self, the pressure of other biological factors determining the growth of secondary sex characteristics, and especially the pressure exerted by the return of oedipal wishes in the adolescent, there is ego regression, characterized by a re-emergence of oral, anal, and phallic derivatives, and increased efforts to erect new defenses against the resurgence of drives.

Anna Freud (1958) said: "I take it that it is normal for an adolescent to behave for a considerable length of time in an inconsistent and unpredictable manner; to fight his impulses and to accept them; . . . to love his parents and to hate them; to revolt against them and to be dependent on them; to be deeply ashamed to acknowledge his mother before others and, unexpectedly, to desire heart-to-heart talks with her; to thrive on imitation of an identification with others while searching unceasingly for his own identity; to be more idealistic, artistic, generous, and unselfish than he will ever be again, but also the opposite: self-centered, egoistic, calculating. Such fluctuations between extreme opposites would be deemed highly abnormal at any other time of life" (p. 275).

The adolescent must now keep even greater distance from his parents than he did in latency, because for the first time he has the biological capacity for procreation; hence the parents as the objects of sexual incestuous drives become real objects rather than fantasy objects. Thus the adolescent isolates himself in his room, gets involved in philosophical thought and discussion with others, relates primarily to peers, develops crushes on new heroes further removed from the home, and identifies with groups sponsoring social causes. This is a period of ego upheaval, and the adolescent's speech often reflects it; he may be loud and boisterous; he may be rebellious; he may use only anal terms, he may become stilted and compulsive in the manner of his speech; or he may have a return of stammering, a misuse of words, a confusion of speech; or he may even speak in an ascetic manner. Generally, in the postpubertal period of adolescence, there is a further ego consolidation, with a loss of regression and improvement in speech patterns.

We can see a pathological extension of the speech patterns mentioned in a thirty-five-year-old man described in a paper on simultaneous analysis of a father and son (Kolansky and Moore, 1966): Mr. B. was a rigid, compulsive man who appeared timid, overly respectful, cautious, and very frightened. He was thin, balding, wore metal-framed glasses, appeared hunched over, and "showed evidence of a lifelong struggle over his impotent efforts to assert his masculinity." He came for analysis because he wanted to leave his father's business, but was anxious about the consequences this action would have on his and his father's welfare. He was unconsciously rebellious, but manifestly obedient to his father's every wish. He was sexually impotent; he had a fate neurosis which manifested itself in a continuous feeling (frequently acted out) of people abusing him; and through the mechanism of identification with the aggressor he constantly acted in a harsh and sadistic manner toward his eldest son Dick. His speech contained numerous misuses of words, incorrect words, newly coined words, and confused sentence structure, all belying his college education. One day he began to rediscuss what he considered to be a most interesting recent article on dreams and REM phenomena which he had read in the magazine section of the Sunday New York *Times*. He said that the article indicated that Freud's analytic work was now being proven on a physiological basis. His speech lapsed into an archaic form, e.g., "proven out." Immediately thereafter he stressed the high percentage of sexual dreams in males, and probably in females as well. The proof for the sexual nature of dreams in the male was obtained by the use of mercury gauges attached to the penis. These registered erections. He stressed that the article also mentioned heart attacks occurring with some frequency, presumably during nightmares. Then he said that perhaps he should not read this material because he might misinterpret it and overemphasize it and cause some trouble for himself. I asked whether he thought reading about it would bring on a heart attack in himself, to which he said: "My God, my father could die in a nightmare and never would know what killed him. It could happen to me as well. My thought was 'what I don't know won't hurt me.' " I asked what he meant, how it would affect his health simply to know. He said, "It will always leave me hoping that I won't have a nightmare."

Again during this discussion he made mistakes in the use of language, an indication of his continuing anxiety, and I used the material in the following way: I reminded him of the previous session when we also discussed the dream material from the New York *Times*. At that time he had indicated the danger of bad dreams and the possibility of death, and I quoted the use of his mixed-up speech on that occasion as follows: "Dreams it can pose as a danger with bad dreams, with the adrenalin pouring out—like my God—my father

—could die—or me." I had also interpreted his speech confusions in relation to death ideas toward his father and punishment ideas toward himself. I reminded him that at the time I had mentioned a possible fear of heart attacks during intercourse as well, and I said that today he tied the two together in speaking about the prevalence of sexual dreams and the prevalence of death. I quoted his use of language in the previous session to show its confusion when he discussed sexual intercourse; he had said: "With Dick out of the room next door to the back of our room, the embarrassment of having him next door, together that we have, is here that he isn't there with the hearing of the sex intercourse." (Meaning, that since his son moved out of the room next to the parents' bedroom, Mr. B. could have intercourse with his wife without embarrassment at the thought of being overheard.) He was shocked to hear his own language repeated and could not believe that he talked in this manner. I stressed his intelligence and his good ability, but at the same time told him that under the impact of his conflict over sexuality, which had the unconscious meaning of trespassing into the realm of adults and his father's world, he regularly showed disintegration and disorganization of thoughts.

I further indicated that I felt he had experienced a learning problem in growing up, which reflected itself in a variety of ways including the learning of incorrect words, the disintegration of thoughts and words under the impact of sexual anxiety, and the restriction of learning as exemplified in his comments today: "What I don't know won't hurt me," and that here we were seeing an example of his wish to restrict his reading (another of his symptoms), under the impact of learning about sexuality, having increased sexual wishes, and possibly dying of a heart attack, which was related to the fearful wish that his father would also read the article and die. Then I quoted his misuse of any number of words in the past, including the following: "remembrance" for memory, "arousement" for arousal, "tumult" for turmoil, "revolvement" for revolving, "analyzation" for analysis, "jungle" for jumble, "presentment" for presentation, "lackadaisial" for lackadaisical. I said that most of these words were not words at all, and those that were, were used incorrectly. He was shocked and dismayed, never having realized the extent of his misuse of language. Moreover, I reinterpreted his old wish to protect his father from death, because of his death wishes and the frustration of not being able to protect his father from dreaming, unlike his previous ambivalent attempts to stop his father from eating foods containing cholesterol. I indicated that his learning difficulty as exemplified by the use of language must have been a way of limiting himself as if to say to his father, "I am no threat to you; I'm not even very bright; I won't surpass you"; that in relation to his firstborn son, Dick, he had somehow conveyed to Dick the same idea of limiting his learning and intelligence; and that Dick has complied by using language equally inappropriately and by failing in school. I reminded him of the first dream he had in his analysis, actually several months after the analysis began: His father was lying down and began to drowse and mumble while playing cards with his partner. Mr. B. anxiously shook his father to see whether he was alright. This made his father angry and confused about where he was. In his associations Mr. B. revealed his apprehension about a feeling that his father was losing his memory, as his grandfather had, and that his father would not wear glasses although he was losing his vision. His father did not protect his health, often stayed up too late playing cards. His father often withdrew from important decisions, as if lying down on the job, leaving the decisions to his partner. This had in fact happened on the day of the dream, and Mr. B., acting like a watchdog, had asked his father why this happened, only to get a gruff retort. The partner told Mr. B. that his father was no longer very capable and that more would be expected of Mr. B. Mr. B. said that he knew he was overly concerned about his father's health; however, he had also noticed some cloudiness in his father's eyes!

The dream showed both Mr. B.'s reaction formations against his death wishes toward the father and the elimination of the father from the card game. He was being "dealt out" by his son and felt insulted. In brief, Mr. B.'s father perceived this as a castration threat. Mr. B. mentioned that he also acted as a watchdog toward Dick, but Dick rebelled primarily because his father acted as if he were castrating him by emphasizing his faults and by preventing him from becoming independent. He had forgotten the dream, but remembered the associations.

Throughout this, I said, we could see in his misuse of language a similar desire to show his father that he had not surpassed him. His affect was one of amazement, shock, anxiety, and agreement with what I said. Then he remembered that he actually began to have difficulties in learning between the ages of ten and twelve, that is, in the prepubertal period, during which time, as I reconstructed, he had been most actively masturbating and most actively smoking, while feeling the need for punishment. He said he remembered this as a period when due to competition with his sister, he only and sorely wanted his father's attention and affection. I said that could be explained on the basis of not simply the competition with his sister, but the desire to undo the implicit rivalry with and rebellion against his father, exemplified in the smoking and masturbation, i.e., doing the forbidden thing, and that in fact he had to say to his father: "Look what a good little boy I am; you have no need to fear my rivalry. I won't even learn enough to ever be a rival to you."

As a result of my reconstructions, he actually dated the beginning of his learning and speech difficulty to the same period as his active masturbation.

In the following analytic session he remembered that at the age of eleven or twelve while he was in the sixth grade, he began to stammer very severely at the beginning of sentences, and especially over the use of the word mother! He was embarrassed by it, worked hard to correct his stammer in speech classes, and no longer stammered by the age of sixteen!

Thus, in this example, we see misused words and confused speech, in addition to a stammer, as equivalents of neurotic symptoms, as a consequence of a man's death wishes to his father, and sexual wishes toward his sister and mother in his prepubertal and pubertal periods of development. His aggressive killing thoughts brought with them an ego inhibition in speech and learning. This served the superego well, in that he appeased his father, for wanting to surpass him. This also represented an upward displacement to his mouth (embarrassing language) from his penis. He had been so embarrassed over the small size of his penis that he had avoided locker rooms during the same period of time.

Summary

We can view speech from many vantage points. Speech contributes to various aspects of ego development and functions including self-observation, differentiation of self and external object, sense of reality and reality testing, secondary-process thinking, synthetic function, and of course control over action or impulse, and separation-individuation. The vicissitudes of each psychosexual stage contribute to the normality or deviations of speech, including the negativism of the anal-sadistic stage, the consolidation of masculinity or femininity in the phallic stage, the limited use of speech as communication with the parent during latency and adolescence, while consolidating peer relationships and new ego ideals outside the home.

In the clinical situation speech is a useful aid in the diagnosis of disparate conditions; for example, total lack of speech, perseveration, clang associations, and misuse of pronouns make us think of early infantile autism, while speech reflecting the voices of several people with whom the individual appears to identify makes us think of a symbiotic psychosis. Immature speech leads us to consider prelatency fixations or neurotic regressions. Confusion in speech leads us to consider ego disturbances or neuroses, while stammering generally puts us on the track of a neurosis.

In analytic therapy itself we carefully observe the patient's use of speech, and analyze specific speech patterns such as the misuse of words, the transference and resistance implications of various speech phenomena such as a whining complaint, a sudden stammer, an inability to think of a common word, a gruff tone, an imitative style, and other variations.

Through configurations of speech or its absence, we also have a research medium in clinical practice, as can be seen in the interesting implications for the steps of development which occur beyond our awareness in the normal child, but which are broadly illuminated in the development of the psychotic child.

Finally, Peller (1966) epitomized many relevant points in her paper on Freud's contribution to the theory of language:

> The following points may have been expressed before; however, for me, they represent new facets, arrived at by combining recent findings about language with those indicated by Freud. Academic psychology stresses how much language widens our knowledge of the external world. Now we add that language deepens greatly our awareness and knowledge of our inner world and that the two developments are interdependent. The tool of language enables

us to take a position of distance from our own physical and mental acts. Of course, the clarity of self-awareness differs greatly for different people and for the same person at different times. Language gives us both a distance from and a new intimacy with our own selves. Because language permits us to make mental processes public it also enables us to keep them private. And the defense mechanism of repression is predicated upon language. . . . Once the child has [language], . . . his store of information about the world around him grows by leaps and bounds . . . because language makes possible the conceptual organization of what he sees and hears [p. 462].

BIBLIOGRAPHY

Blanchard, P. (1953), Masturbation Fantasies of Children and Adolescents. *Bull. Phila. Assn. Psa.,* 3:25-38.

Bornstein, B. (1951), On Latency. *This Annual,* 6:279-285.

Ekstein, R. (1965), Historical Notes Concerning Psychoanalysis and Early Language Development. *J. Amer. Psa. Assn.,* 13:707-731.

Ferenczi, S. (1913), Stages in the Development of the Sense of Reality. *Sex in Psychoanalysis.* New York: Basic Books, 1950, pp. 213-239.

Freud, A. (1958), Adolescence. *This Annual,* 13:255-278.

—— (1965), *Normality and Pathology in Childhood: Assessments of Development.* New York: International Universities Press, pp. 86-87, 111.

Freud, S. (1911), Formulations on the Two Principles of Mental Functioning. *Standard Edition,* 12:213-226. London: Hogarth Press, 1958.

—— (1913), The Disposition to Obsessional Neurosis. *Standard Edition,* 12:311-326. London: Hogarth Press, 1958.

—— (1923), The Infantile Genital Organization: An Interpolation into the Theory of Sexuality. *Standard Edition,* 19:141-145. London: Hogarth Press, 1961.

Kaplan, E. B. (1965), Reflections Regarding Psychomotor Activities during the Latency Period. *This Annual,* 20:220-238.

Katan, A. (1961), Some Thoughts about the Role of Verbalization in Early Childhood. *This Annual,* 16:184-188.

Kolansky, H. (1960), Treatment of a Three-year-old Girl's Severe Infantile Neurosis: Stammering and Insect Phobia. *This Annual,* 15:261-285.

—— & Moore, W. T. (1966). Some Comments on the Simultaneous Analysis of a Father and His Adolescent Son. *This Annual,* 21:237-268.

Madow, L. & Silverman, D. (1956), Child Analysis Seminar, Institute of the Philadelphia Association for Psychoanalysis. Unpublished.

Mahler, M. S. (1952), On Child Psychosis and Schizophrenia: Autistic and Symbiotic Infantile Psychoses. *This Annual,* 7:286-305.

—— Furer, M., & Settlage, C. F. (1959), Severe Emotional Disturbances in Childhood: Psychosis. In: *American Handbook of Psychiatry,* ed. S. Arieti. New York: Basic Books, pp. 816-840.

Pearson, G. H. J. (1949), *Emotional Disorders of Children: A Case Book of Child Psychiatry.* New York: Norton.

—— (1958), *Adolescence and the Conflict of Generations.* New York: Norton.

—— (1966), The Importance of Peer Relationship in the Latency Period. *Bull. Phila. Assn. Psa.,* 16:109-121.

Peller, L. E. (1954), Libidinal Phases, Ego Development, and Play. *This Annual,* 9:178-198.

—— (1966), Freud's Contribution to Language Theory. *This Annual,* 21:448-467.

Spring, W. J. (1935), Words and Masses: A Pictorial Contribution to the Psychology of Stammering. *Psa. Quart.,* 4:244-258.

Wentworth, H. & Flexner, S. B. (1960), *Dictionary of American Slang.* New York: Crowell.

ENCOPRESIS IN A LATENCY BOY

An Arrest Along a Developmental Line

MORTON SHANE, M.D. (Los Angeles)

Introduction and Review of the Literature

The paucity of material on encopresis in the psychoanalytic literature has been the stimulus to report the psychoanalysis of a latency boy who suffered from that symptom. My presentation will be organized according to Anna Freud's (1963a) description of the developmental line "from wetting and soiling to bladder and bowel control." The heuristic and clinical usefulness of her Developmental Profile (1962) is being increasingly established (e.g., Heinicke, 1965; Michaels and Stiver, 1965). I shall present the analysis of a child in which it was possible to distinguish between a flight into health that simulated development and true development that progressed from soiling and wetting to bowel and bladder control. The correspondences and disharmonies with other developmental lines will be disregarded for the purposes of this paper.

Anthony (1957) said, "Clinicians on the whole, perhaps out of disgust, prefer neither to treat them [encopretics] nor to write about them. The literature as compared with enuresis is surprisingly scanty . . . and superficial" (p. 157).

Freud (1908) explicitly mentioned anal incontinence when he wrote that those who exhibit the triad of characteristics that stamp

---

Presented to the Child Analysis Study Group of the Los Angeles Psychoanalytic Society and Institute, May, 1966; to the Los Angeles Psychoanalytic Society and Institute, November, 1966; and at the Midwinter Meetings of the American Psychoanalytic Association, December, 1966, New York.

Member of the Child Analysis Study Group and the faculty of the Los Angeles Psychoanalytic Society and Institute.

I would like to express my appreciation to Dr. Heiman Van Dam who both supervised the treatment and, after a critical reading of this paper, provided me with many helpful suggestions.

the anal character "took a comparatively long time to overcome their infantile *incontinentia alvi* . . . [and] even in later childhood they suffered from isolated failures of this function. As infants, they seem to . . . refuse to empty their bowels when they are put on the pot because they derive a subsidiary pleasure from defaecating" (p. 170). In the subsequent elaborations of the anal phase of libidinal development by Freud (1913), Abraham (1924), Jones (1918), and others, failure in the function of bowel control was not the focus of extensive study. However, I shall limit this review to those contributions that deal specifically with fecal incontinence itself. Of course, many psychoanalytic cases reported in the literature had encopresis as an incidental symptom that was ameliorated in the course of analysis, but in few instances did it become the center of the presentation. Anna Freud and Dorothy Burlingham (1944) stressed that in order to achieve toilet training the child needs the presence of a loving parent surrogate. Erikson (1950) presented two vignettes of encopretics. A more recent example is E. Furman's report (1962).

The first article by an analyst dealing solely with encopresis was written by Lehman (1944). He mentioned that the term "encopresis" was coined in 1926 by Weissenberg, who regarded fecal incontinence as etiologically analogous to enuresis; that is, both are psychogenic in origin. Lehman reviewed the psychiatric and psychoanalytic literature and presented the psychotherapy of four child cases, emphasizing the need for parental love, especially from the mother, to establish control over the bowels. In his psychotherapeutic approach he focused less on the transference than on making unconscious fantasies conscious. Moreover, he helped the parents to be either less compulsively demanding or more lovingly attentive to these children. Their symptoms decreased as a result of the diminished environmental stresses and as they gained an intellectual understanding of their preverbal expression of conflicts.

Fenichel (1945) saw rectal incontinence as a "conversion symptom, expressing . . . instinctual conflicts. If it only happens occasionally, it probably represents an equivalent of an anxiety. If it happens habitually, however, it represents an equivalent or substitute for masturbation . . . a sign of a marked anal erotic organization" (p. 234).

Garrard and Richmond (1952) recognized the syndrome of psychogenic megacolon, differentiating it from the potentially fatal and surgically correctable Hirschsprung's disease. Call et al. (1963), elaborating on this syndrome, stressed failure in the establishment of adequate object relations, erotization of bowel functioning, and traumatic toilet training.

Prugh, Wermer, and Lord (1954) presented the psychotherapy of two encopretics. They mentioned the crucial interaction with the pregenital mother, regression from oedipal conflicts, and obsessive concerns of the mother with bowel controls. They found that fecal smearing is rare in latency, except in psychotic children. Warson et al. (1954) also reported the psychotherapy of an encopretic six-year-old girl. None of these children was seen in analysis.

Anthony (1957) did an intensive study of seventy-six cases, in which he attempted a classification of encopresis based on two factors: (1) whether or not the child had ever achieved bowel control (i.e., discontinuous or continuous types); and (2) the relative pressure the mothers exerted on their children to achieve continence. He states, "Where such [sphincter] control remains defective or dependent on the mother's activity, the child's personality will appear unorganized and amorphous and his behaviour uncontrolled and uncontrollable" (p. 155). The overtrained child who is later encopretic shows a prematurely rigid and structured ego. In Anthony's retentive type of encopretic (a subgroup of both other groups), clean periods turn out to be retentive ones: "a voluminous stool . . . becomes a dramatic highlight in the history of a case" (p. 159). As in enuresis, which occurs frequently with encopresis, the ratio of boys to girls is quite high (6:1).[1] He found that encopresis usually disappears during puberty. In his opinion, children who had never been trained needed training and not therapy. This would suggest a contrast with A. Katan's (1946) views concerning enuretics; she believes that a "continuous" type of enuresis has a worse prognosis and hence requires more intensive treatment. On the other hand, this apparent contradiction might be reconciled by taking account of statements made by Anna Freud (1965). She remarked that in child analysis "the whole range of therapeutic possibilities [is] kept available for the patient" (p. 234). This includes a kind of "corrective emotional

[1] Greenacre (1945) speculated as to why this was so with enuretics. Her thesis, of increased stimulation of the penis and motoric thrust in male urination, would not apply to an equally high incidence of encopresis in males, thus tending to weaken her explanation.

experience" (p. 231) with the analyst seen as a "new object" (p. 38). It would therefore seem that training and therapy are not mutually exclusive. In analysis, the new object aspects of the analyst are secondary to his insight-giving functions but nevertheless need to be considered, especially in cases of arrested development.

Lustman (1966) described the analysis of an encopretic latency boy with hyperactive motoric equipment. This boy exhibited a fragmentation of thinking due to a frequent breakthrough of impulses. Superego formation was inadequate, as demonstrated by an observable lack of shame and guilt. After a stormy first year, during which the patient literally tore up the playroom, the analysis took a more usual form. The child developed into a scrupulously honest boy, capable of adequate shame and guilt, though his behavior retained a certain impulsive quality.

Delineating the line of development "from wetting and soiling to bladder and bowel control," Anna Freud (1963a) mentions four stages: (1) complete freedom to wet and soil; (2) a cathectic shift from the oral to the anal zone so that anal products become highly cathected with unfused libido and aggression; (3) bowel and bladder control accomplished through identification with mother, though dependent on positive relations to her; (4) autonomous control disconnected from object ties. She stresses that as long as the oedipal and preoedipal conflicts are not resolved, the intense disappointments with mother will lead to loss of bowel and bladder control and interfere with development to stage four.

Although such a progression is only a small part of a complete Developmental Profile, it lends itself well to an understanding of the symptom of encopresis in the nexus of psychic organization and development. For example, E. Sterba's (1949) excellent discussion of a case of constipation in a two-year-old boy can be seen in this context. The child was not old enough to have achieved autonomous ego and superego control of bowel and bladder functioning (i.e., he was still in stage three). The shift from oral to anal zone (stage two) was prematurely heightened through excessive anal manipulations. Regression to stage two, with retention of stool, was experienced with object loss of either the nursemaid or the analyst.

A. Katan (1946) reminds us that enuresis is only a symptom and not a diagnosis. The same is true for encopresis. But the symptom does indicate an arrested line of development in bowel control, and is usually associated with arrested lines of development in other areas, especially in object relations.

Michaels and Stiver (1965) presented a Developmental Profile which demonstrated the correlation of psychopathic character traits with aggresive acting on impulse, persistent enuresis, reading difficulties, language retardation, and with a higher incidence in males than females. Similar correlations are seen in encopretic children (Anthony, Lustman). Encopresis indicates a defect in impulse control which is more serious than in enuresis, although the two frequently occur together (in about 50 percent of encopretics, according to Anthony). Denial, prevalent in enuretics, must be utilized even more extensively by the encopretic child who needs to deny, often while fully awake, that his stool affects those around him, thus involving a greater impairment of reality testing.

I have chosen to present this case of Stevie because it seems illustrative of the progression in the developmental line pertaining to bowel and bladder control, including the functional association between encopresis and enuresis which Anna Freud implies.

Case Illustration

The Presenting Complaint

Stevie S. was almost nine when he was referred for a second attempt at treatment. He had been in psychotherapy with a woman analyst, three times a week for over two years. Because his parents were not satisfied with his progress, they withdrew him. His nightmares had disappeared, but the other symptoms that had led to his therapy, at age six, persisted: enuresis, encopresis and constipation, temper tantrums, difficulties in concentrating and reading, and an inability to play without completely destroying his toys. Convinced that there was organic pathology which had been overlooked in his first treatment, the parents sought other consultations. After a negative barium enema, he was referred to me for analysis.

Stevie was enuretic and encopretic almost all his life. He had stopped soiling for short periods, once for a few months during this first treatment, and again following the barium enema. His temper tantrums and aggressiveness, directed toward his parents, his older brother, and his younger sister, began at age five following a severely traumatic time. This involved the abrupt discharge of his lifetime nanny-maid and the birth of his sister.

His former therapist felt she had made some progress in reducing Stevie's anxiety, but she had felt helpless in coping with his "animal-like" outbursts of aggression. Her interpretations had been directed at getting him to appreciate the significance of the loss of his mother-maid, although Stevie had been unable to put his feelings into words. His therapist felt that the mother neglected and mistreated this child, and that his father was distant and uncooperative and eventually obstructive. Mr. S. did not want his son to have further treatment; he threatened to kill Stevie if he did not stop his soiling and swearing.

Stevie would shout obscenities at passersby, and curse at his mother and father, provoking their hitting him or furiously banishing him to his room. In cleaning himself after soiling his pants, he would inadvertently smear feces over the bathroom. Often he hid his shorts in an effort to avoid punishment, and at the same time so that he could be remembered (though negatively) by the pervading odor. Sometimes he would flush his shorts down the toilet, backing up the plumbing. His complaints to his mother about the food she served led to bitter battles and his refusals to eat breakfast and lunch.

In spite of his many troubles at home, Stevie did fairly well in school, although much below his potential. He had some friends and was a leader in sports, at which he excelled, but he found himself much hampered by his great difficulty in adhering to rules. He made collections of pencils, erasers, and rocks. These hobbies, however, were poorly endowed with neutralized energy, for he would frequently steal pencils, or lose them, and throw rocks rather than save them.

Stevie was a handsome, husky boy of average height, who could make direct affective contact that would elicit a warm response. In the same fashion he could, by teasing or direct attack, bring one to a murderous boiling point. Even when he deliberately withdrew, his libidinal contact was evident.

Family Background and Personal History

Stevie's mother immigrated from South America with her mother and younger brother when she was twelve, after the death of her father. Although she finished six years of psychoanalysis, she still suffered from depression, mood swings, bulimia, and phobias. Dominated in the past by her own mother, Mrs. S. still reacted to her mother's depreciation of Stevie, of psychoanalysis, and of "modern" methods of discipline, by identifying with her mother's attitudes. Her first son, Hugh, was a head banger and rocker through his first two years; now in early adolescence he is overly disturbed by girls, emotionally withdrawn, and compulsively neat.

As a child Stevie's father had rarely been thwarted by his mother who had been as frightened of his temper tantrums as Mrs. S. later was. He was not toilet trained until he was five. Mr. S. gambled to a fault, putting his needs well before those of his wife and children, until financial reverses and increasing awareness of his problems led to his seeking analysis soon after Stevie began with me. His own father seems to have been a paranoid character.

The pregnancy with Stevie went well. As with the other children, Mrs. S. did not breast-feed him ("too embarrassed"). He never banged his head, but had trouble sleeping during the first year, crying all night. His mother handled this by yelling at him because she was afraid that Stevie would wake up his father. On the other hand, she recalled pulling the nipple from Stevie's mouth in what to her was an inexplicable effort to enrage him. (In her analysis, she learned that it derived in part from the anger she felt toward her younger brother.) She turned over more and more of Stevie's care to the Mexican-American maid, Lupe. His toilet training, begun at eight months, was never completed and eventually ignored. Enemas and other anal stimulations were not prominent. The mother was aware that her laxity was a reaction to the strictness which she and her brother had been subjected to by her mother. Stevie's speech and motoric development were advanced compared to his brother's. Most events of Stevie's first five years were vague in his mother's mind. Instead of remembering, she took masochistic pleasure in blaming herself that she had allowed Lupe to handle everything. Lupe was a kindly middle-aged woman who apparently set few limits on this boy, recognizing him as her special charge. A prolonged depression and hospitalization of the maternal grandmother contributed much to the crucial withdrawal of Stevie's mother in his second and third year. His three-year-older brother, Hugh, was allowed to beat up Stevie.

Only in the past few years was Stevie strong enough to limit these assaults. According to his parents, Stevie did not show signs of sexual curiosity or masturbation. Nudity was permitted between the children, but not with their parents. Stevie once asked his mother what had happened to his sister's penis.

When he began nursery school, at four, his teachers thought he was too withdrawn. A psychiatric consultant recommended treatment, but the parents could not initiate it. Stevie's behavior changed markedly following Lupe's sudden dismissal. The aggression that was contained in his soiling, wetting, and withdrawal from his mother was directed openly toward his parents after he suffered this overwhelming loss of his mother surrogate and the additional loss of his mother to the care of his new baby sister, Ann.

The Course of the Analysis

Introductory Phase and the Beginning of the Therapeutic Alliance

Stevie was seen four times a week, his mother every other week, and his father occasionally. Stevie knew he was sent for treatment again because his soiling and wetting had continued and was upsetting to his parents. He so grasped this fact that within the first weeks of analysis, like with the barium enema, his fear of being attacked by a man led to his taking a flight into health; he stopped, for the first time in his life, wetting his bed, and by withholding his stools he tried to convince his mother and himself that he was cured. I expressed my admiration for his accomplishment, asked him how he did it, and interpreted his wish to avoid what to him was a dreaded encounter with me. His symptoms then recurred. He initially brought several objects for me to see. One was a dirty rock, full of fossils, that he fondled, speculating on its worth, soiling himself and the office with its dust. Another was a book on astronauts. He thereby expressed his anally fixated expectations as well as his progressive phallic and genital hopes.

He attempted to seduce me to pursue him, first with questions, and later by running out in the hall or leaving early. He said he was afraid I would tell his parents his secrets. He projected criticism of himself onto me (identification with his introject [Sandler and Rosenblatt, 1962]). When he made an error in drawing a design for his mother, he said it was my fault and threw something at me. When he was very excited, this projection seemed to have more the quality of a loss of differentiation between self and object representations, so that he would say, "You're trying to stab me!" at the same time that he was trying to stab me with a pencil. I told him that he thought he ought to be hurt and punished for his secrets.

Stevie's attacks and provocations of counterattacks were defensive, warding off affects of loneliness, depression, and separation anxiety related to the loss of his former therapist and, behind that, the traumatic loss of Lupe. His primitive fears of talion punishment were aggravated by my being a man, thus exciting frightening homosexual wishes in addition to the marked oral demandingness and anal possessiveness. His severe aggressive behavior became the focus of his analysis. It was possible to interpret his identification with his (superego precursor) introject, projection of his aggression onto me, and turning it onto himself (in accident proneness). His anal fixations were clearly exemplified by his unfused and highly ambivalent object cathexes.

There was a suddenness and unpredictability to his aggressive outbursts which made them extremely taxing and frustrating. Because of the threats that closeness to me entailed, it seemed that just when I was making contact with him, he would attack me. But it also seemed he was identifying with the capriciousness of his mother's love, and treating me to the same inconsistency he remembered and was still experiencing. (His mother was capable of warmth and affection, but then could go into a sudden depression.) Later in the analysis, he played the part of a saccharine mother who would punish suddenly after promising sympathetic understanding.

I often attempted, by story or directly, to encourage him to put his feelings into words instead of direct discharge, as Crocker (1955) had done in treating a similarly aggressive child. Whenever my talking brought him too close to an uncomfortable idea or affect, he screamed, "Shut up, shut your ass hole!" which was not only an identification with his father's rage but a goal he truly desired for himself. His lack of impulse control was demonstrated in a domino game when he knocked down one piece to start a chain reaction. I then put into words for him that he was unable to stop himself once he started some action.

Stevie "soiled" freely during his analytic hours, always leaving a mess of papers and broken toys for me to clean up at the end of the hour, but he refrained from actual fecal incontinence. He treated me as if I were his indulgent maid, Lupe, who tended lovingly to his messes. At such times his behavior could almost be seen as approximating Anna Freud's description of stage one in the developmental line from soiling to bowel control. (Of course, this was not freedom to soil as it is in the first year of life, but rather was a regressive pull to such pleasures.) Shame and guilt connected with his lack of control were not overtly apparent. Self-punitive behavior had the unneutralized quality of aggression turned on the self. Yet his reluctance to talk about his soiling betrayed some shame, defended against by denial. His development was arrested mainly at stage two, his anal products and processes being highly cathected, and fixation being more prominent than regression.

Seeing the Analyst as an Auxiliary Ego

The establishment in Stevie's mind of myself as a trustworthy, reliable, external source of control was complicated by fears that I would be summarily dismissed, as Lupe and his former therapist had been. About six months after the beginning of his analysis, Stevie hit upon the idea that I was to be his personal manservant, "Jives," whom he then had power to hire, fire, and order around to do his bidding. Interpretations of this fantasy, as the need for belated mastery, revived for him the experience of his traumatic fifth year when he lost both mother surrogate and mother (through the birth of a sibling). He tried to force me actually to protect him as a child might do in the separation-individuation stage (Mahler, 1963). In one of his rages, he harmed himself by upsetting my desk chair. He accused me by saying, "Why didn't you stop me?" and ran to the bathroom with great anxiety to tend his cut lip. He manipulated me into saving him by falling backward while scaling my toy shelves. This aggressive demand for protection and love, which he still longed for from his mother, was interpreted. His disregard for harmful consequences demonstrated the inadequacy of his reality testing.

Stevie's attempts to provoke me to touch or hit him had an additional value for him; they expressed his masochistic longing for the fights with his much bigger brother, and similar fantasies of being sexually overwhelmed by his loud, threatening father. After he felt sufficiently safe with me, he began to steal some of my pens, pencils, and erasers. This was first interpreted as a defense against separation anxiety, as an attempt to retain a part of our experience together (a transitional object) or a part of me (a need-gratifying object). Later he spoke of the pen's "black magic" qualities, which he hoped would give him better grades in school and better control over his impulses. When I frustrated him by refusing to let him have a pen or pencil, he made open gestures toward grabbing my penis. He saw himself as he saw women, with a damaged genital-cloaca, incontinent of urine and feces, needing an external source of control, in the form of my penis, to achieve power over himself. "I hate girls; they're smelly and stupid."

Identification with the Analyst and the Beginning Internalization of Control (stage three)

His identification with the aggressor underwent a gradual change as Stevie became more conscious of his own aggression and projected it less. He then chose to identify with my therapeutic power, perceived by him as inconstant but helpful. In play, he became the doctor and I was "Joe Farty," who wet my bed and made BM in my pants. He tried to be the helpful one, thereby turning his passivity with me into activity. It took some time in the hour before his aggression and unpredictability would break through and he would then throw me out of his office. This was played several times during the latter part of the first year of analysis, preceding by a few months his giving up both wetting and soiling.

Another aspect of Stevie's identification with me (more as an auxiliary ego than superego) was an increased ability to verbalize. After becoming more conscious of his preoedipal frustrations, he told his mother he would soil himself to get even with her. But he would settle for the words alone, stopping short of actually defecating in his pants. This delay in impulsive action allowed for a greater opportunity to think. To the extent to which he used me as a new object, one could say that he had a "corrective emotional experience." I was seen by him as a source of external control, as a person who reacted, not with counteraggression or withdrawal, but rather with integrative verbal expression. I believe he used my remarks on a primary level, as mediating an exchange leading to object constancy, and, almost concomitantly, on a secondary level, grasping the conceptual meaning of the words themselves. (A. Katan [1961] has highlighted the usefulness of words in child development and treatment.) His father's "temper tantrums" also diminished around this time. With Stevie's beginning improvement, his mother wished to reduce his visits to me. It seemed to echo her earlier pulling the nipple from his mouth. However, she agreed not to interfere.

As Stevie's ability to control impulses increased, his anxiety diminished. He progressed from his preoedipal oral and anal fixations and conflicts to seductive phallic exhibitionism. Even early in treatment, he took pleasure in showing his dirty buttocks to his sister and brother. Now he showed them his "purple penis." Through drawings, he revealed the fantasy that his "bottom" was broken and the loss of his stool was seen as castration. (He earlier saw his stool as a sea monster that would bite him for his own oral aggressiveness.) Following this understanding, he felt safe enough to be more sexually seductive, as well as more tenderly loving, to his mother. She responded to his less aggressive attitudes by some reciprocal friendliness and optimism that aided in breaking their sadomasochistic stalemate. This resulted in Stevie's easier acceptance and internalization of his mother's wishes for his control of phallic and anal drive derivatives. He said that his father was jealous of my seeing his mother every other week. The projection of his jealousy of me onto his father was made obvious as he tried to slash my office paneling with a can opener. Following this he dreamed of losing a tooth. Around this time, he passed a huge stool that stopped up the toilet. This impressed his mother greatly, just as it had when he accomplished the same feat when he was four. It was then possible to interpret his anally tinged phallic competitiveness with his father and me.

The Beginning of Controls Relatively Autonomous from the Analyst (Superego Development) (stage four)

With the working through of his castration anxiety in connection with his oedipal conflicts, both soiling and wetting gradually began to disappear. However, during my summer vacation, one year after analysis started, the trend was reversed; he soiled and wet regularly. This demonstrated the lack of autonomy of this newly emerging control (stage three of the developmental line). A few months after my return, he again regressed, this time to constipation, in reaction to anticipating my inability to give him the birthday present he unconsciously wanted (my magically endowed penis). In this way, he demonstrated that disappointments in me led to an increased cathexis of his own body products (back to stage two).

Fourteen months after analysis began, Stevie reported that each night for one week he had dreamed he wet his bed, and each morning he had awakened dry and frightened that he had lost control. I told him that now he was able to think and dream about losing control without having to do so. Daydreams of wetting and soiling followed; the increased control led to more conscious elaboration of his anal-urethral impulses. (E. Furman [1962, p. 267] comments that dreams can be "the next forum" for a struggle with a conflict when the "ego [is] strong enough to give up a behavior pattern.") He played he was a teacher or mother who shamed and ridiculed me for "making in my pants," enabling me to soften the harshness of his (superego) criticisms without eliminating their effectiveness. For example, as a punishment I had to be banished to my room for 100 years. "That long?" I replied.

By the eighteenth month of treatment, he was more permanently in control of his bowels and bladder. He was concerned that a trip (away from me) to the mountains might precipitate "accidents," humiliating and frustrating him as had happened one year previously. But this time my absence did not abandon him to his impulses. Internalized controls, relatively independent from the loved object, were beginning (stage four).

The Consolidation of Superego (Autonomous) Controls

After Stevie experienced the pride in his accomplishment of bowel and bladder control and a deinstinctualized identification with his mother, he could allow himself to face his homosexual love for me and his father. He became more open in his admiration of my phallic qualities, at times in a slavish homosexual thralldom. He would defend himself by his characteristic reversal of roles and identification with the aggressor. In play, he was an admired and powerful (though in reality purportedly homosexual and sadistic) movie actor, and I, the adoring girl who wanted his autograph, a kiss, and a rendezvous in his apartment. He was made more conscious of his fear of closeness to me and the castration he felt it entailed. He would experiment with how close he could get to me without being overwhelmed by his feminine castration wishes. We would play we were in a time machine going to Mars or Hell. I was instructed to throw him a rope to help him across a precipice. The danger of his falling to his death increased as he was pulled closer toward me. Another time, as he kicked a hole in my door, screaming in a high feminine voice, I told him I now understood why he did that; he was afraid that I would kick a hole in him and that it would turn him into a girl. The understanding of this homosexual aspect of his identification with the aggressor led to an increased ability to control his actions, through a de-erotization of the superego introject of his father.

To the Present

Stevie has been in analysis three years, and has been in control of his bowels and bladder for well over a year. He still tries to provoke me to stop him from giving in to his impulses. The wish to have me stop him from uncontrolled masturbation (with both negative and positive oedipal fantasies) is inferred from his play and allusions.

Stevie still finds it difficult to put his thoughts and feelings into words; but he has developed increased patience and control, shows more interest in games and age mates, and is less involved with his family. Occasionally he throws papers on my floor. His saving his bowel movements to coincide with his hour demonstrates a partial persistence in stage three within the transference. Preadolescent problems (he is now twelve) threaten him with a fresh loss of control of preoedipal impulses, especially with his delay in attaining the achievements of latency (Blos, 1965). He presents the familiar problem in child analysis of correctly evaluating what changes are derived from analytic work, what from development and maturation that would have occurred under any circumstances, and what from environmental changes, such as altered parental attitudes (for example, through his father's analysis and his mother's continued therapy).

Discussion

Stevie's encopresis would be seen by Anthony as a "continuous type" (in that he never achieved control over his bowels) with retentive tendencies (constipation), but such a descriptive classification seems to add little to our understanding. At the beginning of his analysis, Stevie was arrested at stage two in the developmental line, never having internalized his mother's controls. Due to her own reaction formations, she was uncertain in making demands for cleanliness on both sons. When she finally did insist with Stevie, it was in association with the traumatic loss of his mother surrogate and the birth of a sibling. But his difficulties with impulse control began in his first year. His mother repeatedly and deliberately frustrated him, thus precipitating his poor sleeping and excessive crying. This probably also led to a faulty differentiation from, and establishment of, representations of his mother as a need-gratifying object. She insisted too early on his (reflex) compliance in bowel control, at eight months, and then abandoned him when an adequate object relationship with her would have enabled him to develop bowel (and bladder) control in his second year. The maid, as a surrogate mother, perhaps saved Stevie from worse traumatization by his mother's periodic depressive withdrawals. Separation anxiety, before and during his analysis, was reacted to by aggressive smearing or retention. These symptoms probably protected him from a more serious regression to a narcissistic withdrawal or autism. His object relations were predominantly on an anal level. Spitz and Wolf (1949) have postulated that infants orally turn to their stool as a replacement for the lost object. Such a heightened cathexis of anal products could have occurred in Stevie in reaction to his mother's repeated depressions (although no history of excessive fecal play in the first two years could be elicited). The attentions of Lupe to his anal messes further increased this cathexis.

The sudden loss of Lupe, during his oedipal phase, along with the birth of a younger sister, must have augmented Stevie's turning to his father for a masochistically gratifying resolution. Stevie's lack of impulse control stimulated his father to similar outbursts of aggression, making superego introjection difficult. Disappointed in his attempts to win his father's love, Stevie regressed to excessive gratifications of his already fixated soiling, wetting, and aggressive outbursts. In these, he had been indulged by Lupe and so was trying to bring her back magically. In analysis, after working through his preoedipal fixations, he did reveal his oedipal interest in his mother and the severe castration anxiety associated with it. The regression to anal discharge of these phallic impulses was overdetermined, not only by his own strong anal fixations and by the homosexual fantasies of penetration by his father, but also by his adapting to his mother's unconscious anal conflicts, "forming the only type of relationship that is possible in view of the mother's own psychopathology" (Nagera, 1964, p. 238).

The short period of bowel control achieved in his first treatment indicated the beginnings of his entrance into stage three of the developmental line, but without the resolution of his oedipal (and preoedipal) conflicts no permanent structuralized control was accomplished. Stage four, autonomous control, relatively independent from objects, perhaps cannot be said to be definitely accomplished until Stevie has successfully terminated with me. He has retained the characterological impulsiveness that has been noted by Lustman (1966) (and, in enuretics, by Michaels and Stiver [1965]) and that in my experience with encopretics is stubbornly retained through adulthood. For example, an adult man, encopretic until age seven, in terminating his analysis regressed to impulsiveness and sloppiness. He openly expressed a wish to be "prodded" by me. Thus, threatened by object loss, he relinquished autonomous control (stage four) over derivatives of anal drives, and reverted to stage three, where controls were dependent on positive relations to his (mother) analyst.

Stevie's case indicates that when an arrest in development is undone by analysis, development then progresses through the developmental line landmarks, rather than suddenly jumping to age-appropriate behavior and attitudes. The step-by-step progression has also been observed in recovery from temporary ego regression under stress, such as hospitalization (Anna Freud, 1963b, p. 103). (Wolfenstein [1966] finds the same in the treatment of arrested adolescent development following the death of a parent.) Anna Freud (1963a, p. 255) stresses that bowel and bladder control become autonomous only when object constancy has been achieved and consolidated. "Preoedipal anal control remains vulnerable and, especially in the beginning of the third phase, remains dependent on the objects and the stability of positive relations to them." This stability is not accomplished until the oedipal phase is satisfactorily resolved. "A child who is severely disappointed in his mother . . . may not only lose the internalized urge to be clean but also reactivate the aggressive use of elimination." As demonstrated in Stevie's case, such regression carries with it a considerable loss of other advances, such as secondary-process thinking, age-appropriate defenses, superego controls, and (fleetingly) self-object differentiation. The symptom of encopresis itself is often so provocative to the parents that it can foster even further regression in the child. This regression can stem either from a reaction to the real object loss of hostile, withdrawn parents, or from the gratification of the child's masochistic desires through the parents' overly harsh punishment.

Summary

The first three years in the analysis of an eight-year-old suffering from encopresis were presented. The literature was reviewed. Anna Freud's developmental line "from wetting and soiling to bladder and bowel control" was used to organize the clinical material. Encopresis could then be seen as an arrest along this developmental line. Progress in the analysis seemed to derive primarily from insight via interpretation but also from reactions to the analyst as a new object. Regression from oedipal conflicts did much to reinforce the prominent anal fixations. Autonomous internalization of bowel control was accomplished only after these oedipal conflicts had to some extent been resolved. Progress then occurred in a stepwise fashion along the developmental line.

BIBLIOGRAPHY

Abraham, K. (1921), Contributions to the Theory of the Anal Character. *Selected Papers on Psycho-Analysis.* London: Hogarth Press, 1954, pp. 370-392.

—— (1924), A Short Study of the Development of the Libido, Viewed in the Light of Mental Disorders. *Selected Papers on Psycho-Analysis.* London: Hogarth Press, 1954, pp. 418-501.

Anthony, E. J. (1957), An Experimental Approach to the Psychopathology of Childhood: Encopresis. *Brit. J. Med. Psychol.,* 30:146-175.

Blos, P. (1965), The Initial Stage of Male Adolescence. *This Annual,* 20:145-164.

Call, J. D., et al. (1963), Psychogenic Megacolon in Three Preschool Boys. *Amer. J. Orthopsychiat.*, 33:923-928.

Crocker, D. (1955), The Study of a Problem of Aggression. *This Annual*, 10:300-335.

Ekstein, R. (1966), *Children of Time and Space, of Action and Impulse*. New York: Appleton-Century-Crofts.

Erikson, E. H. (1950), *Childhood and Society*. New York: Norton.

Fenichel, O. (1945), *The Psychoanalytic Theory of Neurosis*. New York: Norton.

Freud, A. (1962), Assessment of Childhood Disturbances. *This Annual*, 17:149-158.

—— (1963a), The Concept of Developmental Lines. *This Annual*, 18:245-265.

—— (1963b), The Role of Regression in Mental Development. In: *Modern Perspectives in Child Development*, ed. A. J. Solnit & S. A. Provence. New York: International Universities Press, pp. 97-106.

—— (1965), *Normality and Pathology in Childhood: Assessments of Development*. New York: International Universities Press.

—— & Burlingham, D. T. (1944), *Infants Without Families*. New York: International Universities Press.

Freud, S. (1908), Character and Anal Erotism. *Standard Edition*, 9:167-175. London: Hogarth Press, 1959.

—— (1913), The Disposition to Obsessional Neurosis. *Standard Edition*, 12:311-326. London: Hogarth Press, 1958.

Furman, E. (1962), Some Features of the Dream Function of a Severely Disturbed Young Child. *J. Amer. Psa. Assn.*, 10:258-270.

Garrard, S. D. & Richmond, J. B. (1952), Psychogenic Megacolon Manifested by Fecal Soiling. *Pediatrics*, 10:474-483.

Greenacre, P. (1945), Urination and Weeping. *Trauma, Growth, and Personality*. New York: Norton, 1952, pp. 106-119.

Heinicke, C. M. (1965), Frequency of Psychotherapeutic Session as a Factor Affecting the Child's Developmental Status. *This Annual*, 20:42-98.

Jones, E. (1918), Anal-Erotic Character Traits. *Papers on Psycho-Analysis*. Boston: Beacon Press, 1961, pp. 413-437.

Katan, A. (1946), Experience with Enuretics. *This Annual*, 2:241-255.

—— (1961), Some Thoughts about the Role of Verbalization in Early Childhood. *This Annual*, 16:184-188.

Lehman, E. (1944), Psychogenic Incontinence of Feces (Encopresis) in Children. *Amer. J. Dis. Child.*, 68:190-199.

Lustman, S. L. (1966), Impulse Control, Structure, and the Synthetic Function. In: *Psychoanalysis—A General Psychology: Essays in Honor of Heinz Hartmann*, ed. R. M. Loewenstein, L. M. Newman, M. Schur, & A. J. Solnit. New York: International Universities Press, pp. 190-221.

Mahler, M. S. (1963), Thoughts about Development and Individuation. *This Annual*, 18:307-324.

Michaels, J. J. & Stiver, I. P. (1965), The Impulsive Psychopathic Character According to the Diagnostic Profile. *This Annual*, 20:124-141.

Nagera, H. (1964), On Arrest in Development, Fixation, and Regression. *This Annual*, 19:222-239.

Prugh, D. G., Wermer, H., & Lord, J. P. (1954), On the Significance of the Anal Phase in Pediatric and Child Psychiatry (workshop). In: *Case Studies in Childhood Emotional Disabilities*, ed. G. S. Gardner. New York: American Orthopsychiatric Association, 1956.

Richmond, J. B., Eddy, E. J., & Garrard, S. D. (1954), The Syndrome of Fecal Soiling and Megacolon. *Amer. J. Orthopsychiat.*, 24:391-401.

Sandler, J. & Rosenblatt, B. (1962), The Concept of the Representational World. *This Annual*, 17:128-145.

Spitz, R. A. & Wolf, K. M. (1949), Autoerotism: Some Empirical Findings and Hypotheses on Three of Its Manifestations in the First Year of Life. *This Annual,* 3/4:85-120.

Sterba, E. (1949), Analysis of Psychogenic Constipation in a Two-year-old. *This Annual,* 3/4:227-252.

Warson, S. R., et al. (1954), The Dynamics of Encopresis (workshop). *Amer. J. Orthopsychiat.,* 24:402-415.

Wolfenstein, M. (1966), A Research Project on Parent Loss. Presented to the Child Analysis Study Group of the Los Angeles Psychoanalytic Society and Institute.

MASTURBATION FANTASIES

Their Changes with Growth and Development

HENRY WERMER, M.D. and SIDNEY LEVIN, M.D. (Boston)

The interest which analysts have shown in masturbation and masturbation fantasy goes back to the beginnings of psychoanalysis (Levin, 1963). In fact, there is no analytic case in which the topic of masturbation is not an issue involving considerable conflict for the patient. In 1908 Freud discussed masturbation in terms of two basic components: (1) the return of early autoerotic activity; (2) the merging of a later sexual fantasy with the autoerotic activity. He believed that the renunciation of masturbation involved not only the giving up of autoerotic activity but also the repression of the associated fantasies, either of which could then be revived in the form of symptoms. Arlow (1953) has stated: "From the point of view of the dynamic, defensive functioning of the psychic apparatus, masturbation and symptoms have much in common. Both demonstrate how the ego operates in attempting to achieve a satisfactory solution of the conflicting claims of the instincts, the pressure of the superego, and the demands of reality. Masturbation and symptom formation both portray the end product of a complicated and overdetermined set of mental operations in the ego, operations which proceed according to the principle of multiple functioning [Waelder, 1930]" (p. 45).

It is well known that the act of masturbation and the fantasy accompanying or preceding it may become separated from each other and that defenses may then be directed against either the fantasy or the physical activity or both. Furthermore, a variety of fear fantasies and defenses against them may also arise, reflecting the castration anxiety evoked by masturbation, as in the case described by Bornstein (1953) of a five-and-a-half-year-old boy whose fear of masturba-

---

From the Department of Psychiatry, Harvard Medical School; The Psychiatric Service, Beth Israel Hospital, Boston; and the McLean Hospital, Belmont, Mass.

tion was expressed through a fantasy of wolves lying under his bed, observing all his movements.

If we study masturbation fantasies, as Eidelberg (1945) has done, it becomes obvious that they reflect not only the drives and their particular fixations but also a mosaic of ego defenses such as regression, displacement, condensation, and reversal. Under the influence of the ego certain impulses may be excluded from consciousness or be disguised to an extent that their true nature can be brought out only through a step-by-step analysis of the manifest content. If this is done, the analysis of masturbation fantasies can become a royal road to the unconscious, as the analysis of a dream or a symptomatic act is. By "unconscious" we mean not only the drives but also the unconscious defenses of the ego, and the unconscious aspects of the superego.

It is of some importance to distinguish between erotic fantasies in general and masturbation fantasies in particular. Erotic fantasies consist of all ideas of a sexual nature, including those which can be realized if the object becomes available. Masturbation fantasies, on the other hand, can often not be fulfilled in any reality relationship with another individual. The aim of masturbation fantasies is that of autoerotic gratification, often of pregenital impulses; and individuals frequently make little or no effort to translate these fantasies into action. As early as in the 1912 discussion on masturbation Stekel noted that individuals fixated to perverse fantasies often find masturbation their only sexual outlet. Using an example of a patient who masturbated with a fantasy of cutting off his father's head, Stekel pointed out that such a fantasy could certainly not be gratified in reality (see A. Reich, 1951).

We shall present selections from analytic material which has been gathered from two young children, one adolescent, and two adults. Brief vignettes will be used to illustrate some of the issues discussed by Arlow, Eidelberg, and Stekel, and to accent two main points:

1. The variety of changes which masturbation fantasies may undergo as a person passes through various phases of psychosexual development.

2. The major influence which masturbation fantasies of childhood may exert upon the development of later ego-syntonic interests.

I

The first three cases to be presented illustrate some of the changes which masturbation fantasies may undergo in the course of development.

Case 1

A four-year-old child, Mary, came into treatment because of phobic symptoms which significantly interfered with her freedom to function in the absence of her mother. She was an unusually bright, extremely verbal child who developed a strong positive relationship to the analyst. She did something rather unique for a child of this age: she wrote the analyst a few letters during his vacation, berating him for not having written to her.

In the analyst's office Mary carried out a repetitious play. She built a playhouse under the analyst's desk by surrounding herself on all sides with a set of pillows taken from a chair and couch in his office. She then asked him to enter the house by finding an opening between the pillows. She admitted that the game she was playing was very much like a daydream which she frequently had before going to sleep. It involved a combination of fairy tales. She is a princess and the prince approaches her by overcoming her or by passing through some underbrush which presents a variety of obstacles. She cannot go to sleep when she has this daydream because she cannot stop twisting. However, when the prince finally reaches her, nothing happens because she then falls asleep. This is a rather typical fantasy of a little girl at the height of her oedipal wishes toward her father. One can already see the ego's influence on her instinctual needs. The father is changed into a prince and the access to her castle and to herself is made difficult by the underbrush in her fantasy and by the pillows in her play.

Let us take a look at the same child about two years later, when she was a bright, conscientious first-grader. While she had previously been convinced of her inexhaustible charms, she was now openly concerned about how her teachers and the analyst regarded her. At four, she had referred to herself as "sugar and spice and all that was nice." At six, since she had entered the latency period, she spoke of herself as being more "like snakes and snails and puppy-dog tails." In this view of herself she expressed both self-criticism and a denial of her femininity; and the masturbatory daydreams concerning the prince and princess were now replaced by entirely different fantasies which reflected some of the influences of her developing superego. In describing these fantasies she remarked: "I am a teacher, I am a nurse, I am very strict with the boys and girls." The sexual impulses which she had previously expressed openly had undergone a major alteration, but they had not entirely vanished. Her teacher and nurse fantasies were accompanied by considerable sexual excitement, carried a certain amount of sadism, and again kept her from falling asleep because she had to get up and urinate.

This girl was also seen for a few visits at the age of twelve, shortly after the onset of puberty. At that time her fantasies at bedtime dealt with the theme of being a "fancy lady" who was dancing and being admired by an audience. These fantasies were described as a means of "lulling" herself to sleep. Whether masturbatory activity accompanied them was not ascertained. The animated way in which she related the fantasies, however, and the fact that she found it necessary to lock her door before going to bed suggested that such activity was probably present. The significant contribution of maturation to the development of these fantasies was indicated by two facts: (1) The patient had recently begun to participate in stage appearances at school, a new activity from which she derived considerable age-appropriate satisfaction. (2) Her drawings during the interviews depicted primarily female actresses, with major emphasis on the development of the breasts, indicating a strong preoccupation with her own bodily changes of puberty.

Case 2

In this case, the influence of the fundamental maturational step of puberty could be observed with considerable clarity. Johnny, who is now in his early twenties, came into analysis at the age of ten with a severe obsessional neurosis which nearly paralyzed him. Johnny's history was replete with traumatic experiences. During his second year of life his mother became ill while she was pregnant, and the father, who gave every indication of being an ambulatory schizophrenic, took on the responsibility of caring for Johnny. He did so in a somewhat bizarre manner. He toilet trained his son between the ages of eighteen and twenty months in what he described as "doggy style" by rubbing the boy's face into his soiled diapers on three occasions. When Johnny was five, he regressed under the impact of oedipal strivings and became phobic of dirt, especially feces. In the middle of latency he developed the habit of what he called fishing in his rectum. Consciously, this was determined by his desire to get rid of all fecal material, but it also constituted a return of anal-erotic impulses since the compulsive action became a gratifying form of stimulation, namely, anal masturbation.

We shall now describe this boy's masturbation fantasies at five periods of his development: at the age of ten; at age twelve, just before puberty; at age thirteen, shortly after he became an adolescent; at age fifteen, in the middle of adolescence; and at age sixteen, one year later. While actual genital masturbation was absent prior to adolescence, the prepubertal fantasies to be described were repetitious and accompanied by sensations in the pelvis, culminating in an excited feeling throughout the body.

At the age of ten, when the ego was in such dominance over the id that the erotism was largely disguised, Johnny reported the following fantasy: "There was a house that had all sorts of electronic controls and a central switchboard (it was like our hi-fi system which I am not supposed to touch). The house was like a castle and like a factory and it was owned by a queen who was everybody's boss. In the basement was a bomb factory and next to it was a vault in which the queen kept all her money. She let me play with the controls of the bomb factory and when I pressed the buttons the periscope went up. But I was careful and did not let any of the bombs fall out. Then the lady told me to stop and I did." Johnny illustrated this daydream on the blackboard and the rising periscope was dramatic in its phallic symbolism.

At the age of twelve Johnny was under pressure of the impending instinctual awakening of adolescence, and had regressed somewhat to the anal-sadistic level. He had already developed pubic hair and had shaved it off because he found it "so ugly." He played out the second fantasy as a game, using a pillow and an electrically driven toy car which could be backed up to the edge of the pillow. The analyst had given him such a toy as a Christmas present, and the game Johnny played in the analyst's office was identical with the game he played at home. In the fantasy the patient and the analyst are driving through the North Shore of Boston and are backing up the car to a cliff overlooking the ocean. They stay there for a while and then decide to go home. When they try to leave, they find that the rear wheels are stuck in the sand and begin to spin, causing sand and rocks to be cast off into the ocean. As a consequence, the cliff recedes more and more, while the car always remains in the same position in relation to the cliff. The ocean then engulfs the territory where the cliff used to be, inundating more and more land and killing thousands, even millions of people. The patient became conscious of the anal significance of this play when he linked up the sound of the rocks falling into the ocean with the sound of feces falling into the toilet. Furthermore, in describing the water rushing inward from the ocean, he compared it to the flushing of the toilet. What was more impressive was the shift from the earlier highly disguised anal fantasy of the latency period to the more blatant anal-sadistic fantasy of early adolescence.

A few months later, at the age of thirteen, Johnny informed the analyst that he had experienced ejaculations. Previously, he had never shown any interest in the toy medical equipment in the office. Now he began to use an injection syringe, by filling it up with water which he then squirted into the sink. He also inserted his finger in a half-empty tube of ointment and represented ejaculation through squeezing out the ointment. His daydreams of the car had now vanished, and he reported that he had a new fantasy. He would think for hours of his mother's closet, visualizing her many elegant shoes and boots. One can note here the similarity between the lady who had all the money in the basement and his mother who had all the shoes. These fantasies were very exciting to Johnny; whenever he visualized the shoes, he would experience an erection and an urge to rub his penis inside them. It was clear that, as Johnny's phallic interests asserted themselves, the basic fixation at the anal level was not relinquished, as indicated by the fact that a strong preoccupation with the smell of the shoe leather was an important component of the new fantasy. These preoccupations established a bisexual fetish in which the masculine component was emphasized through the importance of the height of the heels and the feminine component was emphasized through a desire to put his penis inside the shoes. Johnny was aware of the developmental significance of the new fantasy, since, when the analyst indicated through his mannerisms some concern about the newly found interest, the patient reproached him. He argued that, after all, the analyst had shown some misgivings about the habits he had with his rear end and therefore should not be troubled by a shift from the rear to the front. The very nature of the reproach seemed to validate the analyst's assumption that the new fantasy constituted a progress over the old one.

It would be beyond the scope of this paper to discuss the fetishism that Johnny displayed. We wish only to stress the fact that even though there was progression from a purely anal to a phallic masturbation fantasy, the anal fixation was not completely abandoned. Furthermore, it seemed that the shift to a higher developmental level could not be considered to result solely from the analytic process or any particular interpretation that was made.

As Johnny progressed further into adolescence, he abandoned the shoe fetish and replaced it with heterosexual fantasies and activities in which he gradually emerged from a very passive position to that of a slightly more active male adolescent. At this time, when he was fifteen years old, his masturbation fantasy conformed to an actual experience which he had had with his six-year-old sister and which the analyst had prohibited, for the sake of both of them. He and his sister had played a game in which he would pretend that he was a slide and would lie down on the staircase, whereupon his sister would slide down his body and thereby touch his genitals. The recurrent fantasy of playing this game with his sister disappeared after a year or so and, at age sixteen, was replaced by the common *Tea and Sympathy* fantasy of being taught sex by an older woman, reflecting a re-edition of the oedipal yearnings. It appeared that these modifications had resulted largely from the continuing maturational effect of puberty.

Case 3

An eighteen-year-old boy, George, started a second analysis after being expelled from college for poor grades. His first analysis was started in another city at the age of six and continued for many years with frequent interruptions. George stated that this first analysis was initiated because of a series of fearful thoughts which dominated his thinking prior to sleep. He was aware that while he talked of fears he was actually describing exciting and sexually stimulating childhood fantasies. In these fantasies he saw himself surrounded by giants who threatened him and attacked him by eating away his flesh. In a mixture of fear and excitement he fantasied himself being devoured more and more. Eventually, nothing but his penis remained. In order to attenuate his anxiety he demanded the presence of his mother, who stayed with him at bedtime while he daydreamed about the giants. During latency these exciting fantasies subsided, but they never completely disappeared. When he was under some stress, he would conjure them up again, arouse excitement in himself, and again obtain tender care from his mother.

Between the ages of eight and twelve the giant fantasy was replaced by daydreams of wrestling with his older brother, as he had actually done on several occasions. He was always defeated by his brother, both in fantasy and in reality, and he experienced strong sexual excitement in both. With the onset of puberty there was a further change in his fantasies, which were now accompanied by genital stimulation. He pictured himself struggling with a stronger girl who overwhelmed him physically, handling his genitals and bringing about orgasm. As he passed from adolescence into maturity, the fantasy was again modified. He now saw himself as an active seducer of a woman, but as his excitement increased he became confused about whether he was the male or the female. At the present time, at eighteen years of age, his fantasies are primarily of heterosexual intercourse. Furthermore, although he is quite inhibited sexually he recently had some satisfactory heterosexual experiences.

In his current analysis it was fascinating to notice the degree to which the early masturbation fantasies had infiltrated his personality. He would skip classes and postpone work and then fantasy that his instructors or the analyst, like the giants, would approach him forcefully, attack him in "biting fashion," and thus force him to study and fulfill his academic obligations. There was no doubt that he was suffering from a severe neurosis and that the forces that had determined his fantasies as a child were still present. However, the change from the primitive oral-sadistic fantasy to the bisexual and eventually heterosexual fantasy of adolescence and young adulthood appeared to have occurred largely on the basis of biological maturation.

The question may be raised concerning the effect which his first analysis had in fostering his development and changing the nature of his fantasies. His first analyst, who was a woman, stated that the analysis had to remain rather superficial and that the changes of fantasy seemed to occur quite spontaneously. When the patient now looks back at this early treatment, he feels that it was an opportunity to grow up in a safe and nonthreatening environment.

One might ask the question how much of the change in fantasy observed in the above three cases was due to inherent maturation and how much was due to the influence of experience. It is apparent that this distinction really cannot be made. If we assume that the maturational changes of latency and puberty are largely biological phenomena, we still have to recognize that the environment inevitably reacts to these biological phenomena and contributes in many ways to the process of maturation.

II

The cases presented so far have illustrated the changes which masturbation fantasies may undergo as a result of maturation. The clinical material to follow illustrates how these fantasies can become desexualized in adult life and eventually achieve a state which is closely linked to the autonomous functions of the ego.

Case 4

A twenty-six-year-old graduate student entered analysis because of indecision in regard to marrying his current girlfriend. After a brief period of analysis he broke off treatment, married, and moved to a Pacific island where he pursued his studies.

As a young boy between the ages of five and seven he had a recurrent exciting daydream which he felt was connected with his reading of the story of the Swiss family Robinson. In this daydream he saw himself and his large family on an island which was being attacked by enemies. The attackers, having numerical superiority, overwhelmed the defenders one by one, killing and mutilating them, and eventually he alone was left. Then the rescuers appeared and he was saved. He recalled playing out this fantasy through violent gestures, including pounding the pillows and blankets and rubbing against them.

During early latency the patient developed an intense interest in geography and found it fascinating to study the location, the climate, and the products of various faraway countries. He covered the walls of his room with maps and, while doing mediocre work in reading, writing, and arithmetic, became an expert in geography. This interest continued throughout his school years and eventually shifted to a study of the native languages of some of the Pacific islands.

When he was nine or ten the original sexual fantasy dropped away; it reappeared in a somewhat different form in puberty when he saw himself as the superman master of a small island, who could command sexual obedience from all the inhabitants. When he reached adulthood, this fantasy was replaced by an activity free of apparent sexual connotations. He became the only white man on a small island; and although he was there ostensibly to study the natives, he and his wife became the central authorities for the native population. He taught them English and promoted their cultural development.

Case 5

This patient, aged fifty, had grown up in a foreign country and as a young child had been exposed to a carnival environment which offered him abundant opportunity to observe, with interest and excitement, many forms of sexual behavior. His interest in these experiences persisted throughout the latency period, after the family moved to a new environment. Trapeze artists, clowns, and couples engaging in sexual activity formed the nucleus of his early masturbation fantasies.

During adolescence these fantasies disappeared, but evidence of their continued existence, in a desexualized form, was later found in his adult professional activity. For a period of time the patient had been involved in research which required him to take scrapings of the skin of people afflicted with dermatological disorders. Even when he was not doing this work, he was preoccupied with it in the form of fantasies of partially naked female patients. However, the major excitement in these fantasies was not the visualization of the naked body but rather the scraping of the skin and especially the viewing of the scrapings under the microscope. Even though this activity was largely desexualized, it aroused sufficient conflict and guilt so that he had to alter his work. He then developed a new technique for the microscopic study of living bacteria, an activity which was far enough removed from the original voyeuristic interests to permit him peace of mind and professional success.

Discussion

Two issues have been discussed: first, that the natural process of growth and development brings about changes in the content of masturbation fantasies; and second, that masturbation fantasies may make important contributions to the formation of ego interests, i.e., to hobbies, ambitions, professional activity, etc.

In all the material presented the masturbation fantasies contained a considerable degree of pregenital coloring. Even in the first case of the relatively normal-neurotic girl, the early latency fantasies of being a nurse or teacher included elements brought forth from the anal phase of development and gave her fantasies a sadistic cast. She thus became the punitive teacher in her fantasies. In many little girls this emergence of sadistic impulses and the denial of passive feminine feelings are characteristic of their growth and development from the oedipal period to latency. This shift says little or nothing about the important question of health or pathology. All one can say is that with maturation a change in fantasy content occurs and that this change reflects a modification of the child's conflicts and defenses. In the cases of Johnny, whose preadolescent fantasies included intense sadistic elements, and of George, who was obsessed with and excited by the giants, the pregenital material was abundant. In the two older patients (the man who migrated to a Pacific island, and the bacteriologist), the pregenital interests were built into the character structure and were manifested largely through occupational interests. In these patients, as a result of sublimation, the masturbation fantasies had entered the autonomous ego activities of adult life. It was only through a step-by-step analysis of the character defenses that the intimate connection between these adult interests and the early fantasies could be established.

Masturbation fantasies in their dynamic structure resemble the dream, and in this way become a royal road to the unconscious. That there are also major differences between dreams and fantasies is obvious. However, the study of masturbation fantasies, especially the observation of their changes or progression, offers us an opportunity to learn much about the vicissitudes of instincts as well as the development of the ego and its integrations. In "A Child Is Being Beaten" Freud (1919) described some of the changes which masturbation fantasies concerning "beating" may undergo in the process of development. He spoke of the beating fantasy as an "infantile perversion" and explained it in part on the basis of constitution and fixation. He also noted that these fantasies may undergo developmental changes, and remarked that "beating-phantasies have a historical development which is by no means simple, and in the course of which they are changed in most respects more than once," and "an infantile perversion of this sort need not persist for a whole lifetime; later on it can be subjected to repression, be replaced by reaction-formation, or be transformed by sublimation." In referring to adult patients he added, "as a rule the phantasy remains unconscious, and can only be reconstructed in the course of the analysis." The same statement can be made concerning a variety of childhood masturbation fantasies which later disappear and become incorporated into the adult personality. Once such changes have occurred, only a careful analysis of the ego-syntonic interests of adult life can enable one to bring these early fantasies to consciousness and to demonstrate how they have been incorporated into the adult personality.

In discussing the developmental modification of beating fantasies, Freud (1919) noted that in two of his female cases an artistic superstructure of daydreams had been imposed on the original fantasy. In expanding upon this issue, Anna Freud (1922) described how a girl's early beating fantasies were in latency transformed into elaborate daydreams which she distinguished by the name "nice stories." In the course of her further development, the theme of these daydreams found its way into stories which the adolescent girl wrote—now clearly directed to an audience.

Anna Freud (1949) noted that when, under the influence of castration anxiety, masturbatory activity is severely inhibited, "the masturbation-fantasy is deprived of all bodily outlet, the libidinal energy attached to it is completely blocked and dammed up, and eventually is displaced with full force from the realm of sex-life into the realm of ego-activities." The cases which we have presented demonstrate that such displacement of fantasies to ego activities may also occur when masturbatory activity is not seriously inhibited but has become disconnected from the fantasies. In many cases, however, the masturbatory activity itself is inhibited or has undergone major modifications. Bornstein (1953) discussed an eleven-year-old girl in whom the derivatives of repressed genital masturbation appeared in the form of repeatedly caressing her arms and legs and strongly pursuing intellectual interests, with the underlying sexual fantasies being totally severed from the acts.

A. Reich (1951) and Anna Freud (1949) have pointed out that sometimes the only residual evidence of an early masturbation fantasy is found in the patient's "acting out." A. Reich described a female patient whose childhood masturbation fantasy of having her father, a surgeon, operate upon her had been repressed but was later acted out by having her husband, also a surgeon, perform an abortion upon her.

In referring to the displacement of masturbatory excitement to nonsexual activities, A. Reich stated: "Often physical activities which involve a certain risk of danger, such as flying or reckless driving, lend themselves well to such a purpose." In discussing the same issue, Bornstein (1953) pointed out that excitement itself is often "the only residue of the substitute for the relinquished sexual activity." In the adult cases which have been reported in the present paper, the high level of nonspecific excitement which accompanied the ego-syntonic interests led the analyst to suspect that these interests had been derived from earlier masturbation fantasies. It is often this excessive nonspecific excitement which gives the analyst the initial clue which eventually enables him to exhume the childhood and adolescent masturbation fantasies.

BIBLIOGRAPHY

Arlow, J. A. (1953), Masturbation and Symptom Formation. *J. Amer. Psa. Assn.*, 1:45-58.

Bornstein, B. (1953), Masturbation in the Latency Period. *This Annual*, 8:65-78.

Eidelberg, L. (1945), A Contribution to the Study of the Masturbation Phantasy. *Studies in Psychoanalysis*. New York: International Universities Press, 2nd ed., 1952, pp. 203-223.

Freud, A. (1922), The Relation of Beating Phantasies to a Daydream. *Int. J. Psa.*, 4:89-102, 1923.

—— (1949), Certain Types and Stages of Social Maladjustment. In: *Searchlights on Delinquency*, ed. K. R. Eissler. New York: International Universities Press, pp. 193-204.

Freud, S. (1908), Hysterical Phantasies and Their Relation to Bisexuality. *Standard Edition*, 9:155-166. London: Hogarth Press, 1959.

—— (1919), 'A Child Is Being Beaten': A Contribution to the Study of the Origin of Sexual Perversions. *Standard Edition*, 17:175-204. London: Hogarth Press, 1955.

Levin, S. (1963), A Review of Freud's Contributions to the Topic of Masturbation. *Bull. Phila. Assn. Psa.*, 13:15-24.

Reich, A. (1951), The Discussion of 1912 on Masturbation and our Present-day Views. *This Annual*, 6:80-94.

Stekel, W. (1912), [Contribution to] *Die Onanie: 14 Beiträge zu einer Diskussion der Wiener psychoanalytischen Vereinigung*. Wiesbaden: Bergmann, pp. 29-45.

Waelder, R. (1930), The Principle of Multiple Function: Observations on Overdetermination. *Psa. Quart.*, 5:45-62, 1936.

CLINICAL CONTRIBUTIONS

VISUAL HALLUCINOSIS IN CHILDREN

A Report of Two Cases

HARRY Z. COREN, M.D. and JOEL S. SALDINGER, M.D.
(San Francisco)

Introduction

Relatively few cases of hallucinatory reactions in children as a response to an acute psychological stress have been reported. There is a paucity of information (1) on the problem of symptom choice, and (2) on the interrelationship of the visual hallucinations with other symptoms. Our experience in a pediatric clinic and a psychiatric clinic shows this syndrome is not rare. Among the patients seen with this syndrome, we have had the opportunity to follow intensively two boys, aged five and twelve, with visual hallucinosis, and we are presenting these cases to elucidate the problems of symptom choice and the interrelationship among symptoms.

We shall describe the close clinical relationship among visual hallucinations, paranoid delusions, and phobias in these patients in the attempt to answer the question: Why do these patients manifest visual hallucinations rather than the more common phobias?

We shall approach the problem of symptom choice via the dynamics and the following structural characteristics of the symptom:

(a) the perceptual sphere of the symptom;
(b) the reality of the event which precipitated the symptom;
(c) the relative defects in reality testing shared with the mothers and the subculture;

From the Department of Child Psychiatry, Mt. Zion Hospital and Medical Center, San Francisco, Calif.

We would like to thank the members of the Department of Child Psychiatry of the Mt. Zion Hospital and Medical Center for their helpful suggestions, interest, and illuminating ideas.

(d) the intensity of conflict without reasonable help from the environment to find solutions;
(e) the reworking of the trauma during an altered ego state.

Case Report: Hank H.

Hank, a five-year-old Negro boy, was admitted to the Mt. Zion Pediatric Ward because he was experiencing intense anxiety and "seeing" snakes following an acute psychological stress.

Family and Background Information

At the time of the stressful incident, Hank lived in a housing project with his mother and three siblings—an eight-year-old sister, a seven-year-old brother, and a two-month-old half brother.

Hank's mother was an attractive, seductive twenty-nine-year-old divorced Negro woman who took a great deal of pride in keeping herself and her children looking neat and well dressed as well as keeping a clean, orderly home. She was born in Mississippi, was the oldest of six children, and had been her father's favorite.

Mrs. H. recalled that she was afraid of thunder, lightning, violence, and death: she often dreamed and imagined the face of someone who had died. These fears intensified in her adolescence and have persisted to this day. Sometimes when awakening from her dreams, she would be unable to differentiate the dreams from reality for quite some time. She had been told by her mother and grandmother a number of spooky superstitions regarding dead people who return. She was so frightened of death, violence, and rape that she often felt she had to have someone sleep in her bed with her. So for the first five years of Hank's life, he often slept with his mother. Besides being anxious Mrs. H. suffered from headaches whenever she felt tense. The headaches began in her late teens and have persisted to the present. She also had to deny her angry feelings and guard against her aggressive wishes.

Her marriage had been very stormy, including violent fights. When Hank was seven months old, his father was imprisoned for shooting someone, and Mrs. H. left her husband and moved to San Francisco.

Hank's early development was unremarkable. He was cared for

by his mother and grandmother up to seven months of age. Then the family moved and Mrs. H. went to work and he was cared for by an aunt from seven months to one and a half years, at which time Mrs. H. stopped working. He experienced no further losses until he was three and a half years old when he and his sister and brother spent a three-week Christmas vacation with their grandparents in Mississippi, without their mother. Hank's sister, who was six years old at the time, developed visual hallucinations of raccoons crawling on her, and she required sedation. The hallucinations persisted throughout the three weeks but subsided by the time the children returned to their mother.

When Hank was almost four years old, the children and their mother returned to Mississippi for a summer vacation because the grandfather was seriously ill. Hank began to wet his bed. When the family returned to San Francisco, Mrs. H. began seeing her current boyfriend. Hank's enuresis intensified when at the age of four and a half he learned that there was going to be a new baby in the family. His mother told him that the baby would be born at the same time as his fifth birthday and that the baby would be his birthday present.

Four months prior to the outbreak of hallucinations, Hank was hospitalized for three days for a cardiac catheterization for a murmur which turned out to be functional. He was described as a quiet, drowsy, cooperative child in the hospital.

Two months prior to the hallucinations, his half brother was born, the family moved to a new house, and Hank started kindergarten, where he was described as a quiet child who usually followed routine. One month prior to the hallucinations, the baby was hospitalized for a week because of respiratory distress. Hank immediately noticed that his mother was upset and asked her whether the baby would ever come home again. Hank was very relieved when the baby returned. Hank did not show any hostility or jealousy toward the baby. This, then, was the state of the patient when the following acute stress occurred.

Presenting Illness

One Saturday, in the late afternoon, Hank witnessed the following real episode. A mouse ran out of its hole in the kitchen and ran into the living room. It ran around Hank's mother several times and then ran up her leg under her slacks. She became quite terrified and jumped up on a chair. The mouse finally ran down her leg and under the carpet. Hank's aunt took off her shoe and hit and killed the mouse; she then picked up the mouse by the tail and threw it in the garbage.

About a half hour later Mrs. H.'s boyfriend, Mr. B., came into the house and Hank re-enacted the whole scene, jumping up on the chair and showing how afraid his mother had been. Hank seemed his usual self that evening and went to bed at his usual Saturday bedtime of 10 P.M. His mother and Mr. B. went out on a date, returned about 2 A.M., and about a half hour later (while they were in bed) Hank came out of his room and said drowsily that he was afraid and wanted to sleep with his mother. He did not appear to be upset. His request to sleep with his mother was not unusual for him. From the time he was a baby, Hank had often slept with his mother because she was afraid to sleep alone. He would often go to sleep in his own bed in the room he shared with his seven-year-old brother; but when his mother was ready to retire or when Mr. B. had left her, she would usually pick Hank up from his bed, take him to urinate (because of his frequent bed wetting), and then take him to bed with her. Occasionally he would come into her bed on his own initiative.

This time Mrs. H. and Mr. B. sent Hank back to his room, but he returned almost immediately, appearing very frightened and wide-eyed and screaming that he had seen a big black snake in his brother's bed. Despite reassurance by his mother and Mr. B., Hank continued to scream he had seen a snake; then he said that the snake was right there in the corner of the room they were in.

Mr. B. tried to reassure Hank by taking a knife from the kitchen, pretending to kill the snake in the corner, and then throwing it in the garbage. Instead of being reassured, Hank became even more anxious. Mr. B. left, and the mother continued to try and comfort Hank—to no avail. He would not lie in bed because he thought there was a snake on the sheets and would only lie directly on top of his mother. He was unable to go to sleep and whispered to his mother that there was a little boy in the room with a knife who was trying to kill him. (Here it is interesting to note that the only other person in the room was his two-month-old half brother.)

Hank spent a sleepless night with his mother. He became afraid of his mother's bedroom and would not set foot on any of the rugs in the house. In desperation, his mother took him to his aunt's house early Sunday morning, where he continued to be anxious, complaining that snakes were after him. Later that morning he was brought to the emergency room. It was noted there that he appeared healthy and was afebrile, but that he was very anxious and said he had seen snakes in his bed, in his brother's bed, and in his mother's bed. The diagnosis was "gross stress reaction," and he was given phenobarbital and sent home. During the day he was somewhat less anxious and slept intermittently during the afternoon.

Then again that night he had difficulty sleeping and hallucinated snakes. His mother brought him back to Mt. Zion Monday morning. This time, in addition to the anxiety, it was noted that he had a low-grade temperature and a mild ear infection. He was again sent home, but was very upset, often clutching his ankles and yelling that snakes were on him. His mother called the hospital, and he was finally admitted to the pediatric ward.

On his first hospital day (this was a day and a half after the onset of the hallucinations), he went through the usual admission procedure and then was sedated heavily for a lumbar puncture and EEG. All the tests showed no abnormalities. He slept most of that day. The next morning he awoke screaming that snakes were crawling on him. He was somewhat calmer when held. A few hours later he was screaming he saw a dead rat; and still later, when taken to the bathroom, he said there were snakes there. In the evening he said there were snakes in his pajama pants. At bedtime he screamed as soon as he was left alone in his room. He screamed most of the night, saying there was something on his legs. He masturbated frequently. It was noted that he was calmer and did not hallucinate when he stayed in the corridor near the nurses station, and eventually he fell asleep in a chair in the corridor.

On the third hospital day he continued to hallucinate snakes crawling on him, but seemed calmer in the afternoon after speaking to a child psychiatrist and saying he had a devil in his pants. In the evening he was seen by myself (H.Z.C.). Hank immediately told me that a rat had been killed at home, that he had seen snakes, and that he was very frightened of the snakes. He began to play a game of looking through blown-up balloons and then asking me to do the same. He repeated the game over and over, to which I commented that it seemed he wanted to know if I could see the same things he saw. That evening when put to bed he again screamed that there was something in his pants and in the bed, and he jumped out of bed and asked the nurse to stay with him. He again spent most of the night in a chair near the nurses station, but it was noted that he was not as disturbed as on the previous night.

The next morning, his fourth day in the hospital, he seemed less anxious and much more chipper. When I saw him he again told me about the rat and the snakes. Then he said he wanted to go home. He told me about his home and he drew some pictures on a blackboard. With great excitement he drew a picture of a person with a dingle (genital). He said his daddy (his mother's boyfriend) had a book with pictures of naked women and you could see dingles and titties. He and his brother often looked at the book. He also liked to look at the dingles of the girls in the neighborhood. Toward the end of the session he asked whether I had a car and whether we could see it by looking out the window. He seemed quite concerned when I told him it was not in sight, and I pointed out his concern to him.

Hank was free of hallucinations most of the day and was less anxious. Later in the evening he said that the snakes in his brother's bed were the largest, but that there were also snakes in his mother's bed and that there were small ones in the baby's crib.

Over the next six days Hank became much less anxious and hallucinated snakes or mice only occasionally, mostly at night. He began to talk more in a paranoid fashion, saying that a little boy had tried to kill him with a knife. He also said there was a man inside his stomach. During his sessions with me he talked about witches changing the colors of toys. The themes of "Can you see what I see?" and "Where is your car?" continued. He also was anxious when he saw a baby doll, and insisted we give it to a girl to feed. Toward the end of his hospital stay, it was noted that he became increasingly negativistic and aggressive with the nurses when they would not let him keep the light on in his room. He visited my office in the outpatient clinic, after which psychotherapy sessions were scheduled. He was finally discharged from the hospital after a stay of ten days.

Therapy

The patient was seen twice a week and the mother once a week for psychotherapy. During therapy various themes and conflict areas became prominent. These I have artificially separated into the following areas: anger, castration anxiety, scoptophilia, the wish to be the only one, and the wish to be grown up versus the wish to be a baby. The examples of play given have multiple determinants but are listed under the principal theme for heuristic purposes.

It became apparent that Hank was a very angry boy. He had been unable to give vent to his anger until therapy was under way. Then, for the first time since the baby was born, Hank showed that he was angry at the baby by telling his mother that they should chop up the baby and put him in the garbage. In therapy Hank also showed anger at his mother's boyfriend by drawing a picture of him and then hitting it vehemently over and over again with a pencil. But he also showed some control over his anger by defensively scotch-taping all the "aggressive" instruments in the room, for example, the stapler, the scissors, the toy rubber knife. However, his anger would erupt: he would throw temper tantrums and try to break things in the office. He would also untape the stapler at times and bang it with his fist. Sometimes at the end of a session he became sullen and angry, refused to go back to his mother, and would just lie on the floor.

Hank's intense castration anxiety was even more prominent than his anger. From the beginning he worried about things that might be missing. When playing cards if he saw he did not have an ace, he became anxious and disrupted the play. He took a noisemaker that did not work, had me fix it for him, and then in later sessions he checked whether the toy was all right. He drew pictures similar to the one he had drawn in the hospital of the man with his dingle, but now they were pictures of a man with "a big old balloon" and a man with a gun. He also reassured me that Dick Tracy's car could not be damaged, that even if a wheel did fall off, it could be fixed. When drawing, he became anxious when a pencil point broke or one of the pens skipped; eventually he drew with a hand full of pens, pencils, and crayons all at the same time. Just before Easter, he brought a paper bunny hat from school and wanted to staple on longer ears.

However, he then became worried that they would fall off. He showed great delight in playing a game in which he stole play money from me and had me tell him "Stop thief." He then shot me dead! The game eventually changed to one in which I was to attempt to steal the play money from him while he was asleep. He kept the money between his thighs and then woke up and shot me dead, just in time. The theme of "seeing is believing," which had started in the hospital in reference to my car, was further elaborated in reference to guns in the toy cabinet and tape in the drawer. This theme was also linked with an anxiety attack provoked by his sister's teasing him about a mouse in the kitchen, to which he responded by not letting his mother put his pants on him for half a day and then leaving his fly open during a therapy session. During psychological testing he drew a picture of a man with a long body but with no appendages (see Fig. 1). Later in therapy, Hank played with the toy doctor kit and asked me for Band-Aids. He eventually told me that he was afraid he might get hurt and showed me the scar on his arm from the cardiac catheterization, which had occurred over a year before. He talked a lot about how he had been afraid that it might hurt when the doctor removed the sutures from his arm, but that it had not hurt him.

Hank showed his scoptophilia in his interest in looking, toys, sex play with dolls, and his drawings. The magnifying glass became his favorite toy. He had the dolls kiss, hold hands, and go to bed. When these games made him too anxious, he would interrupt them and play cards instead. Defensive action continued and he had to scotch-tape the cards as he had done with the magnifying glass and toy bed earlier. He put these toys in his personal storage box and thereafter rarely played with them. In the drawing on the psychological testing, his man and woman showed very large, prominent eyes (see Fig. 1).

Another important theme was his "wish to be the only one." His box became most important to him. It contained all the objects he had taped for safety. The formally defensive taping acquired the new meaning of possessiveness. This incident and others show the fluidity of defensive functions. He taped pictures to the wall, claiming the room as his own. He often asked if other boys came to the room and would screw on the cap of the tinker toys hard so that no other boy

FIGURE 1

could use them. He talked about the baby clinic where babies are fed and said he did not like it when the baby was alone with his mother while he was at school. He also worried that the candy he got from me would not be enough because his older brother would take some away from him.

Hank alternated in his wish to be grown up and his wish to be a baby. His mother said Hank had always shown a greater desire to remain a baby than did his two older siblings; for example, he wanted to wear diapers when he was three and a half and he wanted a bottle when the baby was fed. He also told his mother that he wished the baby would grow up quickly so that he would be the baby again. In therapy he often wanted me to wait on him and do simple things for him that he could do himself, such as get toys from the cabinet, put his shoes on for him, and carry his papers. But he also wanted to do the complicated things I could do, such as loading the stapler. He became concerned when he could not make things such as a Batman hat and utility belt as well as I did. He liked to take my chair but worried about the danger of tilting it as I did. He said he wanted to be strong like Batman and played a game in which he cut off my hand and ate it and then became the strongest man in the world. At times he was contemptuous of the baby, laughing at how the baby was a pig.

During the course of therapy Hank initially talked about his many fears—for example, about Santa Claus, the Bible, the bathroom, monsters, flying snakes. Often in connection with his fears he would talk about loving the baby to reassure himself. This catharsis helped him to become less fearful and less angry, and his enuresis improved. At this point I encouraged the mother to let Hank sleep alone and he was able to do so. He became more interested in school and picnics and enjoyed telling me about his renewed interests.

The mother's reaction to his improvement is noteworthy. She wanted to have Hank circumcised. She said she felt uncomfortable because she thought Hank's foreskin was too tight, although this was not so and Hank showed no discomfort. I successfully dissuaded her from this course.

Psychological testing performed during the middle of therapy showed Hank's phallic concerns with intense castration fears and his fluid neurotic defense system. There was no evidence of a schizophrenic process.

Symptom Dynamics: Predisposition

Prior to the trauma, Hank was frequently exposed to an intense amount of visual sexual stimulation in his home. He could watch his mother's sexual activities with her boyfriend through an open door. Hank also slept with his mother and was repeatedly made aware of the anatomical sex differences. I learned of his interest in looking at the book with pictures of nude women that Mr. B. had left in the home and in peeking under the skirts of girls in his neighborhood. As previously mentioned, his scoptophilic interest was a clear theme in treatment. However, visual curiosity was by no means solely pleasurable. Hank's looking made him very anxious because he had seen the "reality" of castration; i.e., a woman does not have a penis. The strength of this castration anxiety came out clearly in the therapy. Hank also saw that at times his mother went to bed with someone else. His rage at being excluded may explain why his wish to be the only one played a major part in his therapy, as did his anger toward his mother's boyfriend.

The baby's birth also generated a great deal of anger in Hank which he had to repress. During her pregnancy Hank's mother told him that the baby would be a birthday present. Mothers give this ambiguous explanation frequently and with surprising frankness. It implies the mother's wish to share oedipal fantasies with her son. She condones his unconscious fantasies and accepts her own wish to elevate him to the rank of her mate and of the new baby's progenitor. This crossing of boundaries between generations increases the boy's fears of his adult rival. In the attempt to deny and evade her forbidden wish, the mother develops a castrating reaction formation in her attitude toward her son, which makes the boy's situation doubly precarious and exposes him to the dangers of castration from both adults. If the boy accepts the baby as a special gift from his mother, then he also has to accept the injunctions against exhibiting rage and disappointment at the adults; for with his guilt, he is in danger of losing all love and approval. Rage against the intruder is, of course, equally forbidden.

Hank did not show any anger toward the baby or toward Mr. B. He held it all inside. Hank reacted to his particular situation with the fears of the "magical" retribution for his forbidden wishes and feelings. The baby's week-long hospitalization may well have reinforced Hank's fear of his aggressive wishes toward the baby. The intensity of Hank's fears was one of the factors which impaired his sense of reality. This break with reality will be discussed further under the section on Symptom Choice.

Therefore at the time of the trauma Hank was experiencing intense castration anxiety and an increase of aggressive impulses with no form of discharge. This combination of internal factors and external events, both acute and chronic, predisposed Hank for further transformations.

Symptom Dynamics: Symbolic

The trauma of seeing a mouse run up his mother's leg and then get killed could be interpreted in various symbolic ways. Freud (1900) pointed out that small animals can represent unwanted small siblings. Feldman (1949) also supported the view that a mouse can symbolize a baby.

To Hank, the trauma symbolized primarily that the baby could be killed: that his smoldering conflictual wish, which was being defended against by repression, could become a reality. This conflictual wish was verbalized when, following the resolution of the psychosis, Hank was able to say he wished the baby could be chopped up and put in the garbage, which was the fate of the mouse. On the first level of trauma, then, the mouse was equated with the baby.

However, there is another symbolic equation: that of mouse and penis. That the mouse is an unconscious symbol for a penis is well known (Freud, 1900). Feldman (1949) stated that the fear of mice can be related to castration anxiety. Harvey Lewis (1958), in his paper on the loss of the first deciduous tooth, gives good evidence that the mouse is a penis symbol because it goes in and out of holes, because it is hairy, and because of its general shape. He also shows that the mouse frequently occurs in folk legends concerning the compensation for the lost tooth precisely because of its phallic symbolism. Therefore, on a second level, the symbolic trauma for Hank of the mouse running out of his mother's pant leg and getting killed is none other than castration. During his illness and during his therapy, Hank showed an extreme degree of castration anxiety. This amount of castration anxiety could not be explained only by the level of castration anxiety prior to the trauma, but must also have received a good deal of impetus from the trauma itself, in that the mouse's death was symbolically understood as damage to his own penis. Additional evidence is that in the hallucination he saw an even more blatant phallic symbol, a snake.

The reasons Hank equated the mouse's death with his own castration anxiety have to do with his strong unconscious wishes and his fantasied retribution. The exciting sexual games he played in therapy point to his wish to penetrate his mother like the "naughty" mouse.

Hank noted that his mother was very frightened when the mouse ran up her leg. The anxiety a woman experiences at the sight of a mouse has been shown by Feldman (1949) to arise often because of the unconscious symbolism of mouse-equals-penis. In other words, she is afraid the mouse will run up her leg and penetrate her vagina —in short, a rape fantasy. Thus, for Hank's mother, the reality of a mouse running up her leg is very close to the unconscious fantasy of rape. Once more mother and son shared the same fantasy which became "real." That the mother perceived his intent on an unconscious level may also be surmised from her attempt, during therapy, to have him circumcised.

Hank's wish to get rid of his mother's boyfriend was more open in therapy, and there were many times when he expressed anger toward the boyfriend. He also talked about his fear of Mr. B.

It is noteworthy that Hank did not begin to hallucinate immediately following the mouse incident, but did so later in the night following a rejection by his mother. When he wanted to be close to his mother for reassurance, she sent him away because of her preference, at the time, for her boyfriend. The affects aroused while he was in this drowsy state may well have been the final increase in anxiety and in angry impulses that overwhelmed the weakened ego. (This will be discussed further under Symptom Choice.)

Symptom Dynamics: Restitution

The attempt at restitution came in the form of hallucinations of snakes. Symbolically this hallucination was a denial and undoing of all levels of the trauma. He saw a phallic symbol (the snake), which was "visible truth" that his penis was intact; i.e., there had been no castration. Here it is interesting to note that during therapy, whenever his castration anxiety was aroused, Hank reassured himself by visually ascertaining that his penis was present. The theme of "seeing is believing" also pointed up his concern with visual reassurances. Moreover, since snake equals mouse, the fact that Hank saw snakes was an attempt to deny that the mouse was killed; on a symbolic level, it meant the baby was alive and wiggling. However, the resurrection of his victim was not enough reassurance, and Hank had the delusion that a little boy was after him with a knife. This delusion maintained that the little boy was alive and also reversed the possibility that the little boy, the baby, was vulnerable and could be killed like a mouse, but asserted that the little boy was the attacker. This projection of his impulse toward the baby onto the baby is a familiar defense against unacceptable impulses.

The castration anxiety was also projected out and experienced first as a concomitant anxiety with the snake hallucination, then as anxiety attached to a number of shifting phobias. The extreme fear experienced during the hallucinations showed that this projection of castration anxiety was not a very effective defense. The ego was being flooded by the eruption of anxiety. Hank found himself in a similar situation as the beholder of the Medusa's Head as described by Freud (1940). There, too, although the phallic object (the snake) is seen, the beholder experiences anxiety. His attempt to deny female castration has failed. As he projects his castration anxiety onto the external symbol, he once again experiences anxiety.

Case Report: Neal N.

Neal, a twelve-year-old Negro boy, was treated by the psychiatric consultant in the Pediatric Clinic because Neal began to "see" devouring, frightening snakes one week after he saw a man killed by knifing.

Family and Background Information

At the time of the onset of the visual hallucinations, Neal lived with his mother and three sisters—a seventeen-year-old sister, an eight-year-old half sister, and a two-and-a-half-year-old half sister.

Mrs. N.'s life was a history of desertions and chaos. She lived in the South and was cared for by her maternal grandmother because both her parents went North after they were divorced. She felt that her mother had deserted her and was very dependent on her maternal grandmother. Her grandmother's influence led her to be very active in the Baptist Church.

Neal's mother had two marriages, both ending in desertion. Her first husband, Neal's father, left when she was pregnant with Neal. She and her maternal grandmother moved to San Francisco, where she could obtain employment more easily. The grandmother, the woman who had taken care of her, now took care of Neal.

When Neal was four years old, his first half sister was born. A year later Mrs. N.'s maternal grandmother died, and shortly thereafter Mrs. N. remarried. She then began to take care of Neal herself. When Neal was nine years old, his stepfather deserted the family in much the same manner as Neal's father had, leaving when Neal's mother was pregnant. Thereafter the stepfather sporadically visited the family.

Neal's mother was frequently sick; she was obese and had hypertension, and was a regular patient at the medical clinic. The doctors thought that, in addition to her organic disease, she had emotional problems which were expressed by somatic symptoms, i.e., headaches.

She was a very passive, self-sacrificing woman who tolerated no anger in herself or her children; for example, she responded to being deserted without any display of anger toward her husband, merely saying that God would punish him.

Her main interest was in attending church and funerals. She went to the funerals not only of friends and relatives, but also of people she scarcely knew. She was very superstitious and magically believed that death and illness were punishments for sins, committed by both herself and others. She taught Neal these beliefs and took him to evangelical-type religious services, where internal feelings and stimuli were said to come directly from God.

Neal was a quiet, passive, inhibited, smiling boy who showed no anger. His mother called him a "good" boy. He was fearful of bodily injury and avoided competitive sports, which he considered dangerous. He also avoided any situation in which he might get angry or might annoy others because of his fear that someone might get hurt.

During the year preceding the outbreak of the visual hallucinations of snakes, Neal became pubertal and had severe nightmares of people chasing him. These nightmares intensified and became pavor nocturnus. Neal's mother was worried about the severity of the nightmares, but did nothing.

Four months before the outbreak of the hallucinations, Mrs. N. was hospitalized for a month for an acute hypertensive episode. Two months later, Neal's seventeen-year-old unwed sister was discovered to be three months pregnant. There was a great deal of turmoil in the family, and Neal's mother asked for casework help from the social work department of the clinic.

Presenting Illness

Neal was brought to the pediatric clinic because he was extremely fearful and had been "seeing" snakes for a month. An organic etiology for the hallucinations was ruled out on the basis of normal findings in the examinations, tests, and an EEG; and Neal was referred to the psychiatric consultant (J.S.S.).

The mother related, and Neal later confirmed, that one week prior to the outbreak of the hallucinations, Neal had been playing near his home when he saw a man knifed to death. Obviously terrified, he had run home to his mother. He then had become diffusely anxious that he also might be injured. This anxiety was followed by the paranoid delusion that people were out to get him and to hurt him deliberately. The paranoid delusional state had lasted one week when Neal began to "see" frightening, devouring snakes.

Therapy

When I saw Neal for the first time, he had been hallucinating for a month. He appeared extremely anxious, to the point of panic. He constantly looked around him, as if he saw something. He talked a little about how terrified he felt and about the imaginary quality of the hallucinations. He tried to differentiate the hallucinations from real objects.

Neal continued to be haunted both day and night for the next six weeks by the same visual hallucination of snakes. Sometimes he seemed uncertain whether the snakes were real or not, and he attempted each week to get reassurance from me that the snakes were not real. He talked about his terror of the snakes and gradually with this catharsis, reassurance, and reality testing, the hallucinations became less frequent and then disappeared. In their place, Neal began to talk more about his feeling that people were out to maliciously kill him or hurt him. These paranoid delusions were ego syntonic and he did not question them. He also believed that his mother meant to harm him. He was preoccupied with magic. He was curious about it as a hobby but was unsure whether magic was make-believe or real.

The delusions began to subside, but when a friend of his was injured, Neal became transiently more delusional. Gradually, with therapy, Neal talked less and less about his delusions and more about his fears of bodily injury. He talked about his original concerns of being injured during competitive sports. I learned from him how he had continuously restricted his life by avoiding any situations in which he might get angry. He felt that a little bit of anger was extremely dangerous since it could "blow up" and people could hurt and kill each other. He felt that he too could lose control of his anger and hurt others.

Five months after therapy began, Neal lacerated his arm while playing ball. He became extremely anxious and again developed the paranoid delusions that people were out to hurt him and would deliberately attack his injured arm. He had the ideas of reference that he could determine who his attackers would be by their gestures. He felt he could almost read their minds. Again through the catharsis, reality testing, and reassurance that therapy provided, he became less delusional.

Neal gradually improved and by the eighth month of weekly psychotherapy he was able to tolerate consciously some annoyance at his younger half sister. He was less fearful of competitive sports, and wrestled, pushed, and wisecracked with other children. He showed increased capacity for sublimation in his learning to use a skateboard and in his interest in science. He enjoyed looking at insects and studying them minutely.

Now when he saw a friend injured he did not become delusional but merely became more anxious. Neal narrowly escaped having his hand injured by a firecracker. Even with this stress his anxiety did not get out of control and he did not become delusional; however, he did develop transient headaches. In general, he was less inhibited in all his activities.

An interesting memory emerged during his therapy. He recalled that when he was five or six he had gone on a hunting trip with his uncle in the South and was very frightened upon seeing a big black snake. This snake was the same one that appeared in his hallucinations. Neal's mother confirmed that Neal used to go hunting with his uncle and had once been frightened by a snake.

Symptom Dynamics

Neal is a twelve-year-old boy who grew up in a household where anger or aggression were qualities to be feared and avoided at all costs. His character structure before the onset of gross symptoms was dominated by extreme passivity, avoidance of competition or aggressive situations which might provoke anger, and a marked lack of conscious feelings of anger, jealousy, or envy. In these respects he was truly "his mother's child," although he had not yet adopted her attitude of "God will punish them." He felt, rather, that there was no need for punishment. He externalized his own problem with aggression by saying the real problem was the other boys: they were too competitive, they cheated, they got angry over the slightest things, and so on.

It was with this character structure that Neal faced a series of stresses in the year preceding the visual hallucinations. His early pubertal growth was one general stress, intensifying many conflicts. The birth of a sibling was marked by intensification of his conflicts over tolerating envious, jealous, angry, or competitive strivings. His mother became increasingly ill, and Neal felt increasing guilt (the sin being the presence of hostile thoughts), since illness and punishment were equated in his family. Finally, his mother's month-long hospitalization produced feelings of abandonment, further intensifying the conflict. Finally, his sister's pregnancy placed increased pressure on the whole family, and revived fears of desertion (which had occurred with the mother's pregnancies). All of these incidents intensified the conflict over aggressive drives, and Neal developed a number of symptoms, e.g., phobias and nightmares. Finally, actually seeing someone killed undid the controls from the environment that Neal depended on for his precariously balanced repression of aggressive wishes, as well as seductively stimulating these very same precariously repressed and denied aggressive drive derivatives. The result was a regressive shift, with phobias first, paranoid delusions next, and finally hallucinations.

In the paranoid delusions and the hallucinations the aggressive impulses were projected onto outside objects, so that Neal was not faced with his own aggressive drives. Quite striking was his early focus on his mother in his delusions. The visual hallucinations symbolized a primitive, devouring oral aggressiveness—the snake. This perceptual memory trace was also determined by the association of hunting and killing. His fear of bodily injury was given concrete visual form in the snake which was out to attack his body. The fact that the snake was intact may also have symbolized that he, too, would remain intact—that an aggressive object could survive. The snake may also have been partly determined by the recent pregnancy with the unconscious equation of baby, penis, and snake.

As therapy progressed, the striking shifts in Neal were a beginning conscious awareness of his own aggressive and competitive strivings and an awakening sublimation. With therapy, Neal no longer regressed to hallucinations, even under pressures which intensified the conflicts. The ongoing therapy provided him with a wider range for handling aggressive drives, and placed him in a more flexible situation to cope with his major problem, the conscious toleration of aggressive drive derivatives.

Symptom Choice

The problems of symptom choice will be dealt with by attempting to answer the question: Why do these patients manifest visual hallucinations rather than the more common phobias?

The first problem is the interrelationship among symptoms. Both patients had an admixture of paranoid delusions and phobias during the resolution of the hallucinations. There was a rapid shift in symptoms and symbols. This continuum of symptomatology is central to the problem of symptom choice. If the choice of visual hallucinations is not a qualitatively different phenomenon than the choice of phobias, then the question of why visual hallucinations rather than phobias can be answered in quantitative terms.

Rapaport, in his book *Emotions and Memory* (1942), sheds light on this issue. He summarizes Freud's concepts and also elucidates the clinical finding in our cases and others (Esman, 1962; Weiner, 1961; Brenner, 1951), that the hallucinations are closely followed by delusions and phobias in the resolution phase. Rapaport states:

> The varied projection phenomena apparently form a continuous chain: hallucinations, delusions, phobias, dreams, day dreams, imagination, selective perception, memory errors and transformations, and organization of unorganized material.
>
> Projection was thus conceived by Freud as the extreme case of a subject's organizing his percepts, memories, and behavior according to the "pleasure principle," and attributing to the outside world that which is painful and tension-creating [p. 240f.].

We also favor the above view that the symptoms form a continuum. This then allows us to reformulate the question of symptom choice into the quantitative terms: What factors favor the more extreme end of the continuum (the hallucinations) over the less extreme (the phobias and anxieties)? The quantitative aspect is not to be thought of in solely "economic" terms, but rather is to be considered as a balance between the weakness of the ego (particularly the reality-testing apparatus) on the one hand, and the strength of the drives and conflicts on the other hand.

However, we think there is one drawback to considering the problem in quantitative terms only. That these patients experienced real events is of major significance, for the experiencing of a real event specifically favors the outbreak of hallucinations.

Modell (1958) reviewed Freud's contributions to the theory of hallucinations. Two main points were: (1) the hallucination represents the return of the repressed; and (2) the hallucination re-creates an actual piece of reality. Freud originally showed in *The Interpretation of Dreams* (1900), and restated in "Jensen's *Gradiva*" (1907), that when a dream reaches such an intensity that the belief in the reality of the dream image persists unusually long, then the dream refers to a real event which occurred.

The corollary to this hypothesis is that when a real event occurs, there is the possibility of its being reproduced as a hallucination, particularly if the real event connects with repressed conflicts and provokes strong affect. Under these conditions the real event may be "remembered" and dealt with by a hallucination.

Rapaport (1942) has suggested a similar hypothesis, based on the work of Silberer,

> When affects become all too strong, or when transient or developmental "insufficiencies" facilitate their operation, they mani-

> fest themselves by making for a symbolic reproduction of ideas [p. 243].
>
> Symbolism is a representation, or in other words reproduction, of an idea in visual images using the available memory-traces for this purpose [p. 242].
>
> Thus, according to Silberer's theory, in states of tiredness or primitive development, and under the pressure of affects inhibited in their free manifestation, the revival of memory-traces may occur in symbolic form [p. 243].

Both boys experienced a shocking, highly charged real event (a violent death) which provoked strong affects. It also gave expression to fantasies and conflictual wishes which were being defended against. It appears that when this happens the ego is particularly prone to being overwhelmed and must resort to more primitive defenses, such as those on the extreme end of the continuum—the hallucinations and delusions. This real event which produces such a psychological shock is similar to the trauma of the traumatic neurosis. Gill and Brenman (1959) have stressed that the trauma of a traumatic neurosis activates a repressed drive, and the hallucinatory reliving of the trauma gains impetus from the drive seeking expression. Thus the real event triggered and reinforced an impulse into a hallucination, which expressed the same dynamic content as the event.

As was shown in the discussion of symptom dynamics, the real event was extremely close, symbolically, to several powerful drives and anxieties, and became easily associated with the main conflicts of the patients. When reality and repressed fantasy coincide, the distinction between fantasy and reality becomes blurred and the reality-testing function is shaken, particularly in these boys who have no stable internal reality-testing apparatus of their own, but must rely on gross external reality-testing methods and on the reality-testing apparatuses of other people. The shaken reality-testing apparatus is then unable to differentiate internal perception from external perception and is prone to further regression, which allows internal stimuli to be projected outward and "perceived" as external stimuli; hence the symptoms of delusions and hallucinations both of which involve projection of impulses. The shift from phobias to hallucinations can be viewed as a topographic regression to the perceptual mode following an acute stress. Despert (1948) noted that the auditory hallucinations in some of her patients symbolized the demands from the conscience which followed acute increases in anxiety and guilt.

Another important factor favoring the more extreme form of symptomatology is the pre-existing lack of ego strength of the patients, or, in Silberer's terms, their "primitive development." The first defect is the relative lack of reality testing. Freud (1917) also considered this defect an important contributing factor, stating that for a hallucination to occur in a schizophrenic there may be a disturbance of "that institution of the ego" which is concerned with reality testing.

There are numerous factors which, in children, result in serious defects and weaknesses in reality testing. The sense of reality is generally less well established in children than in adults, particularly before they reach latency, and it is to be expected that intense emotions lessen the fleeting awakening of this function in children whose latency has been delayed or is still incomplete.

The overstimulation of Hank's scoptophilia no doubt delayed his latency and interfered with the stability of his reality sense. This stability was further diminished by the "voodoo" atmosphere of fear and superstition with which his mother surrounded him. Fears of ghosts, rape, violence, and any form of aggression frequently overwhelmed her, and there is no doubt that Hank sensed her fears. His mother could hardly contribute to or correct his hold on reality, since she had difficulty in differentiating dreams from reality herself.

Because there was no stable father in either family, the patients were more at the mercy of their mothers' poor reality testing. In these homes, wish was often equated with fulfillment, and the very existence of aggressive wishes was vigorously denied and guarded against to avoid the magical fate of wish coming true. For example, during her therapy, Hank's mother was worried that the baby might die during the night or that he might get sick. She was afraid that he was not breathing correctly and she often stayed awake at night, listening to him breathe. She also brought him to the pediatric clinic frequently. Gradually she revealed that she had had a very difficult labor. Moreover, she had wanted a girl, and when she was told that her baby was a boy, she felt disappointed and for a moment wished he were dead.

These families, with their own defective reality-testing apparatus, tend to give reality validation in other ways to the projected impulses of their children. For instance, these adults attempted to handle the hallucinated snake by throwing it out of the window. Neal's mother gave consensual validation to her son's paranoid delusions that other boys were out to get him at school by actually encouraging her son to stay home, fearing as he did that the boys would deliberately attack his wounded arm.

We have noticed that other children with hallucinations have been reared in evangelical churches and have been exposed to grown-ups who continually give reality credence to internal stimuli, claiming they have been "visited by God." This background undoubtedly contributes to later problems in differentiating internal perceptions from external perceptions, with hallucinations being a prime example of projecting internal drives outward. Wilking and Paoli (1966) have arrived at a similar conclusion. They state: "it seems that it is an adult's direct interference with development of the sense of reality in the child which actually produces the hallucinatory experience" (p. 433).

Besides the defect in reality testing, there were general ego defects in the control of impulse discharge. These children were continually being overstimulated by viewing sexual relations and witnessing overt violence. This overstimulation, coupled with a lack of suitable stable models for identification, prevented these children from developing stable mechanisms for delaying discharge of impulses. They used massive denial for controlling impulses, as did their mothers. The lack of a stable father may have placed an additional burden on both boys to control their death wishes toward a young sibling and their oedipal wishes toward their mothers. The father's absence may also explain why the wishes remained somewhat unmodified. (The absence of a father and the exposure to violent aggression produce difficulties similar to, but less extreme than, those in patients who have had incest relations. The primitive impulses in both are always close to the surface and apt to be expressed in reality, and they must be defended against by very primitive means.) These children, then, showed a precarious control of impulses, using primitive defenses. The sudden regression in both these boys was precipitated by seeing a violent act, which both destroyed the external controls and acted as a seductive pull on a precariously repressed impulse. The "magical" fulfillment of actual violence led to mounting anxiety with the boys' own emerging aggressive drives, which was handled by paranoid delusions and then outright hallucinations. Wilking and Paoli (1966) have also stressed the importance of the faulty ego development for the development of hallucinations in children.

Another aspect of symptom choice involves the perceptual sphere: Why were the hallucinations visual?

In discussing auditory hallucinations Freud (1917) said that the hallucinated voices were related to a hypercathexis of the verbal representation of objects. Esman (1962) extended this point to show that the visual hallucinations of some of his cases were related to the conflict-laden hypercathexis of the visual sphere of perception. The onset of the visual hallucinations in both of our patients was precipitated by the visual stimulus of seeing an object killed (in the first, a mouse; in the second, a man). The initial restitution, the hallucination, was in the visual sphere. (A similar matching of the traumatic perceptual sphere by the restitutive perceptual sphere was shown by another patient, a six-year-old boy who heard a plane crash in his backyard and then developed auditory hallucinations.)

Both patients also showed a predisposing conflict-laden hypercathexis of the visual sphere, as illustrated by the intense visual stimulation in the home, scoptophilia, reassurances by visual means, and a concomitant anxiety induced by viewing threatening scenes (see Symptom Dynamics).

Another aspect of the problem, seen in Hank, but not documented in Neal, was that the hallucinations occurred for the first time when Hank was in a sleepy state. In the cases reported by Brenner (1951) and Weiner (1961), the hallucinations began at night. As Rapaport (1942) noted, the revival of affect-laden memory traces may occur in symbolic form in states of tiredness. This weakened ego state is to some extent similar to the "hypnoid state" that Breuer and Freud (1893-1895), at least initially, felt to be a possible factor contributing to the psychological trauma and fostering the outbreak of hysterical psychosis.

In sum, a number of factors contributed to Hank's reviving the memory of a mouse being killed in the symbolic form of a visual hallucination of a snake. These were

(a) the pressure of strong anger toward the baby and mother's boyfriend;
(b) the lack of an outlet for the anger;
(c) a five-year-old's incomplete ego development;
(d) poor models of reality testing;
(e) conflict-laden hypercathexis of the visual sphere;
(f) drowsy state;
(g) the shocking effect of the real event which acutely undermined reality testing.

This hallucination represented the re-creation of an actual piece of reality, the death of the mouse, and the return of the repressed, the death wishes toward the baby, and his castration anxiety.

There was a significant difference in the expression of anxiety following the resolution of the psychosis: the twelve-year-old experienced primarily "body anxiety" while the five-year-old experienced primarily "castration anxiety." This difference is probably a function of age- and phase-specific dynamics and ego development. Certain practical aspects in the management of the acute phases were pointed up in these cases. The reassurance by the presence of an adult is paramount. If the child requests other aids in reality orientation, such as a night light, he should receive them. As Esman (1962) said, the adults should not attempt to "reassure" the patient by entering the hallucinatory world and attempt to "kill the snakes" or perform some other act intended to drive away the hallucinated animal, for this only serves to further undermine the child's sense of reality. Since it is important to minimize further trauma, the physician should try to keep the medical procedures performed on the child to a minimum, and have the child treated primarily with psychotherapy.

Summary

Two cases of visual hallucinosis as a response to acute psychological stress are presented. The dynamics and structural aspects are discussed and the problems of symptom choice and the interrelationship among symptoms are considered. In addition to corroborating a number of previously expressed hypotheses, another key mechanism was elucidated. That is, when a reality event occurs which mirrors the internal conflict of a child, specifically the repressed id impulse, the psychological trauma is very great, particularly to the reality-testing apparatus, and necessitates a rapid shift in defense mechanisms which often fails. The "remembering" of the reality event then may take the form of a visual hallucination.

BIBLIOGRAPHY

Brenner, C. (1951), A Case of Childhood Hallucinosis. *This Annual,* 6:235-243.

Breuer, J. & Freud, S. (1893-1895), Studies on Hysteria. *Standard Edition,* 2. London: Hogarth Press, 1955.

Despert, J. L. (1948), Delusional and Hallucinatory Experience in Children. *Amer. J. Psychiat.,* 104:528-537.

Esman, A. H. (1962), Visual Hallucinoses in Young Children. *This Annual,* 17:334-343.

Feldman, S. S. (1949), Fear of Mice. *Psa. Quart.,* 18:227-230.

Freud, S. (1900), The Interpretation of Dreams. *Standard Edition,* 4 & 5. London: Hogarth Press, 1953.

—— (1907 [1906]), Delusions and Dreams in Jensen's *Gradiva. Standard Edition,* 9:57. London: Hogarth Press, 1959.

—— (1917 [1915]), A Metapsychological Supplement to the Theory of Dreams. *Standard Edition,* 14:217-235. London: Hogarth Press, 1957.

—— (1940 [1922]), Medusa's Head. *Standard Edition,* 18:273-274. London: Hogarth Press, 1955.

Gill, M. M. & Brenman, M. (1959), *Hypnosis and Related States: Psychoanalytic Studies in Regression.* New York: International Universities Press.

Lewis, H. A. (1958), The Effects of Shedding the First Deciduous Tooth upon the Passing of the Oedipus Complex of the Male. *J. Amer. Psa. Assn.,* 6:5-37.

Modell, A. H. (1958), The Theoretical Implications of Hallucinatory Experiences in Schizophrenia. *J. Amer. Psa. Assn.,* 6:442-480.

Rapaport, D. (1942), *Emotions and Memory.* New York: International Universities Press, 1950.

Weiner, M. F. (1961), Hallucinations in Children. *Arch. Gen. Psychiat.,* 5:544-553.

Wilking, V. N. & Paoli, C. (1966), The Hallucinatory Experience: On Attempt at a Psychodynamic Classification and Reconsideration of Its Significance. *J. Amer. Acad. Child Psychiat.,* 5:431-440.

OBJECT CONSTANCY AND PSYCHOTIC RECONSTRUCTION

RUDOLF EKSTEIN, Ph.D. and SEYMOUR FRIEDMAN, M.D.

> There is a tide in the affairs of men,
> Which, taken at the flood, leads on to fortune;
> Omitted, all the voyage of their life
> Is bound in shallows and in miseries.
> —SHAKESPEARE

When Theresa Esperanza, our patient, was a little girl less than ten years of age, she lived with her maiden aunt in a swank apartment on the Paseo de la Reforma in Mexico City, near the Statue of Independence. She loved that monument and its golden angel on top which had been shattered into many pieces during one of the violent earthquakes but was now completely restored and as good as new, at least on its shiny and glittering surface.

That was between 1956 and 1958, years before she started treatment at the Reiss-Davis Child Study Center. Later, when psychotherapy became a desperate necessity, her aunt gave a vivid description, a condensed account of the child's life at that time. The aunt had given the child a charming little poodle which they owned for about two years. Theresa gave the dog the name Trampa, the Spanish equivalent of Tramp, the Disney character in the movie *The Lady and the Tramp*. The dog had been bought originally because Theresa had wanted a dog, but soon, without anybody knowing why, the animal became attached to the aunt. Recently Theresa told her aunt how she had threatened the dog by making motions to throw him out of the ten-story apartment window right on the Paseo de la

Dr. Ekstein is Director of Project on Childhood Psychosis, Reiss-Davis Child Study Center, Los Angeles, California; Training Analyst, Los Angeles Psychoanalytic Society and Institute, Los Angeles, California.

Dr. Friedman is Director of Clinical Services, Reiss-Davis Child Study Center, Los Angeles, California.

Reforma and had dashed the animal's body against the tile floor; that she got on the floor and devoured his food; and when this had become uncomfortable, she had deprived the dog of his raw meat, taken it to the table, and eaten it like a dog. All these observations helped Theresa's aunt to realize how ill the child had been. The aunt found herself devoted to the little animal and she recounts how, some two years later, this dog died in Ecuador, having caught a fish hook in its throat when he was on a boat as they were out fishing with Theresa and her little cousins. He was rushed, not to a veterinarian, but to regular doctors because everyone was so devoted to him. It was Sunday and the animal was hospitalized in a regular hospital, where he died from the effects of anesthesia after the surgeon had removed the hook.

At the time of this interview, the social worker[1] had felt that the aunt's awareness of the child's deepening illness was covered with a deep distrust of doctors who cannot help.

For our present purposes, though, we want to take these observations as a quasi-independent account of an adult observer who thus describes to us the strange love-hate relationship that Theresa developed toward the little animal. We are thus in possession of an observed fact, an actual episode of that phase of the child's life, a piece of personal history, a fragment of a continuum in the life of an individual who struggles with the problem of *acquiring constant self and object representation,* of restoring some continuity in her life by means of restitutive processes, the *psychotic patient's equivalent of reconstructive activity* (Ekstein, 1966a; Chap. 16).

In this paper we shall follow Theresa and her therapist through two sessions, treatment hours 578 and 580, to observe the specific psychic work she must accomplish in order to re-establish her relationship with him each hour, to restore the continuity of her life by gaining access to memories until then unavailable and dreaded, to make these memories serve the selective purpose of restoring object and self constancy, and of regaining the capacity to function in her current situation.

If we were to analyze a dream, we would try to move from the manifest content of the dream to its latent meaning. In this specific example, we have put the latent meaning ahead when we described

1 We are grateful to Mrs. Beatrice Cooper for the use of her records.

the murderous situation between her and the dog. We now return to the actual psychotherapeutic material in order to show how this psychotic girl's mind works its way from the current psychotic life situation to the restoration of appropriate memory, and how we attempted to bring this process about.

Theresa came to the 578th interview[2] about half an hour late. She had canceled her two preceding appointments by telephone. The patient started the hour acting apologetic. She feared that she had disappointed the therapist, referred to the weather and complained of the heat and mugginess. Her manner was that of a petulant, frightened, reluctant girl on a date, deeply involved in a silent love relationship, with a passionate yearning for the lover to whom she cannot and dare not openly confess her need, but to whom she can only make protests, irritated excuses, and complaints of discomfort, and finally end up with the impulse to escape and postpone the contact for another day. She can remain committed to therapy only if she dictates its structure and has the freedom and power not to turn the relationship into therapy, but to make a safe situation for therapy. Although the patient sought to convey that this contact was more like a casual chance meeting in the street that began with chit-chat and irritated complaints about the heat and muggy weather, she inwardly yearned, as well as feared, to restore the love relationship with the therapist and to confess that she loved him, yet could not see what he looked like and what he really was.

The therapist endeavored to convert this brief encounter into a therapeutic session by reacting to her comments about the weather as a metaphoric expression of her inner and outer psychological and emotional climate, and by attempting to re-establish the severed contact from the last therapy session. He reminded her of her intent at the end of the last hour to relate something important to him in the next session. This led Theresa to her customary borrowed fantasy from a TV show, her characteristic mode of reconstituting the transference by love-hate relationships, and her defensive and adaptive establishment of optimum distance to withstand maximum closeness.

Theresa related her fantasy version borrowed from a film depicting the destruction of Pompeii by volcanic eruption and devastating

[2] Previous accounts of our work with Theresa appear in Ekstein (1966a, Chaps. 3, 8, 12, 14, and 22) and Ekstein (1966b).

earthquakes. Her account revealed her confusion and vagueness regarding details, facts, and persons involved, reflecting her tremendous inner anxiety and lowered intellectual functioning, as well as communicating the subordinate relevance of the content of the fantasy to its transference meaning and purpose. As if in a hypnotic trance, she essentially gave this account to the therapist.

Somewhere in a park in the vicinity of what she identifies as a planetarium in Los Angeles (actually her misinterpretation of the TV show—a misconception in the service of recollection of aspects of her own life and the transference position), a street sweeper, cleaning up a mess, rummaging in the sand for trash, comes upon a stone hand which turns out to be part of a statue of a Roman soldier dating back to the ruins of Pompeii, buried under volcanic lava. As the statue is removed via truck to a museum it comes to life, becomes violently destructive and murderous, and has to be restrained and confined. The therapist's interventive comment during the patient's account of the story, that this story impressed him so much in demonstrating that there was no protection against danger in being a lifeless statue, since it became alive and angry and could do great harm, brought from the patient the retort that it was a ghost from the past, and that after the orgy of killing, either to comply with or to escape from the vengeful, destructive wrath of the people, it walked into the ocean and slowly began to vanish and disappear, as it seemed to melt into the water. The therapist's repeated attempts to focus her attention on his interpretation of its meaning and relevance for her identification with the immobile, lifeless statue and her fear of her own anger, destructiveness, and consequent self-destruction are countered by her own need to control the interpersonal process and the therapist's participation by her repeated interruptions.

She continued by enumerating a variety of factual details, in this way warding off the therapist's interpretative intervention and explanation of the fantasy and its relatedness to her life because she herself had experienced a catastrophe, like an earthquake. After again interrupting his attempts to explain her need to be lifeless and immobilized, she remembered having been in a terrifying earthquake in Mexico, followed by an agonizing nightmare in which she desperately but unsuccessfully tried to awaken the aunt in order to be comforted and protected. The nightmare had ended in the death of the aunt, the dog, and herself, as well as the destruction and collapse of the building.

The therapist successfully continued his effort to explain her need to be a lifeless, immobile statute, paralyzed for work, school, and other normal activities, out of fear that, alive and active, she could become destructive and harmful and make other people angry with her, wanting to destroy her in their vengeful wrath. As a lifeless statue, paralyzed and harmless, she remains safe and at peace, a good girl who is not angry and who is even enshrined eternally in a museum. She appeared to accept the interpretation, as well as the therapist's reaffirmation of his wish to help her so that her mind and body can be safeguarded from both outside and inside earthquakes, but she ended by wanting to relate a spooky love story which she promised to tell from the beginning in the next session. The love story ended with the danger that the girl would vanish into the sea together with the restored lover from the past, but she is saved by the police as the deadly lover disappears.

Theresa's fantasy communicates her explanation, justification, and rationalization of her inability to come to this hour on time and to enter actively and openly into its therapeutic purpose and goals, just as her whole life has been confined to a paralytic stalemate of active-passive ego inactivity and expectant waiting (Ekstein and Caruth, 1966). In the fantasy she inadvertently reveals her theory regarding her *lack of object and self constancy:* that it is the consequence of a violent and catastrophic blow from the outside, as if she had been trapped in a vise by an accident of fate and of nature—a grandiose and omnipotent rationale to restore self-esteem in the infantile experience of complete helplessness and impotence, loss of control and of self-esteem. The patient's theory and rationale, however, succeed no more in restoring her self-esteem than the interpretative activity of the therapist, who attempts, via interpretation,[3] to establish or

[3] Psychotherapy can become addicted to the explanatory function of the interpretation which unsuccessfully attempts and only deceptively appears to restore self-esteem and object constancy. For purposes of productive research and incentive, we must resolve to give up *explanation constancy* as a condition both of research and therapeutic activity, with the conviction that the objective of psychotherapy and of our research is not to explain but to understand the working of the mind and of the therapeutic process. Interpretation facilitates contact, process, and object relationships, and therefore creates object constancy; explanation provides quasi-mastery, disrupts contact in

re-establish the effective functioning of the mind and with it object constancy as well as constancy of the therapeutic process and of the therapist as the object.

Via the metaphor of digging in the ruins and cleaning up the mess, the patient permits re-establishment of the therapeutic situation, reconstitutes the object, restores the past and its reservoir of old objects, presumably dead, lifeless, and buried. Thus, in her varied and apparently distant, irrelevant, and trivial communications, equivalent to the fragments, stones, and trash of the fantasy, the patient provides us with her imagery that becomes the psychoanalytic tool for reconstitution of objects, past and current, and furnishes the deceptive façade concealing the past and its relationship to the live and lived-out process in the current relationship with the therapist.

The themes of identity formation and object constancy run through and are dealt with in the patient's material. The therapist is regarded as a god of Roman antiquity who creates the weather, to whom the patient responds by bringing her irritated, depressed complaints of discomfort and fear. The reconstitution of the object of the therapist permits the emergence of archaic shadowy memories and affective experiences out of which the therapy relationship arises. Rather than recalling, talking about, and reflecting upon the theme, the patient lives out the problem of object constancy with the therapist in the present. For psychotic and borderline patients, object constancy is externally represented by their content in whatever form of ideation, whether of love, politics, films, trash or weather, that serves to maintain the contact with the therapist. Contact between patient and therapist constitutes the agent of both inner and outer negotiation and interaction, out of which emerges the psychological construct of object constancy. And just as the agent for contact can be represented by any communication, each of equal value, so can the object remain constant yet be represented by the opposite images of the warrior hero of Roman imperial grandeur with a sword in his hand, or by the clean-up man who gathers up the trash with a broom and shovel in his hand.

In a normal or less disturbed personality development, founded

---

process, and fosters object separation rather than constancy, establishes the omnipotence of the therapist, and may, in the total process, impede the formation of mutuality (Ekstein, 1959).

on more stable and reliable object constancy, object and self are in mutually accepting relationship to each other, surviving changes in roles and adapting to each other in whatever role each may appear. In psychotic and borderline patients the relationship between object and self remains not mutual but antithetical and reciprocal, in which both together form a unit and can survive in a united relationship only if a rigid equilibrium is maintained in which the net change is zero, and the equilibrium of the combined forces remains static and immutable. As on a teetertotter or seesaw, the equilibrium of the closed system must remain unchanged so that, if one goes down, the other must go up. If one member is active and alive, the other must remain inactive and lifeless. If one is omnipotent, the other must remain impotent. If one becomes too much alive, the other must die; if one is active, the other must remain passive. In the archaic reciprocal autistic-symbiotic relationship, the equilibrium can be maintained only by following the dictum, "You do what I tell you, no more and no less." So it is with the internal equilibrium reached by the various roles comprising the object. The world as extension of self and as object responds to the psychotic patient as he manipulates its roles. If the world as object becomes alive, it becomes dangerous and has to be returned to the world of the dead via the omnipotent, delusional power of the psychotic ego to perceive in a manner that serves its needs for survival, or the self must become dead. To remain constant and to retain self and object in equilibrium, one of them must be dead. In the therapeutic struggle the therapeutic goal is lost in the battle of quasi-self-constancy which can be achieved only by wiping out the object. Yet, conversely, the only means of keeping the therapeutic relationship and process alive is by maintaining this equilibrium between live and dead partners, active and passive participants.

The problem of object constancy in the psychotic and borderline patient lies in this closed struggle between motion and stagnancy. We usually attribute the disturbance to the psychotic patient feeling threatened by the omnipresent, persistent, and fluctuating loss of object, the ever-present threat of loss of object constancy. What we begin to see, however, as a *core problem* is the rigid persistence and implacable constancy of the destructive, dangerous object (having grown out of negative introjects), which by its danger to the ego and patient and world must constantly be destroyed lest it destroy. Life destroys and must in turn be destroyed. Only in psychic death and lifelessness can object constancy be maintained.

Object constancy is not to be understood in terms of the fixed, permanent position of the object in time or space as external fixtures that can be identified in a person, thing, place or time dimension, but rather as an internal psychological ego process which in the normal situation remains vital, dynamic, and in flux, and permits the object to assume and to consist of many varied roles, images, and attitudes. By contrast, the psychotic ego is rigidly rooted in the past, stagnated in a position of constant adherence to and recognition of only one role, image, and attitude, that of inevitable, terrifying destruction, and permitting no modification, changing imagery, or additional role increments to the object in the course of time and in the present.

The fantasy related by Theresa via the destruction of Pompeii perhaps illustrates the familiar etiological theme of the original trauma, the volcanic and earth-destroying upheaval that originally destroyed the psychic life of the patient—and coincidentally the world—not as a completed event but as an enfeeblement of the ego's vitality and capacity for continued development and maturation, leaving it in a paralyzed state of shock, petrified into stone and impotent rage, overwhelming her psychic apparatus into passivity, stagnation, and suspended deanimation, a form of psychic death. As if to justify her attitude of interminable, inert waiting to be rediscovered by future events, fortune or therapy, she acts as though she borrows from the legend of the Dybbuk to explain her passive waiting to be released, as if by exorcism, from its stultifying imprisonment of her life energies in order to free her psychic apparatus to complete its life task of actively conquering its rage or giving vent to its murderous destructiveness, to seek safety in the mother ocean which was denied in the original trauma, and to complete its life cycle by achieving its progressive life goal at the same time it returns to its peaceful intrauterine reunion with the mother. As an idealized statue she can gain entry into a museum; as a live human she can only become an agent of the dead and must return to the dead, which paradoxically also saves her life.

In Theresa's psychotic illness we see the problem of object constancy manifested in her inability to perceive and meaningfully to appreciate as a reality the emerging new roles of the object as they become manifest in the course of time. Rather, she can perceive and react to, as reality, only the object's rigid roles of the past in the form of destruction, catastrophe, terror, panic, and death. In Theresa, as in other psychotic patients, rigidity maintains constancy; constancy is equated with psychic death. Stagnation, paralysis, and immobility guarantee safety and survival. The object is permitted to exist and has the power to exist only if it remains rigidly unchanged in terms of past perceived reality. Imminent perception of the object's new roles, even, or particularly, of a positive, health-identified nature in terms of love, reliability, trustworthiness, commitment, etc., immediately leads to the ego's flight from, denial of, and wiping out of the object, or overwhelming it under a barrage of irrelevance and triviality, or violently destroying it in fantasy, thus guaranteeing the *status quo* of the original traumatic object, and in effect experiencing the loss of the new object. The object is allowed to be only that which the psychotic ego prescribes its role to be—i.e., an echo—and if the object attempts to change, it must be destroyed. The psychotic ego cannot accept or realistically perceive the new object, but permits it to exist only as a mirror or reflection of the object of the past that is seen only in terms of hate, fear, and death. The psychotic patient cannot accept the new object as it is. Instead, the new object has to be to the psychotic patient what it is not, and therefore cannot in reality exist. A dilemma thus arises: although the patient is in constant threat of losing the real object as it is because the object has to be what it is not, that is, a copy of the real introject, he can maintain object constancy only by maintaining the object, not as it is in reality, but as it was in the past. The conception of the past object also need not have corresponded to reality, but may have been shaped by fantasy and delusion. The situation is comparable to the task of having to erect a building on a foundation of quicksand.

In the normal object representation, the ego can perceive the object in its manifold roles, has the capacity to accommodate them to each other, to accept each of the many roles on its own integrity and merit, and to synthesize them into a consistent entity. This capacity is absent in the psychotic ego which, to maintain constancy, has to maintain rigid and unchanging image representations of the object and to turn all roles and images into the devil, the witch, the creature or some delusional destroyer.

Object constancy depends upon the capacity to accept changing object images and representation as they emerge in the external reality of the patient's life. Object constancy depends on the synthesis between the enforced imposition of the image and the real person with the capacity to determine in reality what the object really is. In normal object constancy the ego has the capacity to perceive equally the two sides of the coin—buffalo and Indian head—as together constituting the coin. In the psychotic ego, object constancy depends on perceiving and accepting only one side of the coin and on vigorously excluding the other side. The function of normal object constancy makes possible the integration and synthesis of present objects seen in totality and reality with the memory of past objects and object representations. It can be likened to the two-headed Janus who simultaneously looks to the past and the present, *integrating and synthesizing memory and perceptions into one effective object entity.* In the psychotic process, only the powerful, raw, past images predominate and the present perceptions are rigidly cloaked in past images.

Object constancy therefore must be understood not in terms of external realities of space and time, in such external objects as mother, bottle, feeding schedule, place of existence, and other external events—although these are necessary external conditions that mirror the internal process—but as an inner reality in psychic function, the achievement of the ego's capacity for synthesis of permanent, fixed images of the past with impressions and perceptions of the present in the service of creating realistic object representations for optimal ego functioning.

The therapeutic task in childhood psychosis is thus to transform the psychotic concept of constancy that is equated with stagnation and death to the realistic view of constancy as a dynamic *synthetic function* that makes possible an active fulfillment of life. Object constancy is thus seen not as an agent of cure of the psychotic illness as provided by mother, therapist, appointment time or therapeutic commitment, but as the achievement of the ego created by the cure for which the agent, techniques, methods, and psychological tools of the therapeutic process still remain a largely unexplained mystery and provide us with the goals of our research interests, efforts, and reasons for collaborating in a research project.

Much of what we have been presenting here was the result of discussions that took place in our research group. As we realized that Theresa was struggling with the restoration of that time described at the beginning of the paper, we were acquainted by the social worker with her version of what the aunt had told us about this phase. The social worker was certain, and all of us agreed with her and thought the same, that Theresa, standing on the balcony of that apartment house on the Paseo de la Reforma, had taken the little French poodle in sudden anger and had thrown him down to the pavement. We were convinced that she struggled with the recollection, that painful memory, repressed, distorted, and under the dominance of the primary process, of the murder of the dog. It is indeed a curious thing that a whole group of people, including the therapist, must unquestionably accept the distorted account of the murderous fantasy, the memory of the fusion of object and self, in such a way that it appears to be secondary process memory, an actual fact outside, thus for a moment shifting our analyzing attention from the internal process to an external traumatic event. Our invention of *quasi-fact* was a kind of *metaphoric representation* on a secondary process level of a *psychotic state of mind.* We were nevertheless able to use that quasi-fact, expressed in our language and within the framework of our logic, in order to enter the mind of the child and to reconstruct what must have happened within that mind. The invention of outer reality, then, becomes the metaphor which permits us to guess inner reality. In this case, the progression which forced us to introduce our kind of reality testing actually forged the inner facts, but was nevertheless in the service of the therapeutic ego, the reconstructive ego which permitted us to understand the psychic work of the reconstituting ego, that psychotic substitute for reconstruction.

As we were preparing the final draft of this paper, our scientific conscience suggested that we check the established memory against the recorded data. For a moment we identified with the feeling that Freud must have had when he discovered that his assumption of sexual etiology in the neurosis of hysterics was related to fantasy, to inner reality, rather than to an external fact. This peculiar error, in our case a distortion of our own memory and not the patient's, rather than standing in the way of understanding the material, was our way of coping with the attempt to understand the patient, such as her strange way of "remembering" via the fantasy material, borrowed and delusional, which helped her to get back to the past, to separate past and present, and to create continuum out of chaos.

We follow therapist and patient and enter the consulting room in the midst of the 580th hour, in order to see how the patient completes the reconstructive work with the therapist.

Treatment Hour 580

T. You sleepy? You're yawning.
P. Umm. Yeah. I'm always tired.
T. Did you get enough sleep these days?
P. No, I still go to bed late.
T. Oh, well, no wonder.
P. But I decided that one day I'm going to start going to bed early. I don't know why I—
T. Well, how many hours of sleep do you like to have?
P. A lot! Why can't I just be like—I mean, want to be like—I just feel like if I—am an animal.
T. You are like a little kid.
P. Yah, I know. Sometimes I feel like a little child. Other times I feel like an infant all born again—
T. Theresa, even children sleep enough, and animals—
P. And I also feel like an animal, and sometimes I feel like a—like a ghost—like I'm an old woman. The woman who never was—a ghost! I feel like all different persons.
T. That's right, but the animals sleep. Maybe ghosts don't sleep, but animals sleep enough. You ever had an animal at home?
P. The last animal I had was this little baby poodle dog.
T. Oh, yah? Did he sleep a lot?
P. But I didn't care for him. He died. He got killed, because of me. I feel that I'll always still blame me for it.
T. Oh, really.
P. Yeah. He died.
T. Did you feed him enough? What did you do wrong?
P. Well. . . . You see, he was supposed to be my dog. My aunt gave me that dog to be for me. I always wanted one, but the kind of dog I always wished for was a collie or a German shepherd. You know, those big dogs? The only thing is that they cause a lot of problems in taking care of them. Then, one thing my aunt keeps mentioning, mostly when we talk about these dogs, she says one of the worst things that I found about these dogs is that they shit in

the house. They shit everywhere (laughing). They shit all the time. They never stop shitting. You have to give them a pound to eat of food, a pound of food, not the (inaudible).

T. Those big dogs. . . .

P. And when they shit (laughing) they shit (inaudible) (laughing). And that's true. But, at that time that's the kind of dog I wished for, and she really knew the right thing and she never really. . . . And she tried to tell me the problem in having one of those dogs. She tried to show me. And she really insisted on knowing. She never really wanted to get me one. She never did. So she got me this little poodle dog, see, because I like poodles also. And she got me this cute little baby poodle. And right after I had seen *The Lady and the Tramp,* that Walt Disney picture; you know, the Tramp.

T. Yes, I remember it very well.

P. That male dog? Well, I haven't even (inaudible) like the Tramp in the Walt Disney (laughs). I haven't even tramped a single (inaudible) in Spanish because I like them when they're sorta cute (inaudible) a little Tramp. When he was a baby dog, though, he was the cutest thing, Trampa was. So it was when he grew bigger that I didn't care for him anymore, because I thought he wasn't so cute. I don't know, I didn't like his looks (inaudible).

T. Well, that was the time when you didn't—

P. (loudly) That's the time when I didn't care for him anymore when he grew bigger. I didn't go for it anymore, and somehow it wasn't like it took my place and kept on with it. And I used to be mean to him many times, and I also used to wish to kill him, and I used to wish that he was dead. I couldn't stand him like this. I hated him. But I was a very sick child at that time. I was a child, and I was sick. Something was wrong with my head, and nobody knew. Everybody thought I was normal as can be (inaudible) normal when I was a two-year-old or three or four. No. Maybe. I was normal, but as I kept growing from there is when I started to get rocks in my head. As I kept growing that's when I started to get rocks in my head.

T. That's why you got afraid to grow up, because—

P. Then finally the day came I had to kill myself, which I find wholly a mystery. And I still can't believe that if I'm dead, how can I be alive. I never heard of such a mystery, did you?

T. Yes, that was the black Theresa.

P. Well, it's not my mind that's dead.

T. I know, but the white Theresa doesn't want to do it. It's only the black Theresa.

P. That's why I live such a rotten life, because I'm dead. I'm just a dead corpse. I—I—I'm—I'm a ghost. I happen to be a ghost, but one of those kind of strange ghosts that really never existed and then finally it does, it came to, and it does exist.

T. Yes.

P. I'm a new kind of ghost, I guess.

T. But we want to make that Theresa ghost alive again and the white ghost—

P. Because ghosts are usually invisible and transparent, they can just pass through one wall and another, but not me. I'm the kind of ghost who can't. Because I'm made out of flesh and bones and blood. I bleed when I cut myself like any human being does, when I hit myself it hurts, and I yell with pain, and I yell.

T. So. . . .

P. So, I'm a very strange ghost. I'm a human one, which means I'm a flesh and blood and bone human ghost.

T. That's right. You're the kind of ghost that can. . . .

P. Isn't that strange?

T. . . . come to realize this.

P. Though I know it's true, I still can't believe it, it's hard to believe especially when it happens to you and not to someone else. You find out that someone else . . . and you try to make them believe it, which is different than. . . . He doesn't have the problem that you have. And when you have it, that's when it's really hard to believe that it's true. Because you're in it already. But if mysteries exist, especially the biggest one, because this isn't a little mystery. This isn't the tiny baby one. It's one of the hugest, most enormousest mysteries that could ever exist in life. . . . One of the biggest, in fact maybe. . . . I don't think it's possible, but it's one of the hugest. It's a gigantic giant.

T. Except that you and I will make out of this whole—

P. It's a fact of life totally. It grows out of the world. It's a fact of life.

T. But you and I will make out of that, these three ghosts, a real person again.

P. And that's why I am like this?

T. That's right, but you also want to be a new person. Where the white Theresa will be stronger than the black Theresa and the purple Theresa and all the other Theresas. And I guess that's hard to believe, too, isn't it?

P. (long pause) Well . . . I think I'll—

T. You think you'll keep on fighting with me so that we can get you to be as fully and thoroughly forever and ever the complete Theresa rather than the Theresa ghost.

P. (long pause) Well, that little poodle dog that I had which was supposed to be mine. . . . Why when he died, why didn't he fall in the same case I fell in? (crying) Why . . . when he died, he didn't remain at the same time alive? If that would have been— Now this is another example I want to give. If that would have happened to him first before it happened to me, then I could see as an example. Well, that is a very strange mystery. Golly! You know what I mean. And then I would never know what happened to me. Suddenly, but then let's say a while after it happened to him, it happened to me suddenly, and then I would understand better, you know what I mean? Because I, I, I would have seen it before . . . happening to someone else, a little animal . . . or a human being. And that would make it easier. Then I wouldn't have such difficulty in believing it . . . in believing that it's true . . . and taking it hard.

T. You took it hard that you lost the dog forever?

P. I would . . . you know—

T. You reproached yourself because you hated the dog, you know. You really also loved the dog. You reproached—

P. No, I didn't hate the dog.

T. Well, you said sometimes you hated him.

P. Well, I really didn't. It's my illness that hated him.

T. It was really your illness that hated him, but you loved him. The ghost of you hated him, but the real Theresa loved him.

P. Yeah, yeah.

T. And I think it was a terrible thing—

P. So, that's what I'm saying. To give you an example, if I really would have seen this same mystery that happened to me. If I really would have seen it at first in him, happening to someone else . . . after that, then it happened to me, I would understand better, and I would take it easier to believing it.

T. You would have taken it easier—

P. But, it never happened to nobody, never. Only to me. So that's why I—I—I . . . It's hard to me to take. That's why.

T. It's harder to understand—

P. And if I would have seen it on someone else before.

T. It's harder to understand.

P. I—I also believe that the mystery of Juan Diego, this little Mexican Indian of Mexico, that had gotten into this strangeness, the mystery that happened to him of the Virgin of Guadalupe appearing, which was a mystery. Yes.

T. Yes. I think—

P. And I think . . . I also find it a great mystery when she, she put her image in this beautiful cloth mantle that she showed to everybody. That's the only way they would believe it.

T. But he won out.

P. He won.
T. He won, and you will win, too, like him.
P. Then they finally believed him.
T. That's right—
P. That was a big mystery, too. I believe it was.
T. And the ghost became real.
P. That was a. . . . No, let me tell you. I do believe that that was some . . . thing of a mystery, and I believe that it was a big mystery —But I also believe that it wasn't the big mystery as mine. I still believe that. Though his mystery was quite strange and big, I still believe that mine is even twice bigger than his.
T. Could be, but maybe that you and I—
P. Twice bigger, it is!
T. Theresa, but it just means that you and I have twice as big a task. But then, we're two people. He was only one (pause).
P. Now, he somehow got help then in, in with the mystery—
T. Well, but we want to get other things—
P. And I really haven't reached up there—
T. Theresa, may I remind you next Tuesday about what we talked about, so that we can continue it?
P. Sure.
T. Would you like me to? Good. Now we know a little better what it means to carry a burden. Bye-bye, Theresa.

Freud (1937) speaks of the *technical activity of reconstruction* in the following terms: "When one lays before the subject of the analysis a piece of his early history that he has forgotten. . . ." He also refers to the process of working through, which permits us to help the patient restore continuity between the past and present as well as the future.

To what degree are such patients as Theresa, who suffer from the lack of object constancy which characterizes their peculiar psychotic transference manifestations, capable of restoring this continuum?

Rather than answering this question and commit ourselves to undue therapeutic optimism or nihilistic therapeutic pessimism, we want to suggest that our material poses a scientific question, the answer to which lies in the careful study of long-term analytic treatment of patients such as Theresa by committed therapists, a study which must allow for the objective evaluation and analysis of records by the therapist, supplemented by the taped research data, by psychological retesting, through the participating team, and independent research observers.

The question concerning the individual capacity of a person for object constancy and reconstruction, a study really in ego psychology, has been anticipated by Freud. As we followed Theresa's attempts to establish a kind of archaeology of her mind, we recall Freud's frequent comparison of the work of the psychoanalyst with the work of the archaeologist. One of these comparisons, an analogy which allows us to formulate new questions, may help us in rediscovering that *reconstruction* implies restoring the patient's access not only to past events but also to the *then available ego organization* which "wrote" that personal history. Freud (1930) suggests in *Civilization and Its Discontents:*

> . . . that everything survives in some way or other, and is capable under certain conditions of being brought to light again, as, for instance, when regression extends back far enough. One might try to picture to oneself what this assumption signifies by a comparison taken from another field. Let us choose the history of the Eternal City as an example. Historians tell us that the oldest Rome of all was the *Roma quadrata,* a fenced settlement on the Palatine. Then followed the phase of the Septimontium, when the colonies on the different hills united together; then the town which was bounded by the Servian wall; and later still, after all the transformations in the periods of the republic and the early Caesars, the city which the Emperor Aurelian enclosed by his walls. . . .
>
> Now let us make the fantastic supposition that Rome were not a human dwelling-place, but a mental entity with just as long and varied a past history: that is, in which nothing once constructed had perished, and all the earlier stages of development had survived alongside the latest. This would mean that in Rome the palaces of the Caesars were still standing on the Palatine and . . . the beautiful statues were still standing in the colonnade of the Castle of St. Angelo, as they were up to its siege by the Goths, . . . the observer would need merely to shift the focus of his eyes, perhaps, or change his position, in order to call up a view of either the one or the other. . . .
>
> There is one objection, though, to which we must pay attention. It questions our choosing in particular the past history of a *city* to liken to the past of the mind. Even for mental life our assumption that everything past is preserved holds good only on condition that the organ of the mind remains intact and its structure has not been injured by traumas or inflammation. Destructive influences comparable to these morbid agencies are never lacking in the history of any town, even if it has had a less chequered

past than Rome, even if, like London, it has hardly ever been pillaged by an enemy. Demolitions and the erection of new buildings in the place of old occur in cities which have had the most peaceful existence; therefore a town is from the outset unsuited for the comparison I have made of it with a mental organism. . . . The fact is that a survival of all the early stages alongside the final form is only possible in the mind, and that it is impossible for us to represent a phenomenon of this kind in visual terms.

Perhaps we are going too far with this conclusion. Perhaps we ought to be content with the assertion that what is past in the mind *can* survive and need not necessarily perish. It is always possible that even in the mind much that is old may be so far obliterated or absorbed—whether normally or by way of exception—that it cannot be restored or reanimated by any means, or that survival of it is always connected with certain favourable conditions. It is possible, but we know nothing about it. We can only be sure that it is more the rule than the exception for the past to survive in the mind [pp. 15-20].

BIBLIOGRAPHY

Ekstein, R. (1959), Thoughts Concerning the Nature of the Interpretive Process. In: *Readings in Psychoanalytic Psychology,* ed. M. Levitt. New York: Appleton-Century-Crofts, pp. 221-247.

—— (1966a), *Children of Time and Space, of Action and Impulse: Clinical Studies on the Psychoanalytic Treatment of Severely Disturbed Children.* New York: Appleton-Century-Crofts.

—— (1966b), The Orpheus and Eurydice Theme in Psychotherapy. *Bull. Menninger Clin.,* 30:207-224.

—— & Caruth, E. (1966), Activity-Passivity Issues in the Treatment of Childhood Psychosis. In: Panel on Activity-Passivity, rep. P. Gray. *J. Amer. Psa. Assn.,* 15:709-728.

Freud, S. (1930), *Civilization and Its Discontents.* London: Hogarth Press, 1946.

—— (1937), Constructions in Analysis. *Standard Edition,* 23:255-269. London: Hogarth Press, 1964.

SCHOOL PHOBIAS

Classification, Dynamics, and Treatment

MELITTA SPERLING, M.D. (New York)

School phobia is actually one variety of the group of phobias. A systematic study of the phobias, which is the most widely encountered neurosis in children and adults, is still lacking. The classical concepts, valid to this day, were developed by Freud (1909) almost sixty years ago in his account of the indirect treatment of Little Hans. According to these concepts, a phobia is the neurosis of the oedipal phase and deals with castration anxiety and the conflicts of this phase.

The analytic study of young children has enabled child analysts to observe directly phobic manifestations in children of preoedipal age (Bornstein, 1935; Wulff, 1927). In my analytic work with children of preoedipal age (1952a), I could study the sources of anxiety which led to the onset of phobia before the oedipal phase. It is my impression that pregenital impulses and pregenital fixations are of major significance in this neurosis. In the treatment of psychosomatic patients, children as well as adults, I found that there is a dynamic interrelation between the psychosomatic symptoms and phobic behavior, often with an alternation between the somatic manifestations and the overt phobic behavior. This is the case particularly in mucous and ulcerative colitis and in bronchial asthma (M. Sperling, 1950a, 1952b, 1955, 1961b, 1963a).

I have come to consider phobias as a neurosis which is related to the anal phase of instinctual development, and even more specifically to the anal-sadistic phase. A new version of the earlier conflicts about separation appears at and belongs to the anal phase of development

---

Clinical Professor of Psychiatry, State University of New York, Downstate Medical Center, Division of Psychoanalytic Education.

(roughly between age one and one half to three). It is during this phase that the motor equipment necessary for active separation—walking away from mother—develops, and when the ambivalence conflict concerning the anal instincts is at its height. It is the conflict of whether to hold on or to let go of feces (unconsciously equated with objects). During the oral phases there is only passive dependence because the child lacks the equipment for initiating any active separation from mother in reality.

I would suggest classifying the phobias as being midway between the obsessive-compulsive and the hysterical neuroses, but closer to the first. The main mechanism of defense in phobias and in obsessive-compulsive neuroses are similar—namely, displacement, isolation, and projection. In 1909 Freud described a mechanism characteristic of the phobias, i.e., the externalization of an instinctual internal danger, which then can be avoided as an external danger. The high degree of ambivalence and narcissism, the persistence of the fantasy of omnipotence, and the exaggerated need for control are characteristic pregenital (anal-sadistic) features of this neurosis, and provide the link with other pregenitally fixated disorders (character disorders, certain perversions such as fetishism) and with psychosomatic diseases, especially with asthma and colitis. In all these conditions, separation anxiety is a crucial issue, and its persistence interferes with a satisfactory resolution of the oedipal conflicts.

From this it follows that school phobia has to be considered a psychoneurosis in the true sense; that is, that it is based on unconscious conflicts and fantasies and that the reasons a phobic child gives for his behavior are rationalizations, while the true reasons are unknown to him. Although this concept is shared by many workers in the field (Coolidge et al., 1960; A. Freud, 1965; Greenbaum, 1964; Johnson et al., 1941; Kahn and Nursten, 1962; E. Klein, 1945; Waldfogel et al., 1957; Suttenfield, 1954; Talbot, 1957), it is essential to emphasize this very strongly because there is the temptation to treat a school phobia with a common-sense approach, such as reassurance, reasoning, persuasion, reward or punishment. It should be obvious that none of these can really be effective or have *lasting* results, although it may be possible to bring a child back to school by any of these means. I am aware of the importance of inducing a phobic patient to return to the phobic situation as soon as possible; the aim of treatment, however, cannot be limited to this goal. It is our responsibility not only to bring the phobic child back to school, but also to make it possible for the child to remain in school without *too much* anxiety. An inordinate degree of anxiety interferes with the child's ability to function properly and inadvertently leads to other pathological behavior and symptoms, which, because they may not be as apparent and disturbing as is the school phobia, may go unnoticed at first and not be regarded as consequences of the school phobia by the child's environment. Psychosomatic manifestations are frequent substitutions for school phobias; "real" illness is a "legitimate" reason for absence from school.

It is unfortunate for school-phobic children that many of those who professionally deal with them do not seem to realize that a phobia is a neurotic illness, often more painful and crippling than a "real illness," and that bringing the child back to school "by hook or crook" is not the answer (Eisenberg, 1958; Leavitt, 1964; Waldfogel et al., 1957). Serious characterological and other maldevelopments are the consequences of untreated or poorly handled school phobias.[1] I shall deal with this aspect of the problem further in the discussion of the treatment of chronic school phobias.

For the purpose of choosing the most expedient approach to the management of school phobias, it is necessary to differentiate between acute and chronic school phobia and between a common or induced school phobia; moreover, the child's age must be taken into consideration: whether the onset of the phobia occurs in prelatency, latency, or adolescence.[2] As far as adolescence is concerned, it includes not only high school but also college students. The onset of a school phobia in college students is not a rare occurrence; it may be masked by other symptoms, especially by somatic manifestations of various kinds and characterological symptoms, and may culminate in a "mental breakdown." At any rate, whatever the overt symptoms may be in each case, the underlying dynamic factor is the inability to accept separation from a parent figure and to function

[1] In this connection, a recent report on "Desensitization Techniques in the Treatment of School Phobia" (Garvey and Hegrenes, 1966) is pertinent because it exposes the fact that these authors believe that the removal of the symptom is identical with the elimination of the neurosis itself.

[2] In this context, the chapters on "Assessment of Pathology" in *Normality and Pathology in Childhood* by A. Freud (1965) are particularly relevant.

independently away from home. The purpose of leaving school and returning home is usually achieved, even if only temporarily.

Acute school phobias can occur at any age, during any time of the year, not necessarily at the start of school or after school vacations. There is usually no history of prior school-phobic behavior. In all cases of acute school phobia, I favor a direct and analytic approach, regardless of age. I am aware of the fact that this is not always possible and that such children can be and are brought back to school by other approaches. In "Analytic First Aid in School Phobias" (1961a), I have explained why I consider an analytic approach in acute cases particularly important, and I shall briefly recapitulate here some of the salient points:

In the acute school phobia, it is often possible to detect, in one or in a few interviews, the unconscious significance of the precipitating event and to interpret it to the child. The traumatic event is usually one that represents a danger to the child's ability to control reality; that is, a danger of loss of control over a situation or object (usually the mother). In the final analysis this extreme need for control reveals itself as a wish for control over life and death, and the fear of the phobic patient (child or adult) as a fear of death. The precipitating event may be real or feared illness or death of a parent or a person unconsciously representing a parental figure, or illness or an accident, or surgery performed on the child, which to the child has the meaning of having barely escaped death. In other words, the event represents an acute separation threat and, to the child predisposed to phobia by its fixations to the anal-sadistic level, has the meaning of impending death (of the parent or of the child himself). The fixation to the anal phase has other implications: object relationships are highly ambivalent, the narcissistic orientation has persisted, and so has magical thinking (omnipotence of thought), which means that the child equates his unconscious death wishes with actual reality.

I consider an acute school phobia as a "traumatic neurosis with school phobia as the presenting symptom." The intense anxiety caused by this trauma leads to an increase in the need for magical control (control over life and death), which the child is attempting to achieve by the phobic behavior.

Seven-year-old Peter's school phobia began suddenly one day in school during assembly. He became panicky and ran home looking for his mother. The next day he was reluctant to go to school. In school he became panicky and ran home again. This repeated itself, and after a few days he refused to go to school at all. When I saw him he had been out of school for nearly three weeks. In retracing the circumstances under which he had his first anxiety attack in school, I learned that it had occurred in assembly when he heard the teacher play the piano. He suddenly felt "funny," very sad, and had an irresistible urge to see his mother. He associated the music with a funeral, and more specifically with the funeral of a neighbor, a lady who had committed suicide while her child was in school. For the purpose of bringing him back to school it was sufficient to make him aware of his fear that this could happen to his mother and to link it with the unconscious wish by remarking casually that boys sometimes when they are angry have such wishes and are afraid that they might come true. His phobia cleared up immediately. There was a rather strong probability that Peter might have sensed the depressive mood of his mother and that his sudden phobia was also a sort of realistic protection for her. I have illustrated with case material (1961a) that it is possible to bring an acutely school-phobic child back to school rather quickly by this method, which to some extent might even have a preventive effect and forestall the development of a later insidious neurosis. Exposure of the unconscious death wishes results in a devaluation of the magical qualities attached to unconscious thought processes.

It is important to differentiate this type, the traumatic or common type of acute school phobia, from what I would call *"induced" school phobia.* "Induced" school phobia is not an infrequent occurrence, especially in younger children. From the point of view of a differential diagnosis, the most significant factor is the absence of a manifest external precipitating event (which by its unconscious meaning for the child has such a traumatic effect) in the "induced" phobia, in contrast to the "common" acute school phobias. The onset of acute, induced school phobia is a much less dramatic event than that of an acute traumatic school phobia, because in the first case we are dealing with a more insidious traumatization of the child due to the pathological parent-child relationship. "Induced" school phobia can also occur at any time during the school year. In these cases we usually find indications of some phobic behavior in the past; therefore, even if such a child is brought for treatment as soon as the school-phobic behavior becomes more apparent, we are really not dealing with the acute onset of the phobia any longer. In these cases, because of the neurotic needs of the person, usually the mother (but not too infrequently also the father), who induces the phobic behavior of the child, the indirect approach through therapy of the parent—especially with young children—is not only preferable but imperative. The real acute phase of such an induced school phobia one gets to see only accidentally, in which case it may be possible to resolve it *in statu nascendi*. I would like to give an example of an acute, induced school phobia in a five-year-old boy.

The inducer, in this case, was the father, who was in analysis during the time when John developed an acute school phobia. Mr. J. was very distressed about the situation and blamed himself for his son's phobia, thinking that he was the cause of it because he had not devoted enough time to his son. John now was clinging to his father, and requested that he stay home with him and not go to work. He could not give a reason why he did not want to go to kindergarten, which he had previously attended willingly. In fact, he said that he liked the teacher, and that the children were okay. Attempts to get him to school failed. Even when his mother could get him into the car and take him to school, John refused to enter the school. In this case, my knowledge of the father's personality and of the family dynamics made it possible to understand the development and meaning of the child's phobia and helped to resolve it rather quickly through the help given to Mr. J. in his analysis.

Mr. J. had been a phobic person since childhood, but had managed to cover up his phobia rather cleverly by manipulating his environment. His wife, apparently because of her own needs, lent herself to play in with the patient's phobia. She was always at home taking care of the house and children. At the time of the acute onset of John's phobia, Mrs. J. as a result of her husband's analysis had become much freer and was even considering beginning some activities which would take her away from the house for brief periods of time. John was the youngest of three children and the only boy, and there had been talk about having a fourth child. Manifestly, this was a strong wish expressed by Mrs. J., but Mr. J.'s analysis revealed that it was unconsciously intended by him as a means of tying her to the house and limiting her newly regained mobility, so that he was very ambivalent about whether to impregnate her or not. The patient himself was at a critical phase in his analysis, which at that time dealt with the core of his phobia, i.e., the early relationship with his mother displaced onto his wife and, in the transference, onto his analyst. He seemed to come closer to a resolution. He had begun to drive alone and to go places by himself, and he had even taken a plane trip recently. (He had never traveled any place before and had always managed to have someone go along with him in the car.) He felt trapped in the analysis; giving up the phobia meant giving up magical control and resolving the infantile tie with mother (his wife and his analyst), that is, to finish his analysis. The deepest meaning of the phobic relationship, as I see it, is to maintain the infantile tie with mother forever, that is, the avoidance of any change, any termination. In the final analysis, this equals the avoidance of accepting the reality of death.

My patient had always identified himself with John. He felt that John looked like him. He also thought that John was rejected by his mother as Mr. J. had felt rejected by his own mother. He had always been closer to his father. He looked like his father and felt that his father preferred John among all the grandchildren. Analysis revealed that at this critical point in his analysis Mr. J. had passed on his phobia to his son. He continued the phobic relationship with John by playing the part of the solicitous father. This was a piece of clever acting out. Instead of resolving his phobia, Mr. J. arranged for a phobic relationship with his son. This could be convincingly and effectively interpreted to him. He became aware that by his anxiety and overconcern about John, he had been transmitting to John his unconscious wish for the phobic dependence. The most startling thing for Mr. J. was what he called John's paradoxical reaction. Without any intervention from the outside, there had been a dramatic change in John's behavior. John, who previously had been whining and fearful in the morning, reluctant to get dressed and to leave the house, now was as happy as a lark, more carefree and relaxed than before the onset of the phobia. This change occurred when Mr. J. was able to disengage himself from his pathological involvement with John and to treat him more casually. The child responded with immediate relief, and directed his interest back to his playmates and outside activities. The extra interest, devotion, and time given to him by his father had apparently been correctly interpreted by John as a premium for his compliance with his father's unconscious wishes.

Certain aspects of Mr. J.'s analysis during this period are of particular interest for the further understanding of the phenomenon of induced school phobia. These aspects dealt with Mr. J.'s relationship with his father, which he had conspicuously neglected in his analysis. He had always considered his father the more independent and the more considerate parent and had had a manifestly positive relationship with him. The conscious hatred and hostility he felt for his mother had occupied a large part of his analysis. He now remembered that his father would often belittle the mother in his presence and that he would tell on his mother to his father. His father used to take him on his business trips and have him sit for hours in the car waiting for him. The patient had insisted on looking at this as a proof of love and had never before admitted to himself that he felt that his father was phobic and inconsiderate and was using him as a tool in his phobic manipulation. To admit this would have meant to acknowledge the same concerns in himself. He could now understand that he had been trying to do the same with John.

John's phobia served many functions in his father's mental life and in the family's neurotic needs. At this point I want to mention only the following:

1. In identification with John, Mr. J. could maintain his own phobia, the maintenance of which was threatened by the analysis.

2. Mr. J. perpetuated with John the relationship he had had with his own father; that is, he transformed what he had experienced passively into an active experience; he did with John what had been done to him by his father.

3. The phobic child also could substitute for the fourth child, the new baby, by fulfilling the purpose of limiting the freedom of the parents.

4. John's phobia served Mr. J. as a punishment of his wife (mother) and analyst because he implied that Mrs. J.'s rejection of John and, in the transference, my rejection of the patient, caused John's phobia. It was as if he said: "My wife is a bad mother to John and you are a bad analyst to me." He clearly manifested this attitude by assuming the role of the good father with John—being even better than a mother. He felt, and it would seem that Mrs. J. shared this feeling, that John's behavior exposed her as he had exposed his own mother by his behavior in childhood. A further significant meaning which he brought out in the analysis was that now I would have to treat John for his school phobia so that I really had nothing to gain by insisting that he finish his analysis. In this way, the relationship with me (the tie with mother) would not terminate but would continue through John and forever.

I would now like to illustrate the dynamics and the handling of a case of induced school phobia in a child of latency age. Six-year-old Ann developed a phobia at the start of the first grade in school. According to the mother, Ann had gone to nursery and kindergarten without too much difficulty.

Mrs. A. related that on the first day of school they met a little boy on the way to school who was crying, "I don't want to learn the ABC's. I don't want to go to school." Mrs. A. was disturbed by this, but to her surprise Ann went into the auditorium of the school willingly. The mother started to wink at her and wave good-bye, whereupon Ann wanted to come over to her mother, but was prevented from doing so by the teacher. In fact, two teachers grabbed her. Mrs. A. brought Ann to school the next day, and since the line had not yet formed, she brought Ann to her classroom and stayed with her until the other children came. She noted that Ann was uneasy. Ann did not mix with the other children, and she cried when her mother left. The next day Mrs. A. did not take Ann to school. When she came for treatment, Ann had been out of school for two weeks.

The mother thought that Ann's phobia was related to a baby sitter they had had a few weeks prior to this incident. Ann never stayed with anyone in the family, not even her father or the maternal grandmother. With the exception of her mother, Ann would stay only with a baby sitter who lived on the same floor. Several weeks ago, when this girl was not available, the mother hired another baby sitter. Mrs. A. seemed to have strong feelings about this girl whom she described to me in great detail. Mrs. A. was shocked when Ann, who knew this girl, accepted her readily. A week later when this girl came again, Ann was very upset and did not want her to stay. Although Mrs. A. had no special plans for that evening, she insisted that the baby sitter stay with Ann. Ann threatened to vomit, but the mother left her. However, Mrs. A. returned immediately because she felt that she should not have left and found that Ann had vomited. The vomiting was then repeated for several nights, Ann getting up at the same time each night and vomiting.

I then learned that Ann had had a period of nightly vomiting when she was about eleven months old, and that the pediatrician had implied to the mother that she must be doing something wrong with the child. Ann would vomit only during week nights when the house was quiet and she was alone with her mother. Mr. A. was working nights at that time. On weekends, when the house was full of people, the child never vomited. When Ann was about three or four she was very active and often said, "I want to play on the street. I want to go there. I want to do this by myself." Yet at night she always clung to her mother, who had to come into Ann's bedroom innumerable times. This would end up with the mother becoming angry, yelling, and spanking Ann.

When I pointed out to Mrs. A. that it appeared to me that she was overconcerned with Ann and seemed to be holding on to her tightly, she said, "She's my only child. I am now married fourteen years, and I had to wait seven years until I could conceive." When I remarked that she seemed to want an exclusive relationship with Ann, into which nobody was to intrude, not even her own mother or husband, she said, "Ann is crazy about her father, but she wouldn't stay with him alone. In fact, he doesn't want to stay with her, because he wouldn't know how to handle her." She then related that Ann was willing to stay with her father or even to go out with him provided her mother stay at home. Ann had to know where her mother was and that she would find her in the same place. In her second interview, Mrs. A. traced the onset of Ann's phobic behavior back to the time when Ann was ten months old and Mrs. A. had left her with a baby sitter for the first time. It was then that the vomiting, which the doctor had diagnosed as purely emotional, began.

The mother felt that the intensification of the phobia occurred after the last baby sitter had stayed with Ann. Since then, Ann was getting up nightly and would not stay with her father or grandmother in the evening, though she did not mind doing so during the day when she knew where her mother was. On several occasions Ann had recently wanted to come into her mother's bed, and although Mrs. A. knew that she should not accede, she gave in to Ann's demands.

After the second interview I suggested to Mrs. A. that she take Ann back to school. She reported that Ann refused to go into the school building, but when Mrs. A. said, "Then let's go home," Ann became angry at her. Ann did not want to go home and stayed in school. Then there was a holiday after which Ann refused to go back to school. Mrs. A. wondered whether she should do homework with Ann or put her into a private school so that she could stay with her in school. She talked of the close relationship she had with Ann. She then began to talk about her marriage and her feelings about her husband. Her husband has a very bad temper, he gets very upset when he has to stay with Ann because he has to clean her up after she vomits. There are frequent scenes between them. At this point Mrs. A. began to cry and then related that she had been unhappy when she got pregnant after seven years. She did not like the child. She was melancholy. Everything in the house appeared strange to her. Previously she had never stayed much at home; she did not even cook at home, they always ate out. She thought that she had finally become used to having the child. Last winter Ann had had the whooping cough and Mrs. A. had been with her constantly. During this and the next interview Mrs. A. became increasingly aware of her own need for Ann's phobia, which kept Mrs. A. from running away and leaving her husband. She had suffered from a chronic untreated depression since the birth of Ann. Although after the third interview Mrs. A. was able to convey to Ann that she no longer needed Ann as a protection and Ann returned to school promptly and without any fuss, I felt it necessary to refer the mother for psychotherapy, both for her own sake and to make sure that she did not fall back on Ann for security.

In this connection an experience with a patient whom I treated successfully for a severe school phobia when she was an adolescent is of interest. I saw this patient again eleven years later when she consulted me because her oldest child aged four years was reluctant to go to nursery school. It was possible to clear this problem up in one interview because the mother realized that she was having difficulty in separating herself from this child, to whom she felt very close. She had been aware that she had felt jealous and slighted when the child had at first very readily accepted the teacher and the other children (M. Sperling, 1961a). I saw this patient again ten years later, a few months after her youngest child had started kindergarten. There had been no school-phobic problems with any of her children during the intervening years. Being aware of her tendency to hold on to her children, she had been able to handle herself admirably. She came this time for herself, because she had been feeling jittery during the past few months and realized that this was her reaction to "there being no children in the house." This case is also interesting as a twenty-one-year follow-up of an adolescent school phobia, but cannot be dealt with further within the framework of this paper.

In cases of chronic induced phobia in an older child in the late latency or prepuberty period the situation differs from that of the previously presented cases. It then becomes necessary to treat the child himself as well as concomitantly the parent (inducer). If the parent who needs the phobia of the child for his or her own neurotic reasons is unavailable for treatment, the prognosis for the child is poor because such parents will withdraw the child from treatment at the time when their equilibrium is threatened by the child's improvement (M. Sperling, 1959). I would like to illustrate this briefly with the case of nine-year-old Harry, whose school phobia had become very intense during his last school year.

In Harry's case, the pathological relationship was with his father, who gave the developmental history and brought the child for consultation and treatment. Mr. H. had been very close to Harry from infancy and had obviously been instrumental in Harry's developing severe reaction formations against anal-erotic and anal-sadistic impulses, as early as the age of two. The father was particularly proud of the fact that Harry had never displayed any overt manifestations of derivatives of anal impulses. He was delighted by the two-year-old child's "innate consideration and kindness." Harry never broke or destroyed anything and he was so clean that he never wiped himself because "he would become disgusted and nauseated." I learned later that for this reason Harry had never used the toilet in school for defecation. Harry was the older of two children. Two other siblings had died, one shortly after birth and the other in infancy when Harry was two years old. These events seemed to have played a part in the parents' latent anxiety about Harry and also, I believe, in Harry's phobic response to it. When Harry was not quite four his father left for the army. Sometime thereafter a baby sister was born who took up the mother's time and attention. At that time the family lived with the maternal grandparents, who genuinely cared for Harry. He did well during these two years when his father was away.

When Mr. H. returned, he resumed his preoccupation with Harry. The father seemed disappointed that Harry had "learned to get along without me" and that he liked school and being with other children. Harry's first neurotic reaction to his father's return manifested itself in a sleep disturbance, the dynamics of which will be discussed in connection with the manifest school phobia which he developed later. Harry's sleep disturbance seemed to have complemented his father's severe insomnia. Both Harry and his father would be up and together for parts of the night while the mother and sister slept in another room. Harry began to miss school when he developed frequent colds and complaints of sore throats. At seven and a half years he had a tonsillectomy. At the same time the family moved and Harry was transferred to a new school. He now showed a manifest reluctance to going to school and complained about the teachers. Mr. H., who could not tolerate any overt neurotic behavior in his son, now became very punitive and forceful with Harry. At this point Harry developed bellyaches and diarrhea. The diarrhea made it nearly impossible for him to remain in school, particularly because he had even earlier refused to use the toilet in school. Now he came running home from school several times a day to use the toilet. After a few weeks of this, Mr. H., feeling that the school authorities were not forceful enough with Harry, decided to take Harry to school himself and to stay with Harry to prevent him from running out. But as soon as the father left Harry would run after him. Threats, beatings, bribes, changes of school were of no avail. During that year Harry ran away several times whenever an attempt was made to keep him in school forcefully. By this time the father had induced the school authorities to handle Harry rather harshly (Jarvis, 1964). The father did everything except follow the advice to seek psychiatric treatment for Harry.

From the history, the child's behavior, and my observations of father and child, I gained the impression that this father, prompted by his own intense neurotic needs, had induced a very severe school phobia in his son. Mr. H. openly devalued psychotherapy, which he considered a treatment for weaklings. He could not accept that his son was neurotic, which to him meant a weakling. What he wanted was a magical formula for returning Harry to school quickly. The mother was unavailable physically and emotionally. She was tied up with her baby daughter and entirely pushed into the background by her husband.

The psychological records, including a Rorschach taken when Harry was eight and a half years old, showed that he was struggling with tremendous repressed aggression and lived in terror of being overwhelmed by his impulses. A tendency to withdraw was noted, but there were no concrete evidences of disturbed thinking or deterioration in reality testing at that time. Clinical exploration indicated that a rapid deterioration of personality had taken place in the intervening half year. In defense against overwhelmingly strong destructive impulses (of a homicidal and suicidal nature) Harry was using somatic pathways for discharge. In addition to the bellyaches and diarrhea, he had also begun to wheeze as if he were developing asthma. His dreams, usually of a nightmarish character, were of such intensity and vividness that he often woke up confused and unable to differentiate between dream and reality. His dreams dealt with violence and death. In daytime, moreover, he seemed to have brief lapses of memory, which to me appeared like the beginning of petit mal. I found that there was a very close physical contact between Harry and his parents; his mother was still bathing him and cleaning him after bowel movements, and the father was both overly seductive and sadistic with him. Between Harry and his father there was a strong latent homosexual tie, which apparently covered up Harry's positive oedipal wishes and murderous impulses against the father.

The intensity of the oedipal conflict and of his castration anxiety manifested itself in the severe sleep disturbance which Harry developed after his father's return home. Turning toward the seductive and sadistic father in (masochistic) submission was his attempt to deal with his intense aggressive impulses directed primarily against his father. The fear of loss of control and of something terrible happening (somebody getting killed) was an outstanding feature of his nightmares as well as of his school phobia. This was also expressed and acted out in the loss of control over his bowels. Both the waking up from the nightmares and the running home from school were attempts to gain control over an uncontrollable situation—his repressed impulses threatening to break through. The inescapable internal, instinctual danger was externalized in his sleep by the nightmares and in the daytime by the school phobia, so that he could escape the danger. This Harry did by staying up and avoiding sleep (nightmares = the phobic situation) and escaping the danger in sleep by waking up. In avoiding going to school and, when forced to go, in running from school, Harry used the same mechanisms.

After several weeks of treatment during which Harry's panic lessened and he apparently accepted me as his therapist, Mr. H., feeling threatened by this, I believe, decided against psychotherapy and put Harry in a military school. Mr. H., who appeared to me to be a borderline psychotic with marked depressive and paranoid trends, was inaccessible to any psychotherapeutic interventions. His sadistic inclinations were scarcely concealed by his insistence on obedience and discipline. He once tied Harry to his bedpost for several days and on another occasion beat him mercilessly, commenting with pride that any soldier would have succumbed, but Harry did not budge. I felt that under the circumstances separation from the sick father was therapeutic in itself.

Chronic school phobia, whether of the induced or the traumatic (common) type, is an indication of a serious personality disturbance and is a difficult condition to treat effectively, requiring skill, patience, and time (Coolidge et al., 1960; Greenbaum, 1964; Kahn and Nursten, 1962; Messer, 1964; M. Sperling, 1961a). Treatment should be regarded as successful only when it brings about favorable changes in the personality and character disturbances associated with chronic school phobia and not on the basis of whether the child does or does not return to school quickly—that is, the removal of the presenting symptom. The emphasis in the treatment of chronic school phobia has to be placed on the treatment of the total neurosis, of which the school phobia is only one manifestation, just as a persistent fever or cough may be only one symptom of a chronic progressive tuberculosis. The behavior of children with chronic school phobia of the induced type may resemble that of children with symbiotic schizophrenia, and there is a similarity in the dynamics of the parent-child relationship in these two conditions. In planning treatment of a child with chronic school phobia of the induced type it is important to keep this in mind (M. Sperling, 1963b). Unless the pathological tie with the parent (inducer) can be resolved or at least appreciably modified, treatment will not be successful even though it succeeds in returning the child to school for shorter or even longer periods of time. There will be inevitable recurrences and severe setbacks, especially at those times when in the course of normal development the child's ability to relinquish the attachment to the original love objects and to form new relationships is being tested, that is, at puberty and adolescence. Here again, the similarity with schizophrenia as well as with children suffering from psychosomatic disorders is apparent (M. Sperling, 1949, 1950b, 1951).

In all these instances we are dealing with children with unresolved symbiotic preoedipal fixations. Such children cannot resolve their oedipal conflicts and are unable to utilize the progressive forces of puberty and adolescence. Puberty and adolescence are critical phases for these youngsters because instead of progressing they may, under the influx of the biological and psychological stresses of these phases, regress to the preoedipal relationships (A. Freud, 1965). The onset or recurrence or intensification of phobic, psychotic, or psychosomatic manifestations is a frequent occurrence in puberty and adolescence (M. Sperling, 1955). It cannot be emphasized enough that the aim of speedily removing the presenting symptom of school phobia before any appreciable change in the parent-child relationship and in the ego structure of the child himself has been achieved could be a disservice rather than a service to such a child. In these cases there is a resistance to treatment on the part of both the child and the parents because treatment is a threat to the continuation of the pathological relationships, and return to school is often used as a rationalization for discontinuing treatment. The chronicity of the case may be an indicator of the intensity of the need for the persistence of this relationship. I would like to illustrate this briefly with the case of fifteen-year-old Fred, who is rather typical of the more severe cases of this kind.

Fred's phobic attachment to his mother already manifested itself in nursery school. He had some difficulties in the early school years; but he still managed with shorter or longer absences until he was nine and a half, when he had a severe setback, developed psychosomatic symptoms, mainly nausea and vomiting, and stayed out of school for a prolonged period of time. He received brief psychiatric treatment of a supportive nature and medications and returned to school, though with many difficulties and rituals. His mother had to stay home and be available whenever he wanted to call her so that she could take him out of school when he felt sick. At thirteen he had what appeared to be an acute psychotic episode with some paranoid ideas accompanied by anorexia and weight loss. He returned to the psychiatrist who had treated him earlier. When the latter recommended hospitalization, the parents consulted another psychiatrist, who felt that he could treat Fred on an ambulatory basis. His school attendance was now very irregular, he was out for long stretches of time, and there was also a marked change in his personality. Fred was treated mainly with tranquilizers and was hospitalized at one time when he became more difficult at home. Since his intelligence was superior, he could keep up with his grades. Whenever he returned to school, the parents felt that the problem was solved, refusing to recognize the progressive deterioration of Fred's personality until he refused to go to school altogether.

Psychological tests, including Rorschach, taken when he was fourteen years of age revealed superior intelligence in a boy who was in a state of massive regression and failing defenses, especially the phobic and psychosomatic ones. In the case of a boy in such a precarious balance it was unwise to insist on his return to school, a factor that may further contribute to his deterioration.[3] Unable to cope with the realities of school, especially on a social level, and with the demands of adolescence, Fred was teased and made fun of by his classmates, which he experienced as persistent failure and continuous narcissistic injury and which only increased his need for further regression and withdrawal from reality. His case would seem to illustrate particularly well the point I have tried to make earlier, namely, that a child with such psychopathology and without adequate treatment will react with severe exacerbation or even with a psychotic break to the stresses of puberty and adolescence. I was consulted when Fred was fifteen years old and the parents had been advised to place him in a hospital away from home. I was able to convince the mother to accept treatment for herself and psychoanalytically oriented psychotherapy for her son.

In my twenty-six years of child psychiatric practice I have seen quite a number of such cases and I have learned that proper assessment and treatment plans are essential for a successful outcome. I have found that in the case of prelatency children, indirect treatment, that is, treatment of the parent-inducer, is the treatment of choice and leads to excellent results, even in chronic cases. This approach may still be effective with latency children, although for this age group I favor the direct approach, that is, treatment of the child himself with prior or concomitant treatment of the parent (inducer). This method still works with puberty children, although in their case and particularly in that of adolescents I prefer to have minimal contact with the parents, especially the parent-inducer, during treatment of the youngster. My aim is to establish a therapeutic alliance with the parent(s) before I start treatment of the child. If the parent is in need of continued treatment, I refer the parent for therapy and make the suggestion that the parent-child relationship should be specifically focused upon. If the parent later wishes to have further treatment for himself, this can then be arranged for in the conventional way as psychotherapy or psycho-

3 In this connection a paper by Rodriguez et al. (1959) is of interest. These authors insist upon early return to school and do not hesitate "to invoke the legal authority of the school to compel attendance." They do not believe that school phobia in a child of latency and prepuberty age is a serious matter. Such thinking contributes to a neglect of early symptoms and their prognostic significance.

analysis, whichever is advisable. The type of treatment to which I am referring here, in which the parent is treated as the senior partner in the pathological partnership with the child, is goal directed and focused on his specific relationship to the child (M. Sperling, 1949, 1951, 1959, 1963b). In cases of older children and especially of adolescents, it is preferable to assign the child and the parent to different therapists, who have a similar orientation regarding the theoretical concepts and technical approaches, and who collaborate as a team (see Burlingham et al., 1955; Hellman et al., 1960; Levy, 1960; Sprince, 1962).

The differential diagnosis between induced chronic and common chronic school phobia is not always easy to make because once the school phobia has been in existence for some time the circumstances under which the acute onset occurred are usually not remembered, and if they are remembered, the accounts are distorted. Upon surface examination the children suffering from common chronic school phobia appear to be less disturbed than those suffering from induced chronic school phobia. In fact, if it were not for the presenting symptom, they would seem to be functioning well in other areas to the casual observer, and even to their families. On closer observation, however, it becomes evident that in these cases, too, the total personality is affected. The school phobia is used as a safety valve by means of which the child manages to maintain some sort of equilibrium. The school phobia in these cases has the function of keeping the neurosis localized to one area, while in the induced chronic school phobia the school phobia is one more overt symptom in a *manifest* total personality disturbance. This differentiation is of dynamic importance because in cases of common chronic school phobia it is obviously unwise to attempt the removal of the school phobia before working on the latent personality disturbance. In these cases the removal of the presenting symptom without sufficient therapeutic work endangers the precarious balance that is maintained with the help of the school phobia. Actually these children react to attempts to return them to school prematurely with panic and may develop transitory somatic symptoms as emergency discharges of anxiety.

In this connection I want to point again to the definite dynamic interrelation between certain psychosomatic disorders in children and school phobia (M. Sperling, 1950a, 1952b). In fact, the onset of a psychosomatic illness can in some cases be traced back to the start of school, or to similar separation traumata which induce other children to develop overt school phobias. In consequence of their psychosomatic illness these children have a poor attendance record, with absences from school often ranging from months to years. I have found that at a certain phase in the treatment of these children, when the somatic symptoms begin to subside, the underlying phobia and symbiotic relationship with the mother emerge and must then be resolved before regular school attendance can be achieved and maintained. To this group belong children with ulcerative or mucous colitis and bronchial asthma, and others (M. Sperling, 1950a, 1952b, 1961b, 1963a).

Analytic study of children suffering from common chronic school phobia reveals that they acquired the disposition to react with a phobic response to traumatic situations early in childhood, but in these cases the object relationships and the instinctual and ego development during the oral and anal phases have been much more satisfactory than in the case of the induced type of chronic school phobia. In common school phobias, the conflicts mobilized by the trauma or series of traumatic experiences are mainly related to the oedipal phase. There are transitions between cases of induced and common chronic school phobia. If a common school phobia has been in existence for a long time, there will inevitably be character changes with emphasis on secondary gain from illness, as we find them in chronic traumatic neurosis of adults.

It is necessary to keep in mind that we are dealing with more or less severe personality disorders and that long-term therapy is required for a lasting result. The treatment of choice, in my opinion, for such a psychoneurosis is psychoanalysis, if possible, or psychoanalytically oriented psychotherapy. The aim in psychoanalysis is to analyze and to modify the main mechanisms of defense—in these cases, repression, isolation, projection, externalization, displacement, etc.—and to bring about structural changes in the ego and superego. The unconscious conflicts are then gradually brought to the fore, and the child whose ego has been strengthened by the therapeutic relationship is enabled to deal more appropriately with his conflicts and to find more suitable solutions for them in reality. It would be desirable, especially in view of the fact that there is some controversy concerning the applicability of psychoanalysis in puberty and early adolescence, to give a full account of the analytic treatment of such a case. It is impossible, however, to do this within the framework of this paper. I shall have to limit myself to indicate the essential points concerning dynamics and technique. As an illustration I shall use material from the analytic treatment of a twelve-and-a-half-year-old boy, who had a common chronic school phobia.

Peter was referred because of a school phobia that had become increasingly evident over the past two years. During the past six months he had attended school only two days a week. His mother had to take him and call for him and be available for his calls from school to take him home in case he felt sick. For the past six weeks he had refused to go to school altogether. His attendance record had been poor for some time because of frequent colds, which turned to near-pneumonia, headaches, bellyaches, feeling faint, etc. On the surface he gave the appearance of a rather mature and well-adjusted boy. It soon became obvious that he had been fighting a losing battle against the spreading phobia and that he was in a state of constant anxiety, at times reaching panic proportions. He had been using counterphobic defenses and rationalizations in the attempt to conceal from others and himself the degree and intensity of his anxiety. He was afraid of doctors and dentists, injections, new places, elevators, water, getting lost, etc.

Psychoanalytic investigation revealed that there was repression of intense aggression and that his precarious balance was maintained mainly by reaction formations. There were occasional breakthroughs of destructive impulses, especially in self-destructive behavior. He was very accident-prone and had had innumerable accidents, some of a rather serious nature, prior to and continuing for some time during his analysis. Once he nearly blinded himself. He had obsessional thoughts of killing people, and since his father and he himself owned a collection of guns (for hunting), this was a matter of some concern. When cleaning a gun he often had fantasies that it accidentally fired and someone (a man), and less frequently he himself, was killed. Although it became apparent rather early in his analysis that his major problem stemmed from a very intense, unresolved oedipal conflict with repressed and displaced parricidal impulses, which gave a paranoid cast to his castration fears, this problem was not dealt with until late in the analysis. The anal-sadistic features were very marked and contributed to the severity of the oedipal conflict. Peter's personality was characterized by a high degree of narcissism and the persistence of the fantasy of omnipotence which made it dangerous for him to know his thoughts, feelings, and impulses. He also had a number of rituals and he carried a rabbit's foot with him as a magic charm.

I kept Peter out of school a term and a half in order to prevent repetition of the experience of failure to attend consistently and of continual narcissistic injuries resulting from it. I had the full co-operation of his parents and the school authorities in this matter. When Peter returned to school, his narcissism, his magical thinking, and his anxieties were considerably reduced due to the persistent analysis of his defenses. His attendance from then on was remarkable. He seemed to have developed a special immunity to colds from which he previously had so frequently suffered. It was not until the second year of his treatment that he could to some extent curb and bring into analysis a symptom which proved dynamically very significant and therapeutically more stubborn than his school phobia—namely, a persistent enuresis. Peter had been successfully bladder trained at the age of two and became enuretic when he was not quite four years old, following a hernia operation and during a vacation in which he shared the parents' bedroom. He had been enuretic since then every single night. In the third years of treatment he formed a relationship to a girl which enabled us to analyze more fully his relationship to his mother and his attempt to transfer this relationship to the girlfriend, of whom he was very possessive and jealous. He no longer felt so dependent upon his mother. Through the school phobia he had managed to control and possess (the oedipal) mother in a preoedipal (anal-sadistic) way.

In the fourth and final year of treatment it was possible to analyze the oedipal conflict sufficiently for Peter to feel that to be a man did not mean to kill father and to be castrated, that is, to be killed in turn, and that he did not need his phobia which had been a regressive (anal-sadistic) way of possessing, that is, controlling, his mother. Peter had never been away from home, even for one night, until the end of the second year of analysis. He usually became sick in anticipation of such events and would have sleep disturbances and nightmares, indicating an acute intensification of separation anxiety. It was found that the acute exacerbation of Peter's school phobia at age twelve (Peter had shown milder signs of school phobia from the start of school, but these had been disregarded until his phobia became so intense that all concessions and manipulations failed to get Peter to school) had occurred at a time when his father had been away for several weeks and Peter had been left alone with his mother. During his treatment I could observe that Peter became very anxious whenever his wish to stay out of school each time his father left for short trips was revived. Neither Peter nor his environment had in any way connected this with his school phobia. This connection was made at an advanced stage of his treatment when this could be recognized and interpreted as an event that had acutely intensified his oedipal conflicts and as a consequence led to regression to the anal-sadistic stage. Peter had at first considered a college where he could live at home, but he later changed his mind and decided to live on campus.

The treatment of adolescents suffering from this type of school phobia can be limited to the adolescent, and no work with the parents is necessary. This is different in induced chronic school phobia, where the symbiotic tie between child and parent has to be modified before successful treatment of the child is possible. It is necessary, however, to insure the parents' willingness to accept long-term treatment because this is the only guarantee for a successful resolution of the child's neurosis. Peter's parents were genuinely concerned with helping him and supported my efforts without intruding or interfering with his treatment. In the first few months of Peter's treatment I spoke to his mother several times, mostly on the telephone, to help her to disentangle herself from Peter's controlling maneuvers. She obviously had neurotic, and particularly phobic, problems of her own, but these were neither interpreted nor dealt with by me. Because she behaved as though she and not Peter were responsible for his attending or not attending school she needed support and reassurance in order to relax her overcompensations and to let Peter carry this responsibility himself.

In the actual treatment of adolescents, the preoedipal conflicts and relationships should be dealt with first. Owing to the revival of the unresolved oedipal conflicts during puberty and the danger of a breakthrough into consciousness, repression has to be reinforced, and the lifting of this re-repression is strongly defended against. The anal fixations, especially the unresolved separation conflicts, also make the oedipal conflicts more pathogenic in these cases.

These dynamics and techniques also apply to adolescent girls suffering from chronic common school phobia. In such a case we usually find an overprotective, controlling mother and a seductive father, features which contribute to the intensification of the oedipal conflicts. The inevitable resentment and disappointment in both parents increase the girl's need for omnipotent control. The phobic attachment to the mother with its homosexual coloring covers up the underlying hostility and death wishes. In girls, agoraphobic features are more prominent, such as a fear of leaving the house, walking to school, crossing the street; the unconscious wish to run away, to have sexual adventures, to be raped (which in the final analysis reveals itself as a fear of death), comes out in the fear of getting lost, of being in crowds or in wide open spaces.

In acute cases it is often possible to connect the onset of the phobia with the precipitating event or events—usually those that trigger off such unconscious wishes and fears related to the oedipal conflict. While it may be possible in re-establishing this connection to make conscious some of the underlying sexual wishes and to relieve the anxiety to such an extent that a speedy return to school can be effected, this first aid (M. Sperling, 1961a) has to be followed up by further exploratory and interpretative work to prevent the phobic core from retaining its pathogenicity. The fact that some girls react in this specific way to certain experiences to which many others are exposed as well and to which they react differently indicates that there is a latent phobic disposition and that the trauma has a specific unconscious meaning and has been interpreted in this specific way (O. Sperling, 1950).

A frequent etiological factor in these cases is the identification with a phobic parent. In the case of a fourteen-year-old adolescent girl, Paula, who had a severe chronic school phobia and whom I treated in successful analysis for three and a half years, the mother was an agoraphobic. It is of interest that Paula behaved as if she were unaware of this fact, as if she tried to repress this knowledge. Her mother had been in therapy off and on during Paula's childhood and had returned to her therapist at the time of Paula's referral to me. There is a quality of secrecy and denial associated with the way agoraphobics deal with their handicaps. Paula applied the same tactics to her own phobia. I would like to repeat again that in the chronic cases of this type of school phobia one has to be careful with the interpretation of sexual material. One should first analyze and devalue the pathological defenses and the inordinate narcissism and need for omnipotent control. Furthermore, one has to resist the pressures exerted by the parents, the school, or even the patient for a quick return to school. This technique was applied in Paula's case.

I had an opportunity to see Paula some fifteen years later, when she consulted me because of problems in her marriage. I learned that she had gone to college, had finished graduate work, and was pursuing a career. She had two children, and there seemed to be some conflict between her career and her children. This conflict was related to her feelings about her mother. I learned that her mother was still phobic and manipulating and that her sister (who had always been held up to Paula as a model) had also developed agoraphobia. Paula was very critical of both her mother and her sister, but it appeared to me that her overemphasis on her career had a defensive function and that she was using it as a protection against her fear that she might repeat such a pattern with her own children. I am mentioning this here to indicate that such phobic patterns can be so persistent and pervasive that they affect whole families and are perpetuated through generations.

Summary

This paper is an attempt to study school phobias comprehensively. It was undertaken in the hope that a fuller understanding of some etiological, dynamic, and therapeutic factors might enable us to deal more effectively with these problems. I consider school phobia to be a neurosis characterized by fixation to the anal-sadistic phase of development, persistence of ambivalence, narcissism, and magical thinking (fantasy of omnipotence), and more closely related to the compulsion neuroses than to anxiety hysteria.

I have divided the phobias into acute and chronic and into induced and common (traumatic) school phobia. In the induced type, the traumatization is insidious and results mainly from a pathological parent-child relationship. In the common type, the acute onset follows a trauma or a series of traumata and resembles a traumatic neurosis with the presenting symptom of school phobia.

The indications for the type of treatment to be chosen depend upon the differential diagnosis and the age of the child at the onset of the school phobia, whether in prelatency, latency, or at puberty or adolescence. These factors determine whether the child or the parent(s) should be treated and, if both are to be treated, whether the parent should be treated prior to or concomitantly with the child, whether by the same or by a different therapist, and whether by psychoanalysis or short-term psychoanalytic psychotherapy. I questioned the value of symptomatic treatment and the emphasis on quick return of the school-phobic child to school without treating the total neurosis, of which the school phobia is one manifestation.

BIBLIOGRAPHY

Bornstein, B. (1935), Phobia in a Two-and-a-half-year-old Child. *Psa. Quart.*, 4:93-119.

Burlingham, D., Goldberger, A., & Lussier, A. (1955), Simultaneous Analysis of Mother and Child. *This Annual*, 10:165-186.

Coolidge, J. C., Willer, M. L., Tessman, E., & Waldfogel, S. (1960), School Phobia in Adolescence: A Manifestation of Severe Character Disturbance. *Amer. J. Orthopsychiat.*, 30:599-607.

Eisenberg, L. (1958), School Phobia: Diagnosis, Genesis and Clinical Management. *Ped. Clin. N. Amer.*, 5:645-666.

Freud, A. (1965), *Normality and Pathology in Childhood: Assessments of Development*. New York: International Universities Press.

Freud, S. (1909), Analysis of a Phobia in a Five-year-old Boy. *Standard Edition*, 10:3-149. London: Hogarth Press, 1955.

Garvey, W. P. & Hegrenes, J. R. (1966), Desensitization Techniques in the Treatment of School Phobia. *Amer. J. Orthopsychiat.*, 36:147-152.

Greenbaum, R. S. (1964), Treatment of School Phobias: Theory and Practice. *Amer. J. Psychother.*, 18:616-634.

Hellman, I., Friedmann, O., & Shepheard, E. (1960), Simultaneous Analysis of Mother and Child. *This Annual*, 15:359-377.

Jarvis, V. (1964), Countertransference in the Management of School Phobia. *Psa. Quart.*, 33:411-419.

Johnson, A. M., Falstein, E. I., Szurek, S. A., & Svendsen, M. (1941), School Phobia. *Amer. J. Orthopsychiat.*, 11:702-711.

Kahn, J. H. & Nursten, J. P. (1962), School Refusal: A Comprehensive View of School

Phobia and Other Failures of School Attendance. *Amer. J. Orthopsychiat.,* 32:707-718.
Klein, E. (1945), The Reluctance to Go to School. *This Annual,* 1:263-279.
Leavitt, A. (1964), Treatment of an Adolescent with School Phobia. *J. Amer. Child Psychosom. Med.,* 11-377-385.
Levy, K. (1960), Simultaneous Analysis of a Mother and Her Adolescent Daughter. *This Annual,* 15:378-391.
Messer, A. A. (1964), Family Treatment of a School Phobic Child. *Arch. Gen. Psychiat.,* 11:548-555.
Rodriguez, A., Rodriguez, M., & Eisenberg, L. (1959), The Outcome of School Phobia: A Follow-up Study Based on 41 Cases. *Amer. J. Psychiat.,* 116:540-544.
Sperling, M. (1949), The Role of the Mother in Psychosomatic Disorders in Children. *Psychosom. Med.,* 11:377-385.
—— (1950a), Mucous Colitis Associated with Phobias. *Psa. Quart.,* 19:318-326.
—— (1950b), Children's Interpretation and Reaction to the Unconscious of Their Mothers. *Int. J. Psa.,* 31:36-41.
—— (1951), The Neurotic Child and His Mother: A Psychoanalytic Study. *Amer. J. Orthopsychiat.,* 21:351-364.
—— (1952a), Animal Phobias in a Two-year-old Child. *This Annual,* 7:115-125.
—— (1952b), Psychogenic Diarrhea and Phobia in a Six-and-a-half-year-old Girl. *Amer. J. Orthopsychiat.,* 22:838-848.
—— (1955), Psychosis and Psychosomatic Illness. *Int. J. Psa.,* 36:320-327.
—— (1959), A Study of Deviate Sexual Behavior in Children by the Method of Simultaneous Analysis of Mother and Child. In: *Dynamic Psychopathology in Childhood,* ed. L. Jessner & E. Pavenstedt. New York: Grune & Stratton, pp. 221-242.
—— (1961a), Analytic First Aid to School Phobias. *Psa. Quart.,* 30:504-518.
—— (1961b), Psychosomatic Disorders. In: *Adolescents: Psychoanalytic Approach to Problems and Therapy,* ed. S. Lorand & H. I. Schneer. New York: Hoeber, pp. 202-216.
—— (1963a), A Psychoanalytic Study of Bronchial Asthma in Children. In: *The Asthmatic Child,* ed. H. I. Schneer. New York: Harper & Row, pp. 138-165.
—— (1963b), Some Criteria on the Evaluation of the Treatment Potential of Schizophrenic Children. *J. Amer. Acad. Child Psychiat.,* 2:593-604.
Sperling, O. E. (1950), The Interpretation of the Trauma as a Command. *Psa. Quart.,* 19:352-370.
Sprince, M. P. (1962), The Development of a Preoedipal Partnership between an Adolescent Girl and Her Mother. *This Annual,* 17:418-450.
Suttenfield, V. (1954), School Phobia: A Study of Five Cases. *Amer. J. Orthopsychiat.,* 24:368-380.
Talbot, M. (1957), Panic in School Phobia. *Amer. J. Orthopsychiat.,* 27:286-295.
Waldfogel, S., Coolidge, J. C., & Hahn, P. B. (1957), The Development, Meaning and Management of School Phobia. *Amer. J. Orthopsychiat.,* 27:754-780.
Wulff, M. (1927), A Phobia in a Child of Eighteen Months. *Int. J. Psa.,* 9:354-359, 1928.

AN INFANTILE FETISH AND ITS PERSISTENCE INTO YOUNG WOMANHOOD

Maturational Stages of a Fetish

NANCY TOW SPIEGEL, M.A. (New York)

A young woman's manipulation of an inanimate object from early childhood on offers material which is of clinical and theoretical interest for considerations of female fetishism. Object losses, excessive sexual exposures on the part of adults, together with constitutional proclivities led the patient to concentrate on an inanimate object which gradually developed into a fetish in adolescence. Fixation to the fetish was loosened during the course of analysis, especially of her resistances, of which the foremost were denial, projection, and turning against the self. The fetish was slowly devalued by the patient, ultimately lost its prestige, and was finally relinquished. The rather lurid material appeared as part of her free associations.

It is noteworthy that the patient's fetish, a shoestring, deviates in two respects from the usual one. In contrast to the supposedly habitual attainment of orgasm through a fetish, it is not certain whether the patient did or did not have an orgasm with her fetish. Second, an unusual stress on its defensive aspect, i.e., undoing, seems to distinguish it from the classical fetish (Freud, 1927).

Fetishism has been subjected to extensive scrutiny since Freud's masterful delineation of it in *The Three Essays on the Theory of Sexuality* (1905). On February 24, 1910 Freud wrote to Abraham: ". . . it must be emphasized that the female foot is apparently a substitute for the painfully missed, prehistorically postulated, female penis" (p. 87).

Clinical Instructor in Child Psychiatry, Albert Einstein College of Medicine.

A version of this paper was presented at the Hampstead Child-Therapy Clinic, London, May 25, 1966. Presented at the New York Psychoanalytic Society, June 13, 1967.

The pregenital nature of the patient's fetish receives a good deal of attention in this paper, and certain comments by Gillespie (1940), E. Glover (1939), Bak (1953), and Greenacre (1953, 1955, 1960b, 1966) are of particular relevance. Gillespie asks whether fetishism may not come from more primitive levels than the phallic phase. Glover emphasizes pregenital fixations of an anal and urethral type. Displacements to such objects are influenced by anxieties arising during early stages of reality development. Greenacre (1953) considers fetishism to be the result of a rather definite combination of genetic influences in disturbances of pregenitality. Bak (1953) says: "The symbolic significance of the fetish corresponds to pregenital phases and thus may represent separately or in condensation: breast-skin, buttocks-feces, and female phallus" (p. 286). He emphasizes disturbances in the mother-child relationship as a possible source that "results in increased clinging to the mother totally, or to a substitute part of her as a *pars pro toto*" (p. 286).

Turning now to the literature concerning female fetishism, Fenichel (1934) says: "The problem of fetishism in women has not been sufficiently studied. The fact that female fetishists are rare is obviously explained by Freud's theory of fetishism. The little experience we have had of these rare forms suggests that in this condition, . . . the chief rôle is played by the castration complex, with the usual characteristics of that complex in women . . . the fetishist refuses to acknowledge that a woman has no penis" (p. 267).

Hug-Hellmuth (1915) noted the symbolic nature of the foot for a female fetishist with the consideration that in its role as a substitute for the idealized organ of the mother, the pregenital phallus, the fetish must remain hidden.

Greenacre (1955), in a footnote, said: "Forms of fetishism which are not always clearly linked to the genital functioning . . . and even those linked to the genital activity but not demanding the objective fetish—such as set fantasies or rituals preparing for masturbation or intercourse, seem to occur in female as well as male" (p. 188). Dickes (1963) describes a degree of fetishistic behavior in females whose penis envy seemed overwhelming.

Relevant as well to this paper are references to fetishes and fetishistic practices in children. These in large part reinforce the idea that object loss and the need for a "concrete" and tangible object play an important role.[1]

Winnicott (1953) distinguishes between the pathological forms of fetishism and the love of things in early infancy. He describes the fetish in terms of a persistence of a specific object beyond the transitional field and as linked with the delusion of a maternal phallus.

Lorand (1930), Wulff (1946), Buxbaum (1960), and Sperling (1963) describe childhood fetishes and fetishistic practices.

Anna Freud (1965) speaks of the early origin of the adult fetish and its persistent nature. It is this "persistent" nature of the fetish that is given especial emphasis in this paper.

Case Presentation

The existence of the fetish (called "string" by the patient) and its significance were discovered incidentally during the course of the analysis. Nora T. had come for other reasons and consequently her comments on the string were peripheral and casual. She attributed no significance to it, although it gradually became evident that it was of special importance to her. She had not referred to the string in an earlier period of treatment (from about the age of eight on).

Nora, a pretty girl of nineteen, came into treatment not only because she frequently felt "empty" and could not do anything, but primarily because of her agitation about what she considered to be her excessive masturbation (Fenichel, 1938). It was while Nora reproached herself for her masturbation that she casually mentioned the string. She said: "I turned to my string. It made me feel pure." The context in which the string appeared led me to inquire about it, and after she expressed a certain degree of diffidence about it, tactful scrutiny brought to light the shoelace's central importance.

It gradually emerged that she had occupied herself with a string since she was about two and a half years old. The string was always a shoelace. She took the first one from her mother's brown shoe almost directly after the occurrence of certain traumatic events. The birth of a male sibling was of particular significance. Subsequently

[1] In a personal communication, Dr. Greenacre underscored the *concrete* nature of the fetish.

she used strings from her own shoes, and as she grew older she surreptitiously removed shoelaces from females' shoes.

Over the years the style of manipulating the string varied. When Nora was little, between the ages of two and a half and four, she remembered that she held it between the thumb, index finger, and third finger of her right hand. Later, between five and eight, she held and twisted it between these fingers as it rested in her pocket, or as she gazed at it in bed. During these years she kept a string with her at all times since it was essential for her to have the sensation of touching it. Without it she would have "nothing" and be "nothing." She discarded some strings, casually left them about to be seen, and then always sought a replacement from another shoe. From puberty on she no longer toted a string around with her. She manipulated a string only at special times, and *only* in combination with a complicated and elaborate body ritual together with a fantasy, which she called "pure."

Two sets of contrasting conditions led Nora, in her adolescent period, to turn to her shoelace or, as she put it, "to play with my string." One set can loosely be called *negative* and the other *positive*. On the one hand, she "played" with her shoelace when she felt bad (i.e., morally bad): because of anal masturbation, because of an urge to steal, because of feelings of hate against those who exposed her to narcissistic humiliations, parents and especially females. On the other hand, she used her string as an expression of joy when she had mastered some realistic task; e.g., swept a room, read a few pages, was on time, made a decision, etc.

Out of a number of partial descriptions of the manipulation, of the body ritual, and of the essential "pure" fantasy, the ensuing composite picture is synthesized.

In a lighted room, the patient, completely clothed, lay at an oblique angle across the bed (Freud, 1916). She closed her legs tightly, making them stiff. She said: "I arrange my body so I won't feel the lower part at all. I only feel my head from my shoulders up. This part can't relax at all." When the lower part felt "nothing," she focused on the upper. She fixed her elbows at right angles on a line with her head and clutched her "string" with the fingers of both hands, making certain that it was out of her range of vision. Her eyes had to be wide open, unblinking, and staring at a blank part of the wall. Her pursed lips were set in a sucking position, her tongue made stiff so that mouth and tongue hurt. From time to time she cracked her jaws so that she heard them "click." She was now arranged to twirl the string, and while she did so her fingertips tingled, her head whirled, and she elaborated her "*pure*" fantasy: After having endured numerous humiliations, she goes on an auto trip with a young man, a mother, and the mother's little son. There is a bad accident in which the mother is injured and bloody. The patient goes for help, leaving the little boy to look after their mother. On her return the mother is dead. She now takes care of the boy. The three of them stay together, i.e., the young man, the little boy, and she. However, she sleeps only with the little boy. After a while she gives birth to a girl baby without any man being involved. Now she has two children and considers herself to be good and "pure."

Through this combination of ritualistic activity and, in her words, pure fantasy, the patient achieved a feeling of purity, peace, and quiet. This state of mind was attained when she felt sore, exhausted, and numb. When Nora reached this point, she stopped the ritualistic activity with the string and her absorption with her fantasy.

Of course, neither activity nor fantasy was as "pure" as she believed. Obviously, a breakthrough of sexual elements in both was covertly present. These appeared in frank form in another ritualistic activity. The "sinful" effect of this second activity was undone by repeating the first purifying one.

In the *second* practice, the patient, now stark naked, placed herself in a prone position, on her knees, with her buttocks raised up. She squeezed her eyes shut till they stung, while she made sucking sounds with her tongue and lips. She either tugged at her breasts or fingered her anus. She experienced a degree of wetness, but one could not precisely elicit whether this was vaginal, rectal, or urethral.

Lurid, perverse, and pathetic fantasies accompanied this anal-masturbatory act. An old shriveled man was frequently the chief protagonist and victim in these fantasies. In one fantasy a tiny old man had to procure a virile man for his cruel, full-breasted wife. The old man secretly watched them and, while they performed fellatio, he masturbated and wept. It will become apparent that this fantasy was a primitive transmutation of an early object loss. In this clearly masturbatory act both the activity and the lurid fantasy made her feel as if she were "dissolving" and being "emptied out."

The string itself played *no* role in this second ritualistic activity. In fact, "it" had to be kept out of this act so as to be preserved from contamination and degradation. The patient called this second act "a perversion. You feel it's wrong, it's sinful. It makes you want to stop, but it is exciting, you can't stop. You know you'll feel bad afterward, but you do it anyway."

It is clear that the two rituals can be put together, the masturbatory act *without* the string which made her feel "bad," and the ritual act *with* the string which made her feel "good and pure." Obviously, the two ritualistic acts fall under the well-known compulsive doing and undoing which frequently are part of compulsive masturbation (Freud, 1926).

Up to now what has been described has been an act of masturbation resulting in a feeling of guilt, and an undoing of this act resulting in a feeling of purity. But this feeling of purity was achieved by a ritualistic act with a string which itself sounded masturbatory (namely, stiffening and squeezing legs together).

In order to understand the developing function of the string which concealed a masturbatory act, it is necessary to offer both a clinical picture of the patient and to consider the patient's life history.

Nora, pretty and rounded, made a somewhat old-fashioned impression with her wispy-ashen hair tucked up in Edwardian style. Her features, though delicate, had a sort of housemaid look. This unconsciously assumed look appeared to serve as a degradation of and contempt for her intellectual and snobbish family. The housemaid air was also evident in the exaggerated swaying of her hips and projection of her buttocks. Her schooled speech was demure, but as time went on it became peppered with obscenities. As the complaints increased, her voice rose till it culminated in a scream.

In addition to the dominant complaint, her excessive masturbation, Nora harped on her feelings of emptiness, not knowing who she was, her inability to work, read or think. She felt she was stupid and "nothing." "Nothing" meant she had nothing, neither a worthwhile body nor a mind. She expressed irritation with everyone and everything and shrieked at the slightest frustration. From time to time she resembled an infant, wet, flailing, wailing, and inconsolable.

She condemned the abhorrent envelope of her body which she frequently pinched and pummeled. In her words, her breasts were "sexless, nothing there," whereas her mother had "huge, sexy ones." Her buttocks were viewed as identical with her mother's "big and common." She considered her clitoris insignificant and avoided references to it. She concluded the diatribe against her body by saying: "I wish I could tear this skin off. If I didn't have this stupid body, I would be as pure outside as I feel inside."

After finding fault with her body she renewed her reproach against her mind for being stupid. As soon as she used her mind to read, her eyes betrayed her; they itched, blurred, burned, shut or fell asleep. If her eyes could only see, she might have something. Obviously, in reproaching her mind, she was still preoccupied with her body.

The patient's irritation with inanimate objects was as intense as with animate ones. She raged at machines that did not work or that she could not control: typewriter, record player, locks, scissors, needles, toilets. Above all, the telephone was censured. She often wished she could pull the wires out so she would not hear it ring or click. And indeed it emerged that the telephone played a role in her fetishistic preoccupation. Mention of the telephone brought to her mind frequent calls between her mother and the maternal grandfather which dealt largely with the patient's abdominal cramps and for which he recommended, "Give her an enema." She was systematically subjected to enemas from about nine months on till she was eight years old, when she refused to let her mother administer them any longer.

The enema procedure furnished a highly significant clue to the patient's fetish. The following is a somewhat paraphrased version of the agitated accounts she gave of it.

As far back as she could recall she screamed when she had abdominal cramps. Mrs. T. would call her father and Nora would hear them speaking of enemas, particularly to "give her an enema." She would watch the telephone cord and at once think of water flowing out of a tube. She felt like "exploding," but also wanted to press tight, to hold in. Right after the call her mother would speak two cue words: "Hurry, hurry." These made Nora slow up immediately. She quickly squeezed her legs together and experienced a feeling of "wetness." The words "hurry, hurry" were repeated, and she went docilely to be given the enema. Her accounts focused on the following points: her mother was invisible standing behind her; she had something long in her hand (evidently the enema tube). The patient screamed in anticipation of the enema. She maintained that her father was always present and watched. She was sure mother also gave her father enemas.

As time went on, it could be seen more directly that these enema scenes played a prime and modeling role in her life. Reverberations from them persisted into her fantasies, and often her moods were rooted in them (Abraham, 1921).

Enemas were not the only factor contributing to the intense anal atmosphere in the family. Both parents were preoccupied with money. Her father felt done in by his own pathologically stingy and compulsive mother, who had hidden money in undisclosed places. He claimed to have been cheated by his avaricious family. He earned little or no money. Nora's mother vacillated between excessive generosity and agitated concern about being left destitute by her own wealthy but penurious father who controlled people with his "money." The patient herself stormed at every aspect of money, getting, having, taking, spending, and losing it. She too felt that she was constantly being "cheated."

This pervasive atmosphere of anality, a two-generation inheritance of pathological preoccupation with money, weighed heavily on the patient. Furthermore, lofty morality, exhibitionism, and excessive indulgence were concomitant features of the family structure (Jones, 1918).

The patient's early development was considered uneventful.[2] Nora was considered to be content, smiling, and responsive. She never sucked her thumb, ate and slept well, and was agreeable. Only the following points clouded an otherwise benign account of her early infancy.

For two weeks after Nora's birth Mrs. T. was afraid to touch the infant lest she drop her.

Enemas were instituted at about eight months, directly after weaning.

[2] Mrs. T. furnished historical material and corroborated the patient's rather agitated accounts of actual events.

Shortly after the patient was weaned from the breast at eight months, the mother observed the child twisting a string with beads on it and staring at it unblinkingly. Mrs. T. spoke of this last incident with unusual intensity and concluded with the statement: "She was transfixed. It's as though she always twisted something and stared" (Hoffer, 1949).

Nora, in whom a hypersensitivity to a lack of love seems to have prevailed from almost the beginning of her life, may have been especially sensitive to a lack of true mothering at this crucial period of development, and then turned with unblinking preoccupation to a string toy.[3] In later life she spoke of her mother's feeling toward her as a fraud and a pretense. "She tried to be real, but it was only a game she played. She never felt real love."

Aside from the administration of enemas nothing of especial traumatic consequence was reported to have happened until about the age of two, when a sequence of traumatic events took place. First of all, the patient suffered from severe separation anxiety when her mother placed her in a nursery school. Nora felt afraid, lonely, and deserted. One of her memories was of wetting herself all over and remaining seated in a puddle till a teacher picked her up.

Secondly, concurrent with separation from her mother, Nora's maternal grandfather moved away from the neighborhood. (The patient believed that her mother had forced him to move.) This was the grandfather whom Mrs. T. telephoned and who recommended "giving enemas." Because of his exceptionally small size the patient appeared to have converted him into a sort of Rumpelstilzkin who had magic (Niederland, 1956). Contact with him up to about two and a half was seductive and overstimulating. He had her bathe with him and fondled her in a provocative way. She could not recall seeing his genitals, but it seems difficult to avoid the thought that her head reached to his penis and scrotum.[4] (It will be recalled that in her later ritualistic behavior, Nora had to fix her eyes on one spot without seeing anything and then alternated by shutting her eyes tight.)

[3] In a personal communication Dr. Marianne Kris said she had the impression that the mother must have been totally unaware of the infant's stare at her face while she nursed Nora, and only became aware of the infant's piercing look when she observed Nora "transfixed" by the beads.

[4] Dr. Marianne Kris, in a personal communication, suggested that the little man of the lurid fantasy could mean the shriveled penis of the old man as well.

The grandfather appeared to be the prototype of the little shriveled man who was the betrayed victim in her perverse fantasy, perhaps as a punishment for his early abandonment of her. Throughout her analysis Nora expressed feelings of love and hate for the "little man"! She spoke of him as a sadist and as a seducer. Later visits to his home invariably led to revivals of fantasies about the telephone, the enema, the filled enema bag, and a frequent need for her string.[5]

Not long after her grandfather left ("abandoned me to her," in Nora's words), Mrs. T. went away. Nora stayed with relatives, and recalled that she did not know why all this happened: "They didn't tell" anything. When she returned home, she was dismayed to find mother had brought back a "boy-baby." She denied any knowledge of having seen her mother's full abdomen, and throughout her treatment avoided references to pregnancy.

The final loss was a feeling of losing her mother's breast. Nora referred to this loss with intense feeling. She said: "When she nursed that boy, I felt she took my breast away and gave it to him. I hated to see her give him my breast. She left me nothing." She recalled screaming while her mother nursed the infant. The only thing Nora could do was tap his head without letup.

The need to touch and finger seems to have been a reaction formation against Nora's wish to punch and hit her infant brother, and perhaps a displacement from touching his penis. She tapped the boy's head and fingered his hair for long periods of time, a practice she continued to a late age. She said: "I always had to touch his head, tap it and then his hair. I wanted to bang his head, but I stroked it. When he got a little bigger, he let me do it for awhile, but then he would turn on me. . . . It reminds me of my cat. I would stroke and tap her head, and she would let me, but by and by she would turn on me, too. I think I touched my string like that, too. Anyway 'it' was better. I could do just as I liked with 'it.' "

References to the lost breast were frequent. Nora was preoccupied with fantasies of huge breasts and her own lack of breast development. From time to time (especially when she used her grandfather's bathroom) she would have intense, visual memories of a full, warm

5 Dr. Walter Stewart, in his discussion of the paper, felt that the bisexual conflict was established and reinforced by the enemas as well as by the fusion of identification of the mother and the grandfather.

enema bag and immediately thereafter of her mother's large full breasts, suggesting the proximity of anal and oral elements.

It was soon after these painful events that Nora took her first shoestring from her mother's brown shoe. She herself connected her taking of the string with object losses. "I felt I had nothing left, so I took a shoestring." Except for her fingering the string Nora remembered nothing else about it, neither taste nor smell. From that time on, however, she picked her nose and ingested mucus. It is therefore likely that the smell and the taste of the shoestring were displaced onto these autoerotic activities. Like the string, these autoerotic activities also compensated, to a small extent, for her object losses.

At above five a new symptom appeared: fright. Nora was afraid of spiders, noises in the parental bedroom, and especially of her mother doing "terrible" things to father. The dark frightened her and she had to have a light on. A set of ritualistic, compulsive behavior mechanisms, which she called "habits," became manifest and slowed her up: touching walls, counting steps, mouthing names, lip biting. It is likely that the patient instituted the habits primarily as means of warding off masturbatory wishes and also as a retaliation against her parents.

At this same age sexual excitement seems to have been heightened by episodes involving animal pets. She saw them copulating, giving birth, bleeding, and saw some die. She herself alternately fondled and provoked them, tapped their heads, let them lick her, licked them, and tried to control their movements.

Her string was of particular comfort to her between the ages of six and seven. Nora felt relegated to second place, alone and not certain of who she was. The string in particular appeared to serve the patient as a way of establishing an identity. She recalled that when she held her string, she was able to feel that "I was me."[6]

The string took on an additional attribute when Nora was left alone with her father. She was ashamed to be seen with him in public because he looked different and odd. Still he inspired awe in her by his wisdom. When he had once remarked that he could not get any money and casually spoke of everything having strings attached, her

[6] Dr. Stewart, in his discussion, suggested that during the development from the anal to the phallic phase the string functioned as a stabilizer of self and object representations. It represented both the self and the object.

string acquired a special, sanctioned meaning and she was convinced that "it" was truly a magical, special part of her. It is significant from the point of view of idealization that from this time on she could not look at her father's face, but felt "he was sort of God."[7]

Nora's longing for her mother continued unappeased and she felt "empty" without her. Apparently she could to some degree overcome her emptiness only by turning to her string. She related an actual incident which made her feel deserted by her mother and "emptied out."

"My mother took me to a new school and left me alone behind a glass door. I wanted her to stay with me, stay home from work because I was lonely without her. But she just left me alone, went out with my brother and never looked back at me even though I spoke her name in my mouth and glued my eyes on her back." She had forgotten to take her string and felt none of her magic worked without that special part of herself.

She dated another recurrent fantasy from that time. She is jealous of her mother's girlfriends because her mother feeds them. She rushes to the kitchen after they leave. There is a long loaf of her mother's homemade bread. She wants to steal a piece and chew it hard. The thought of being caught stealing a piece and being punished for it makes her heart beat fast. She imagines the words "hurry, hurry" at which her tongue begins to stiffen and she makes sucking noises with her lips while pressing her legs together. She reaches out and tears off a piece of bread. She no longer wants it. What she wanted was for "mother to give it to me."

This fantasy reproduced to a noticeable degree the sensations she experienced with the enema and hints at a wish to obtain the fantasied object (breast, pregenital phallus). It also shows her unappeased wish of getting something from her mother, as well as her oral way of attaining the longed-for object (Fenichel, 1936). After this fantasy she turned to fondling her string.

One can scarcely say that Nora entered the latency period in the true sense of the word. Sadomasochistic sexual activities with girls and then with boys preoccupied her, and by the time she entered prepuberty she was in a tense and overexcited state. In the first part of

7 E. Glover (1938), says: "Primitive idealizations have a specially close relation to anal sadism, highmindedness and anality."

the latency period, about age six, she engaged in activities of a primarily homosexual nature. Nora attached herself to little girls, stroked and fondled them. If they acknowledged her, she became submissive to them. She recalled that some girls tried to masturbate her clitorally, but she refused. She did, however, beg them to give her an enema. They were incredulous, derisive, and ran away from her. She was humiliated and enraged by their desertion. The initial submissiveness to them gave way to hate, and in revenge she threw stones at their heads to see them bleed.

In the second part of her latency, beginning at age eight, it seems likely that because of the girls' rejection Nora repressed her interest in them and turned to boys, but was similarly rejected by them. She chased little boys and demanded that they show her what they had. When they refused, she became downcast. She also felt outrivaled by her brother, who boasted about his manner of urinating. It would seem that her envy at not having a penis led to a denial of what it looked like. Nora said: "I never saw anything." This denial made it relatively easy later on to deny knowledge of her own sexual encounters, and strengthened her disavowal of not possessing the longed-for organ. After these frustrations from girls and boys she relied even more on fingering her string for comfort and relief.

Despite this pathological behavior she spontaneously took exceptional steps in the direction of health. At eight she refused to permit her mother to give her enemas any more. She screamed till her mother desisted, and from then on never was given another enema. She felt they were "making me crazy." She also determined to be "purer" than the adults, whose casual nudity and open talk about sex shocked and frightened her. In order to "be pure" and "good" she forced herself to renounce the string as well.

A general forward push in her development then ensued. She improved in her schoolwork, she was less fearful, she wrote rescue fantasy stories which dealt with the search for a lost object. It hardly seems possible to account for this improvement, which occurred despite the regressive pull of severe pathology, except on the basis of some innate capacity for health. This assumed innate strength showed itself again during her analysis in a certain capacity for realistic action and moderately sustained object relations (A. Freud, 1965).

Regrettably the forward movement lasted only about a year. Nora took up her string again, and reverted to the habits she had developed at five (touching, counting, mouthing, etc.). A period of inconsolable and mystifying weeping ensued, both at home and at school (Greenacre, 1945). Under the sway of this regressive pull, the growth and the sublimatory advance came to an abrupt halt.

It is not easy to account for the cessation of this brief advance. Nora implied that she felt "it's no use" since no one acknowledged her accomplishments. More significant seems to have been the shock of a car wreck. (This wreck may have been incorporated in the "pure" fantasy.) Though neither she, father, nor brother were injured, the car itself was demolished and she thought at first that her father and brother had been killed. Her mother was not with them. Other factors impeding her forward development may have been chronic overstimulation, early breast development, anticipated menarche: a host of prepubertal excitations with their characteristic reinforcement of sadomasochistic trends which increased the pull of regressive forces.

The parents, frightened at Nora's ceaseless weeping, her screaming, the return of the "habits," which virtually immobilized her, sought ambulatory treatment for her. But when no improvement took place, they consented to a precipitous psychiatric hospitalization for the nine-and-a-half-year-old girl without preparing her. This act reinforced Nora's ever-present fantasies of abandonment and loss, for now she had unmistakable proof of her parents' hostile intentions. It is significant that the shock of actual abandonment, the reality, the fright, shook her out of her tearful depression, for shortly after hospitalization she felt quite calm. This response again suggests a certain degree of health.

One occurrence during her brief stay in the hospial remained a beacon in her mind and casts light on the "pure" fantasy which accompanied her fetish manipulation. She claimed that the children in the ward lifted her up on a table and gazed at her in wonder while they called her angel. She felt like an idol, worshiped and pure. She transferred this "pure" feeling to her string. It was pure and she too was pure.

Having stayed at the hospital for about a month, she returned home and managed better. She got on at school, had crushes on boys, was somewhat better liked, had a girlfriend or two, and even showed some aptitude in an artistic area.

After her menarche, at about twelve and a half, she took up with or was enticed into joining a group of very tough girls. They dolled her up and made her a decoy for night-haul drivers. She thought the men were kind to her and recalled nothing sexual in these encounters. Her father found out about these excursions and intercepted her with the accusation that she was a slut. She felt he shamed and humiliated her with his derision and contempt. She stood even more in awe of him than before, but secretly determined to revenge herself on him whenever she could.

Numerous forces asserted themselves between fifteen and eighteen. There was an alteration between masochistic, exhibitionistic acts and perverse, hostile ones. She stole sweaters from girls who she fancied had large breasts like her mother. These thefts excited her as the enemas had. She felt impelled to steal shoestrings from these same girls' shoes and was aroused sexually by these acts. It was at this time that the two rituals previously described became full-blown.

However, sporadic healthy moves manifested themselves as well. She finished high school, was admitted to college, and embarked on an artistic course. She formed an affective relationship with a young man. The anal fixation, however, was evident, in that sexual relations with him were almost entirely limited to anal intercourse.

Apparently the sexual relation and the emotional expenditure became too burdensome for her, as did recurrent perverse sexual encounters with men and failure in her competitive struggles with girls. She was beset by a fear of being empty, being "nothing." An inertia overtook her similar to the one she had experienced in prepuberty when she had wept inconsolably. By the time she entered analysis, she suffered from the complaints already described, felt oppressed by her masturbatory activities, and was preoccupied with her ritualistic practices.

Stages in the Evolution of the Fetish

The patient's fetish, meager and insignificant as it objectively was, served a number of functions. In the course of time one use was layered onto another, so that the fetish became interwoven with the patient's life in complex ways.

The first and primary role of the string was to substitute for object loss.[8] It will be recalled that around the age of two and a half to three the patient felt left by her mother, lost her preferred place at the breast to a male sibling, and felt abandoned by her grandfather. The effect of these losses may have been due not only to their own inherent traumatic quality. Immediately after weaning, the infant may have begun to develop abdominal cramps which led to her being given repeated enemas. The sequence of "loss of breast" followed by "loss of stool" may well have rendered her particularly sensitive to object loss. Furthermore, the early administration of enemas occurred before a firm separation of external and internal had taken place (Mahler, 1961), likewise heightening the patient's vulnerability and sensitivity to object loss (Hoffer, 1949; Rochlin, 1953).

Fantasies of umbilical cords were frequent when the patient occupied herself with her string.[9] In some of these she strangled an infant with an umbilical cord. In others she throttled her mother with "the umbilical cord I'm attached to her with." The string itself may have symbolized an umbilical cord, permitting her to remain an attachment of her mother. This suggests that fantasies of being attached to her mother by way of the enema tube played a significant role in inhibiting separation from the love object.

The sensitivity to object loss continued into later life when she had a feeling of having lost everything, of having nothing. This anguished feeling of loss appeared whenever anything was lost: earrings, addresses, papers, money, directions, and time. In fact, Nora managed to lose a number of things, to have them taken, to be robbed, "to be eaten out of house and home," suggesting a need to repeat the trauma of object loss.

In the next stage, around mid-latency, the string functioned as a kind of talisman, and as an apotropaic device (A. Freud, 1936). Then it seemed to protect her from threats and humiliations from girls, against attacks by her brother, and even against her destructive and hostile wishes against her parents.

[8] J. Glover (1927), Weissman (1957), and Muensterberger (1962) trace the interest in the fetish to the fear of object loss.

[9] References to laces, strings, thongs, and their symbolic meaning occur in the works of several writers: Kronold and Sterba (1936), Sharpe (1937), Róheim (1948).

At this time the fetish assumed another and significant meaning. It became an *idealized* object. Certain occurrences contributed to this elevation. The father's statement of a general nature, "everything has strings attached," sanctioned the string. Nora said it became a pure part of her. It made her special. The feeling of uniqueness of herself, and in consequence of the string, was reinforced during her hospital stay. This quality of her own uniqueness and contempt for others became even more prominent in late adolescence.

From the age of thirteen on, the fetish, though used with much less frequency, took on special aspects. On the one hand, it seemed to have a life of its own and Nora felt irresistibly drawn to it. On the other hand, she controlled it as she had dominated her pets in the past. Thus depending on "its" power over her or her control of "it," she could say: "My string made me *do* this," or "I made my string help me from thinking about masturbating."

It was at this time that her autoerotic activities received the compulsive imprint of doing and undoing. As already stated, it was during adolescence that the separation between anal masturbation with salacious fantasies but without string, and the ritual with string and a so-called "pure" fantasy, became clearly demarcated.

The patient entertained alternate feelings of affection and hostility toward the fetish. If she felt the impulse to masturbate, she avoided doing so by resorting to the "good" fetish and said she was performing a "pure" act. If, however, she succumbed to the anal, digital practice with scatological fantasies, she hated her "bad" fetish and accused it of being useless, of not stopping her from masturbating, and being responsible for all her "dirty" actions.

It will be recalled that the fetishistic ritual took place under a variety of special circumstances: after anal masturbation as an undoing of guilt, after feeling morally bad for nonsexual reasons, and alternately as an expression of joy for having accomplished something in reality. This later unusual manifestation appears connected with the "idealized" component of the fetish (E. Glover, 1938).

The patient likewise experienced different body sensations in the ritual with the string. The conditions which led to these variations in sensations were not clearly recalled, but either of the following group of sensations can be understood as the fulfillment of possessing an illusory phallus. In the one set of sensations her *whole* body felt stiff, and in the other set she had specific sensations in her head *alone,* during which it felt either full or hollow, expanding or contracting. Then with the twisting of the string her head felt like her own and she felt "*whole*" (Bak, 1953; Fenichel, 1945).

It is conceivable that with the inclusion of the total body in the ritual there occurred a sort of packaging of sensations she had experienced over the years. The patient's body itself could function as a phallus to avoid her fear of castration. The view of her body as phallus is supported by certain features of her ritual position while she handled her string: the stiff body in the oblique position; the sensations of tightening and stiffening ("I was frozen stiff"); the open eyes, fixed and staring—to this she said: "I feel blind, I can't see a thing." A state of self-hypnotization can be presumed (Bernfeld, 1928). In this state she thought "nothing" and only engaged in motor activity. Moreover, she manipulated her string so that she never saw it, she only felt it, a reinforcement of the illusion of having and being a phallus (Lewin, 1933; Fenichel, 1936).

An enumeration of the elements that entered into the ritualistic activity with the string will show the high degree of complex organization which the fetish finally assumed. In the string ritual can be seen elements from all libidinal phases, oral, anal, and phallic, trends toward omnipotence and idealization,[10] disavowal of castration, undoing of guilt. The latter, i.e., the undoing of guilt, came about as a result of the preceding anal masturbation and as an *apparent* aid in the avoidance of masturbation, while Nora actually attained a partial satisfaction from it through thigh pressure.

The oral element can be seen in the emphasis the patient placed on the role of the tongue in the ritual with the string, during which time it had to be stretched out in her open mouth with lips puckered. In this way the patient could attempt to restore the early, sucking child-mother bond (Abraham, 1916).

The string, which derived vitality from its relation to the sexually arousing enema tube, was purified of its anality by being *elevated,* out-of-sight, during the ritual. Thus the fetish became an idealized object (E. Glover, 1938).

[10] Dr. Stewart speculated that in the pure fantasy with the string there might have been illusions of a virgin birth and immaculate conception. Nora had associated her "pure feeling" to feeling "like the Virgin Mary."

It is probable that the string was also endowed with strong *phallic elements.* The patient's insistence that she had "nothing" but that she felt she had "something of her own" when she used the string, the alternate contracting and expanding of her head during the ritualistic activity, the feeling of total body rigidity, point to the string having the meaning of a phallus.

It would appear that in the full-blown, dual, autoerotic activity, features close to Freud's ideas formulated on the fetish were dramatized. Freud (1927) states that the fetishist in one area of his psyche affirms the castration of the woman, while in another denies it. By masturbating anally the patient avoided the affirmation of her castration. In the so-called "pure" phase, by using her body as a phallus, she retained an illusory one.

While the ritual with the string was designed to protect against anal masturbation, it will be noted that the squeezing of the thighs suggests clitoral masturbation, certainly a step above her frank anal masturbation.

The Passing of the Fetish

In the course of time the patient was impressed by connections that were made during analysis—connections which had not occurred to her at all—namely, those between the trauma of the enema, the jangling telephone, excitements generated by mother and grandfather.

As an example: the mother's admonishing words, "hurry, hurry," and the ominous feelings of filling up and dissolving were related to her chronic struggle with *time.* She raged at time for running out, for being "wasted." She was reminded that her string was viewed as a prime "loser" of time; that in addition to loving it, she hated it because of her perpetual absorption with it: "it" wasted her time. Her characteristic of rarely being on time, being either too late or too early, was also connected to the early struggle.

Mouthing the words "hurry, hurry" when she had to get a "move on," catch a train, etc., aroused memories of the past and induced feelings of heightened tension and excitement which manifested themselves in two opposing responses: on the one hand, she responded by *holding back* from what was to be done, and on the other, she felt stimulated to use her string to *lose* her excitement.

After a time these and other interpretations began to bear fruit and she felt less need for the fetish and used it less frequently. She spontaneously offered the explanation that she must really have thought that having the string was like having a part of her mother. She now began to accuse me of robbing her, of making her look and see, of trying to make her rely on herself. She said: "You've taken my pleasure away. I can't go back to my string. You are making me like all the rest of the females, drab, gray, and ordinary. I might love without my string and then I'd be weak."

The relinquishment of her fetish, her feeling of "specialness," forced her to seek some gratification through the mastery of reality. In order to master reality she had to see more accurately, hear clearly, and know where she was. In fact, parallel to the renunciation of the fetish, a gradual improvement of ego functions took place. She complained less of blurring of vision, loss of time, loss of things, and feeling lost. She was able to re-enter college, take examinations, get a job. She established somewhat more lasting object relations.

At the same time she became disgusted with anal masturbation and the rituals, as a result of which a marked diminution of both took place. Nonetheless, the early magical power of the fetish persisted, and the patient felt that something *bad* might happen if she achieved too much by herself without it.

It took an actual event to put the final quietus on the string. On her birthday, a day charged with pain and portent, her somewhat smart but eccentric boyfriend insisted that she look at him parade naked before her with his penis erect. She said: "I stood frozen stiff. I had to look. I never saw it before. I was horrified at my own fright." She had the same feeling of fright when she heard a poem about "a snake spitting." She was reminded of her fear of looking at her father. She now admitted that she had believed a penis was like an enema tube, pendulous and flexible. The actual confrontation indubitably convinced her that the male organ had other properties, that it was not a replica of a rubber tube.

It seems that at this juncture she accepted the fact that she did not possess a phallus. She now said: "I'm through with that string. My perversion is of no use to me. I'll have to get along in the world without it." It was indeed astonishing to see the ease and painlessness with which the fetish dropped away. It was as though she had never needed it. Her rituals dropped away. Her fantasies became restricted, meager, and ultimately repressed. In her case the relinquishment of the string provided a necessary push toward reality. However, she continued to deplore this closer contact with the inevitable realities of life. She often said: "Now I know how plain life is and you can't give me more."

She took up with a frail young man whom she viewed as an appendage. She said of him: "He is my dangling man. I can make him do anything I want and he is mine. He is my monkey on a string." Anna Freud, in her discussion of this paper, suggested that in this object relation the patient did not altogether relinquish her fetishistic preoccupation. It is fairly clear that she took a male object as her phallus (her fetish). This suggests the inverse of the situation reported by Josine Müller (1925) where the female patient imagined that she herself was the penis of her august father. For the patient reported here, it can be viewed as an advance to have chosen to have some relation to a human object rather than to an inanimate one. One can say that the ease with which she gave up the shoestring was due to having "a man on a string." On the other hand, it is also possible to say that she found a young man on a "string" because she gave up the inanimate object.

When I left on a vacation, despite a lengthy preparation for it and a prolonged discussion about her response to being left, the patient intensely resented my leaving her. The problem of loss and desertion reappeared and she retaliated with anger, first by threatening to leave and then by acting on it, regrettably terminating analysis at this point. It would have been of continuing benefit to the patient to tap certain elements of her newly gained psychic improvement. However, with the relinquishing of the shoestring and its multiple functions, the patient also gave me up and was thus able to achieve some degree of separateness from the love object.

Addendum

As an addendum to the theme of the string I would like to conclude with a fragment from a session with a nine-year-old boy suffering from severe castration anxiety.

During the session the question of relying on oneself rather than expecting a motor, a mechanical object to work for one, arose. At this point the boy reached up into the air and said: "See, I have a magical string." Empty-handed, he began a series of playful stunts with the imaginary string, using it in the service of sublimatory trends while defending himself against anxiety about his genital. In rapid-fire exclamations he said: "I've got you. You're my magic string, invisible. It can do anything I want it to. When I don't need it, I shove it into my pocket." He lunged into the air a few more times, evidently pulling more and more invisible strings down. "There's another and another. I can weave them together. Braid them and have a rope. . . . Now you guess what I can do."

From then on he did "something special" with the imaginary string. He accompanied every movement of his fantasy object with the appropriate act and with gestures of exceptional grace. "I'm a camera . . . I'm a plant . . . I'm a flower . . . I'm a vase . . . a binocular . . . a towing truck . . . a snake . . . a ladder . . . a lasso hauling in a bucking broncho." (Laughing he pulled and strained and distorted his face, tugged and shouted, "I've got that bucking boy.") He ended his performance with a portrayal of Jack and the Beanstalk.

As he was about to leave the session, he said: "I can't leave without my string." At this he reached up into the air and grabbed for the imaginary object. "I have it. I would have missed it."

Summary

A case illustrating the development of a fetishistic practice in a young woman has been presented. At an age of two and a half a string consoled the patient for object losses. In latency it became an apotropaic device, in adolescence a fetish. Idealized during late latency, it served in adolescence as a narcissistic defense to deny feelings of castration and to conceal masturbatory activity.

Following a gradual awareness of the ways in which the fetish limited and constricted her life, the fetish was gradually relinquished, as were obsessive rituals and fantasies attending its use. The result was an improvement of ego functions.

BIBLIOGRAPHY

Abraham, K. (1910), Remarks on the Psycho-Analysis of a Case of Foot and Corset Fetishism. *Selected Papers on Psycho-Analysis*. London: Hogarth Press, 1949, pp. 125-136.

—— (1913), Restrictions and Transformations of Scoptophilia in Psycho-neurotics; with Remarks on Analogous Phenomena in Folk-Psychology. *Selected Papers on Psycho-Analysis.* London: Hogarth Press, 1949, pp. 169-234.
—— (1916), The First Pregenital Stage of the Libido. *Selected Papers on Psycho-Analysis.* London: Hogarth Press, 1949, pp. 248-279.
—— (1920), Manifestations of the Female Castration Complex. *Selected Papers on Psycho-Analysis.* London: Hogarth Press, 1949, pp. 338-369.
—— (1921), Contributions to the Theory of the Anal Character. *Selected Papers on Psycho-Analysis.* London: Hogarth Press, 1949, pp. 370-392.
Bak, R. C. (1953), Fetishism. *J. Amer. Psa. Assn.,* 1:285-298.
Bernfeld, S. (1928), Über Faszination. *Imago,* 14:76-87.
Buxbaum, E. (1960), Hair Pulling and Fetishism. *This Annual,* 15:243-260.
Dickes, R. (1963), Fetishistic Behavior: A Contribution to Its Complex Development and Significance. *J. Amer. Psa. Assn.,* 11:303-330.
Fenichel, O. (1934), *Outline of Clinical Psychoanalysis.* New York: Norton.
—— (1936), The Symbolic Equation: Girl=Phallus. *The Collected Papers of Otto Fenichel.* New York: Norton, 1954, 2:3-18.
—— (1938), On Masturbation. *The Collected Papers of Otto Fenichel.* New York: Norton, 1954, 2:81-88.
—— (1945), *The Psychoanalytic Theory of Neurosis.* New York: Norton.
Freud, A. (1936), *The Ego and the Mechanisms of Defense.* New York: International Universities Press, 1946.
—— (1965), *Normality and Pathology in Childhood: Assessments of Development.* New York: International Universities Press.
Freud, S. (1905), Three Essays on the Theory of Sexuality. *Standard Edition,* 7:125-244. London: Hogarth Press, 1953.
—— (1910), Letter of 24.2.10. In: *A Psycho-Analytic Dialogue: The Letters of Sigmund Freud and Karl Abraham 1907-1926.* New York: Basic Books, 1965, pp. 86-88.
—— (1916), A Connection between a Symbol and a Symptom. *Standard Edition,* 14:339-340. London: Hogarth Press, 1957.
—— (1926), Inhibitions, Symptoms and Anxiety. *Standard Edition,* 20:77-105. London: Hogarth Press, 1959.
—— (1927), Fetishism. *Standard Edition,* 21:149-157. London: Hogarth Press, 1961.
—— (1931), Female Sexuality. *Standard Edition,* 21:225-243. London: Hogarth Press, 1961.
—— (1938), Splitting of the Ego in the Process of Defence. *Standard Edition,* 23:271-278. London: Hogarth Press, 1964.
Gillespie, W. H. (1940), A Contribution to the Study of Fetishism. *Int. J. Psa.,* 21:401-415.
Glover, E. (1938), A Note on Idealization. *Int. J. Psa.,* 19:91-96.
—— (1939), *Psycho-Analysis.* London: Staples Press, pp. 258-259, 275.
Glover, J. (1927), Notes on an Unusual Form of Perversion. *Int. J. Psa.,* 8:10-24.
Greenacre, P. (1941), The Predisposition to Anxiety. *Trauma, Growth, and Personality.* New York: Norton, 1952, pp. 27-82.
—— (1945), Pathological Weeping. *Trauma, Growth, and Personality.* New York: Norton, 1952, pp. 120-131.
—— (1953), Certain Relationships between Fetishism and the Faulty Development of the Body Image. *This Annual,* 8:79-98.
—— (1955), Further Considerations Regarding Fetishism. *This Annual,* 10:187-194.
—— (1960a), Regression and Fixation: Considerations Concerning the Development of the Ego. *J. Amer. Psa. Assn.,* 8:703-723.
—— (1960b), Further Notes on Fetishism. *This Annual,* 15:191-207.
—— (1964), A Study on the Nature of Inspiration. *J. Amer. Psa. Assn.,* 12:6-31.
—— (1966), On Nonsense. In: *Psychoanalysis—A General Psychology: Essays in Honor*

of Heinz Hartmann, ed. R. M. Loewenstein, L. M. Newman, M. Schur, & A. J. Solnit. New York: International Universities Press, pp. 655-677.

Hoffer, W. (1949), Mouth, Hand and Ego-Integration. *This Annual,* 3/4:49-56.

Hug-Hellmuth, H. (1915), Ein Fall von weiblichem Fuss-, richtiger Stiefel-Fetischismus. *Int. Z. Psa.* 3:111-114.

Jones, E. (1918), Anal-Erotic Character Traits. *Papers on Psycho-Analysis.* London: Baillière, Tindall & Cox, pp. 413-437.

Kronold, E. & Sterba, R. (1936), Two Cases of Fetishism. *Psa. Quart.,* 5:63-70.

Lewin, B. D. (1933), The Body as Phallus. *Psa. Quart.,* 2:24-47.

Lorand, S. (1930), Fetishism in statu nascendi. *Int. J. Psa.,* 11:419-427.

Mahler, M. S. (1961), On Sadness and Grief in Infancy and Childhood: Loss and Restoration of the Symbiotic Love Object. *This Annual,* 16:332-351.

Muensterberger, W. (1962), The Creative Process: Its Relation to Object Loss and Fetishism. In: *The Psychoanalytic Study of Society,* 2:161-185. New York: International Universities Press.

Müller, J. (1925), Atheism in Childhood and Faulty Character-Development. *Int. J. Psa.,* 8:521-522, 1927.

Niederland, W. (1956), Clinical Observations on the "Little Man" Phenomenon. *This Annual,* 11:381-395.

Rochlin, G. (1953), Loss and Restitution. *This Annual,* 8:288-309.

Róheim, G. (1948), The Thread of Life. *Psa. Quart.,* 17:471-486.

Sharpe, E. F. (1937), *Dream Analysis.* London: Hogarth Press, pp. 55-56.

Sperling, M. (1963), Fetishism in Children. *Psa. Quart.,* 32:374-392.

Weissman, P. (1957), Some Aspects of Sexual Activity in a Fetishist. *Psa. Quart.,* 26:494-507.

Winnicott, D. W. (1953), Transitional Objects and Transitional Phenomena. *Int. J. Psa.,* 34:89-97.

Wulff, M. (1946), Fetishism and Object Choice in Early Childhood. *Psa. Quart.,* 15:450-471.

CONTENTS OF VOLUMES I–XXI

——— & BARRON, A. T.
A Study of Identical Twins: Their Analytic Material Compared with Existing Observation Data of Their Early Childhood (1963) *18:*367–423
——— GOLDBERGER, A., & LUSSIER, A.
Simultaneous Analysis of Mother and Child (1955) *10:*165–186
BUXBAUM, E.
Transference and Group Formation in Children and Adolescents (1945) *1:*351–365
Technique of Child Therapy: A Critical Evaluation (1954) *9:*297–333
Hair Pulling and Fetishism (1960) *15:*243–260
The Parents' Role in the Etiology of Learning Disabilities (1964) *19:*421–447
BYCHOWSKI, G.
Patterns of Anger (1966) *21:*172–192
See also E. KRIS (1954)

CASUSO, G.
Anxiety Related to the "Discovery" of the Penis: An Observation. With an Introduction by *Anna Freud* (1957) *12:*169–174
COLEMAN, R. W., KRIS, E., & PROVENCE, S.
The Study of Variations of Early Parental Attitudes: A Preliminary Report (1953) *8:*20–47
COLONNA, A., *see* NAGERA & COLONNA (1965)
COOLIDGE, J. C., TESSMAN, E., WALDFOGEL, S., & WILLER, M. L.
Patterns of Aggression in School Phobia (1962) *17:*319–333
CROCKER, D.
The Study of a Problem of Aggression (1955) *10:*300–335

DANN, S., *see* FREUD & DANN (1951)
DAUNTON, E., *see* SANDLER, DAUNTON, & SCHNURMANN (1957)
DAVISON, C., *see* E. KRIS (1954)
DAWES, L. G., *see* LINDEMANN & DAWES (1952)
DE SAUSSURE, R.
J. B. Felix Descuret (1946) *2:*417–424
DEMAREST, E. W. & WINESTINE, M. C.
The Initial Phase of Concomitant Treatment of Twins (1955) *10:*336–352
DESPERT, J. L.
Dreams in Children of Preschool Age (1949) *3/4:*141–180
DWYER, T. F., *see* BIBRING, DWYER, HUNTINGTON, & VALENSTEIN (1961)

EISSLER, K. R.
Ego-psychological Implications of the Psychoanalytic Treatment of Delinquents (1950) *5:*97–121
Notes upon the Emotionality of a Schizophrenic Patient and Its Relation to Problems of Technique (1953) *8:*199–251
An Unusual Function of an Amnesia (1955) *10:*75–82

——— & ANDERSEN, I.
The Uncompromising Demand of a Three-year-old for a Real Mother (1945) *1:*211–231
PEARSON, G. H. J.
A Survey of Learning Difficulties in Children (1952) *7:*322–386
PELLER, L. E.
Incentives to Development and Means of Early Education (1946) *2:*397–415
Libidinal Phases, Ego Development, and Play (1954) *9:*178–198
The School's Role in Promoting Sublimation (1956) *11:*437–449
Daydreams and Children's Favorite Books: Psychoanalytic Comments (1959) *14:*414–433
Freud's Contribution to Language Theory (1966) *21:*448–467
PETO, A.
Variations of Archaic Thinking in Neurotics, Borderline Patients, and Schizophrenics (1964) *19:*73–92
PETTY, T. A.
The Tragedy of Humpty Dumpty (1953) *8:*404–412
PINE, F. & FURER, M.
Studies of the Separation–Individuation Phase: A Methodological Overview (1963) *18:*325–342
PLANK, E. N.
Memories of Early Childhood in Autobiographies (1953) *8:*381–393
——— & HORWOOD, C.
Leg Amputation in a Four-year-old: Reactions of the Child, Her Family, and the Staff (1961) *16:*405–422
——— & PLANK, R.
Emotional Components in Arithmetical Learning as Seen Through Autobiographies (1954) *9:*274–293
PLANK, R.
On "Seeing the Salamander" (1957) *12:*379–398
See also PLANK & PLANK (1954)
PRENTICE, N., *see* JESSNER, LAMONT, LONG, ROLLINS, WHIPPLE, & PRENTICE (1955)
PROVENCE, S. & RITVO, S.
Effects of Deprivation on Institutionalized Infants: Disturbances in Development of Relationship to Inanimate Objects (1961) *16:*189–205
See also COLEMAN, KRIS, & PROVENCE (1953), RITVO & PROVENCE (1953)
PUTNAM, M. C., RANK, B., & KAPLAN, S.
Notes on John I.: A Case of Primal Depression in an Infant (1951) *6:*38–58

RAMZY, I. & WALLERSTEIN, R. S.
Pain, Fear, and Anxiety: A Study in Their Interrelationships (1958) *13:*147–189
RANGELL, L.
A Treatment of Nightmare in a Seven-year-old Boy (1950) *5:*358–390